Essays in Stylistics **文体学研究论丛 ❹**

前进中的文体学
——第五届文体学国际研讨会暨第九届全国文体学研讨会文选

Stylistics in Progress
—Papers from the 5th International & the 9th National Conference on Stylistics

主编 吴显友

上海外语教育出版社
外教社® SHANGHAI FOREIGN LANGUAGE EDUCATION PRESS

图书在版编目(CIP)数据

前进中的文体学：第五届文体学国际研讨会暨第九届全国文体学研讨会文选/吴显友主编. —上海：上海外语教育出版社,2016
(文体学研究论丛)
ISBN 978-7-5446-4195-1

Ⅰ.①前… Ⅱ.①吴… Ⅲ.①文体论-国际学术会议-文集 Ⅳ.①H052-53

中国版本图书馆 CIP 数据核字(2015)第 316781 号

出版发行：**上海外语教育出版社**
 （上海外国语大学内） 邮编：200083
电　　话：021-65425300（总机）
电子邮箱：bookinfo@sflep.com.cn
网　　址：http://www.sflep.com.cn　http://www.sflep.com
责任编辑：奚玲燕

印　　刷：上海信老印刷厂
开　　本：700×1000　1/16　印张25.5　字数440千字
版　　次：2016 年 4 月第 1 版　2016 年 4 月第 1 次印刷
印　　数：1 100 册

书　　号：ISBN 978-7-5446-4195-1 / H · 1942
定　　价：53.00 元

本版图书如有印装质量问题,可向本社调换

中国修辞学会文体学研究会策划

文体学研究论丛 4 (Essays in Stylistics, Vol. 4)

《前进中的文体学》编委会

序

2014 年可谓是文体学的丰收年,有三项标志性成果可鉴。

一是第五届文体学国际研讨会暨第九届全国文体学研讨会在重庆召开,吸引了来自中国、英国、美国、荷兰、澳大利亚等国家 100 多所高校的 200 余名代表参加。大会主题为"新世纪初文体学研究的新进展",议题涉及文体学诸多分支学科,充分展示了 21 世纪初国内外文体学研究的新方法、新趋势和新成果。归纳起来,本次盛会有如下亮点:(1)中外学者热情参与,中青年学者崭露头角,与会者提交的论文数量、质量高;(2)研究视野开阔,理论视角新颖,研究方法多样。既有理论探索又有实证研究,分析语料文学文本与非文学文本并重,既有中外经典文本,也有当下流行的影视文本、网络文本;(3)文体学的部分分支学科,如文学文体学、功能文体学、认知文体学、叙述文体学等,成为本次会议的热点议题,成果丰硕;(4)文体学的一些前沿研究,如语料库文体学、批评文体学、多模态文体学、英汉文体学对比研究等已进入中外学者的研究视野,并收到了丰厚的回报。

二是剑桥大学出版社推出的《文体学手册》(*The Cambridge Handbook of Stylistics*)。该书充分认识到文体学研究的跨学科特性,结合了语言学、心理学、社会学、人类学、教育学、计算机方法、文学批评等相关领域的知识和理论,较为全面地介绍了文体学的理论、发展、特点和方法。该书由英国诺丁汉大学文学语言学教授 Peter Stockwell 和谢菲尔德大学语言与文学方向讲师 Sara Whiteley 共同编写。中国文体学研究会前任会长、北京大学申丹教授在为该书撰写的推介语中称其是"一部难得的文体学参考书"。该书除绪论和后记外,正文包括五个部分,共有 37 篇研究论文,对文体学研究的方方面面进行了述评。

三是劳特里奇出版社推出的《文体学手册》(*The Routledge Handbook of Stylistics*)。该书除绪论外共包括 32 篇论文,分别就文体学的研究历史、核心问题、当代话题及发展趋势四个方面对文体学进行了系统的介绍。该书展现给读者的不是一般的按照诗歌、小说、戏剧等文类编排的学术论文集,而是一本详尽的文体学研究指导手册。该书由国际诗学与语言学学会前任会长、荷兰乌特勒支大学修辞学教授 Michael Burke 担任主编,邀请了全球文体学领域的 38 位专家学者作为撰稿人。笔者在为该书撰写的推介语中对该书的创新性给予了高度评价："知识的不断更新对每一个学科都是至关重要的，Routledge《文体学手册》正是这样一部与时俱进的著作。该书内容充分反映出文体学作为一个成熟学科的强大生命力。"

由此可见，文体学已经发展成为一个独立学科。根据我们现在的认识，文体学是研究文学风格和语言体裁的学科。其研究内容涉及文学、语言学、社会生活等领域。在文学领域，文体学研究有诗歌、小说、戏剧之分；在社会生活方面，有广告、计算机和种种特殊用途语言等分野；在语言学方面，有形式、功能、语篇、语境、认知等分支。目前，除了文体学的理论基础和核心问题之外，新媒体文体学、多模态文体学、情感神经文体学等新兴领域的研究也为人们所期待。另外，文体学与修辞学、诗学、叙事学、符号学、传播学、伦理学、宗教学、图像学和建筑学等学科有诸多交叉，它们既相互借鉴，又各自独立，形成了众多的分支研究领域与问题。

例如，文体学与修辞学剪不断、理还乱的关系是个有意思的问题。西方修辞学源于古希腊的雄辩术，已有两千五百多年的历史。公元前二世纪后，古罗马也开设了许多修辞学校，向贵族奴隶主阶级的子弟传授演说、辩论的技巧。从亚里士多德开始，历史上的修辞学家、文学批评家和文学研究者对文学语言进行了大量的、卓有成效的研究，一门完全涵盖语言学、文艺学的新学科——文体学早已在历史中得到长期孕育，它的成熟和独立是水到渠成的事。现代文体学是由索绪尔的学生、瑞士语言学家巴依创立的。他在《法语文体论》中对文体学的研究任务、研究对象和研究方法作了明确的阐述。

尽管有学者不愿承认文体学与传统修辞学的联系，但两学科的研究范围确有不少重合。从研究语言表达的手段来看，传统修辞学可谓古人的"文体学"，而现代文体学则是在传统修辞学的基础上吸收了现代科学成果而发展起来的，两者既有联系又有区别，区别在于：一是研究内容不同，文体学研究语言风格，修辞学侧重研究演讲、写作艺术；二是研究目的不同，修辞学注重"净化语言"、树立标准，文体学则强调适合原则。

其实，文体学可以说是修辞学的延伸和扩展。修辞学从古代的"演讲艺术"至今天的"写作艺术"，为语言的发展、净化起了巨大作用，且富有无限生命力。但由于修辞学拘泥于公式化的修饰手段和模式、忽视语言的社会交际情景，束缚了人们的活跃思想，阻碍了情感的自由表达，与节奏越来越快的现代社会不大合拍，因而不断遭到批评与抵触。

文体学则注重语言的交际环境，所观察、研究的就是什么样的语言适用于什么样的场合，从而冲破了修辞学条条框框的束缚。可以说，文体学是在人们对修辞学的不满情绪中应运而生的学科，是对修辞学的挑战。由修辞学到文体学的发展,是一场突破性的革命。

修辞学为文体学的发展提供了积淀和基础,而文体学的创立也开扩了语言工作者的眼界,冲击了传统的修辞学。修辞学注重语言素材本身,在方法与技巧上给演讲艺术和写作艺术提供有益的准则;词、句的提炼是修辞的前提。文体学视点则从单词、单句中跳脱出来,从宏观角度将语音、语义、结构及其他因素有机结合起来,形成高于修辞学的境界。因为语言的灵活性、微妙性、深邃性是远非修辞框框所能够束缚的。两门学科分别从不同的角度观察、分析语言,只要正确认识与处理,修辞与文体的关系以及修辞学与文体学的关系就能相辅相成、并行不悖。

文体学同其他学科一样,同人们丰富多彩的社会生活一样,也会赶时髦! 每过一段时间就会出现一个或几个热点话题,如,多模态文体学,文体学与情感表达、神经科学交叉研究,文体学与修辞学交叉研究,等等。与此同时,文体学也不断在此过程中丰富、发展、充实和完善自己。

文体学,与时俱进!

参考文献

Burke, M. 2014. *The Routledge Handbook of Stylistics*. London: Routledge.

Nørgaard, N., B. Busse, & R. Montoro. 2010. *Key Terms in Stylistics*. New York: Continuum Publishing Corporation.

Stockwell, P. & S. Whiteley. 2014. *The Cambridge Handbook of Stylistics*. Cambridge: Cambridge University Press.

Wales, K. 2011. *A Dictionary of Stylistics*. London: Pearson Education ESL.

胡壮麟. 2000.《理论文体学》. 北京:外语教学与研究出版社.

刘世生. 2015.《什么是文体学》. 上海:上海外语教育出版社.

刘世生,吕中舌,封宗信. 2008.《文体学:中国与世界同步》. 北京:外语教学与研究出版社.

申 丹, 2008.《西方文体学的新发展》. 上海:上海外语教育出版社.

苏晓军. 2013.《文体学研究:实证 认知 跨学科》. 上海:上海外语教育出版社.

王守元,郭鸿,苗兴伟. 2004.《文体学研究在中国的进展》. 上海:上海外语教育出版社.

吴显友. 2016.《前进中的文体学》. 上海:上海外语教育出版社.

俞东明. 2010.《中国文体学研究:回顾、现状与展望》. 上海:上海外语教育出版社.

于善志. 2012.《文体学研究:探索与应用》. 上海:上海外语教育出版社.

刘世生

2015 年 11 月 28 日于

清华大学外文系

Table of Contents

Part I　Theoretical Studies

Part II　Cognitive Stylistics

Part III　Literary Stylistics

Part IV Functional Stylistics

Part V Pragma-stylistics

Part VI Style and Translation Studies

Part I   Theoretical Studies

Advances in the Stylistics of Literature Reading

Geoff Hall   (The University of Nottingham Ningbo China)

Abstract: Stylistics research has become increasingly interested in questions of readership in describing and accounting for the meaning of literary texts. The paper reviews a historical move from more textual earlier understandings of stylistics to acceptance of the need to look at literary communication as discourse in contexts, including questions of readership. Two broad research traditions are outlined, following Peplow & Carter (2014), one more inflected by psychology and experiment, the other more qualitative in nature, including ethnographies and discourse analysis. An important puzzle raised for stylistics scholarship is the degree to which or how exactly language contributes to meaning making by readers, with apparently contradictory findings coming out of each tradition. The way forward would seem to be mutual interrogation of each research approach by the other with carefully designed studies testing and exploring in more depth some of the apparent contradictions that have appeared around the basic stylistic question of the primacy of language for literary reading experience.

Key words: reading literature; empirical studies of literature reading; language in literature; stylistics of literary reading; the reader of literature

Early Formalist stylistics was arguably more interested in form than in effects (hence the name), though Shklovsky notoriously argued for the defamiliarising effects of foregrounding, while Jakobson later suggested the function of foregrounding as prompting reader concentration on the linguistic forms before the meaning in poetic language use. There is thus still a caricatural image of stylistics in the minds of some literary critics who do not read contemporary stylistics research, as pointless counting of words or identification of recurrent patterns of language use or 'deviant' language items almost for their own sake. It is true that the early linguists who began to elaborate stylistics tended to be interested first in the language and second in the literary meaning. As, increasingly, they did speak about 'the reader', this 'reader' was rather abstract, like the reader of reader response critics to be discussed below, a speculative hypothetical figure or idealized version of the stylistician's own reading persona and seemed rather unproblematic: certain devices would tend to prompt certain responses, it seemed. Even early cognitive stylistics research tended to follow this tradition of a non-empirical reader too often (compare Allington & Swann's (2009) survey of uses of 'the reader' in stylistics papers published by the key journal *Language and Literature*). A stylistic tic of much cognitive linguistic writing is the use of a co-optive 'we' ('we understand', 'we see' etc.) never explicitly identified, but again typically looking suspiciously parochial, actually an 'exclusive we' rather than the apparent 'inclusive we' offered so ambiguously by English grammar: as reader, I often cannot recognize myself as a member of that reading club. Nevertheless, today, Simpson is right to insist, 'contemporary stylistics ultimately looks towards *language as discourse*' (Simpson, 2014: 8). The best stylistic work is very much concerned with the study of readers and reception and interpretation as much as any narrow purely linguistic study of texts 'in themselves' even if that very circumscribed aim were really possible. There is a widespread recognition that meaning is unavoidable and should be accounted for in the stylistician's analysis rather than repressed, ignored or taken for granted as somehow of secondary interest or pretty much predictable. An increasing interest nowadays is in the wider semiotic features of texts in fact, not only the linguistics of a text, because of the wider interest in meaning and meaning effects. With the growth of discourse stylistics, the approach to text as discourse, contexts, including contexts of reading, are very much part of the business of stylistics. 'Stylistics is interested in language as a function of texts in context, and it acknowledges that utterances (literary or otherwise) are produced in a time, a place, and in a cultural and cognitive context. These 'extra-linguistic' parameters are inextricably tied up with the way a text 'means' (Simpson,

2014: 3). The contention of the present writer (GH) is only that the acknowledgement of context needs to go as far in practice as it has in theoretical pronouncements like that of Simpson.

Certainly for stylistics today as throughout its history, literature is first and foremost linguistic text. It is made of words. The key claim of stylistics is that linguistic forms and design must influence or even ' determine ' in stronger or weaker senses, the meanings readers take from texts. The claim is surely uncontroversial if imprecise. Better understandings of reading, readers, and readership are nevertheless informing better understanding of how exactly linguistic meanings may (or may not) influence readings. The fundamental challenge to be faced by stylistics may be phrased as, ' How far is reading language-driven?' The question is unlikely to be answered by any formula or quantitative measure, at least in my estimation, but can be clarified through carefully designed studies and perceptive analyses of data of literary reading events and practices. To anticipate my later argument, more naturalistic studies of literary reading must explore actual readings in context to supplement and fill out understandings gained from more experimental research.

Historically, reader response approaches to literature reading emphasized the importance of readers in proactively determining meanings, and instanced the very different interpretations of different readers, or even the same reader in differing contexts, could produce of the same text. At one end of the scale, Iser (1978) wrote of ' concretisations' and suggested readers follow prompts in the text being read, joining the dots, as it were, rather than any more creative or proactive activity. Culler's (1975) ' literary competence' idea also emphasised that there are better and worse readings of a text, and that these are driven by accepted protocols of reading, expert literary readers having learned what to read for and how to talk or write about that reading. The most extreme and most provocative position in the debate was of course that of Stanley Fish (1981), who argued that the readings communities of readers produce have rather little to do with the texts they are reading and more to do with the preoccupations of that group at that time, so that for Fish accounts by stylisticians were unadventurous at best or self-deluding post hoc rationalisations at worst. (Toolan (1990), and later O'Halloran (2007) provide strong stylistics ripostes to Fish.) Thirty years after Fish, Belsey (2011) seems to suggest something similar in some of her more recent writings when she points to the rather dreary tendency of literature students in universities, and their teachers and supervisors, to identify workings of power, gender and the rest in whatever they read. Feminist reader response (Fetterley, 1978) or others (Gates, 1992) showed in what was at that time a revealing move, the reproduction of dominant power relations in a society and ways of understanding the world through literature reading, particularly literature reading in the university or other institutions (learning to read literature as learning to read from a white male perspective). A fascinating history of reception like Taylor's (1990) account of meanings taken from Shakespeare's writings across the centuries, reinforce this picture of readers valuing and noticing texts or features of texts for rather extra-textual reasons ('contexts' of reading), so that the readings they produce tell later readers at least as much about the earlier readers as about the so-called 'text itself'. More recently Spiro (2011) in a suggestive if somewhat forced quick-and-dirty experiment, shows the importance of contexts to evaluations readers make: her readers of decontextualised poems — like Richards' (1929) Cambridge undergraduates in the 1920s — demonstrably do not rely on the linguistic text alone in coming to judgments of literary value, whatever they or we might want to believe. The basic claim of reader response based on the kind of work reported above, is that readers read differently, with different evaluations and different responses to the same text, and that such readings are not purely determined by the language of the text. The language is only one factor, perhaps not even the most important factor in driving meaning making. To repeat, then, the challenge for stylisticians today is to model and clarify the ways in which language contributes to meaning making in the reading of literary texts, against a wide variety of non-empirical claims that have been made.

One response to this apparent challenge from what I have broadly presented as 'reader response' could be the work of psycholinguists Kintsch & van Dijk (1978, 1983). van Dijk and Kintsch claimed that we all read the same plot of a novel, identify the same hero and minor characters and so on, but we only respond to it differently. This was the idea of the 'proposition base' + 'situation model'. As we inference and elaborate away from the 'facts' of the literary text, our readings will vary because we bring to bear differing world knowledge, textual experiences and so on to help us elaborate our 'situation models'. Text World Theory (Gavins, 2005) is in some ways a more sophisticated later version of that early work, with some of the same roots. The issue is perhaps more clearly set out by such models of literary reading but by no means solved. 'The reader' in the model remains elusive and at least in earlier versions of such work, is still a pre-empirical speculative or subjective figure only and rather unproblematic. Such research helps clarify how variations in reading may occur, but leaves very much still open the need to explore what actual readers do with actual texts, which is all much messier. It is interesting, indeed, in this perspective, to see Gavins in her most recent work appealing to Internet reader comments to help her build a more empirical account of actual readers' readings into her analyses of 'absurd' literature. Absurd literature, it is suggested, is absurd to the extent that readers read it as such, rather than for any essential text-inherent linguistic or genre features (Gavins, 2013). Stylistics has here moved a long way from its Formalist origins, including the study of genre considered then as a primarily or even purely textual phenomenon (Erlich 1978).

In the best introduction to the stylistic study of literary reading to date, Peplow & Carter (2014) distinguish two major traditions of the study of such reading by stylisticians and those in related areas. The empirical study of literary reading (ESL) is their first tradition. Naturalistic study of reading (NSR) is their second. The labels are perhaps not the best. Both traditions are empirical in different ways, and it is unfortunate if there is any unintended implication that NSR might be in some way less or indeed not, 'empirical'. Nevertheless the distinction is an important one and enables a newcomer to the field to see the territory more clearly, as well as understanding better the theoretical positions implied and required to work or even to read in one field rather than another, or more charitably, what is gained and lost by each tradition as it seeks to explore and explain literary reading.

ESL has been the dominant research approach to the empirical study of literature reading to date. ESL is driven in design and procedures by psychology, so that reading in this perspective is seen as an act that takes place within the mind of an individual reader. Who 'the reader' might be and reading in what circumstances and contexts, is of marginal interest for such studies. Real readers are of course used, but they follow the experimenter's instructions, usually reading texts or extracts provided by the experimenter in an institutional setting of some kind and answer questions determined by the experimenter. Reading in one's favourite chair or on a station bench, or reading from a screen or a very expensive illustrated historical edition signed by the nineteenth century author (and so on) are considered secondary or even irrelevant issues for the ESL tradition which is first and foremost concerned with reading as a mental activity in the most limited sense of the term. This description may sound critical but of course the argument from such research is that first the basic outlines and major factors need to be understood; the detail (the chair, the smell and feel of the paper, even time of day etc.) will then only be expected to modify the general picture rather than change it fundamentally. It is an accumulative rather than holistic or ecological view of knowledge building. Parts can be added to parts of understanding until the whole structure becomes clear. The assumption of ESL is the classic stylistic assumption that formal linguistic features of texts should be at the centre of any investigation of literature reading, and so the effects of formal texts in carefully controlled experiments are what ESL research tells us about.

NSR studies, by contrast, seek to investigate as far as possible what happens when people read more naturalistically rather than to the agenda of the ESL researcher. Much NSR research has used book club meetings as a site to study more naturalistic reading, where we might note also, that reading will be more of a social activity and less of a private and individualized event. Peplow & Carter (2014: 442) see this as a 'broadly ethnographic' approach, where research is more about exploration and developing contextualized understandings than seeking to prove or disprove pre-formed hypotheses about reading. A drawback of such approaches may be that the researcher loses control of variables and cannot find answers to the questions s/he started out with, but the advantage is that issues and factors not previously considered or downplayed by academic researchers can come to seem more salient to participants and must therefore be accounted for by such NSR research.

Steen (1991) is now regarded as a classic early call for research and one that necessarily at the time privileged ESL research. Steen gives examples of verbal protocols, 'Think out Loud' experiments and calls for more. For Steen at that time, experimentalist, quantitative testing of the claims of stylistics were needed. He describes coding systems which can be counted and measured as 'empirical'. At best, for Steen at that point, such work might be extended by more qualitative-naturalistic research based on interviews or diary studies, but these are not much discussed and clearly not regarded highly at that point. In any case, not many were being done. The cognitive psychology of Kintsch and students of his such as Rolf Zwaan is also instanced a part of this ESL controlled-experimentalist approach.

Turning first, then, to ESL, since one of the key or indeed defining claims of stylistics has always been the notion of foregrounding, it is hardly surprising that early empirical work looked at foregrounding in literary reading, led notably by van Peer and his colleagues over the years, with important work also coming out of Canada led by Miall, and North America more widely. Important research in this paradigm continues to be published through the journal van Peer founded in 2012, *Scientific Study of Literature* (Benjamins). van Peer (e.g. 1986 and after) gave poems to his original groups of university students asking them to underline words or phrases found 'striking' or 'worth discussion' and then compared these with the words and phrases a stylistic analysis would have predicted to be noticeable as 'deviant' or foregrounded in some way. When prompted like this, the students duly seemed to confirm that stylistic analysis can predict very accurately what a reader will notice (if they are asked to notice something). Miall (2007) and colleagues interestingly extended such work into the investigation of relations between enjoyment and other emotions when reading literary texts and foregrounding, with short stories as well as poetry, claiming, plausibly enough, that feelings are central to literary reading experience and motivation to read more literature. For present purposes, then, the key point to be derived from ESL studies is that linguistic features do influence ordinary readers reading literary texts, and largely in ways that stylistic analysis would predict. Moreover, a range of readers tend to notice the same (foregrounded) features and typically slow down their reading rate to give them more attention; the case for reader variation ('reader response') has been much over-stated in this view. It has been proven time and time again, they would say. Something has been proven, but it probably needs to be more carefully stated than this formulation suggests. I return to the point after considering an overview of the NSR tradition and its own, apparently contradictory, key finding. But even at this point, it is legitimate to ask: Who are these ordinary readers? An important sub-text of all this work for these researchers was to prove that ordinary readers read in certain ways, and that these ways can disprove claims of critical or literary theorists who claim they can read in different ways. Such different ways, for ESL researchers, are sometimes 'expert readings' (a whole branch of research on its own) but more typically mis-representations of reading which need to be shown empirically to be wrong. This discourse of the 'ordinary reader' is now well-established in such studies, but needs always to be treated with suspicion. Is an ordinary reader untrained in literary reading, less highly educated, reading only for pleasure or no particular purpose? The concept is often presented as if its meaning were self-evident but is elusive once we try to define what an 'ordinary' reader might be. Ordinary people are usually other people we find, or the term is used as discursive construct, 'I'm just an ordinary reader'. Internet readers are often instanced now as ordinary readers, but are those who post comments on Amazon or other sites really very ordinary people? In experimental research studies, under what conditions in what circumstances are the ordinary readers reading? Is that really ordinary ('natural'?) reading? ESL has been enormously suggestive and stimulating, and in many ways confirms stylisticians in what they do (and as teachers) but it could be argued that the results of ESL research can be seen as too obviously products of the way the research was conducted.

Thus in 2008 I published my own worries on this topic in a collaborative collection with van Peer and others (Hall, 2008). Taking the example of ESL studies of free indirect speech, I critiqued two suggestive and in many ways exemplary studies of the 'dual voice' controversy. The core of my critique was to suggest that asking experimentees, as these studies did, whether in a decontextualized extract from a novel not known, character A or character B or a narrator was heard, is actually to *assume* that three voices can be identified and distinguished, when in fact the whole object of investigation could be argued to be whether that is actually the phenomenological reading experience of readers in the first place. This kind of 'priming' of participants is problematic to my mind. The question is assuming *a priori* what should rather be investigated first. A clear case of ESL research needing NSR research as much as the other way round, I return in my conclusion to the current chapter. More evidence for the kind of position I claimed there is found, to my belief, in a study such as Zyngier *et al* (2007) , which looked at the perception of foregrounding across cultures. This is a valuable study in the best tradition of academic research because it raises uncomfortable issues for the researchers. In this case, the problem is that the expected degree of universality across cultures in the perception of foregrounding was not confirmed. Netherlands students from northern Europe, with a more highly developed and schooled literary culture (I would hypothesise) were more sensitive to foregrounding features than notional compeers from other parts of the world such as Brazil. Elsewhere I note the contradictions in expert/non-expert reader research: they read differently (we are sometimes told)/they don't read differently (in other studies). Perhaps the very construct of the expert reader is suspect, these contradictory results would suggest, as suspect as the 'expert reader', its conceptual complement.

Turning then to Peplow and Carter's NSR research heading ('Naturalistic' reading), I have already quoted its characterization as 'ethnographic'. The importance of contexts is emphasized in such research, that meanings are related to time and place and emerge from social interaction as much as from interaction of disembodied minds with print. There is a notable cautious retreat from more universal claims in favour of specific studies of more precisely specified groups of readers who may or may not be 'ordinary' (the term is rarer in such reports). Language may or may not mediate meaning construction for such researchers. The claim is not assumed but left open and sometimes there seems to be some evidence for it but the case is not as clearly established as in ESL. Discourse analysis methods are used to study the emergence and construction of meaning in talk around texts. In a sense, for such researchers, the text is not read until it has been discussed and a meaning agreed with others. This is a different picture to the idea of reading by an individual followed by 'post processing' which has to be distinguished from 'reading itself'. For the NSR researcher, reading is a longitudinal, gradual emergent process, not a one off event. Reading begins when a friend recommends a book, or an online review is casually scanned and arouses interest to know more. There is a growing but only limited number of such studies at present, though growing and growing in influence: Allington and Swann's special issue of *Language and Literature* (Issue 3, 2009) ; Peplow, 2011; Whiteley, 2011; Swann, Peplow, Trimarco & Whiteley, 2014; and

Procter & Benwell, 2014, would be some of the strongest examples of this approach. Some studies in history of the book could perhaps be added (Miall, 2006). Jackson (2001) is a fascinating study of the dialogues readers may have with the books they are reading as they scribble furiously in the margins, underline, and 'correct' or exemplify approvingly the text they are reading.

The salient issue for stylistics, however, is here: NSR studies consistently report that readers discussing books in book groups or elsewhere *do not often spontaneously refer to language*. For the most part, only broad references to text are made. Interpersonal social interaction seems to be at least as important to meaning making from reading as the linguistic text itself. Indeed meaning making is ongoing, and open-ended; no fixed final meaning is normally taken from a literary text by its readers. When language is referred to by the readers of these studies it is, perhaps significantly, when a dispute arises, and the text (or that reader's interpretation of the text, to be more accurate) is appealed to in order to 'prove a point'. Evaluations also are often made by reference to language used in the text. Finally, but very relevant for any study of literary reading, clear awareness even self-consciousness is frequently shown about literary schooling and cultural contexts such as literary prizes, critics and reviewers. Even where contesting such culturally privileged readings (which is often done: examples in Procter & Benwell, 2014), readers still show themselves to have been influenced in their readings by the views of others as much as by the text. To make a crude contrast, where ESL tells us that language is central and crucial to literary reading, NSR raises real doubts about the importance of language to meaning making from literary reading. Does NSR research suggest that language, though important, is just not normally consciously noticed? (Then how do we know it is 'important'?) Or that language is at best only a final constraint on more extreme interpretations? Or perhaps just that stylistics has exaggerated the importance of language (as some literary critics might in any case allege)?

Such findings, howsobeit they raise more questions than they answer, as is the nature of such research, need to be incorporated into ever finer understandings of literary reading. They cannot be ignored. It is a classic research methodology paradigm, surely to be followed here too, to suggest that more exploratory qualitative research should lead to rigorous testing of hypotheses arising from such work in a more experimentalist approach. ESL and NSR need to be constantly tested against each other, in dialogue rather than — as too often seems to be the case now — a dialogue of the deaf. Far more data is needed to explore the nature of NSR. The Internet offers unprecedented opportunities here, with exchanges on social media, blogs and the rest. Reading groups, book clubs and the like have been given new impetus by new technologies, and in this rapid development are generating more and more valuable data for those interested in literary reading. (Compare e.g. Stockwell's (2009) brief comments on what metaphors found on the web tell us about literature reading.) Educational research has much to contribute too since education remains one of the key sites for the reading of literature and enculturation into the reading of literature which remains very influential through most readers' lives. One interesting reader variation I have noticed in my own career as teacher is the cultural and linguistic variation in what English as a second language readers take form literary texts as compared to L1 readers in the UK education system.

I close with an example of second language literary reading from Chinese undergraduate students at the University of Nottingham campus in Ningbo, China. I find great student interest in the relatively unknown contexts in which the literature was produced and first read, in culture, history, and so on. There is a related real interest, as might be expected, in what might broadly be referred to as 'postcolonial' topics, such as representations of 'eastern' peoples in Dickens or Conan Doyle. But anecdotally, I am struck by the number of times my own 'natural' readers (if undergraduate students of English literature in China are in any way 'ordinary'!), in this context, refer, unprompted, to the precise language of the texts we have been reading. Tennyson was a particular favourite last year, with students repeating after me the refrain of 'Mariana': 'He cometh not, she said./She said I am aweary, aweary,/I would that I were dead.' (The 'deviant' word 'aweary' was focused on by students not me, and queried.) One student reader came to me after various extracts from 'In Memoriam' had been discussed to stress how beautiful she found the lines: 'An infant crying in the night;/An infant crying for the light.' I had laid no particular emphasis on these lines. They had 'spoken' to the student though, very clearly. Unexpected examples arose, as always in such teaching: why should 'All things bright and beautiful', which I had meant to introduce only incidentally, have proved so fascinating? A final example, a number of students quoted to me and then repeated in essays Jude the Obscure's "I have understanding as well as you. I am not inferior to you." Where the UK student would almost certainly be noticing this as an instance of social class resentment or claim to entitlement, my Chinese students were surely responding to some other aspect of exclusion or perceived condescension in their (educational?) experience. The words were noticed; they had a different meaning for those readers. These are all (admittedly anecdotal) examples of highly contextualized reading acts which an adequate model of language in literary reading must strive to account for. I have tried in this short introductory paper to suggest some of the ways stylisticians are trying, in exciting new ways, to investigate explicit and implicit claims of their discipline about the core activity of literary reading. I would suggest that historically stylistics moved from ideas of investigating 'what the text means', to ideas of 'how the text means' (compare again Culler, 1975, also cognitive poetics), but that now we need to move again to more precise questions of 'what the text means *for who*?' and how or why that might be. This to my mind is the next challenge for the ever more ambitious and more sophisticated discipline of stylistics.

References

Allington, D. & J. Swann. 2009. Researching literary reading as social practice. *Language and Literature*, 18 (3): 219–230.

Belsey, C. 2011. *A Future for Criticism*. Oxford: Wiley-Blackwell.

Culler, J. 1975. *Structuralist Poetics*. London: Routledge and Kegan Paul.

Erlich, V. 1978. *Russian Formalism*. Cambridge, MA: Harvard University Press.

Fetterley, J. 1978. *The Resisting Reader*. Bloomington: Indiana University Press.

Fish, S. 1981. What is stylistics and why are they saying such terrible things about it? In Freeman, D. (ed). *Essays in Modern Stylistics*. London: Methuen, pp. 53–78.

Gates, H. L. 1992. *Loose Canons. Notes on the Culture Wars*. New York: Oxford University Press.

Gavins, J. 2007. *Text World Theory: An Introduction*. Edinburgh: Edinburgh University Press.

Gavins, J. 2013. *Reading the Absurd*. Edinburgh: Edinburgh University Press.

Hall, G. 2008. Empirical research into the processing of free indirect discourse and the imperative of ecological validity. In S. Zyngier, M. Bortolussi, A. Chesnokova and J. Auracher (eds.). *Directions in Empirical Literary Studies*. Amsterdam: Benjamins, pp. 21–34.

Iser, W. 1978. *The Act of Reading: A Theory of Aesthetic Response*. London: Routledge and Kegan Paul.

Jackson, H. 2001. *Marginalia*. New Haven: Yale University Press.

Kintsch, W. & T. A. van Dijk. 1978. Toward a model of text comprehension and production. *Psychological Review*, 85: 363–394.

Miall, D. S. 2006. Empirical approaches to studying Literary Readers. *Book History*, 9. 291 –311.

Miall, D. S. 2007. *Literary Reading: Empirical and Theoretical Studies*. New York: Peter Lang.

O'Halloran, K. 2007. The sub-conscious in James Joyce's 'Eveline': A corpus stylistic analysis that chews on the 'Fish hook'. *Language and Literature*, 16 (3): 227–244.

Peplow, D. 2011. 'Oh, I've known a lot of Irish people': Reading groups and the negotiation of literary interpretation. *Language and Literature*, 20 (4): 295–315.

Peplow, D. & R. Carter. 2014. Stylistics and real readers. In. M. Burke (ed.). *The Routledge Handbook of Stylistics*. Abingdon: Routledge, pp. 440–454.

Procter, J. & B. Benwell. 2014. *Reading Across Worlds: Transnational Book Groups and the Reception of Difference*. Basingstoke: Palgrave Macmillan.

Richards, I. A. 1929. *Practical Criticism*. London: Routledge and Kegan Paul.

Simpson, P. 2014. *Stylistics: A Resource Book for Students* (2nd Ed.). Abingdon: Routledge.

Spiro, J. 2011. Reader response and the formulation of literary judgment. In J. Swann, R. Pope, & R. Carter (eds.). *Creativity in Language and Literature: The State of the Art*. London: Routledge, pp. 231–244.

Steen, G. 1991. The empirical study of literary reading: methods of data collection. *Poetics*, 20: 559–575.

Stockwell, P. 2009. *Texture: A Cognitive Aesthetics of Reading*. Edinburgh: Edinburgh University Press.

Swann, J, D. Peplow, P. Trimarco, & S. Whiteley. 2014. *The Discourse of Reading Groups: Integrating Cognitive and Sociocultural Perspectives*. Abingdon: Routledge.

Taylor, G. 1990. *Reinventing Shakespeare*. London: Hogarth.

Toolan, M. 1990. Stylistics and its discontents; or, getting off the Fish "hook". In J. J. Weber (ed.). *The Stylistics Reader: From Roman Jakobson to the Present*. London: Routledge, pp. 117–135.

van Dijk, T. A. & W. Kintsch. 1983. *Strategies of Discourse Comprehension*. New York: Academic Press.

van Peer, W. 1986. *Stylistics and Psychology: Investigations of Foregrounding*. London: Croom Helm.

Whiteley, S. 2011. Text world theory, real readers and emotional responses to *The Remains of the Day*. *Language and Literature*, 20 (1): 23-42.

Zyngier, S., W. van Peer, & J. Hakemulder. 2007. Complexity and foregrounding: In the eye of the beholder? *Poetics Today*, 28 (4): 653-682.

What Makes Poems Poetic?

Michael Toolan　(University of Birmingham)

Abstract:　Poems are different from other kinds of text. There are things about them that make some people hold them in especially high regard, by comparison with all other kinds of texts equally aimed at a non-specialist audience. There are things about them, also that make a lot of other people shun them like the plague, by comparison with all other kinds of non-specialist text. Are they the same things in both cases? For some time I have been trying to specify some of the stylistic features or resources in poems that seem especially instrumental in causing readers to feel moved, 'immersed', or engaged — features that might lie at the heart of literariness or 'poeticality' or literary creativity. One of these is lexical repetition, echo, and reformulation — where I am trying to develop a model that will distinguish productive and immersive repetition from the many kinds of lexical repetition that are judged to be boring or pointless or unpoetic. I will discuss these issues by looking at a few modern or contemporary poems by Wallace Stevens, Michael Longley, Kathleen Jamie, and Jo Shapcott. There should be some implications for the teaching of English to advanced or high-proficiency learners — e.g., the kind of student of English who can cope with poetry.

Key words:　poems; poeticality; lexical repetition; sample texts

Although the topic of my presentation is poetry, I have to begin with narrative prose fiction, and repetition, and move on from these to looking at poems. This is because in much of my recent stylistics work I have focussed on the role of repetitions of various kinds, in the achievement of literariness (Toolan, 2010, 2012, 2015, and forthcoming). There are plenty of literary scholars who have made a career out of studying para-repetition over time and between texts, and called it intertextuality, or influence, or literary tradition. My own approach might be denounced as New Critical: I am interested in intratextual repetitions, repetitions within a particular text, and the effect they have. Repetition seems to me fundamental to language (Bloomfield famously said so, in his canonical *Language*: 1933: 76), and I believe it is the essence of everything Jakobson says in his famous Closing Statement (Jakobson, 1960); but it is also obviously problematic. Repetition can imply redundancy, needless recurrence, what Americans call 'the same old, same old'. In some respects, repetition is without question to be avoided: a book or piece of music is criticised for being 'boring and repetitive', with a strong implication that it is boring because it is repetitive. Repetitive work is shunned and can do you harm (we have a musculoskeletal condition known as 'repetitive strain injury', with its own acronym, RSI). No artist is praised for being 'creatively repetitive': the phrase is almost oxymoronic, like 'tediously exhilarating' (*tedious* is a collocate of *repetition; exhilarating* is not!).

But no-one chastises Shakespeare for having Macbeth say 'Tomorrow, and tomorrow, and tomorrow', or having Othello say 'Put out the light, and then put out the light' (or, just six lines earlier, 'It is the cause' three times over). So in the appropriate circumstances, what I would call 'full adjacent repetition' is very effective indeed. And no-one would rather have Othello eschew repetition and say 'Put out the light, and then make everything dark.'

Repetition is also strictly illogical, in the matter of propositions. If I tell you that 'Chongqing is one of China's four directly-controlled municipalities', what is the point of telling you the very same thing again? Surely it is inefficient, all cost and precious little benefit? True; but without repetitions there can be no pattern, and patterning does carry benefits. All art forms exploit repetitions in one way or another: in western classical music, one thinks first of those two little vertical dots that appear at the end of section after section of a Mozart sonata, allowing everything to be repeated without further ado. But of course *within* very Mozart composition one can think of, there is rampant, beguiling repetition, repetitions with little differences, local developments, and then sometimes brilliantly unforeseen repetitions, known as modulations and inversions. Even these, sometimes the opposite or counterpart to the original phrase or melodic line, are arguably a form of repetition, a para-repetition; and in a similar vein, I will suggest below that things like antonyms and collocates are forms of repetition too, in language.

Poems are different from other kinds of text. There are things about them that make some people hold them in especially high regard, by comparison with all other kinds of texts equally aimed at a non-specialist audience. There are things about them, also, that make a lot of other people shun them completely, unlike their response to all other kinds of non-specialist text. Are they the same things in both cases, causing the embrace and the revulsion? For some time I have been trying to specify some of the stylistic features or resources in poems that seem especially instrumental in causing readers to feel moved, 'immersed', or engaged — features that might lie at the heart of literariness or 'poeticality' or literary creativity. One of these is lexical repetition, echo, and reformulation — where I am trying to develop a model that will distinguish productive and immersive repetition from the many kinds of lexical repetition that are judged to be boring or pointless or unpoetic.

Alongside my interest in the language of poetry, I have been using corpus stylistic methods to develop some proposals about readers' main resources in making sense of literary narratives (especially short stories). My proposals form the basis of a forthcoming monograph (Toolan, 2016), in which I focus especially on the establishment of narrative situation, lexical repetition and para-repetition, maximally vague mental picturing as readers' rough and ready means of keeping track of the developing narrative situation. In Toolan (2009) I had explored narrative progression in depth; in the new book, on sense-making, I focus on the noted triad of factors (situation, mental picturing, and lexical repetition), but looking in detail at a commonly-occurring moment (or passage), often close to the end of the story, of greatest reader-involvement and ethical-cum-emotional immersion in the story situation (a 'payoff' which justifies the investment of effort made by the reader of the story). This near-final point in the story often seems to deploy a cluster of text-linguistic features, and as a result (I argue) is all the more 'engaging' of the reader. Readers of these passages, particularly, report feeling most drawn into the spatio-temporal situation of the narrative, which is always an occasion of ethical or experiential crisis for one or more of the characters.

I call these passages of high emotional involvement (HEI) passages, and strive to demonstrate how stylistically distinct they tend to be, on a series of characteristics, relative to the rest of the story. They are an most arresting, most affecting moment in the story and — inter alia — they prepare the reader for the termination of the story in the near future. I argue that many stories *have to* have such a passage, high risk though they are for the author (they run the risk of being judged melodramatic, overblown, 'windy'), to give the story a satisfying shape, including a peak of intensity (as distinct from a steady sameness of reader-involvement and character experience). I have found ten features or stylistic characteristics to be prominent in these passages, and list them immediately below.

Summary of HEI passage stylistic features in emotively immersing passages in **stories**:

1. Key projecting verbs are *feel, think, see, want, know*
2. Negation is widespread: *a lack of hope, no comfort, that wasn't what ...*
3. Sentences are longer, and/or grammar is comparatively complex
4. In part *because* sentences/clauses are longer, their internal rhythms tend to be more developed; and this in turn may make the passage feel (be) more poetic, with richer tonality or voicing than adjacent text.
5. More likely that standard sentence grammar may be departed from. Sentences (e.g. lacking a Subject or finite main verb, or easily recoverable ellipsis relative to a previous sentence) may border on the ungrammatical.
6. More temporal staging and simultaneity (marked by *As he did x, he felt y* structures, which typically combine report of a *physical* or external narrated event with report of a mental or internal event/reaction/insight; hence a double telling).
7. Absolute/ultimate words: *everlasting, never, rock-bottom, deeper than she could ever have managed, on and on, all there was ... final*
8. Heat, light and dimension words are prominent: *cold, dark, deep, rock-bottom, inflammation*
9. A higher density of lexical and structural repetition and para-repetition in HEI passages than elsewhere; kinds of para-repetition mean that there are noticeable possibilities of inter-substitutability of words, phrases, within the HEI passage. In effect, the passages are highly rhetorically crafted.
10. Much more likely to find Free Indirect Thought here than in the non-HEI co-text ...

Now let me turn back to poetry, and the stylistics of poetry. Or what I prefer simply to call, echoing the title of Winfred Nowottny's fine book (which I first met when an undergraduate), the language poets use. (The Language Poets Use is the title of a course I now teach to undergraduates in Birmingham). Actually there was a handful of books that I found especially useful general introductions to the language of poetry when I was myself a student at Edinburgh University forty years ago; they included Brooks and Warren's classic *Understanding Poetry*, and what was one of the first student-oriented books in the new stylistics tradition, Geoffrey Leech's *A Linguistic Guide to English Poetry* (1969). Despite all the changes to stylistics wrought by computers, cognitivist thinking and corpus linguistic methods, Leech's 1969 guide, older sibling to Leech & Short's study of style in fiction (1981), remains a richly rewarding read, clear, informed, and balanced in its discussion of rhyme and metre, metaphor, foregrounding, and many other key topics in poetry analysis.

When thinking about the kinds of poems I have been studying with undergraduate students at Birmingham, and thinking also about repetition and High Emotional Involvement passages as crucial in short stories, I began to consider whether and how HEI passages might also operate in poems. In a sense, stories have the luxury of *building* towards an HEI point and passage, usually near the end of the text and thus after several thousands of words of text, many pages, which establish a situation, a set of circumstances, and often a sense of characters negotiating a problem or a lack. But in some other respects, literary stories seem quite like poems, at least if we consider how the former have been characterised by critical authorities. Thus writing in the late 19th century and very much following in Poe's footsteps, Brander Matthews wrote that a short story 'deals with a single character, a single event, a single emotion, or the series of emotions called forth by a single situation'. And more recently the short-story theorist Austin Wright has noted that stories tend to be strongly unified, have plots of small magnitude (static or disclosure plots, Joycean epiphanies, and the like), and leave significant things to inference. As much could surely be said of poems, so that there are similarities of function here, albeit not so many of form.

But very clearly, a fourteen-line sonnet does not have the luxury of such extension: everything is intense, immediate, and encapsulated. There is simply very little time, very little text, in which to establish the conditions that will lead a reader to feel caught up in a moment of crisis, i.e., to feel moved by an embodied ideational and ethical drama. But is there not still scope, even in such a short poem, for a sense of textual contour, and of lexicogrammatical (and cognitive) *build*, from the 'unsaid-ness' that precedes the poem's title, to the sense of vivid and particular completion by the time we have read the last line? This, roughly, was what I wish to consider, in relation to a handful of modern or recent poems.

Short poems I assumed are just as 'immersing and involving', *in their own way*, as short stories, but must do this by somewhat different means; just how different are those means? A preliminary look suggests that some of the ten posited characteristics of HEI passages in fiction, listed above, are also evident in HEI moments in poems. To confirm this, consider the poem *Summer Evening* by Peter Sansom.

Summer Evening

Every summer comes an opaque evening
before the beach is photos and the leaves
let go to relight autumn. It's brisk in Wickes
and the garden centre's scented colours
are loaded in the backs of estates. In parks
that saw offices undress for lunch
lads career in the wake of the World Cup
and wood after deliberate wood finds
a path in its own curve to the jack.
Everywhere is couples, and pushchairs
that make sense of last year or last but one,
till pubs overflow round continental tables
on main roads, laughing like it might last.

Sooner or later, swans on a river
disprove the moon they paddle through,
cameod by willows. The rowing boat
moored there is a temptation you decline,
though all the time you walk, taking
the long cut to the car park, you imagine
being out on that water, the drag
and viscous ripples as you pull,
then shipping oars and just letting it drift.

Here in note form are my stylistic observations about this poem, keyed especially to the HEI characteristics of fiction:

1. The long first stanza mostly unmodalized, *realis*, declarative, factual-descriptive, interpretive of the setting, the exterior. Describing generalities and groups.

2. Stanza 1: groups, pantemporal, multispatial; Stanza 2: focusses on a *you*, at a specific time and place.

3. Very simple direct repetitions in st 1: *every, wood, last* (3). Some para-repetitions in st 2: *temptation/pull; rowing-boat/shipping oars; moor/drift; there/on that water*. Plenty of local alliterative and assonantial repetition throughout.

4. Other than *all the time*, there are few if any 'absolute' words expressing dimension, depth, heat, light, etc. This is one contrast with the story HEI features ...

5. Final lines are modalised, *irrealis*, hypothetical-speculative; interpretive of self, more reflexive (4 *yous*). These same lines are also pseudo-negation, describing what was not ...

6. Extensive 'temporal staging' in the final sentence: *all the time, as you pull.* There was more spatial staging earlier, but now with spatial stability (e.g. the anaphoric *there* st 2 line 4) there is temporal detail and also the double focus on the mental and the material (all the time you *walk* you *imagine* ...)

7. Is there a pun in the final line, *shipping oars? Ors/oars?*

8. The final sentence is the longest and most complex syntactically. Arguably the most complex intonationally too.

The upshot of analysis of the Sansom poem and other poems, to see how many of the narrative fiction HEI characteristics, is that features #1, #2, #5 and #10 seem not to be salient in poetry (projecting verbs, negation, non-standard sentential grammar, and Free Indirect Thought), while feature #9 (kinds of lexical and structural repetition) is if anything even more significant.

Repetition is at least as instrumental in poems as it is in stories. But it may take different forms. In Toolan (2012) I tentatively proposed a distinction between

1. adjacent or distant full repetition (like the earlier Shakespeare examples: this can often be powerfully poetic) and

2. adjacent reformulatory repetition (which risks appearing to be a feeble and imprecise, a kind of self-correcting, which breaches the Gricean maxims in not

being as brief as it could have been without the repetition, while failing to yield, by means of the near-repetition, sufficient enriching implicatures.

More recently I have added to these types of a repetition a third broad type, which following Hoey (1991) I call complex repetitions; these include, besides antonyms and hypernymic relations and strongly collocating pairs (*car* as a kind of repeat of *Jaguar*; the verb *brake* as a kind of repeat of *accelerate;* *hood* and *windshield*) all kinds of later lexical items that can be shown on fairly strict morphological or semantic basis to be relatable to earlier ones (perhaps by contextual substitutability). Non-adjacent (thus non-reformulatory) complex repetitions, like the full repetitions (type 1 above), are I believe at the heart of the literariness of many poems, being prominent in the passages of most foregrounded text. They are a key contributor to what makes poems poetic.

I have only limited space in which to discuss specific examples, but consider the complex' lexical repetitions in the final stanza of W. B. Yeats's great late poem, *The Circus Animals' Desertion*:

> Those masterful images because complete
> Grew in **pure mind**, but out of what began?
> A mound of **refuse** or the **sweepings** of a street,
> **Old** kettles, **old** bottles, and a **broken** can,
> **Old** iron, **old bones**, **old rags**, that raving slut
> Who keeps the **till**. Now that my **ladder's** gone,
> I must lie down where all the **ladders** start
> In the **foul rag** and **bone shop** of the **heart**.

The words highlighted in the stanza above are those which I judge to participate, just within the confines of this stanza, in some form of complex repetition. I have not, however, marked all the repetition links between highlighted items, for example by means of arrow-headed lines; so the reader is asked to identify those linkages themselves. Some of course are obvious by virtue of formal near-identity: the repeated uses of *old*, and the *ladder's/ladders* pairing. Others, such as the antonymic (*pure/foul; mind/heart*) or collocational (*till/shop*) involve more reflection. But the chief point of identifying these patterns is simply to show how pervasive and extensive they are, to the point that they appear to be a key structuring principle of the stanza — and of the poem.

Earlier I talked about focusing intratextually, and certainly one should register all the (complex or full) repetitions in this final stanza in relation to the lexis of the previous four stanzas. That would show you, for example, that however scandalously repetitive it is for Yeats to have used the word *old* as many as five times in this stanza, these only continue what was started earlier, since *old age, old themes*, and *old songs* are named in stanzas 1 and 2 respectively. Likewise the *broken* in this final stanza (which I judge to be an intra-stanzaic complex repetition of *old* and *foul*) harks back to the first stanza, where the speaker describes himself as ' but [sc. no more than] a broken man '. So repetitions across all five stanzas should be tracked, but given limited space I have simply highlighted those operating within the small compass of these eight lines, to show how arresting and cumulative their effect can be: arresting, in that a repeat compels the recipient to read (hear/see/ feel/etc.) again, and for longer, what was already read. Sequence, the poetic line, carries the promise that you will encounter something new, that the content will be different; a repetition enacts that sequencing, that linear continuation, but it does not take you somewhere radically new ideationally, and instead compels you to think more about what has already been introduced — to focus upon it. In a sense, a rhyme — an auditory repetition — does the same. Take the poem's final rhyme: the verb *start* and the noun *heart*, taken separately, have nothing semantically in common and only phonologically identical nuclei and codas; but here we are obliged to take them together, paired up, as if *heart* and *start* had something unexpectedly in common. And in the given textual situation, readers begin to see an uncommon, almost magical, connection between these two ideas.

I will finish with another example, Wallace Stevens's complex but hugely rewarding *Sunday Morning*. By comparison with the one-stanza discussion of the Yeats, I will take a step towards a fuller intratextual analysis by drawing attention to the kinds of coherence and unity that even quite simple repetitions (not complex ones) can create within each of the first and last stanzas and between those two stanzas (bearing in mind also that the poem comprises eight 15-line stanzas, and like much of Stevens, is not always open to straightforward interpretation). For ease of scrutiny of the within-stanza and between-stanza lexical links, I will present the stanzas side by side — whereas in the poem they are separated by as many as 90 lines. Nor, by the way, do I claim that below I have identified *all* the complex repetitions in and between the two stanzas: the more inward one becomes of a poem, the more repetition patterning one tends to see. Thus, for example, only now do I see that the second half of *water-lights* in line 8 of stanza 1 could be classed as a repeat of *dark* in line 6 by means of antonymy and word-class change. Or that the *inescapable* of stanza VIII line 8 could be classified as an antonymic repeat of *free* at the end of the previous line. Again I have opted not to mark up the text with lines and arrows, to underscore just where the repetitions occur, but trust to the reader's alertness to see where they arise; I prefer not to 'doctor' the text too much, beyond introducing the format highlighting, to the point of presenting the text in a form that radically differs from what the ordinary reader encounters.

Sunday Morning

Stanza I

Complacencies of the peignoir, and late
Coffee and **oranges** in a **sunny** chair,
And the green freedom of a cockatoo
Upon a rug mingle to dissipate
The holy hush of **ancient** sacrifice.
She **dreams** a little, and she feels the **dark**
Encroachment of that **old** catastrophe,
As a calm **darkens** among **water**-lights.
The pungent **oranges** and bright, green **wings**
Seem things in some procession of the dead,
Winding across **wide water**, **without sound**.
The **day** is like **wide water**, **without sound**,
Stilled for the passing of her **dreaming** feet
Over the seas, to **silent Palestine**,
Dominion of the blood and **sepulchre**.

Stanza VIII

She hears, upon that **water without sound**,
A voice that cries, "The **tomb** in **Palestine**
Is not the porch of spirits lingering.
It is the **grave** of Jesus, where he lay."
We live in an **old** chaos of the **sun**,
Or **old** dependency of **day** and night,

Or island solitude, unsponsored, free,
Of that **wide water**, inescapable.
Deer walk upon our mountains, and the quail
Whistle about us their spontaneous cries;
Sweet berries ripen in the wilderness;
And, in the isolation of the sky,
At evening, casual flocks of pigeons make
Ambiguous undulations as they sink,
Downward to **darkness**, on extended **wings**.

In a poem where the sense is not always obvious, where readers struggle to grasp the coherent unity of the work and its argument, repetition cohesion can be invaluable. So the reader who notices the *dark* and *darkens* in the opening stanza, and sees them echoed in the flight of birds downward to *darkness* in the very final line, has an important aid to sense-making. They can then ponder on why a ' Sunday Morning' should be occasion of such ' darkness', and piece together the references to sacrifice, that old catastrophe, the blood and sepulchre in Palestine, and postulate a contrast between the ' She' enjoying a ' complacent' Sunday morning of coffee and oranges and a pet bird, and the Christian religious observance built around the re-enactment of Christ's death. There seems no mention of resurrection in the first stanza, and perhaps the poem will go on to reveal that the ' She', the woman, does not believe in any such. Such a conclusion seems to be implied also in the final stanza, where the first stanza's *sepulchre* is now repeated as *tomb* and *grave*, but with no declared assurance that *the old chaos of the sun* in which we live, *the old dependency of day and night*, are ' escapable'. But when complex repetitions between an opening and closing stanza of a complex poem like *Sunday Morning* are put side by side, as here, it is as much the differences embedded within the repeats in the later stanza, as much as the samenesses, that are noteworthy. At the poem's close as at the opening there is a preoccupation with darkness, and with wide water without sound. But now the silence is less than total (a voice cries out about the grave of Jesus, and later the quail's spontaneous cries are noted: *cries/cries* here is another repetition I failed to register above!), and while there are wings still, the birds are different: before, a single cockatoo with green wings, now flocks of pigeons, descending to the earth ambiguously.

My brief conclusions are that only some of the HEI resources used in some stories seem to be equally instrumental in the high point of poems (the latter half of short poems, the final stanza in longer ones). On the other hand, some resources drop out of the picture when we turn from narrative prose to poetry, and other resources may be more prominent — clearly these include rhyme and rhythm, which I have barely touched upon. These narrative vs poetry differences point to the obvious conclusion that difference of genre and of sub-genre (for example, where we can identify a poem's sub-genre) are likely to affect formal choices with respect to HEI-creation. Repetition is perhaps even more important than it is in literary fiction, but it may be deployed differently, for example with full repetitions in the build-up, but complex or para-repetitions (sometimes no repetitions) at the immersive 'peak'. Or a final stanza may repeat or evoke words and phrases from a now-distant initial stanza, as we saw in *Sunday Morning* (and in the Yeats poem discussed, to a lesser extent), but always repeating 'with difference'. Many poems, of course, may not have this 'build to immersion' contour at all — they function quite differently. I would not claim that the stylistic phenomena I have dwelt upon are characteristic of more than a minority of modern poems — but if they are instrumental in a significant minority, then they are surely worth studying.

References

Bloomfield, L. 1933. *Language*. New York: Holt, Rinehart & Winston.

Brooks, C. & R. P. Warren. 1976 [1938]. *Understanding Poetry*. New York: Holt, Rinehart & Winston.

Hoey, M. 1991. *Patterns of Lexis in Text*. Oxford: Oxford University Press.

Jakobson, R. 1960. Closing Statement: Linguistics and Poetics. In T. A. Sebeok (ed.). *Style in Language*. Cambridge, MA: MIT Press, 350 – 377. Also reprinted in R. Jakobson, *Selected Writings, Vol. III: Poetry of Grammar and Grammar of Poetry*, The Hague: Mouton de Gruyter, 1981, pp. 18–51.

Leech, G. 1969. *A Linguistic Guide to English Poetry*. London: Longman.

Nowottny, W. 1964. *The Language Poets Use*. London: Athlone Press.

Toolan, M. 2009. *Narrative Progression in the Short Story: A Corpus Stylistic Approach*. Amsterdam: Benjamins.

Toolan, M. 2010. What do poets show and tell linguists? *Acta Linguistica Hafniensia* 42: 1, 189–204.

Toolan, M. 2012. Poems: Wonderfully repetitive. In R. Jones (ed.). *Discourse and Creativity*. London: Pearson, 17−34.

Toolan, M. 2015. Poetry and poetics. In R. Jones (ed.). *The Routledge Handbook of Language and Creativity*. London: Routledge, 231−247.

Toolan, M. forthc. 2016. *Making Sense of Narrative Text: Situation, Repetition, and Picturing in the Reading of Short Stories*. London & New York: Routledge.

On the Narrative Rhythm of Drama

Xu Youzhi （**Henan University**）

Abstract：Dramatic narrative rhythm is the playwright's rhythmic treatment of all the elements of drama. Such rhythm is achieved through the playwright's arrangement of his/her work's acts and scenes, conflicts and clashes, and development of its characters' emotions and affections. The drama's acts and scenes may be rendered undulating, conflicts and clashes stirring, and its characters' emotions and affections full of ups and downs. But drama is an art of dialogue. Unlike in novels where the novelist may directly describe the novel's actions and events, and comment on characters or editorialize rather freely, in drama, the playwright has to reveal characters and their conflicts/ clashes — that is, he/she has to let characters dramatize the kind of people they are and the kind of events they are engaged in by their own words and actions. So dramatic narratives have to be presented through the playwright's designing of the plot and the characters' acting and conversing, forming the rhythmic movement of tense or relaxed, sad or happy communication between the drama's narrative curve and the reader/audience's emotional response. Thus we have to look at dramatic narrative rhythm from two respects: one, structural rhythm, and two, dialogical rhythm.

Key words：drama; narrative rhythm; structural rhythm; dialogical rhythm

Drama is something written to be performed, by actors on a stage, for an audience. Drama is made possible not only with words but also with physical actions, stage effects, and other bits of theatricality that may involve lights, music, fine arts and dancing etc. to create special effects on the audience.

So, the solitary act of reading drama is certainly a different kind of experience from seeing and hearing a performed drama — a play. We have to face a greater strain on our imagination in reading a drama: to cast characters in our minds, paint in the scenic backdrops, place the furniture and props, and choreograph the action, which is a very compelling literary experience. But as readers, the most important thing for us to do is to come to grips with the hidden dramatic narrative rhythm of the play, as dramatic rhythm is the playwright's rhythmic treatment of all the elements of drama. And I would say that it is the living soul of organic drama.

Susanne K. Langer incisively pointed out: That rhythm is the "commanding form" of the play; it springs from the poet's original conception of the "fable", and dictates the major divisions of the work, the light or heavy style of its presentation, the intensity of the highest feeling and most violent act, the great or small number of characters, and the degrees of their development. The total action is a cumulative form; and because it is constructed by a rhythmic treatment of its elements, it appears to *grow* from its beginnings. That is the playwright's creation of "organic form" (Langer, 1953: 356).

So dramatic rhythm is achieved through the playwright's arrangement of his/her work's acts and scenes, conflicts and clashes, and development of its characters' emotions and affections, one cliffhanger after another. The drama's acts and scenes may be rendered undulating, conflicts and clashes stirring, and its characters' emotions and affections full of ups and downs.

But as I see it, drama is very much an art of dialogue. Unlike in novels where the novelist may directly describe the development of plot, and comment on characters or editorialize rather freely, in drama, the playwright has to reveal characters and the progression of their conflicts/clashes — that is, he/she has to let characters dramatize the kind of people they are, and the kind of events they are engaged in, by their own words and actions. It is clear that dramatic narratives have to be presented through the playwright's designing of the plot and the characters' acting and conversing. Thus we have to look at dramatic narrative from two respects: one, structural rhythm, and two, dialogical rhythm. Both structure and dialogue are clearly assisted by stage directions: for structure, there are division of acts and scenes, scenic backdrops, the furniture and props, the curtain, etc.; for dialogue, there is choreography of the characters' action, or mood, or both.

We know plot in plays usually involves actions, and dramatic structure concerns the organization of them within a limited time (nowadays not more than two to three hours) and space (a limited stage with curtain). A typical dramatic structure involves five distinguishable parts that mark different stages in the progression of plot. The first of these, *the exposition*, presents the situation at the opening of the play, introducing the characters, their relationships in the play, and very often, the main problem confronting them. The second part of dramatic structure, *the rising action*, consists of a series of events that complicate the original situation and creates conflicts among characters or values. The rising action is more and more complicated and quickly leads clashes to a turning point, i. e. the third part of dramatic structure, *the climax*. Then follows the fourth part, *the falling action*, which presents the unwinding or unknotting of the complication. The final part of dramatic structure is the conclusion, or what is called *catastrophe*, when the central contradiction is resolved, a stable situation is reestablished, and the drama is done.

Besides the five dramatic structural divisions that shape the action, most plays also have formal divisions such as scenes. Many classic plays have five acts (called multi-act play), but modern plays tend to have one (called one-act play) or two or three acts, some of which are further divided into scenes. For instance, Shakespeare's *Hamlet* has five acts, each of which contains five, two, four, seven, two scenes respectively. Oscar Wilde's *The Importance of Being Earnest* has just three acts, with no scenes. Moliere's play *The Doctor in Spite of Himself* has three acts; both Act I and Act II have five scenes, and Act III has eleven scenes. Such formal divisions are the result of the content of individual plays — where sharp breaks can be emotionally effective by creating suspense, or giving readers a relief from tension.

Here we can see that the play's division of structure (with the use of curtain's rising or falling) display a certain rise and fall rhythmic pattern. The oscillation between up moments and down moments, between satisfied expectation and sudden surprise, between successes and failures, and between climatic moments and intermission, forms the drama's narrative rhythm.

Such dramatic rhythm is embodied in the playwright's skillful temporal arrangement of plot: the different time allotted for the play's different stages in the progression of events at different spaces; and in his/her control of the characters' emotional ups and downs: how they begin, how they develop, how they reach climax, how they come to an end, and why all these occur, and when there are breaks — there is a keeping to the cause and effect logic of real life and a wholeness of story in them.

Depending on the playwright, in some parts such as the exposition, the rising action, and the climax, the progression of plot may be gradually quickened, which benefits an increasingly intense and speedy description of the plot, whereas in other parts like the falling action and catastrophe, the progression of plot can be slowed down by degrees, which is displayed in a leisurely, or unhurried unwinding or unknotting of the complication. So, the play's structure and division moves in a rhythmic tense vs relaxed way, embodied in a tranquil — tense — relaxed — tense again — climactic — relaxed again — easing off way. Even within the exposition, there is likely a gradual rising — tense — climax — falling progression. These manipulations of plot produce the ups and downs of the emotional rhythm of the play, which sustains the readers/viewers' interest and holds their rise and fall of emotion. Their mood goes up and down according to the main characters' successes or failures in the pass/fail cycle — what may be referred to as the drama's overall introduction — rising action — climax — denouement narrative curve, and the readers/viewers' emotional response to it. Hence the attractiveness of the dramatic rhythm.

But as drama is an art of dialogue, and what we read in drama is chiefly conversational give and take, so we have to construct the plot of the play, and the characters' relationship, ideas, activities, habits, eccentricities, and personalities from what they say, with, of course, some hints on their action or mood given by stage directions. Even when we watch a performed drama — a play, though we can directly see the characters' acting, including their facial expressions and body movements, what we hear is still chiefly characters' conversings. So we can say that the overall dramatic structure is fleshed out and enacted by dramatic dialogue.

Dramatic dialogue displays certain literary and stylistic traits.

First, dramatic dialogue reveals the theme and advances the action of the play. A series of conversational exchange is not simply a string of remarks of alternating speakers but a series of moves to promote the development of plot, to present conflicts and clashes, and to reveal the characters' relationship, ideas, activities, habits, eccentricities, personalities, their rich and mixed mental and physical activities, and changes in their relationship.

Secondly, dramatic dialogue displays the characters' characteristic social positions and special interests by varying the speakers' language in tone and expression, and brings out the particularity of each speaker's speech.

Thirdly, dramatic dialogue gives the impression of naturalness of the characters' speeches by couching them in a concise, condensed, sometimes poetic, sometimes colloquial language, heightening its artistic appeal, or increasing its emotional strength, or imbuing them with the rich flavor of life.

So besides the designed rhythmic plot movement and thematic and character development promoted by characters' conversing, we should also notice the playwright's rhythmic presentation of characters' different tone and expression, as well as the dialogue's realistic or unnatural feel to make characters' speech long or short, strong or weak, elegant or pompous, casual or vulgar, sloppy or banal, so as to reflect the drama of everyday life.

In pushing the advancement of plot, the playwright exploits rhythmic use of cyclic turn-taking patterns, making the dialogic interplay beginning slowly or unhurriedly, and then getting increasingly quickened and sharpened, and in this way bring out the thematic movement, intensify the contradiction of the plot, and reveal through these various feelings of the characters, making the characters' conversing most arresting.

So from the very beginning, as readers/viewers, our curiosities and feelings are quickly aroused. See how the very opening scene of Moliere's play *The Doctor in Spite of Himself* immediately interests us as readers/viewers in seeing whether or not the couple in the play are on good terms:

> SGANARELLE: *No, I tell you I won't do anything of the sort, and I'm the one to say and be the master.*
>
> MARTINE: *And I tell you that I want you to live to suit me, and I didn't marry you to put up with your carryings on.*
>
> SGANARELLE: *Oh, what a business it is to have a wife, how right Aristotle is when he says a wife is worse than a demon!*
>
> MARTINE: *Just listen to that smart fellow with half-wit Aristotle!*
>
> SGANARELLE: *Yes, a woodcutter who knows how to reason about things, like me, who served a famous doctor for six years, and as a youngster knew his*

elementary Latin book by heart.

>MARTINE: *A plague on the crazy fool!*

>SGANARELLE: *A plague on the slut!*

>MARTINE: *Cursed by the day when I went and said yes!*

>SGANARELLE: *Cursed by the hornified notary who had me sign my own ruin!*

And how their quarrel quickly leads to a climatic situation just within the first scene: challenge and abuses on the part of the wife, and sarcasm, threat, and finally brutal action on the part of the husband:

>MARTINE: *And you, you drunkard, do you expect things to go on for ever like this?*

>SGANARELLE: *My good wife, let's go easy, if you please.*

>MARTINE: *And me to endure your insolence and debauchery to all eternity?*

>SGANARELLE: *My good wife, you know that my soul isn't very patient and my arm is pretty good.*

>MARTINE: *You make me laugh with your threats.*

>SGANARELLE: *My good little wife, my love, you're itching for trouble, as usual.*

>MARTINE: *I'll show you I'm not afraid of you.*

>SGANARELLE: *My dear better half, you're asking for something.*

>MARTINE: *Do you think your words frighten me?*

>SGANARELLE: *Sweet object of my eternal vows, I'll box your ears.*

>MARTINE: *Drunkard that you are!*

>SGANARELLE: *I'll beat you.*

>MARTINE: *Wine-sack!*

>SGANARELLE: *I'll wallop you.*

>MARTINE: *Wretch!*

>SGANARELLE: *I'll tan your hide.*

>MARTINE: *Traitor, wiseacre, deceiver, coward, scoundrel, gallowsbird, beggar, good-for-nothing, rascal, villain, thief, ...*

>SGANARELLE: [Takes a stick and beats her.] *Ah, so you want it, eh?*

>MARTINE: *Oh, oh, oh, oh!*

>SGANARELLE: *That's the right way to pacify you.* (I.i)

We are becoming worried about the outcome of the brutal action, when a neighbour comes in to her help. But to our great surprise, the good-hearted neighbour is slapped for his meddling.

MONSIEUR ROBERT: *Hey there, hey there, hey there! Fie! What's this? What infamy! Confounded the rascle for beating his wife that way!*

MARTINE: [Arms akimbo, forces MONSIEUR ROBERT back as she talks, and finally gives him a slap.] *And as for me, I want him to beat me.*

MONSIEUR ROBERT: *Oh! Then with all my heart, I consent.*

MARTINE: *What are you meddling for?* (I.ii)

The poor neighbor is even slapped by the husband too. The couple seem to make peace. But the next scene (I.iii) shows immediately that the wife is not pacified; she wants to take revenge on her husband, by successfully making others believe that he is a capable but capricious doctor, and his capriciousness has to be beaten out of him. In this way the husband is beaten to become a doctor — a doctor in spite of himself!

The following extract from Oscar Wilde's *An Ideal Husband*, through the gradually quickening interplay of ideas and personalities of the character conversing, the theme is made clear, the characters are vividly presented: Sir Robert Chiltern is shown as appearing to be at first cold, then indignant, then irritated, then apprehensive, and in the end unnerved, whereas Mrs Cheveley is shown as possessing an unhurried, nonchalant, contemptuous and overbearing attitude.

MRS CHEVELEY: [In her most nonchalant manner.] *My dear Sir Robert, you are the man of the world, and you have your price, I suppose. The drawback is that most are so dreadfully expensive. I know I am. I hope you will be reasonable in your terms.*

SIR ROBERT CHILTERN: [Rising indignantly.] *If you will allow me, I will call your carriage for you. You have lived so long abroad, Mrs Cheveley, that you seem to unable to realize that you are talking to an English gentleman.*

MRS CHEVELEY: [Detains him by touching his arm with her fan and keeping it there while she is talking.] *I realize that I am talking to a man who laid the foundation of his fortune by selling to a stock Exchange speculator a cabinet secret.*

SIR ROBERT CHILTERN: [Biting his lip.] *What do you mean?*

MRS CHEVELEY: [Rising and facing him.] *I mean that I know the real origin of your wealth and career, and I have got your letter, too.*

SIR ROBERT CHILTERN: *What letter?*

MRS CHEVELEY: [Contemptuously.] *The letter you wrote to Baron Arnhem, when you were Lord Radley's secretary, telling the Baron to buy Sues*

Canal shares — a letter written three days before the government announced its own purchase.

SIR ROBERT CHILTERN: [Hoarsely.] *It is not true.*

MRS CHEVELEY: *You thought that letter had been destroyed. How foolish of you! It is in my possession.*

— Oscar Wilde, *An Ideal Husband* (I)

And in terms of the impression of naturalness of the characters' speeches, and the displaying of the characters' characteristic social positions and special interests, we can see how Shakespeare purposely makes his major characters speak in iambic pentameter verse, to give them a kind of gravity appropriate to their importance and to the affairs they deal with, as in the beginning of *Measure for Measure*:

DUKE: *Escalus!*

ESCALUS: *My lord.*

DUKE: *Of government the properties to unfold*
Would seem in me t'affect speech and discourse,
Since I am put to know that your own science
Exceeds, in that, the lists of all advice
My strength can give you; then no more remains
But that, to your sufficiency, as your worth is able,
And let them work. ...

— Shakespeare, *Measure for Measure* (I. i. 36)

To rhythmically counterpose the verse paragraphs, Shakespeare makes other characters speak in prose, to show, on one hand, their low status, and to present, on the other, their wit and humour in the art of language, as the speech made by Falstaff in *Henry IV*:

FAL.: *Bardolph, am I not fall'n away vilely since this last action? Do I not bate? Do I not dwindle? Why my skin hangs about me like an old lady's loose gown; I am wither'd like an old apple-john. Well, I'll repent, and that suddenly, while I am in some liking. I shall be out of heart shortly, and then I shall have no strength to repent.*

— Shakespeare, *Henry IV* (I. iii. 113)

And see how N. R. Nash gives the rhythm of his characters' speechways in their conversing: LIZZIE is shown as pompous, H.C. casual, while NOAH vulgar.

LIZZIE: *No sign of rain yet, is there?*

H.C.: *Not a cloud no where.*

LIZZIE: *I dreamed we had a rain — a great big rain!*

H.C.: *Did you, Lizzie?*

LIZZIE: *Thunderstorm! Rain coming down in sheets! Lightening flashed — thunder rolled up and down the canyon like a kid with a big drum! I looked up and I laughed and yelled …! [With a laugh.] Oooh, it was wonderful!*

NOAH: *Drought's drought and a dream's dream.*

LIZZIE: *But it was a nice dream, Noah — and nearly as good as rain.*

NOAH: *Near ain't rain!*

— N. R. Nash, *The Rainmaker*

And also see how Eugene O'Neill even goes so far as to employ eye-dialect to give a hint at his characters' poor educational background and low social position:

LONG: [Indicating it all with an oratorical gesture.] *Well, 'ere we are. Fif' Avenoo. This, ere's their bleedin' private lane, as yer might say. [Bitterly.] We're trespassers 'ere. Proletarians keep orf the grass!*

YANK: [Dully.] *I don't see no grass, yuh boob. [Staring at the sidewalk.] Clean, ain't it? Yuh could eat a fried egg offen it. The white wings got some job sweepin' dis up. [looking up and down the avenue — surlily.] Where's all de white-coller stiffs you said was here — and de skoits — her kind?*

LONG: *In church, blarst 'em! Arskin' Jesus to give 'em more money.*

YANK: *Choich, huh? I useter go to choichonct — sure — when I was a kid. Me old man and woman, dey made me. Dey never went demselves, dough. Always got too big a head on Sunday mornin', dat was dem. [With a grin.] Dey was scrppers for fair, bot' of dem.*

— Eugene O'Neill, *The Hairy Ape* (V)

In dramatic dialogue, all utterances made by characters are likely to be thought of as goal-directed actions, i. e. speech acts, which may be ordering or pleading, threatening or promising, challenging or suggesting, etc. The playwright expertly exploits the patterns of speech act use as a flexible and powerful mechanism to typify the traits of characters and help the reader grasp their social relationships — whether or not they are of roughly equal status, or on good terms. See the playwrights' rhythmic presentation of characters' different tone and expression in the following dramas:

RILEY: [Sharply] *Give me that tape.*

BROWN: *I haven't got one!*
RILEY: *My patience is not inexhaustible!*

— Tom Stoppard, *Enter a Free Man*

FACE: *Believ't I will.*
SUBTLE: *The worst I fart at thee.*
DOL COMMON: *Ha' you your wits? Why, gentlemen! For love. —*
FACE: *Sirrah, I'll strip you —*

— Jonson, *The Alchemist*

Speech acts are often connected together into sequence of turns in conversation. When two or more people are talking everyone seems to know instinctively when and how to swap turns. But if a speaker has the most turns, controls what to talk about and who to talk next, and interrupts others, then he/she is powerful. One who habitually performs the speech act of ordering others to do things is likely to be thought of as bossy. One who always obeys the commands of others and who only limpidly requests others to do things is likely to be thought of as wimpy. The playwright is very skillful at a vivid rhythmic presentation of such traits of his/her characters in revealing their personalities. See G. B. Shaw's rhythmic presentation of the bossy mother — wimpy son conversing at the beginning of *Major Barbara*:

LADY B: *Now are you attending me, Stephen?*
STEPHEN: *Of course, mother.*
LADY B: *No: it's not of course. I want something much more than your everyday matter-of-course attention. I am going to speak to you very seriously, Stephen. I wish you would let that watch alone.*
STEPHEN: [Hastily relinquishing the chain.] *Have I done anything to annoy you, mother? If so, it was quite unintentional.*
LADY B: [Astonished.] *Nonsense.* [With some remorse.] *My poor boy, did you think I was angry with you?*
STEPHEN: *What is it then, mother? You are making me very uneasy.*
LADY B: [Squaring herself at him rather aggressively.] *Stephen? may I ask you how soon you intend to realize that you are a grown-up man, and I am only a woman.*
STEPHEN: [Amazed.] *Only a —*
LADY B: *Don't repeat my words, please? it is a most aggravating habit ...*

— G. B. Shaw, *Major Barbara*

What is more, playwrights are clear about the important role politeness strategies play in making dramas dramatically interesting, so there tends to be quite a lot of rhythmic interplay of politeness and impoliteness in dramatic texts, as a way to indicate characters' relationship or social conduct. At the beginning extract from Eugene Ionesco's *The Lesson*, *the Professor* directs an elaborate display of politeness strategies (use of repeated apologies, begging for forgiveness) towards what is actually a very trivial imposition (by having kept the pupil waiting).

> PROFESSOR: *Good morning, good morning ... You are ... er ... I suppose you really are ... the new pupil?*
> [The Pupil turns round the briskly and easily, very much the young lady: she gets up and goes towards the Professor, holding out her hand.]
> PUPIL: *Yes, Sir. Good morning, Sir. You see I came at the right time. I didn't want to be late.*
> PROFESSOR: *Good. Yes, that's very good. Thank you. But you shouldn't have hurried too much, you know. I don't know quite how to apologize to you for having kept you waiting ... I was just finishing ... You understand, I was just ... er ... I do beg your pardon ... I hope you will forgive me ...*
> PUPIL: *Oh, but you mustn't, Sir. It's perfectly all right, Sir.*
> PROFESSOR: *My apologies ...* (183-4)

The Professor's excessive politeness to the Pupil at the start of the private lesson is soon replaced by his dominating and aggressive pose when the lesson is well under way:

> PROFESSOR: *What is four? Greater or smaller than three?*
> PUPIL: *Smaller ... no greater.*
> PROFESSOR: *Excellent answer. How many units are missing between three and four? ... or between four and three, if you'd rather?* (192)

And near the end of the lesson the Professor shows his true colors — hypocritical, superficial, pretentious — and, launches a storm of unmitigated impoliteness demanding careful attention from the pupil while heaping warnings and threats on her. Any of the pupil's effort to participate in the interaction draws only admonition:

> PROFESSOR: *Every language, Mademoiselle — note this carefully, and remember it till the day you die ...*
> PUPIL: *Oh! Yes, Sir, till the day I die ... Yes, Sir ...*

> PROFESSOR: *… and again, this is another fundamental principle, every language is in fact only a manner of speaking, which inevitably implies that it is made up of sounds, or …*
>
> PUPIL: *Phonemes …*
>
> PROFESSOR: *I was just about to say so. Don't show off, airing your knowledge! You'd better just listen.*

By now, even the pupil's response is not allowed:

> PUPIL: *Yes, Sir.*
>
> PROFESSOR: *Be quiet. Sit where you are. Don't interrupt …* (202)

In drama, the fluctuation of emotion and feeling hovering around the playwright's heart, achieved with his/her arrangement of the drama's structure and division, either quick or slow, rise or fall, and with his/her designing of characters' dialogue, indicated by some timely stage directions, either strong or weak, apparent or concealed, pompous or casual, elegant or vulgar, bossy or wimpy, will represent a moving rhythmic resonance of emotion of the play, and produce an echo in the heartstring of the reader/audience, forming the rhythmic movement of a tense or relaxed, sad or happy communication between the drama's narrative curve and the reader/audience's emotional response.

References

Bain, C., J. Beaty, & P. Hunter. 1991. *The Norton Introduction to Literature* (Drama). New York & London: W.W. Norton & Company. 1089−1909.

Langer, S. 1953. *Feeling and Form*. London: Routledge & Kegan Paul.

Prince, G. 1988. *A Dictionary of Narratology*. Aldershot: Scholar Press.

Short, M. 1996. *Exploring the Language of Poems, Plays and Prose*. London & New York: Longman.

Simpson, P. 1989. Politeness Phenomena in Ionesco's 'The Lesson'. In Carter & Simpson (eds). *Language, Discourse and Literature*. London: Unwin Hyman Ltd.

Xu, Y. 2012. On Rhythm: Its classification, essential property, and formation. 载于善志（主编），《文体学研究：探索与应用》. 上海：上海外语教育出版社. 304—317.

Xu, Y. 2014. On the Narrative Rhythm of Fiction. 载苏晓军（主编），《文体学研究：实证认知跨学科》. 上海：上海外语教育出版社. 172—185.

胡润森. 1994. 戏剧节奏论.《艺术百家》(2):52—60.

姜耕玉. 2002. 叙事与节奏：奇正张弛起伏——艺术辩证法之一.《东南大学学报》(3).

凯瑟琳·乔治(Kathleen George). 1992.《戏剧节奏》. 张全全译. 北京:中国戏剧出版社.
冉东平. 2009. 西方现代派戏剧的叙事节奏.《外语研究》(6):96—100.
苏咏鸿. 2005. 论记录片叙事结构的节奏美.《许昌学院学报》(1):75—78.

自由间接言语的语义两面性和叙事双声性

辛　斌　（南京师范大学）

On the Semantic and Rhetorical Ambivalence of Free Indirect Speech

Xin Bin　(Nanjing Normal University)

摘　要: 本文从形式上的不确定性和语义语用上的双重性对自由间接言语进行了分析,认为虽然人们通常把自由间接言语视为一种介于直接言语和间接言语之间的转述形式,但是其充满了不确定性,在语篇中判断是否自由间接言语主要应参照该语境上下文。在语义和语用功能上,自由间接言语也有其独一无二的特点,由于它与其他转述形式相比最大程度地掩饰了自己的转述特征,从而获得了与说话者或转述者话语很大的相似性,经常被转述者用于将一种观点表述为一个事实,以表达自己的立场观点。

关键词: 自由间接言语；两面性；语义；修辞

Abstract: This article is an analysis of the formal, semantic and pragmatic ambivalence and indeterminacy of free indirect speech (FIS). Though it has been generally accepted that FIS is a speech reporting form that bears some resemblance both to direct speech and indirect speech, it does not have a definite stable set of formal features and we often have to rely on contextual semantic and pragmatic clues to determine its status as FIS. FIS also has its unique rhetorical function. In addition to the often-mentioned functions of producing an ironic effect and a sense of immediacy (which may also be produced by direct speech), its ambivalence and indeterminacy are often exploited, especially in news reporting, so that it may masquerade as the narrator's (or reporter's) speech to convey an attitude or opinion as if it was a fact.

Key words: free indirect speech; ambivalence; semantic; rhetorical

Leech & Short (1981)把"言语转述"(speech reporting)分为五种形式：直接言语(direct speech, DS)、间接言语(indirect speech, IS)、自由直接言语(free direct speech, FDS)、自由间接言语(free indirect speech, FIS)和言语行为的叙述性转述(narrative report of speech act, NRSA)，并按转述者声音的介入程度将它们排序为 NRSA-IS-FIS-DS-FDS。如果以 DS 为常态,则右边的 FDS 就具有更大的自主性,就好像转述者撤离了舞台,只剩下人物或被转述者在说话;越向左离原话转述越远,转述者的介入力度就越大。Vandelanotte (2004a:490)指出,FIS 处于 IS 和 DS 之间,"其语言特征散乱而难以把握"。其实,FIS 不仅在形式上难以把握,在语义和语用上也具有两面性和不确定性,既难识别又不易理解。

1. FIS 形式上的不确定性

在形式上,FIS 兼具 DS 和 IS 的特点,它既非对原话语的再现,也非其纯间接的表述。FIS 跟其它转述形式一样最早是对英语等西方语言加以分析的。英语中的 FIS 通常是指把 IS 的转述句删去之后剩下的被转述部分,其动词时态和人称代词与 IS 一致,其它一些词汇语法成分则与 DS 相似,经常保留体现人物主体意识的成分,如疑问句、感叹句、不完整的句子、口语化或带感情色彩的语言成分,以及原话中的时间、地点状语等。请比较：

(1) He said, 'I'll come back here to see you again tomorrow.'

(2) He said that he would return to the hospital to see her again the following day.

(3) a. He would return there to see her again the following day.

b. He would return there to see her again tomorrow.

c. He would come back there to see her again tomorrow.

(Leech & Short, 1981: 320–325)

例(1)是 DS,例(2)是 IS,而例(3)中的句子都可视为 FIS,其共同特点是,句法上本应该为从句的"被转述言语"(reported speech)变成了主句,并带上了一些 DS 才具有的语法和语义特征,例如(3b)和(3c)中的"come back"和"tomorrow"。

Volosinov（1973：141－159）把 FIS 叫做"准直接话语"（quasi-direct discourse），并提到早在 19 世纪末人们就认识到了这种转述形式。例如，Tobler 在 1887 年把准直接话语定义为"直接和间接话语的一种混合"，这种混合形式有 DS 的语调（tone）和语序，而其动词时态和人称代词则与 IS 一致。Bally（1912，1914）认为准直接话语是标准 IS 的变种，其形式并非一成不变，与 DS 的相似度或大或小。Volosinov（1973：142）反对把准直接话语视为 DS 和 IS 的混合形式，指出准直接话语并"不是这两种形式简单机械的混合，而是对他人话语的一种全新的积极的接收，是转述言语和被转述言语之间相互关系动态运动的一个特殊方向"。

即使从语法的角度看也不能简单地把 FIS 视为 DS 和 IS 的混合形式。Leech & Short（1981：327）指出，FIS"在小说中的特点似乎总是使用第三人称代词和过去时，但更准确地说，其代词和时态的选择应与 FIS 出现的叙事形式相符合。"例如，在第三人称叙事中也可能出现动词为现在时的 FIS；另外，第三人称代词也不是必须的，也有第一人称代词的 FIS，关键是要适合于叙事的语境上下文。因此，Leech & Short 倾向于不为自由间接引语规定任何具体的形式特征："我们将从'家族相似性'的角度定义自由间接言语，而不是要求它必须拥有某种具体特征"（1981：329）。

由于汉语动词没有时态标记，人们通常只能根据人称代词来识别 FIS。然而，即使是人称代词也经常帮不上忙，因为汉语中人称代词的使用远远少于英语，请比较（4）中的例子：

(4) a. 没有，绝对地没有锁上，不然，为什么她记忆中没有这个动作啊？没有把保管箱锁上？真的？这是何等重要的事！

b. She had not, definitely not, locked it; why else did she have no recollection of this movement? Had she left the safety deposit vault unlocked? Really? How serious!

（Hagenaar, 1996：296）

例（4a）中只出现了一处代词"她"，而在例（4b）中却有 4 处："she"（3）和"it"（1）。其实，在（4a）中我们主要依赖其它线索来识别 FIS，包括词汇线索（如"啊"），句法线索（如疑问句和感叹句），指示词（如"这"），语境线索（如对"她"的记忆的指涉）。Hagenaar（1996）和王勇（2004）等都认为在汉语中语境上下文对识别 FIS 起着不可替代的作用。例如，在（4a）中我们要确定"没有把保管箱锁上？真的？这是何等重要的事！"这段话是否 FIS，就必须参照前一句话"没有，绝对地没有锁上，不然，为什么她记忆中没有这个动作啊？"

Fairclough（1988，1992）提到了新闻语篇中的一种常见现象，即显然是他人的话语内容却没有明确地标记为转述言语，显得就像是报道者的话语。他将其称为"无转述标记的话语"（UNSIG（nalled）），其中包括 FIS。黄敏（2012）根据这一观点认为，FIS 既表述了人物言语，同时又具有与报道者叙事相似的文本特点，由于这种言语表征经常没有任何形式标记，因此只要文本中有语境线索表示某段文字不是报道者的言语而是出自他人之口，就应该是 FIS。Leech & Short（1981：331）甚至指出："的确可以构思出这样的例子，其中能表示它是 FIS 的东西也许仅仅是一个单词或者一个形式特征。"

2. FIS 语义上的两面性

FIS 删去转述句，把原本处于从句地位的 IS 变为主句，使之获得了几乎与 DS 或者转述者话语一样的独立性和自主性。这种转述形式允许转述者的声音介于被转述者和读者之间，导致了两个视角。Vandelanotte（2004a）认为，FIS 虽然兼具 DS & IS 的特征，例如语气（mood）和语序与被转述者相联系，而人称和时态则与转述者相联系，但"事实上自由间接言语更接近直接言语。我认为与被转述者相联系的特征在数量和重要性上都要超过与转述者相联系的特征：事实上，自由间接言语中的与转述者相关联的转述句的那些特征本身的意义也有所减弱。"Vandelanotte 提出三点理由来支持其观点。首先，对第三方的指称往往出于被转述者的视角，而且这种指称不一定需要明确。例如：

（5）He was going to make *her* sorry for that, he thought.

（Vandelanotte，2004a：493）

这里"her"的指称不是来源于转述者，而是源于被转述者；对后者而言，"her"的所指在原始语境中是已知的，而该句子的读者则需要从语境上下文中推导出其所指。由此可见，选择 FIS 中的代词时所参照的指示中心不一定是转述者。其次，对时态的选择确实通常以转述者的说话时间为参照，但从表义的角度看，在许多情况下时间却与被转述者的话语内容和语境相关。例如：

（6）How her heart was beating *now*! She thought.

（Vandelanotte，2004a：494）

虽然例（6）中的被转述句和转述句中的动词都是过去式，但"now"表明其在语义上是以被转述者的说话时间为参照的。最后，FIS 中涉及说话者和听话者之间交流的小句功能（如语态（mood））和人际含义（如情态（modality））主要与被转述者相关，与 FIS 的命题内容相关的一些评价意义，如"正当性"（validity）、"或然性"（probability）和"必要性"（necessity）等，主要属于被转述者的意识范围。例如：

(7) He *mustn't* stay out late or she would punish him the next day, she said.

(8) Was she *really* going to cry now, he asked.

(9) Could he help in any way? He asked.

例(7)中的"mustn't"表达的是被转述者（she）对"he"的一种行为（stay out late）的禁止；例(8)中"really"对一种可能性程度的推测显然属于被转述者而非转述者；而例(9)的被转述句中的语气显然是由被转述者原来选定的，而在间接引语中被转述句中的语气是由转述者控制的，例如：

(10) He asked whether he could help in any way.

Volosinov（1973）把 FIS 称为"准直接话语"表达的是类似观点。他认为，FIS 在法语中的出现是为了弥补法语语法上的不足，而不是作为一种可以自由选择的修辞手段。在中世纪晚期的法语中，叙述者和人物的立场观点是不能混淆的，两者之间应泾渭分明，情感要服从理智。但是随着欧洲文艺复兴运动的兴起，个人主义抬头，人们试图以转述言语表达情感意义，叙述者试图与所描述的人物联合，站在人物的立场上说话。到了 17 世纪，文艺复兴的非理性主义受到了理性主义的抵抗，人们开始提出限制 IS 中时态和语气的严格规则，从而在客观主义和主观主义、在客观内容分析和主观态度表达之间建立一种和谐的平衡。

人们通常认为 DS 具有转述者和被转述者两个"指示中心"（deictic centre），而 IS 只有转述者一个指示中心。但是，FIS 似乎与两者都有所不同：它虽然在语气和情态上经常与被转述者相联系，但其动词的时态有时以转述者的说话时间为参照，有时则与被转述者的说话时间为参照。例如：

(11) China, Japan and ROK are important trading partners for one another, while the latter three either have already established or intend to set up a free trade area with ASEAN, said Wen.

(*China Daily*, October 8, 2003)

(12) Even when safety is not an issue, money is. According to D. C. Public Works Director Larry King, the city is spending $10,000 to $15,000 every week on overtime pay for garbage collectors. It eventually would be cheaper to fix the trucks and hire enough workers to staff them.

(*The Washington Post*, July 16, 1995)

在例(11)中,被转述言语中的现在时显然是以转述者的说话时间而不是"Wen"的说话时间为参照的,紧随其后的转述句中的动词时态选用一般过去式也是以转述者的说话时间为参照。但在例(12)最后一句的 FIS 中,过去将来时的选择显然是以被转述者"Larry King"的说话时间为参照的,情态成分"eventually"也基本属于被转述者的主体意识范围内。FIS 在语义上表现的这种两面性为转述者留下了广阔的介入空间。

3. FIS 叙事上的双声性

Leech & Short(1981:332)认为英国文学作品中的 FIS 由 Jane Austen(1775—1817)首创,在 Fielding 的作品中被广泛使用。大量使用 FIS,是因为这种形式与 IS 相比给人一种身临其境的感觉并可避免重复转述句。Volosinov(1973:151)对 FIS 修辞功能的探讨首先关注的是法国作家,认为这种转述形式最早见于法国古典作家 La Fontaine(1621—1695)的作品中,被用于平衡主客观描述:"取消转述动词表明叙事者对故事中人物的认同,使用过去式(相对于 DS 中的现在式)和与间接言语一致的人称代词表示叙事者的独立立场,即他没有把自己完全融会在其人物的经历中。"在 La Bruyère 的作品中,FIS 具有强烈的讽刺效果,他以这种转述形式表达对一些人物的憎恶和他本人相较于这些人物的优越感。在 19 世纪中叶法国作家 Flaubert 的作品中,FIS 的功能更为复杂。Flaubert 往往关注那些令他厌恶或反感的事物,但其作品也经常表达出他对所描述的那些即可恨又可鄙的事物的认同感。由于 FIS 可以同时表达对事物的亲近和疏远、认同和排斥,所以非常适合 Flaubert 用以表达自己与人物之间的那种既爱又恨的关系。Lerch 从语义内容上将 FIS 定义为"作为事实的言语"(speech as fact),认为与 IS 相比 FIS 的优势在于其产生的印象的生动性和具体性,作者可以通过 FIS 中动词的省略来暗示其本人很严肃地看待所转述的人物话语,表明重要的不仅是说了什么话,还有事实:"以这种形式转述的言语,其内容就像作者自己在传达事实。"(Lerch,1914;引自 Volosinov 1973:147)Lorck(1921)视 FIS 为"经历的言语"(experienced speech)、DS 为"重复的言语"(repeated speech)、IS 为"传递的言语"(communicated speech),认为 FIS 就是对他人言语的经历的"直接描绘"(direct depiction),是唤起对他人言语生动印象的一种转述形式。

我们今天对 FIS 修辞功能的认识与 Lorck 和 Lerch 等前人相比虽有加深但并无实质性的超越。Clark & Gerrig(1990:764)认为,"典型的引语"(prototypical quotation)其作用在于展示:"引语是一种展示。就像你展示网球的发球、朋友的跛行或者钟摆的摆动,你也可以展示一个人在说话时的作为。"人们可以通过三种方法实施言语行为:指示(indicating or pointing)、描述(describing)和展示(demonstrating)。指示是指出事物的所在,其主要功能是标示(designate)事物;描述必须使用语言,侧重思想内容的表达,而展示不一定通过语言,其作用是能够"使他人体验所描绘的对象"(1990:765)。展示是一种描绘(depiction)行为而非描述(description)行为。描绘通常与被描绘的事物具有一定的相似性,但描述则没有。人们在理解描绘时往往会在一定程度上依赖直观感觉,而理解描述则不必。Clark & Gerrig(1990)认为 DS 是一种展示,而 IS 是一种描述;FIS 在一定意义上也是一种展示,只是这种形式采用的是转述者而不是被转述者的视角。

了解 Halliday,Sperber & Wilson 关于转述言语和非转述言语的论述有助于我们理解 Lerch 对 FIS 的定义,即"作为事实的言语"。Halliday(1994)把"转述"(reporting)叫做"投射"(projection)。就语义而言,投射不是对(非语言的)经验的直接表征,而是对一种(语言)表征的表征:"被投射的小句在这里只是一种'措辞'(wording):就是说,它所表征的是一种词汇语法现象"(1994:250)。虽然"投射小句"(projecting clause)表征的是一种经验现象,是对被经历的第一级现实(the first order reality)中事物和现象的描述,但"被投射小句"(projected clause)自身就是一种表征,它所表征的是"元现象"(metaphenomenon),是一种二级语言现实的现象。Sperber & Wilson(1986)把语言运用区分为"描写性的"(descriptive)和"解释性的"(interpretive)。任何语言都能以两种方式表述事物:通过表达的命题直接表述事态或者通过转述他人话语间接表述事态。语言的描写性用法涉及的是语言与现实的关系,命题的真实性依赖于事态本身的真实性;其解释性用法涉及的是命题和命题之间的关系,用一句(些)话来表述另一句(些)话,两者在形式结构或命题内容上具有相似性。DS 与原话在形式和内容上都具有相似性,而 IS 与原话通常只在命题内容上具有相似性。用于表述他人话语的话语没有真值,所表达的命题不能被判断为真或假,因为它不是对现实世界中事件或状态的描述,但是我们却可以对它是否或者在多大程度上与原话具有相似性做出评价。

根据上述观点,DS 和 FDS 是"重复的言语",具有展示功能,从中我们听到的主要是被转述者的声音;IS 和 NRSA 是"传递的言语",具有描述"元现象"或者他人话语内容的功能,反映了转述者对原话语的理解和阐释,从中我们听到的主要是转述者的声音;而 FIS 则与其他转述形式都不同,它不仅带有被转述者的原话特征,也含有转述者对转述内容的态度或评价,因此我们听到的是转述者和被转述者的双重声音。其实这也正是 Volosinov 的观点,转述者在 FIS 中给被转述的话语强加上了自己的声音,在同一种语言结构中转述者的声音与被转述者的声音发生了碰撞,前者对后者进行了干预:"在准直接话语中,与其说我们是通过信息内容不如说是通过被转述者的'重音'(accentuation)和'语调'(intonation),通过其言语的'评价取向'(evaluative orientation),来识别出另一个人的话语。我们感知到作者的'口音'(accent)和语调被另一个人的价值判断所打断……我们完全可以……体会出其每一个词的双声色彩"(Volosinov, 1973:155)。

　　FIS 的这种双声特点赋予了转述者充分的空间发挥其修辞功能。Leech & Short(1981:326-327)指出,小说中常见的是以 IS 开始,慢慢过渡到 FIS,这样的方式既方便了转述者对转述话语的介入又向读者呈现了一些被转述话语原来的风味,不过其后果往往使读者难以确定这是人物的话语还是作者的话语。这种现象其实在非文学语篇里也十分常见,下面这段话来自一篇新闻报道:

> (13) For example, Linderman says, her office hears criticism that ENABL should be offered to 10-year-olds in communities with very high rates of teen pregnancy. *Other communities have complained that talking to 14-year-olds about sex is inappropriate.* "You really see differences in various communities," she says.
>
> (*Los Angeles Times*, July 12, 1995)

例(13)以 IS 开始,以 DS 结束,但中间这个句子的性质却不明确:这是谁的话?虽然我们倾向于认为这依然是转述 Linderman 的话,是 FIS,但却无法排除它是该消息的作者对现实的直接描述的可能性。在中文新闻语篇中类似的例子也十分常见,例如:

> (14) 该市教育局负责人称,该市新的中考政策将一改以往单凭学生考试成绩"论英雄"的状况,变为"学业考试成绩+综合素质评价"的双轨制高中录取标准。此举表明了分数不再是评价和选拔学生的唯一标准,而是以学生学业成绩和综合素质评价为主要依据,全面关注学生发展状况。
>
> (《光明日报》2005 年 2 月 2 日)

例(14)是一篇题为《温州学生上高中不再以分数论英雄》的报道中的一段。它以 IS 开始,转述动词是"称",消息来源是"该市教育局负责人"。但第二句话是什么?它既可能依然是该负责任人的话,是 FIS,也可能是报道者的评论。如果是 FIS,那么这种做法在新闻报道中可以有效降低语篇的转述

性,增强其原创性。下面是一个更长的例子:

(15) 据北京大学宽禁带半导体研究中心张国义教授介绍,氮化镓(GaN)基激
光器是波长最短的半导体激光器,波长为 405 纳米左右的蓝紫光。GaN
基激光器是发展下一代大容量高密度光存储信息技术的关键性器件,在
国防建设、生物、环境、照明、显示、打印和医疗等领域,也具有广阔的应
用前景和巨大的市场需求。研制 GaN 基激光器是国家高科技攻关的重
要项目之一。

从 2002 年 4 月起,北京大学先后承担国家 863 重大项目"氮化镓基
激光器"和北京市科技计划项目"氮化镓基蓝紫激光器"的研制任务,针
对宽禁带半导体氮化镓基激光器的难点,进行了氮化镓基激光器外延和
器件结构的计算和优化设计、MOCVD 外延生长和表征、器件微加工技
术和谐振腔结构等方面的探索和研究,在 GaN 基材料系量子阱和超晶
格与波导结构 MOCVD 生长和窄波导激光二极管器件制备等关键性科
学和技术问题方面取得一系列进展。

(《光明日报》2005 年 1 月 30 日第 1 版)

例(15)这篇报道的题目是"下一代'蓝光 DVD'有了激光光源",共有 4 段,
这里是中间的两段。第一段显然是 IS,消息来源是"张国义教授",但第二
段既可能是报道者的话语也可能是张国义教授的话语。鉴于它与第一段
在语言风格上颇为相似,其中含有大量的专业术语,我们更倾向于认为它
是省略了转述句的 FIS。

Goffman (1981)区分了三种说话者角色:"言者"(animator)、"作者"
(author)和"立言者"(principal)。"言者"指现场说出词语者,"作者"指话
语内容的编码者,"立言者"则指话语内容的制定者。在这三种角色言语交
际中即可相互独立又可重叠,说话者往往既是言者又是作者或/和立言者,
但在转述言语中转述者最多可以既是言者又是作者(例如 IS),但一般不会
三种角色同时兼有,即转述者不应该是立言者。但正如例(14)和(15)所表
明的,由于删除了转述句并模糊了其他转述言语的标记,FIS 往往能使转述
者在一定程度上使自己的声音与被转述者的声音重叠,获得立言者的身
份。黄敏(2012)展示了在新闻报道中 FIS 的这一特点是如何被报道者所
利用来把一种观点表述为一种事实:"当引述人物言语时,文本只是表明
'某人说过某话'为真,至于'某话'是否为真则不得而知,可当以自由间接
言语出现时,文本将'某话'与'某人'相脱离,直接断言了'某话'为真,此
时所报道的不是某个言语,而是某个事实。"(2012:76)这种情况一般发生
在转述者同情、认同或支持某一观点或做法的时候。我们可以通过下面这
个例子进一步体会 FIS 的这一特点:

（16）在某校一个 60 多人的班级里，小李同学被分到了前排靠窗的位子，因为离讲台过近，他整天得抬着头斜眼看黑板，坐的位子又太窄，站起来时腿不能伸直，常常会碰着前面的同学，就为这个，他们两人还吵过好多次架。

（《光明日报》2004 年 9 月 29 日第 2 版）

在（16）中从"因为离讲台过近"直至最后的这一部分极有可能是"小李同学"告诉记者的，在这里应该是 FIS，但报道者将其溶于自己的叙事话语中，就像是他或她本人在讲述一个经历过的或观察到的事实。

4. 结语

FIS 无论在形式还是语义语用上都具有两面性，它一方面通过保留原话语的一些语气和情态色彩，令听者或读者能够听到一些被转述者的声音；另一方面，它又通过对时态和代词的灵活选择与 IS 保持一定程度的相似性，为转述者介入被转述者和听者或读者之间留下了充分的空间。FIS 通过省略转述句获得了比 IS 更大的独立性和自主性，从而增强了其叙事性，经常被说话者或转述者用于将一种观点表征为一个事实，以传递自己的立场观点。

参考文献

Clark, H. & R. J. Gerrig. 1990. Quotations as demonstrations. *Language*, 66（4）：764—805.

Fairclough, N. 1988. Discourse representation in media discourse. *Sociolinguistics*, 17：125—139.

Fairclough, N. 1992. *Discourse and Social Change*. Cambridge：Polity Press.

Goffman, E. 1981. *Forms of Talk*. Oxford：Blackwell.

Hagenaar, E. 1996. Free indirect speech in Chinese. In T. A. J. M. Janssen & W. V. D. Wurff（eds.）*Reported Speech: Forms and Functions of the Verb*. Amsterdam/Philadelphia：John Benjamins.

Halliday, M. A. K. 1994. *An Introduction to Functional Grammar*. London：Edward Arnold.

Leech, G. N. & M. H. Short. 1981. *Style in Fiction*. London：Longman.

Sperber, D. & D. Wilson. 1986. *Relevance: Communication and Cognition*. Oxford：Blackwell.

Vandelanotte, L. 2004a. Deixis and grounding in speech and thought representation. *Journal of Pragmatics*, 36：489—520.

Vandelanotte, L. 2004b. From representational to scopal 'distancing indirect speech or thought': A cline of subjectification. *Text*, 24 (4): 547-585.

Volosinov, V. N. 1973. *Marxism and the Philosophy of Language*. Translated by L. Matejka & I. R. Titunik. New York: Seminar Press.

黄 敏. 2012.《新闻话语中的言语表征研究》. 上海:华东师范大学出版社.

王 勇. 2004. 自由间接话语与叙事声音.《山东大学学报》. 第 5 期.

新世纪初文体学研究的新进展
——第五届文体学国际研讨会暨第九届全国文体学研讨会综述

吴显友　彭康洲　谭小勇　（重庆师范大学）

New Advances in Stylistic Research in the Early New Century
— A Review of the 5th International Stylistics Conference

Wu Xianyou Peng Kangzhou Tan Xiaoyong　（Chongqing Normal University）

摘　要： 第五届文体学国际研讨会暨第九届全国文体学研讨会在重庆召开,吸引了来自中国、英国、美国、荷兰、澳大利亚等国家100多所高校的200余名代表参加。大会主题为"新世纪初文体学研究的新进展",议题涉及文体学诸多分支学科,充分展示了21世纪初国内外文体学研究的新方法、新趋势、新成果。归纳起来,本次盛会有如下一些亮点:(1)中外学者热情参与,中青年学者崭露头角,与会者提交的论文数量和质量高;(2)研究的视野宽阔,理论视角新颖、独特,研究方法灵活多样。既有理论探索又有实证研究,分析预料既有文学文本也有非文学文本,既有中外经典文本也有当下流行的影视文本、网络文本;(3)文体学的部分分支学科,如文学文体学、功能文体学、认知文体学、叙述文体学等,成为本次会议的热点议题,成果丰硕;(4)文体学的一些前沿学科,如语料库文体学、批评文体学、多模态话语分析、英汉文体学对比研究等已进入中外学者的研究视野,并收到了丰厚的回报。

关键词： 第五届文体学国际研讨会；热点议题；综述

Abstract： The 5th International Conference and the 9th National Stylistics
Conference was held in Chongqing, China, drawing over 200
experts and scholars from China, US, Holland, Australia, etc.
to the conference. The conference theme is "New Advances in
Stylistic Research in the Early New Century", and the related
issues cover all those stylistic branches, fully demonstrating the
new approaches, trends and findings in stylistic research at the
early 21st Century. To sum up, this grand conference carries the
following features： (1) scholars both at home and abroad show
a ready response to the conference, young scholars come to the
fore and those submitted papers rise to a new level both in
quantity and quality； (2) those papers are conceived in a broad,
new and unique perspective, each with a particular approach.
Those findings cover either theoretical explorations or substantial
studies, and data of study include either literary texts or non-
literary ones, either those classical texts, popular movie/TV
manuscripts, or web texts； (3) Among those heated topics are
those concerning literary stylistics, functional stylistics,
cognitive stylistics, narrative stylistics, etc. and come to fruitful
results； (4) Some pioneering branches of stylistics, such as
corpus stylistics, critical stylistics, multi-modal discourse
stylistics, comparative studies between English and Chinese
stylistics, etc. are touched upon by some sensitive scholars who
enjoy some happy returns.

Key words： The 5th International Conference； heated topics； review

　　由中国修辞学会文体学研究会主办,重庆师范大学承办的第五届文体
学国际研讨会暨第九届全国文体学研讨会于 2014 年 10 月 17—18 日在重
庆万友康年酒店召开。来自中国、英国、美国、荷兰、澳大利亚等国家 100 多
所高校的 200 余名代表参加了本次盛会,包括英国诺丁汉大学、国际著名期
刊 *Language & Literature* 主编 Geoff Hall 教授,英国伯明翰大学 Michael
Toolan 教授,荷兰阿姆斯特丹自由大学 Gerard Steen 教授,教育部长江学
者、北京大学博士生导师申丹教授,全国文体学研讨会会长、清华大学刘世
生教授等,并在大会作主题报告。本次会议的主题为"新世纪文体学研究

的新进展",议题包括:文体学理论研究,文体学各分支学科研究,语体及体裁特征研究,文体学与外语教学,英汉文体学对比研究。大会共收到论文摘要 200 余篇,国内外 14 名专家作了大会主题报告,80 余名学者在三个分会场进行了交流发言,现就研讨会报告做简要综述。

1. 文学文体学研究

20 世纪初由德国文体学家斯皮泽创立的文学文体学,既吸收了早期俄国形式派的文学理论和 Saussure 的结构主义语言学理论,又借用了语用学、话语分析、认知语言学等学科的理论,对文学文本,如诗歌、小说、戏剧等,进行较为客观、系统、深入的文本阐释与评价,它集中探讨作者如何通过对语言的选择来表达和加强主题意义和美学效果,目前已发展成为一门成熟的文体学分支学科,受到国内外文体学界普遍关注。

  Geoff Hall 教授以一篇题为" Advances in the Stylistics of Literature Reading"的报告,揭开了此次研讨会的序幕。他指出,传统的文体学批评更多关注的是"文本(the text)",而不是"读者(the reader)",而由于语言学、符号学和话语文体学方法的运用,越来越多的研究把阅读看作动态的、互动的、基于社会情境的阅读活动,并从读者反应论的视角回顾总结了 Iser、Culler、Fish 和 Spiro 等学者的研究成果,重点介绍了近年来文体学研究中的文学阅读实证研究(ESL, Empirical Study of Literature Reading)和自然阅读研究(NSR, Naturalistic Study of Reading),并以 van Peer、Miall 等学者的文学阅读实证研究为例提出读者身份、阅读环境、阅读条件等需要关注的变量,他认为 ESL 和 NSR 对比研究、网络文本研究、文学文体学教学研究等领域值得重点关注。苗兴伟教授(北京师范大学)采用 UAM Corpus Tool 语料库,对与简·爱个人生活经历相关的八种相互对立的文体标记展开了系统、深入的实证研究,认为文本对立是《简·爱》小说的前景化手段之一。通过人物、事件、观点等的二元呈现(binary representation),小说关于成长、爱、驱逐(exclusion)、不平等、差异和世界观的文学意义实现前景化。孙红艳教授(邯郸学院)认为,斯泰因背离戏剧常规模式,采用拼贴和分割组合方法变异戏剧文本形式,在剧中抹去故事情节、冲突和高潮,使戏剧语言丧失传统戏剧语言必不可少的指称、表现、呼吁和寒暄功能而使其前景化,更加突出戏剧语言的诗学功能,即将观众的注意力吸引到与语言相关的内在节奏和韵律上来,使戏剧成为风景,创造诗歌剧,塑造一位超越时间和空间的、在历史与现实之间建立起一条重要纽带的大地母亲式人物安东尼。巴微副教授(陕西师范大学)分析了藏族诗歌《仓央嘉措情歌》的戏剧化抒情文体特征。《仓央嘉措情歌》是藏族作家诗与"谐"体民歌结合的典范之作,它一改过去藏族僧侣典雅华丽的"年阿体"风格,借鉴民歌的修辞手法和抒情模式,具有意象生动、场景鲜活的表现特征和便于口传的叙事性结构特征,通过意象化抒情、场景化抒情和叙事性抒情实现了戏剧化的抒情模式,强化了民歌对话与交流的文体功能特征,更通过文人创作极大地提升了"谐"体民歌的审美表达力,成为藏民族传统文化积淀中的重要元素,对藏族诗歌的发展具有深远的影响。博士生左进(上海外国语大学)通过解读瓦瑟斯坦剧本的台词中出现的反复性词语,比如女性对自身身份的刻意隐瞒、所遭受的痛苦、幸福生活的伪装等,认为作者选择这一类词语在舞台上呈现出前所未有的女性形象,书写她们的爱情、困惑、悲伤、失望。刘士川老师(四川文理学院)、李小满老师(咸阳学院)等学者也作了交流发言。

2. 功能文体学与语用文体学研究

刘世生教授近年来致力于《世说新语》的多模态象征表达研究,引起了与会者的浓厚兴趣。刘教授在 Hasan 的言语艺术"双层表达"(double articulation)符号模式,即言语艺术符号系统和语言符号系统的基础上,提出了多模态象征表达模型,并以《世说新语》文本和插图为例,归纳总结了八种表达模式,即相互说明、相互强化、逻辑关系松散、图像从属于文字说明、文字从属于图像说明、图像从属于文字和图像从属于小句等,它们共同构成了插图文本新颖、独特的文体特征。杨信彰教授(厦门大学)的报告《变换的功能文体意义》从功能语言学的视角讨论变换的功能文体意义,强调动词的语义特征和语境之间的互动,解释变换结构的语用和语义理据,把变换看作是说话人根据语境作出的一种词汇语法选择,认为变换是语体变异的一种体现,对于变换的研究有助于我们更好地认识结构的文体意义。辛斌教授(南京师范大学)作了题为《自由间接言语的语义两面性和叙事双声性》的发言,他从形式上的不确定性和语义语用上的双重性对自由间接言语进行了分析,认为虽然人们通常把自由间接言语视为一种介于直接言语和间接言语之间的转述形式,但是其形式充满了不确定性,在语篇中判断是否自由间接言语主要应参照其语境上下文。彭宣维教授(北京师范大学),通过实例分析着重考察文学话语中涉及的消息化(主位化和信息化)组织模式,通过个案分析揭示文学话语中相关前景化成分的文体价值,彰显了系统功能语言学的可行性、实效性和发展潜力。

　　杨雪燕教授(北京外国语大学)借用系统功能语法的分析模式,利用

UAM Corpus Tool 工具对比分析了当下热门综艺节目《爸爸去哪儿》中王岳伦和田亮两位父亲给女儿的信函的言语功能、主语人称、态度、参与者、过程、主位等语言选择进行定性和定量分析，认为两位父亲做出的选择存在明显区别，揭示两种不同的父亲形象：王岳伦更溺爱女儿并希望成为女儿的依靠，田亮则倾向于鼓励女儿并希望女儿独立而勇敢。李华东教授（杭州电子科技大学）从语用文体学的角度对戏剧文本的舞台指令及其语用功能展开了深入的研究，认为舞台指令除了能够显示复杂的作者—读者关系，更重要的是，它是戏剧美学效果的重要体现方式，应成为戏剧文体分析的对象之一。张俊副教授（西南大学）认为，作为一种常见的语义—语用现象，夸张的使用受到语境和百科知识的制约，并且在语篇中发挥独特的功能。在语篇信息流中，夸张具有阻断语篇原有信息流，打破语篇接受者原有信息预期的功能，并利用语篇接受者原有信息预期与语篇制造者的欲达信息（intended information）之间反差累积语篇信息流通的推进力；在语篇宏观结构层面，夸张往往与"问题—解决"、"假设—验证"等语篇组织模式相联系，是语篇组织的重要手段。博士生刘楠楠（清华大学）借用Culpeper 的不礼貌策略模型分析了奥威尔的第一部小说《缅甸岁月》中的对话策略，认为运用人物之间的对话凸显了殖民者与被殖民者双方权力的巨大差异，并通过呈现殖民者言语中的不礼貌合法化来揭示大英帝国对于其殖民地肆无忌惮的统治和压迫。博士生黄妮娅（上海外国语大学）借用中西礼貌理论及面子理论分析了曹禺话剧《北京人》中的女性人物曾思懿的礼貌和不礼貌行为，并从词汇、句子和会话结构上分析总结了人物性格发展的过程。吕东莲老师（中国传媒大学）从语体学的角度探讨力士香皂广告文案的历时演变，揭示该广告语体在过去 80 多年中的语言变化，并试图剖析这些变化背后的原因，王月老师（唐山学院）运用及物性系统理论对兰姆斯文《梦中的女儿》的语言特征进行细致解读，旨在说明及物性系统在散文理解方面的重要作用。

3. 认知文体学研究

认知文体学/认知诗学主要研究读者在阅读过程中的假设推理活动以及它们如何影响读者对语篇的意义阐释，认知文体学不断从认知科学、心理学、计算机科学和人工智能等学科吸收理论资源。随着认知语言学的进一步发展，"认知转向"已在哲学、文学创作和文学批评等领域里初见端倪，呈星火燎原之势。

赵秀凤教授（中国石油大学）的报告《绘本叙事中人物视角的多模态表

征——认知诗学视角》，以几米的绘本叙事作品《时光电影院》（2012）为例，采用认知诗学研究方法，在细致的语料考察基础上提出，绘本作者主要运用图形—背景、隐喻和整合三种认知机制操控视角的切换。通过调控图形—背景关系，突显聚焦人物的感知觉内容；通过隐喻，尤其是基于意象图式的基础隐喻标记人物视角；通过启用整合机制，把故事内的物理空间与想象、梦境、记忆等心理空间整合为一个隐喻场景，并通过视觉图像和言语符号使三种机制相互配合和协作，共同构建绘本叙事的语境框架。郭建教授和于华副教授（中科院大学）借助隐喻及概念整合理论来解释诺贝尔文学奖获得者莱辛的作品《玛拉和丹恩历险记》如何展现其语言的形象性、意象性和趣味性，使其小说的意义更加突出，具有"女性经验的史诗作者，以其怀疑的态度、激情和远见，清楚地剖析了一个分裂的文化"。该小说描绘了几千年后的世界令人恐怖的图景，莱辛以未来的灾难警醒人类，不要再对意识形态方面的次级关怀进行无休止的争执，而应该关心决定地球生命得以延续的初级关怀：环境、食品、自由以及人与人之间的关爱。肖燕教授（重庆师范大学）对小说《时间旅行者的妻子》中的时间与人生隐喻进行考察后发现，小说通过时间概念的不同特质，把时间刻画成点、线、面和一股巨大的能量，这些隐喻把时间与人物的人生串联起来，时间是变换的，而人的信念坚守总能在时间的不可控与信念的可控之间找到一个契合点，使两个人既有幻境中错位的同步，也有现实中的真实的相遇。

　　Allison Creed女士（澳大利亚南昆士兰大学）采用认知语言学的理论及方法，分析了澳大利亚红酒评论中隐喻的文本结构、功能和进程（processes）。她指出红酒的语域由体现在红酒评论中的制度框架（institutional framework）组织形成，红酒评论家们采用简短、具有说服力的文本体裁表达对红酒的品鉴和欣赏。在红酒评论中，作为文体手段的隐喻与修辞意义机制一起传递意象和情感，加深消费者对产品的感官印象。魏利霞博士（北方民族大学）从视觉模态、听觉模态和言语模态三方面对E. E. Cummings的视觉诗"1（a"进行认知解读，抽象出"孤独的人是落叶"、"人生是落叶"两个概念隐喻。赵婧副教授（福州大学）认为，《野草在歌唱》建构了一座"荒原"式的文本世界。"铁皮屋顶"、"水"和"野草"等扩展隐喻贯穿全文，系统描述"荒原"上以玛丽夫妇为代表的非洲殖民地人民生存的艰辛和对幸福生活的不懈追求，"荒原"喻指当代西方文明社会，指涉其内在的矛盾不可调和性：光鲜的白人国家机器统治下的性别、种族和阶级歧视等不公正现象。庞玉厚博士（北京外国语大学）运用隐喻理论对福克纳的小说《押沙龙，押沙龙！》的空间叙事的表征形式及叙事功能进行了深入探讨。博士生曹金梅（清华大学）以概念隐喻为理论依托，以斯洛索普、布利瑟罗、恩赞、戈特弗里德等主要人物的行动轨迹为线索,探讨"火箭"意象在小说意义建构、传统"追寻"模式颠覆与重建中的作用,从而加深对品钦式人文关怀的理解。荣榕老师(华南理工大学)以电影《不朽的园丁》中的回忆展现为研究对象,提出了一个综合指示转移理论和情景框架理论的认知文体学分析框架,并在此框架下讨论记忆闪回的文体学特征、功能以及特点。

4. 叙述文体学研究

叙述文体学是近年来文体学研究的前沿分支学科,"叙述学和小说文体学在当代西方小说批评理论中占据了十分重要的地位,其研究成果深化了对小说的结构形态、运作规律、表达方式或审美性的认识,提高了欣赏和评论小说艺术的水平"(申丹,2004:1);Paul Simpson 教授较系统地分析了"叙述文体学(narrative stylistics)"的理论基础、结构规律、叙述技巧和分析框架(情节、话语与文体特征),文体特征包括语篇媒介(电影、小说或其他体裁)、社会语码、行动和事件、视角、语篇结构和互文性等六个方面。(2004:20—22)。

申丹教授以"叙事文体分析面对的新挑战:情节背后的隐性进程"为题,概述了近几年来学界对"隐性进程"叙事研究的关注。她指出,叙事研究不仅要关注故事情节发展,还应该重视隐含在情节背后且贯穿文本始终的暗流,可称之为"隐性进程(covert progression)"。这两种叙事运动构成互补、对抗甚或颠覆的关系。隐性进程的存在,对叙事文体分析构成一种新的挑战。如果忽略隐性进程,无论文体分析多么系统精确,都难免会片面理解甚或误解作品的主题意义、人物形象和审美价值。我们需要打破以往仅仅关注情节发展的思维定式,将注意力拓展到情节背后,着力挖掘是否存在与情节并行的隐性进程。如果存在这种叙事暗流,我们就需要沿着两个不同的方向,同时探讨作者的文体选择在情节发展和隐性进程中的不同主题意义,并关注两者之间的复杂关系和交互作用。Gerard Steen 教授在题为"Three Dimensions of Metaphor, and Its Relation to Style and Other Aspects of Genre"的报告中指出,随着认知语言学的发展,作为修辞手段和思维方式的隐喻研究和文体学研究取得了长足的发展,但除了话语隐喻和概念隐喻两个维度之外,对隐喻的第三个维度即交际隐喻(the dimension of communication)的研究直到最近才引起学界的重视,隐喻的这三个维度之间的关系也并未完全研究透彻。Steen 教授在发言中论述了引入隐喻交际维度研究的必要性,并提出它对与文体和风格相关的思维隐喻和语言隐喻带来的新问题。吕中舌教授(清华大学)结合 Chatman (1980)叙述文本的构成和 Short (1996)小说语篇结构的理论对劳伦斯1914年发表的短篇小说《普鲁士军官》进行了系统的语篇分析。研究发现,小说中的两位男主人翁普鲁士军官与其传令兵由于出身、年龄、家庭背景和社会地位等方面的不同造成性格上的反差,由此产生的两个男人之间的一系列冲突,最后导致小说的悲剧结局:传令兵谋杀了军官。

　　林立红教授和于善志教授(宁波大学)探讨了叙事文本中反事实理解的层级制约问题。叙事所述的基本命题通过作者的修辞聚焦原则蕴含于文本之中(语言世界);对叙事的反事实理解则需要读者或听者大脑中概念世界(心理世界)和现实世界(物质世界)的参与和互动。从叙事文本的语言输入到大脑情节记忆之间的映射是个多维映射过程,涉及多维语言层面(如词汇、短语、句法、语篇)和多维世界(如反事实世界)之间的互动。我们一方面要对叙事小说中的"事实"暂停怀疑,另一方面在理解反事实世界时还需要利用真实世界中的百科知识(如哲学、心理学、篇章语言学、叙事学等)。从文本中激活的大脑情节既有共核的基础情节,也有外围的变异情节。基础成分越大,文本就越容易理解;外围成分越多,读者对叙事文本信息的准确复原难度就越大。映射和激活情节的知识结构可以降低加工成本,并能准确解读文本。语言符号、大脑、外部世界体验之间的这种互动关系是叙事文本理解中的重要问题。康响英教授(湖南第一师范学院)探讨了《讹诈》中隐含作者的隐性建构及原因,提出作者对直接引语、内隐的叙述者等叙事形式的选择与情景语境或作者的整体意义有关而构成"有动因的突出"。叙事策略的"客观化"与"前景化"凸现了隐含作者的态度,是作者的匠心选择与写作技巧高明之处,也是《讹诈》能成为世界经典名作的原因所在。杨建国博士(五邑大学)从理论上探究时间观和叙事结构的呼应关系,继而借助于两部英国荒岛小说——丹尼尔·迪福的《鲁滨孙漂流记》和威廉·戈丁的《蝇王》,在文学实践中对这种呼应关系加以验证。阳利、骆文琳老师(重庆师范大学)讨论了英国当代著名作家珍妮特·温特森的小说《给樱桃以性别》的时空叙事艺术,认为参照物理学时空观的内部矛盾建立的时空叙事话语为小说中的历史编纂叙事和身份认同叙事这两大主题叙事提供叙事原则。时空叙事话语与主题叙事之间的关系表明:在温特森的小说世界里,虽然矛盾和悖论永远存在,但它们可以在艺术中实现调和,艺术的永恒性折射出这部后现代小说对现代性中的永恒性的追求。戴力芬副教授(福州大学)解读了劳伦斯《玫瑰园中的影子》的文本、亚世界及情节的动态发展,谢柳春老师(福州大学)从叙事时间、叙事聚焦、同故事叙述者等三方面探析菲茨杰拉德的代表作《了不起的盖茨比》的叙事特色及艺术效果,马晓颖老师(华北电力大学)从叙事学和文体学的重合面即叙事视角和人物话语表达方式对小说中的叙事话语进行描述性分析,并探讨其产生的文体效果。

5. 理论文体学、教学文体学与翻译风格研究

Michael Toolan 教授以"What Makes Poems Poetic?"为题,通过分析 Wallace Stevens, Michael Longley 等现当代诗人的诗歌文本,深入系统地分析了诗歌文本中的词汇重复(lexical repetition)、回声(echo)和重组(reformulation)等文体特征。作者认为,正是这些典型的文体特征体现了诗歌的文学性、诗性(poeticality)或文学创造性特质。徐有志教授(河南大学)在《谈谈戏剧的叙述节奏》的主题报告中指出,戏剧除了有其语言节奏外,还具有突出的叙述节奏,这表现在剧作家对于戏剧情景和结构、矛盾和冲突、人物情感等的波澜起伏的安排上。戏剧对场景转换可以安排得自然流畅,对事件过程可以安排得扣人心弦,对人物心态可以安排得跌宕起伏。但是所有戏剧叙述节奏都得通过戏剧人物的行为和言语表达出来,即通过剧作家设计的人物对话表达出来,形成叙事曲线与读者/观众之间或张或弛或悲或喜的心灵律动。马菊玲教授(宁夏大学)借用 Stockwell (2009)提出的注意—共鸣模式解读中国古典山水诗共鸣的认知过程,指出山水诗的共鸣主要是图形边界移动的情感体验,并提出共鸣不仅是注意的选择,还是读者对文学客体的心理属性的体验,共鸣的发生是客观景物情感化和读者自由意识发挥的结果。罗怀宇博士(北京化工大学)考察了"意象"作为文学范畴的理论发展,将其与西方文论中的近似因素作了比较,并深入探讨了其在塑造中国明清小说风格维度中的独特作用。袁微老师(中国民航飞行学院)从音韵格律学的角度对英语诗歌的语音象征及其美学效果进行了探讨。

吴显友教授(重庆师范大学)作了题为《认知文体学视角下的文本阐释》的报告。他首先介绍了认知文体学与认知诗学在学科性质、研究范围、研究目的、理论资源和认知框架等六个方面的特点,并借用认知隐喻理论、图形—背景理论和语篇世界理论,对《高级英语》教材中 3 个语篇片段进行了认知文体学阐释。这样的阐释不仅有利于读者正确把握语篇的语言艺术、主题思想和美学价值,而且还可以从一个崭新的视角研究读者的认知推理活动和它们如何影响读者对语篇的意义阐释,同时对培养学生阅读鉴赏能力具有重要意义。戴凡教授(中山大学)以学生习作为语料,认为各种修辞手段是学生写作技巧中非常突出的文体特征,把创意写作与文体学相

结合的教学方法可以从创作角度和文本分析角度帮助学生提高文学创作能力和文学鉴赏能力。曹春春教授（山东师范大学）从"后方法"视角探讨英语课堂生态教学模式的构建问题。建构语言生态课堂的基本原则包括学习者自主、教师自主和教师赋权，从"后方法"的教育理念，即特殊性、实践性和可能性探讨如何根据教学情景最大限度地发挥教师自身的主动性和创造性，优化英语课堂生态系统结构，建立和谐、健康、充满活力的语言课堂生态系统。

　　封宗信教授（清华大学）以"The Style(s) of a Classic in Translation and Back-Translation"为题，关注路易斯·卡洛尔学会在全世界范围内发起的对儿童文学经典《爱丽丝漫游仙境》指定章节的回译活动，对比分析了从印度尼西亚语、希伯来语、意大利语和汉语等译本到英语的回译。封教授指出，通过回译译本的研究，我们可以了解到该文本超过 120 种语言的译本文体和风格。此外，回译文学经典还可对文学翻译风格进行历史和共时研究，这同时也是跨文化研究的有效手段之一。高剑妮博士（首都师范大学）在"语境与翻译——以一篇邀请函的批评性话语分析为例"发言中对 Hatim & Mason 语境分析三层次提出修正，并应用修正后的理论对"首都文化战略研究院揭牌典礼邀请函"展开批评性话语分析。刘晓辉教授（哈尔滨工业大学）归纳了法律语言的四大文体特征：规范性，严谨性，规约性以及格式化，并以实例具体分析了在法律文本的汉译过程中如何通过文体特征实现汉译的准确性。姚小文副教授（广西民族大学）从语音、词汇、句子和整体效果等层面入手，探寻在民歌曲目汉译英实践中如何成功地传情达意——尽量再现原文生动鲜明的语言文化特征并传递其不可或缺的文体价值。李春林老师（上海外国语大学）认为，从认知文体学中的图形—背景理论角度，通过影像凸显、影像和背景的转换可以分析作者及译者的文章构思及语言风格，可以发现译者的主体性特点，对更好地阅读、鉴赏和翻译李商隐《无题》诗歌的语言风格和主题思想有启发意义。

6. 文体学研究的新趋势

刘承宇教授（西南大学）借鉴生态语言学的研究方法，建构生态文体学的理论框架，包含文体的生态学研究和生态话语的文体分析两种研究路径。前者将文体视作一种生态系统，并借鉴生态学的研究方法，探讨文体发生、发展及演变的外部和内部控制机制；后者运用文体学的研究方法，分析生态话语的语言特征及其文体效果，并以美国海洋生物学家 Rachel Carson 的生态学名著《寂静的春天》为例验证生态文体学在生态语篇分析中的解释力。

刘国辉教授(上海海事大学)借用 COCA 和 COHA 两个大型语料库对"X-able"形态的文体分布进行了深入、系统的统计文体学分析。研究发现,不管文体差异还是历时演变,也不管肯定或否定,"-able"形态变体的使用频率始终最高,而"-uble"形态变体的使用频率则处于最低状态。就具体的词汇而言,表达肯定的意义"able, possible"以及表达否定的意义"inevitable, incredible, unable, unintelligible"使用频率始终第一,而且其意义都与人对主客观世界的处理有关。陈历明教授(华侨大学)通过梳理传教士十六世纪以来在中国传教时留下的各类历史文本,发现欧化白话并非学界所普遍认为的那样源于清末民初,而是明末清初,并且与传教士的翻译和写作有着极深的渊源。重新审视这段历史将会看到,旨在传教的西方传教士,以其目标明确的翻译和写作,(有意)无意间促成了欧化白话的生成,并以此为中国文学的现代性开了先河。罗健博士(宁波诺丁汉大学)概述了语料库文体学的理论并论述了如何运用语料库文体学的方法进行叙事研究,提出了一个可用于叙事研究的语料库文体学—认知叙事学人物分析模型。此模型包含五个互相关联的模块:(1)百科图式(人们对于人物的一般了解),(2)文类常规(人物的类型学知识),(3)叙事情景(人物的身份/标识),(4)话语再现(人物简况),(5)表层语言模式(与人物有关的词汇选择)。他从语料库文体学角度对福特 1915 年的早期现代主义小说《好兵》和伍尔芙 1927 年的经典现代主义小说《到灯塔去》进行对比分析,用以说明语料库文体学如何借助计算机来帮助捕捉、分析小说家用于呈现人物说话风格、思维模式以及行为的语言使用特点。曹海燕副教授(连云港师范高等专科学校)以斯坦福大学提供的慕课"世界妇女健康和权益"为语料探究一系列与世界健康、女性情况和女性人权有关的重要议题,涉及割礼、家庭暴力、性工作等敏感话题,其阅读材料大多为国际组织文献,为了清楚说明某做法造成的伤害,激发人们保护女性权益的热情,国际社会往往选用具有一定宣传效果的术语,如使用反讽、借代等修辞手法,突显"荣誉处决"等做法的父权社会背景及其荒谬性,体现"嫁妆谋杀"等现象的女性相关性。

7. 结语

本届国际文体学盛会主题报告高屋建瓴、精彩纷呈,分组讨论气氛热烈、畅所欲言,为国内外学者交流思想、增进友谊提供了难得的机会,充分展示了21 世纪初国内外文体学研究的新方法、新趋势、新成果。归纳起来,本次盛会有如下一些亮点:(1)中外学者热情参与,国内中青年学者崭露头角,与会者提交的论文数量和质量高；(2)研究的视野宽阔,理论视角新颖、独特,研究方法灵活多样。既有理论探索又有实证研究,分析预料既有文学文本也有非文学文本,既有中外经典文本也有当下流行的影视文本、网络文本；(3)文体学的部分分支学科,如文学文体学、功能文体学、认知文体学、叙述文体学等,成为本次会议的热点议题,成果丰硕；(4)文体学的一些前沿学科,如语料库文体学、批评文体学、多模态话语分析、英汉文体学对比研究等已进入中外学者的研究视野,并收到了丰厚的回报。难怪 Jeffries & McIntyre 教授这样自信地说:"文学批评作为一门学科已处于停滞不前的状态,原因是以主观研究方法所得出的结论的不可证伪性以及语篇研究缺乏(语言)关注焦点使其批评讨论成为不可能的事,我们的观点是文体学才是摆脱僵局的出路。"(2010:192)显然,两位专家的评论有些偏激。我们不赞成文本阐释方法非此即彼的逻辑关系,而认为它是一种开放、多元、互补的关系,后者正是文体学批评方法的优势所在。在新世纪里,我们在继续做好上述各方面研究的同时,还应特别关注文体学研究的新趋势,如语料库文体学、认知文体学、叙述文体学、批评文体学、多模态分析、教学文体学等。

参考文献

Jeffries, L. & D. McIntyre. 2010. Stylistics. Cambridge: Cambridge University Press.

Simpson, P. 2004. Stylistics: A Resource Book for Students. London & New York: Routledge.

申　丹. 2004.《叙述学与小说文体学研究》. 北京:北京大学出版社.

Part II   Cognitive Stylistics

Metaphor in *The Cancer Poetry Project*

Gerard Steen **(University of Amsterdam)**

Abstract: In this paper I discuss the relation between metaphor and its role in the poetry written by cancer patients and their caregivers as reflected in the two volumes of *The Cancer Poetry Project*, edited by Karen Miller. I suggest that metaphor may be less important than is assumed by either Susan Sontag and other critical philosophers, Lakoff and Johnson and other cognitive linguists, or Elena Semino and similar cognitive stylistic and poetic approaches. Metaphor is there, and when we focus on it, it has a lot of potential power, both in negative and in positive ways. But the use of metaphor seems to be relatively subsidiary to the more encompassing genre event of writing a cancer poem for a range of different purposes in the experience of cancer. I conclude that metaphor scholars who wish to apply the study of metaphor in medical practice need to pay more attention to these encompassing discourse factors than happens today.

Key words: metaphor; discourse; cancer poetry; medical humanities

1. Illness, Image, Metaphor: *The Cancer Poetry Project*

The topic of this paper, metaphor in *The Cancer Poetry Project*, comes from the Metaphor Lab's interest in application and teaching metaphor research. For the past five years I have been one of the co-teachers of a general Honors Program Bachelor course at VU University Amsterdam called 'Illness, Image, Metaphor'. The course brings together second-year bachelor students from all disciplines from two universities in Amsterdam in order to study metaphorical and visual representations of the experience of cancer in five genres: poetry, novels, biographies, films, and documentaries. We have students from medicine, the life sciences, the social sciences, and the humanities, and they read poems and books and watch films about cancer that they have to analyze for their use of metaphor and visual imagery. Our course includes poetry by cancer patients and those who love them, published in two volumes called *The Cancer Poetry Project*, with published poets and first time poetry writers combined in one book (Miller, 2001, 2013); but also comprises novels like Solzhenitsyn's *Cancer Ward* and Coetzee's *Age of Iron*, biographies like Philip Roth's *Patrimony* and David Rieff's *Swimming in a Sea of Death*, and films like *Biutiful* by Alejandro González Iñárritu.

The goal of this course is for the students to arrive at a better understanding and appreciation of the ways in which cancer is given figurative expression and visual form across this range of distinct artistic genres. For students of medicine this makes them think about the various meanings and values of their healing practices. For students in the arts the point is that their discipline can in fact connect with life-saving practices and be employed for their potential of application in the new area of 'medical humanities'. These different angles are precisely what makes the course interesting and exciting, and the theories and insights of cognitive linguistics, stylistics and poetics form a solid basis for making the course a success from this multidisciplinary perspective.

Our didactic approach includes students writing small personal reviews of the artefacts that they study and a final essay that reflects upon what they have learned. These student activities are framed by a reading of Susan Sontag's *Illness as Metaphor*, originally published in 1978. The gist of Sontag's position is made plain on the very first page of her famous essay (1990: 3):

> My point is that illness is *not* a metaphor, and that the most truthful way of regarding illness — and the healthiest way of being ill — is one most purified of, most resistant to, metaphoric thinking.

The question we pose to the students in the first class is whether Sontag is right (cf. Clow, 2001). In other words, should cancer be handled without the use of metaphorical thought? Is it indeed 'most truthful' to regard cancer directly, without having recourse to some other domain than illness itself? And vice versa, is thinking about cancer by metaphor less truthful and is it therefore something to be condemned?

When we examine the poetry by the cancer patients and those who love them published in *The Cancer Poetry Project*, the answer to these questions is a little different than Sontag may have wanted. For contrary to Sontag's program, metaphor turns out to be ubiquitous in this poetry, often in smart and moving ways. One of my favorite examples from the first volume of *The Cancer Poetry Project* is the following (Miller, 2001: 162−3).

ON THE BEACH
For mother
by Stephen J. Kudless

It was a shark, her disease.
It took her in many bites;
At first, in tiny nibbles —
bit
by
bit
Leaving scars and hope.
Then, the shark, roused by her blood
Became frenzied and bold —
Devouring, obliterating.
She thrashed and cried out,
In the crimson water,
And was gone.

Now the sea is quiet, even peaceful and blue.
The gulls wheel overhead
And the tiny crabs fiddle in the ebb tide.
They are oblivious to what I know.
Children make castles in the sand,
And parents make plans for dinner.

I see it, though, circling,
Its fin just creasing the surface
Out in the distance,
Just beyond the lifeguards' sight,
This shark, fed on motherflesh,
And still hungry.

I fear the water.

This poem employs an extended metaphor, launched in the first line by 'It was a shark, her disease', a variation upon the classic 'A is B' formula for metaphor which has been molded into a more emphatic expression. This basic metaphorical proposition of the poem is grippingly but beautifully developed into a full-blown metaphorical story that displays gruesome, veritable details. Above all, it ends in ineluctable consequences that hold the narrator in limbo. This is one of the best examples of the power of metaphor in the conceptualization of cancer that can be found in *The Cancer Poetry Project*. Why would Sontag and her followers be against this?

Another example that hinges on metaphorical thought, this time from the second volume, is the following (2013: 188-9):

TOUCH ME
by Janine Soucie Kelley

You tell your lover

the long thin scar
dividing your skin
into hemispheres
tattoos the memory of a trip
down the Amazon
where you met
a strange tribe of healers
whose ceremonies
and rites of passage
tested your courage and faith
teaching you a new language.

You faced
the dark night of the soul
the white day with its blind stars
searching for the hidden face of God
near the fabled healing rivers of love
whose Beatitudes wash away
anger and fear.
You left this rainforest of suffering
naked, new-born
an explorer discovering
how to love this new body
how to map its scars into beauty

how to say, *Touch me, Touch me here.*

Cancer as a trip down the Amazon offers a novel, fantastically concrete variant of the conceptual metaphor of illness as a journey. It has a surprising end, leaving the rainforest naked and newborn, which feels like a positive reversal of the story of Adam and Eve and Paradise: even though the naked body is scarred it is carried by an explorer who discovers how to love this new body and map its scars on to beauty. The final line then brings everything back to realistic, fragile and precarious, non-metaphorical dimensions of human relationships and embodied interaction. This is a beautiful poetic achievement triggering extensive metaphorical thought.

Yet it is also true that there is some very powerful cancer poetry that is completely or almost completely devoid of metaphor. Consider, for instance, the contrast between the previous poem about mastectomy with the following poem, from Miller (2013: 65−66):

THREE MEASUREMENTS OF MY BREASTS
by Margaret Ann Towner

1. A WELCOMING
The first time
my sweetheart
touched me,
ran his fingertips
down my breasts,
I discovered
a universe of wants.
Through the opened
door, new possibilities
found me breathless,
face to face
with desire,
and Life
held out its arms
to welcome me.

2. PERFECT FIT
We used to find each other
in the stillness of the night
as you sought refuge
from the day.

My breasts were perfect —
you would tell me —
just the right size and shape
to fit into the palms
of your calloused hands.

3. BODY ART

In pre-op I sit on the edge of the gurney,
waiting for the surgeon, who arrives
with a black leather case of markers
in his hand. He zips it open,
shows me the variety of colors
and tips, proceeds to draw circles
and lines that crisscross my bare breasts,
chitchatting about this and that
as he makes his calculations.
No one has ever drawn on my breasts.
We want to make the correct incisions,
he says, as he admires his artistry.
And not to worry, later we can
tattoo nipples back on.

This poem is very non-metaphorical, with three local exceptions. It is based in a series of three concrete and realistic scenes, with only the first stanza employing metaphorical expressions: a *universe* of wants; opportunities in life as *doors opening*; the speaker standing face to face with desire (personification); and life holding out its hands to welcome the speaker (personification). These local metaphors, however, have little to do with the illness of cancer per se. Instead, the poem as a whole seems to draw its strength precisely from its non-metaphorical directness. If anything, it displays not a metaphorical but a heavily metonymic quality: the three distinct scenes each function as so many milestones, each standing for much more encompassing and moving scenarios in a story about love, life and cancer. Here cognitive stylistics needs to unravel how metonymy can trigger a rich process of figurative thought.

The didactic purpose I therefore have when I teach the poetry in our bachelor course is to make the students aware that the non-metaphorical attitude to cancer advocated by Sontag is indeed quite possible, as is attested by 'Three measurements of my breasts', but that it certainly is not the only possibility. In fact, what the complete course aims to show is that the artistic representation of cancer is highly variable. The various genres in the course program offer entirely different responses to the issue posed by Sontag.

What the course also shows is that poems like 'On the beach' or 'Touch me' are rather exceptional in their innovative use of extended metaphorical thought. They are not really representative. Instead, there are numerous examples of more moderate and conventional uses of metaphor, in the poetry but more evidently in the prose and in the films and documentaries. Their concerted effect, however, is of a ubiquitous presence of metaphor representing aspects of cancer.

2. Cancer and Metaphor

The question arises, therefore, whether this is because these poets have not paid heed to Sontag's injunction to avoid metaphor in writing about cancer. Or is it because they disagree with her and Sontag is plain wrong? In *The Cancer Poetry Project*, we can ask the poets themselves, for one of the attractive features of the second volume is that it has consistent quotations about the poets' motives for writing. Let us first read one of these metaphor-motivated poems and then see what the author note says (2013: 129).

AFTER THE DIAGNOSIS
by Annette Opalczynski

After the diagnosis,
dirty dishes pile up in the sink,
but the dog still needs her walk.
She pokes me with her cold, wet nose:
Remember me?
Outside she runs,
pulling me forward,
her ears flapping in the breeze.
My neighbor waves.
He's mowing the lawn
in his bare feet.
At the corner,
we pause to watch the kids playing

their daily basketball game.
Along the fence,
wild honeysuckle blooms
and I breathe in
persistent summer perfume.

Annette Opalczynski, forty-six, was feeling depressed after her father was diagnosed with lung and bone cancer. "But the dog didn't care; she still wanted her daily walk. For me, it was a metaphor for the way life goes on and demands your attention, no matter how badly you feel." Her father died a year later in 2003.

It is clear that this poet deliberately uses metaphor as a stylistic device to conceptualize and express her thoughts and feelings about the effects of cancer on her life, and explicitly invites us to share this cross-domain mapping as a meaningful comparison between two distinctly juxtaposed conceptual domains (cf. Steen, 2008, 2011, 2013).

There is a lot more deliberate metaphor use in these poems, but it is not often explicitly commented on as such in the notes. For instance, Janine Soucie Kelley wrote her Amazon poem quoted above to honor her daughter's 'resilience, beauty and courage' and to inspire other cancer survivors to 'love and accept their brave new bodies' (Miller, 2013: 189). This motivation is not very different from the one of the non-metaphorical cancer poem by Margaret Ann Towner, author of 'Three measurements of my breasts', who says: 'Losing my breasts was like an amputation. I even experienced phantom breasts. When I was finally able to write, I wanted to show my perception of my breasts before and after cancer, to capture those changes through poetry' (Miller, 2013: 66). It looks as if metaphor is a non-issue to most of these authors, whether they do or do not make use of it, deliberately or non-deliberately, in their poems.

This is of course precisely what is predicted by cognitive linguistic, stylistic and poetic approaches to metaphor, which see metaphor as part and parcel of our conceptual and cultural models of cancer, as is vividly described by Siddharta Mukherjee (2010: 183). What is more, this conventionalized type of metaphorical thought lies at the basis of everyday talk about cancer. This is reflected in the editorial notes from the poets about cancer as cancer:
CANCER IS AN ENTITY THAT COMES AND GOES

When something big like cancer *comes along*,

I wrote this poem, in a sense, to establish that I am the same person now that I
was before the cancer *came to* me,

They make their home in southern Minnesota where cancer is *not welcome*.

Where they all celebrate the fact that Mommy's cancer *is gone*.

Today, he is *managing* his cancer, which *returned* about seven months later, with
more radiation and chemo.

In 2012, the cancer *reappeared*

CANCER IS A PERSON

Cancer has *touched* my life repeatedly

He interviewed hundreds of people *touched* by cancer

We hold poetry workshops and readings at oncology clinics, churches, etcetera for
anyone who has been *touched* by cancer.

CANCER IS AN ENEMY

Wanting to run away from cancer and *hide from* it —

They have hope that "yet another hormonal therapy" *will slow his aggressive*
cancer

Dad had always seemed *invincible*, even *through the entire fight against* cancer

Her husband, Cawood Hadaway, a wildlife artist and avid outdoorsman, was
diagnosed with stage-four lung cancer in 1999, "*fought a courageous battle*"

Terry Godbey, fifty-seven, says poetry helped her *survive her battle with* breast cancer

His doctors expected him to only have three months before the cancer *overtook* his
brain

In 2002, she *lost* her leg *to* cancer and now wears a prosthetic leg.

Poet Tammi Truax, who *lost* her husband *to* cancer,

I have *lost* many — too many — friends and family members *to* cancer and *stand
with* close loved ones *who are currently battling this scourge*

All of these are well-known, conventionalized metaphorical ways of talking
about cancer (cf. Penson, et al., 2004; Reisfield & Wilson, 2004; Hanne &
Hawken, 2007). They typically do not raise any questions about their
metaphorical status. It is true that people can be alerted to that, but that does
take special effort — in cognitive linguistics, stylistics and poetics, metaphors
are supposed to be figurative conceptualizations we live by without noticing.

3. Metaphor in Language, Thought and Communication about Cancer

This is the moment in our course where we draw our students' attention to the insights of contemporary metaphor theory as well as to its connection with contemporary cancer research. I am referring, of course, to the work by Lakoff & Johnson (1980) entitled *Metaphors We Live By*, but also to the volumes published by Andrew Ortony (1979) and Richard Honeck & Robert Hoffman (1980) that are called *Metaphor and Thought* and *Cognition and Figurative Language*. In a true deluge of metaphor research since 1980 metaphor has been shown to be one of the basic, unconscious mechanisms for building and maintaining language systems and conceptual systems. It is especially useful for automatically conceptualizing and talking about all sorts of abstract or complex or poorly understood phenomena (cf. e. g. Gibbs, 2008). This set of phenomena includes illnesses, our concomitant emotions and understanding of them, and their relation to major life issues such as thwarted expectations, possible death, and strained, changing or lost relationships between people who have to deal with all this. At this point in the course, our students realize that Sontag's idea that cancer should be faced by a non-metaphorical way of thought comes across today as at best misconceived and at worst misleading.

This raises questions about the relation between cancer and metaphor, in art and the media but also in medical practice and care. Part of the course is therefore also a discussion of the diverging potential roles of metaphor in the representation of cancer in all sorts of medical situations. Elena Semino, in her *Metaphor in Discourse* (2008: 175 – 178), discusses some of the contemporary scientific publications about the use of metaphor by professionals interacting with sufferers. She claims that 'What tends to be advocated, therefore, is not the elimination of metaphor, but a more conscious, sensitive and effective use of metaphor, …' A little further Semino concludes:

> By and large, metaphors are not intrinsically harmful or beneficial, especially at the level of the individual: what matters is how a metaphor is used, and the extent to which individuals are free and able to select the metaphors that work best for them. (2008: 178)

This is typically what the students in our course also tend to think after eight weeks of reflection on illness, image, and metaphor. It looks like an extremely reasonable position to take.

But is it?

In just a few pages we have moved from (a) a view of the representation of cancer by metaphor as something to be resisted to (b) a view of the representation of cancer by metaphor as something that cannot be avoided to (c) a view of the representation of cancer by metaphor that to some extent may be chosen and used in various ways with various effects by various individuals. So what does that mean? Are all metaphors that are freely selected also metaphors that work best for their user?

It is time for another poem (Miller, 2001: 37) :

THE SPY

by Marlene Rosen Fine

In the photographs the doctors hold
I see the spy.
They have deciphered your code.
They will track you down.
Traitorous cell.
You have set up quarters in my breast.
You send your signals beneath my skin
making small revolutions
in my underground city.

But the generals are conferring
at the foot of my bed.
Cold and brutal,
they will have no pity.
They will never rest
till they cut you out.
They are the forces
pharmaceutical.

The terrible point of this poem is that the speaker's body will turn into a battlefield. Here it is the doctors that do the fighting against the enemy while the patient is the territory on which the battle is being fought. Assuming that the poet has been free and able to select this metaphor, the question is how this can be said to work best for her. Any consideration of the metaphor by itself will raise deeply depressing thoughts and emotions that an encompassing analysis can attempt to describe and explain.

I suggest that we need to broaden our perspective. My argument today is that it is not the metaphor as such that is important in a poem like 'The Spy'.

And 'The Spy' is not alone: there are many other poems like this that use metaphorical thought and language to measure out the details of the disasters of cancer and its consequences, 'On the Beach' being another example. In fact, this is precisely their point. How can these potentially depressing metaphors be seen as working best for their users?

Given their employment in these very personal poems, it would be nonsensical to put a ban on these uses of metaphor, as Sontag wants to do. This says more about Sontag's attitude to coping than about the ways in which patients and their caregivers can be empowered. What I think we should do instead is appreciate these metaphors as just one cognitive means to help express the poet's thoughts and feelings and focus on the latter: as long as that metaphorical conceptualization is useful in the overall process of managing the experiences of cancer, it does not matter what the particular nature of the metaphor itself is.

This is precisely what the poets themselves seem to be saying as well. They focus on the benefits of poetry writing without much attention to the allegedly special role of metaphor in thinking about cancer drawn to the fore by Sontag. In other words, the conceptualization and representation of cancer may not be about the nature of the cancer metaphor and its use, as is examined by Semino, but about the nature of the encompassing discourse genre and its use: whether we are dealing with a poem or a post on a support group site or a view expressed by a patient to a doctor, as long as the discourse event itself is useful in the overall process of coping with cancer, then it is basically immaterial whether there is any metaphor involved, and if there is, whether the metaphor is significant and prominent, or positive or negative, or not. The issue with conceptualizing and representing cancer, I suggest, is not the metaphorical or nonmetaphorical model of cancer itself, but the way people use these models as parts of discourse events related to cancer for their empowerment.

It is interesting to see how this position can be related to an analysis of the linguistic structure of the poems. A computational examination by means of Wmatrix (Rayson, 2009) reveals that when you compare the cancer poems in the two volumes against a general reference corpus of American English, the 11 semantic domains that are comparatively most prominent in the poems, characterizing their predominant semantic concerns, include the following:

anatomy and physiology, pronouns, medicines and medical treatment, plants, colour, disease, clothes and personal belongings, food, moving, coming, and going, parts of buildings, kin

Most of these domains seem to reflect the more general concerns of being ill and much less the metaphorical conceptualization of having cancer, perhaps with the exception of the moving, coming and going domain. This is suggested even more emphatically by the top 25 most prominent words in the cancer poems in the same comparison with general American English:

your, I, you, my, us, cancer, white, breast, me, chemo, god, like, breasts, bald, hair, by, am, body, her, how, skin, fingers, love, hospital, bed

It is starkly non-metaphorical language that these poets have cancer by, metaphor clearly having a very modest role in this comparison. Instead, what matters is the experience of illness and the way that has to be addressed, especially between individual people (note the prominence of the personal pronouns). In an interesting way, this in fact seems to come quite close to what Sontag was advocating in the preface to her famous essay.

4. Metaphor in Cancer Poetry, Therapy, and Communication: The Importance of Genre

The upshot of my exploration of metaphor in *The Cancer Poetry Project* therefore seems to be that metaphor may be less important than is assumed by either Susan Sontag and other critical philosophers, Lakoff and Johnson and other cognitive linguists, or Elena Semino and similar cognitive stylistic and poetic approaches. Metaphor is there, and when we focus on it, it has a lot of potential power, both in negative and in positive ways. But the use of metaphor seems to be relatively subsidiary to the more encompassing genre event of writing a cancer poem for a range of different purposes in the experience of cancer. These may concern ordering one's thoughts and emotions and making them available for expression, whether these are negative or positive; but they may also concern further reflection and sharing of these thoughts and emotions, or addressing them as mental realities that need to be memorized, cherished, changed or combated. The metaphorical or nonmetaphorical representation of cancer in cancer poetry and related genres hence may be less important than the encompassing nature and function of the genre events themselves.

These genre-driven processes of dealing with cancer require a more encompassing scientific approach than just metaphor research. They take place in interactive, social and societal contexts that are drawing an increasing amount of attention in the medical humanities, for instance in connection with media representations (Walter, 2010) and narrative based medicine (Greenhalgh & Hurwitz, 1999). It looks as if these genre-oriented developments in linguistics create more powerful and recognizable frames of reference for dealing with the representation of cancer than metaphor does. That poetry and poetry writing and discussion may be of significant value in this genre-oriented approach is good news for stylistics.

At the same time, the opportunities for resistance to metaphor may not be ignored or underestimated. Conscious metaphorical cognition may be helpful in pointing out undesirable consequences of particular metaphorical models of thought and stimulate people to find alternative perspectives in the same metaphorical model, alternative metaphorical models, or non-metaphorical models of cancer. This too, however, may be exploited in dedicated genre events, such as poetry writing and discussion, live or online meetings of support group, and therapeutic sessions. This would all be another part of the current movement of medical humanities (e. g. Penson et al., 2004), and cognitively oriented metaphor scholars may have to offer interesting perspectives.

In sum, metaphor may be important as a deliberately used form of cognition in specific discourse events, such as patients and their caregivers writing poetry, patients and their caregivers reading and discussing poetry, patients and their caregivers talking about treatment, therapy and life in doctor-patient meetings, therapy sessions, and dedicated visiting hours. These events may in fact be specially arranged for that purpose. However, metaphor as metaphor may be equally insignificant in these very same discourse events if their focus is on the target domain of illness, life and love — as long as those discourse events themselves are monitored and perhaps even coached regarding their genre-specific efficiency. This brings metaphor and poetry together within a more encompassing genre-analytical perspective; both linguists and literary scholars can contribute to this enterprise and perhaps even make it more applicable. It is that perspective of empirically-founded application that can be on our radar a little more if we wish to contribute to medical humanities and people's dealing with illnesses like cancer.

References

Clow, B. 2001. Who's afraid of Susan Sontag? Or, the myths and metaphors of cancer reconsidered. *Social History of Medicine*, 14 (2): 293-312.

Gibbs, R. W., Jr. (ed.). 2008. *The Cambridge Handbook of Metaphor and Thought*. Cambridge: Cambridge University Press.

Greenhalgh, T. & B. Hurwitz. 1999. Narrative based medicine: Why study narrative? *BMJ*, 318: 48-50.

Hanne, M. & S. Hawken. 2007. Metaphors for illness in contemporary media. *Medical Humanities*, 33: 93-99.

Honeck, R. & R. Hoffman (eds.). 1980. *Cognition and Figurative Language*. Hillsdale, NJ: Lawrence Erlbaum.

Lakoff, G. & M. Johnson.1980. *Metaphors We Live By*. Chicago: University of Chicago Press.

Miller, K. (ed.). 2001. *The Cancer Poetry Project, Volume 1*. Minneapolis, Ill.: Tasora Books.

Miller, K. (ed.). 2013. *The Cancer Poetry Project, Volume 2*. Minneapolis, Ill.: Tasora Books.

Mukherjee, S. 2010. *The Emperor of All Maladies: A Biography of Cancer*. New York etc.: Scribner.

Ortony, A. (ed.). 1979. *Metaphor and Thought*. Cambridge: Cambridge University Press.

Penson, R., L. Schapira, K. Daniels, B. Chabner, & T. Lynch Jr. 2004. Cancer as metaphor. *The Oncologist*, 9: 708-716.

Rayson, P. 2009. Wmatrix: A web-based corpus processing environment. Computing Department, Lancaster University. http://ucrel.lancs.ac.uk/wmatrix/.

Reisfield, G. & G. Wilson, 2004. Use of metaphor in the discourse on cancer. *Journal of Clinical Oncology*, 22 (19): 4024-4027.

Semino, E. 2008. *Metaphor in Discourse*. Cambridge: Cambridge University Press.

Sontag, S. 1990. *Illness as Metaphor and AIDS and Its Metaphors*. New York: Picador.

Steen, G. 2008. The paradox of metaphor: Why we need a three-dimensional model of metaphor. *Metaphor and Symbol*, 23 (4), 213-241.

Steen, G. 2011. The contemporary theory of metaphor — now new and improved! *Review of Cognitive Linguistics*, 9 (1), 26-64.

Steen, G. 2013. Deliberate metaphor affords conscious metaphorical cognition. *Journal of Cognitive Semiotics*, 5 (1-2), 179-197.

Walter, T. 2010. Jade and the journalists: Media coverage of a young British celebrity dying of cancer. *Social Science & Medicine*, 71: 853-860.

认知视角中的言辞行为隐喻复合体
——以莫言作品为例

司建国　（深圳职业技术学院）

Speech Activity Metaphorical Compound in Fiction

Si Jianguo　(Shenzhen Polytechnic)

摘　要：概念隐喻理论的一个重要学说是,隐喻在日常语言与诗性语言中本质上没有区别,诗性隐喻基本上使用了与日常语言相同的认知机制,但使前者不同于或超越后者的是,前者对后者的认知机制进行了特别加工。这种加工在小说语言中如何实现? 为回答这个问题,我们以莫言作品为语料,描述性地探讨言辞行为隐喻复合体现象,发现她源于基本的日常隐喻,是对后者综合、修饰与拓展的结果,涉及比日常隐喻更为复杂的认知过程和更丰富的意象,从而超越了后者。言辞行为隐喻复合体至少含有两个以上概念投射及认知过程,就其内部概念结构而言,她可分为序列型、叠加型以及综合型三大类七小类。序列型指多个隐喻映射在同一层面上运行,叠加型意味着概念投射在多个层次完成,综合型最为复杂,是前两种类型的结合。隐喻复合体在某种程度上为文学隐喻何以超越了日常隐喻,莫言何以为富有超然创造力的语言大师提供了佐证。

关键词：隐喻复合体；言辞行为隐喻； 文学隐喻；莫言

Abstract：The theory of conceptual metaphor claims that poetic metaphor basically adopts the same cognitive mechanism as everyday metaphor, and what makes poetic metaphor different from and beyond daily one is that, poetic metaphor processes everyday metaphor in some special and nonautomatic way. But how is this process realized? To answer this question, we focus on speech activity metaphor compounds (SAMC). Based upon a mini corpus of fictions by Mo Yan, a preeminent writer, we found that SAMC derives from everyday metaphor, but by extending, elaborating and composing, it gets more complicated cognitive processes and more images involved, therefore, goes beyond daily metaphor. SAMC has at least two conceptual mappings, and in terms of conceptual structure, is classified into 3 main types: sequential, hierarchical and complex ones. Sequential SAMC refers to the mappings at the same cognitive level, hierarchical one to those at different levels, and complex one to the combination of the first two types. SAMC provides a convincing explanation for how poetic metaphors is beyond everyday ones, and why Mo Yan is regarded as creative master of words.

Key words: metaphorical compound; speech activity metaphor; poetic metaphor; Mo Yan

1. 引言

认知语言学认为,隐喻不仅是一种言说方式,也是思维方式,既是修辞格(figure of speech),更是思维格(figure of thought)(Gibbs, 1994: 359)。隐喻是我们赖以构筑和理解经验概念的基础。"隐喻的实质为借一种事情去理解和体验另一种事"(Lakoff & Johnson, 1980: 5),是人类用一种事物来认知、理解另一类事物的思维方式,是一种由源始域(source domain)向目标域(target domain)的意义映射(mapping)或投射(projection)。与隐喻相比,"转喻对概念的形成和理解、对思维和语言具有更重要的意义"(Barcelona, 2000: 14)。转喻表述邻近(contiguity)关系,即两个实体在空间和时间上的邻近,它是一个易辨认和记忆的认知域(源始项)激活和凸显另一个认知域(目标项),并以前者作为参照点(referential point),为后者提供心理媒介的过程[1]。转喻同时也是一种比隐喻更为普遍和基本的意义拓展模式(Panther & Radden, 1999),因为人们首先通过接触邻近关系来认识事物之间的关系。

所谓言辞行为隐喻[2]是指言辞行为的隐喻性认知或表征,它以言辞行为为目的域、以其他易感知的经验域为源始域。如"They can't put their feelings into words."是基于隐喻言辞即容器(Linguistic Expressions as Containers)。言辞行为涉及繁杂的经验和认知系统,她不但包括言语行为的实施,还涵盖交际目标的实现、言语意义的表达、交际关系的协商等等(Semino,2005:35)。言辞行为隐喻有助于我们更清晰、直接地认知言辞行为的意义和本质,有助于对言辞行为内容产出和理解、对交际者身份及其相互间的权势关系以及交际发生语境的认知。此外,言辞行为隐喻还反映了第二言者(secondary speaker)对第一言者及其言语的态度及评价(Ibid:38)。

言辞行为隐喻在认知语言学享有独特地位。隐喻的认知研究发轫于此。在划时代的《我们赖以生存的隐喻》(Metaphors We Live By)问世的前一年,Reddy(1979)提出的以言辞行为为目标域的管道隐喻(Conduit Metaphor)开启了认知隐喻研究大门;Lakoff & Johnson(1980)关于Argument is War 的论述对概念隐喻研究产生了巨大影响。其后,不断有新的源始域被发现或证明在言辞行为隐喻中起了重要作用,其中,概念域"移动"(motion)被许多学者看好(Goossens, et al., 1995)。

Goossens 和 Semino 都注意到了言辞行为领域隐喻形成的复杂过程。Goossens(1995:159-74)发现某些言辞行为隐喻经过了两个认知过程、先转喻,而后在此基础上,再形成隐喻,他得出的结论是某些(言辞行为)隐喻是隐喻与转喻互动的结果,并由此提出了著名的转隐喻(metaphtonymy)概念。Semino(2005, 2006)借助语料库手段,发现言辞行为隐喻主要通过一组源始域的复杂互动来实现,它们包括:移动、物理性传递(physical transfer)、物理性构造(physical construction)、物理性支撑(physical support)。她认为许多言辞行为隐喻都是在基本隐喻(primary metaphor)的基础上产生的,即基于具有坚实经验根基的简单、基本的概念映射。

相对而言,汉语的言辞行为隐喻研究起步较晚。Jing-Schmidt(2008)研究了汉语词典中的言辞行为语料,发现转喻和隐喻在言辞行为概念化过程中扮演了同等重要的作用,两者的互动为这一过程重要的认知策略。张雁(2012)对汉语嘱咐类动词(如吩咐、交代)的历时研究发现,这类动词的语义演变基本上经历了从物理行为到言语行为的轨迹。这在很大程度上提供了汉语大部分言辞行为隐喻形成的历时理据。另外,Yu(2003)通过分析莫言作品中的通感(synesthetic)隐喻,发现其隐喻尽管新颖独特,但大致上与日常语言的一般性趋势相吻合,只不过对日常隐喻进行了复杂的加工和综合。同一学者(Yu, 2011)还分析了 2008 年北京奥运电视广告片中多模态的隐喻复合结构。

概念隐喻理论的一个重要理念是,隐喻在日常语言与诗性语言中本质上没有区别,诗性隐喻基本上使用了与日常语言相同的认知机制。但前者不同于或曰超越后者的是,她对后者隐喻的认知机制进行了拓展(extending)、修饰(elaborating)、否定(canceling)和综合(composing)。拓展指以增加投射空位(slot)来扩大概念范围,修饰指以特殊方式填充空位完成概念投射,否定意味着对目标域的某种概念化方式被取消,代之以与其反义的隐喻意象(如 Anger as a weapon./Anger as a hot fluid in a container.)。综合在三者中最为有力,她指同一隐喻的超常规组合,具体而言,指多个指向同一目标域的隐喻同时出现在一个段落甚至句子中,从而产生比单个隐喻更丰富、复杂的隐喻联想。重要的是,综合是概念性的,将复杂的隐喻概念综合在一起,而非只是将文字结合在一起(Gibbs,1994; Kovecses,2005:259-64; Lakoff & Turner,1989:67-72)。而且,综合后的隐喻往往是新奇(novel)的、更具有创造性的,更具有特定文化色彩(Kovecses,2005:262)。

但上述研究对于诗性隐喻超越日常隐喻的这几种方式只作了扼要介绍,并未作详尽的描述和分析。对于拓展、修饰、否定尤其是综合产生的原委、运作机制、主要范畴和类型、形成的认知效果、常见的语言表征形式等等重要问题都语焉不详。而且,他们的佐证材料全是诗歌。文学隐喻究竟何以超越日常隐喻,文学隐喻对日常隐喻的特殊加工如何在叙述文学、在非诗歌文学中实现?为回答这些问题,在言辞行为范畴内,我们提出"隐喻复合体"这一概念。

2. 描述与分析

2.1 隐喻复合体定义

所谓言辞行为隐喻复合体(Speech Activity Metaphorical Compound),是指一个句子或段落中两个以上有关言辞行为的概念投射或认知过程。根据莫言作品语料,我们发现,隐喻复合体中的概念之间有三种不同的关系。一种为序列式的,两个或多个概念相互独立,没有依附关系,呈线性排列。另一种为叠加式的,某个/些概念建立在另外一个/些概念之上,她们之间存在依赖或支持关系,概念呈多层面布局。这两种类型的混合构成复合体中的综合型。隐喻复合体是认知意义上的,而非词语层面的,尽管与概念隐喻一样,具有语言表征。言辞行为隐喻复合体源于简单的、基本的隐喻和转喻,主要是对后者综合以及拓展和修饰的结果。我们的支持性语料来

自莫言小说作品,作者被学界认为是富有超然想象力的语言大师(Wang,
2000:487)。

2.2 研究方法

本研究基于莫言作品语料,涉及隐喻复合体的识别、分类和分析。研究的
具体步骤为:以莫言主要作品,包括《丰乳肥臀》、《酒神》、《天堂蒜薹之
歌》、《檀香刑》、《生死疲劳》(莫言,2012)等,建立约一百五十万字的小型
语料库,使用电子软件 Word 中的"查找"等工具对语料中的言辞行为义项
进行检索、集中,然后,采用排除法,对语料进行三次处理:首先,剔除其中
的字面性(literal)义项,然后,排除非言辞行为隐喻义项,其次,去掉非隐喻
复合体义项。最后,对所有隐喻复合体进行识别、分类和分析。认知隐喻
研究采用自下而上的方法,因此,我们对隐喻复合体采取解构
(decomposing)的分析方式,从复合体的隐喻元素入手,对隐喻复合体的内
部机理、构成成分、认知机制进行描述。

2.3 言辞行为隐喻复合体的主要类型及其分析

如前所述,言辞行为隐喻复合体的主要类型包括序列型,叠加型和综合型,
现分而述之。

2.3.1

序列型:多个概念在同一层面依次排列。这一类型包括两种情况:多个意
象描述同一个概念;多个相对独立的不同概念并列,往往各自有自己的修
饰语。

2.3.1.1

多个角度描述一个中心概念,其概念结构或语义结构可图示为:A1,A2…。
下例两个概念的焦点都在于话语冗长,两个隐喻投射都是对这一焦点不同
角度的描述:

> 1) 大人物清清嗓子,慢条斯理地,**把每个字都抻得很长**。他的**话像长长的纸
>   条**在阴凉的东北风中飞舞着。

(《丰乳肥臀》,155)[3]

第一个语言隐喻(linguistic metaphor),即概念隐喻的语言表征"**把每个字
都抻得很长**"基于概念隐喻"话语为有伸缩性的实体"(Speech as Springy
Object),可拉长可缩短。其实,她还暗含了另一个概念隐喻"时间即空间"

(Time as Space)(Lakoff & Johnson，1980)，用实物的空间长度映射话语的时间长度。第二个投射[4]"话像长长的纸条"则明显含有概念"话语即纸条"，强化了"长"的概念，使得目标域"话语"变得更加具体(纸条)。纸条脆弱、廉价的特性意味着言辞的苍白无力。况且，纸条还在"阴凉的东北风中飞舞"，平添了飘忽不定、难以把握之感。这两次投射都是对基本隐喻"言语即实体"(Speech as Physical Object)(Vanparys，1995：24)的拓展与修饰，她们的源始域不同，但目的域相同，从而从不同视角对目的域作了描写。下例尽管出现了两个不同隐喻，但她们的目标概念都指向同一概念——话语突兀：

> 2）所有的**过渡性语**言都被抛弃，好像有些**夹生**，但她**吞下去夹生**，用近乎无耻的口吻说："我有毛病，盐碱地。"

(《酒神》,2)

"过渡性语言"以概念隐喻"言辞即旅途"(Speech as a Journey)(Semino，2006)为基础。旅途的起点、中途和目的地等要素投射到了言辞的预热准备、铺垫过渡和意图毕现等抽象空位。"过渡性语言被抛弃"意味着言辞没有经过必要的酝酿发展便直奔主题。"有些夹生，但她吞下去夹生"则以另一个隐喻为支撑："言辞即食品"(Speech as Food)(Semino，2005)，因为只有食品才有所谓生熟，才可以吞下。食品由生到熟的过程，映射到语言域，表示说话时机由不成熟到成熟、话语由不恰当到恰当的过程。与食品域相关的"吞下"意味着对食品的接受或认可，"吞下去夹生"有悖常理，映射到言辞行为域，意味着对不恰当言语的接受、认可，突显了言者言语行为的怪异和唐突。这两个隐喻一前一后，排列成序，都描述同一个概念，都表示言语行为的直接莽撞。顺便指出，"吞下去夹生"中的夹生含有转喻基础，即"食品特质夹生激活/指代食品"。与上例不同，这里的两个隐喻同述一个概念。

2.3.1.2

多个不同概念并列，意义相对独立，往往各自有自己的修饰语。其意义结构为：A，B …。如：

> 3）小贱人，在我怀里你说过多少**甜言蜜语**？发过多少**山盟海誓**？

(《生死疲劳》,7)

两个隐喻"甜言蜜语""山盟海誓"目标域不同，指向不同的描述对象。前者指情话，后者喻誓言(包括情人间的誓言)，两者在概念上前后并列，没有修饰与被修饰的关系。前者以概念隐喻"言辞即食品"以及通感隐喻"听觉即味觉"(Sound as Taste)为基础，表示情感浓烈；后者以隐喻"誓言即山/海"

（Oath as Mount/Ocean）为基础，将山与海亘古不变的特质映射到誓言之上，意味着矢志不渝。下例两个隐喻依然相对独立，一前一后，各自有自己的修饰语：

4）以免他**脏话连篇**，**造谣生事**。

（《丰乳肥臀》，269）

"脏话"意味着"话语为实物"，"肮脏"与"干净"本来是修饰实物的，当其与抽象概念连用时，就形成隐喻。因为，凡是以具体（源始域）表示非具体（目标域）都属隐喻范畴（Cameron，2003：72—73）。话语这个抽象概念本无所谓肮脏与否，所谓"脏话"即"下流的话"（《现代汉语词典》，2392）。"造谣"即（凭空）编造谣言，它基于类似的概念隐喻"言语表达即实物"（Linguistic Expressions as Object）（Vanparys，1995），与实物的物理构造（physical construction）相关（Semino，2005：53）。英语中的"to make a promise/plea"等，与之同理。"生事"亦如此，有挑起事端、制造麻烦之意。它本身不属言辞行为，却是前面言辞行为（造谣）的结果。

2.3.2

叠加型：多个意象或概念在不同层面上运行，从而形成多层概念结构。这一类型主要包含两种情形：后面的隐喻建立在前面的隐喻之上以及前面的隐喻建立在后面的隐喻之上。

2.3.2.1

后面的隐喻建立在前面的隐喻之上，意义结构可图解为 $\dfrac{B}{A}$

5）小个雀斑女政府的**嗓音尖上拔尖**，与众不同，很容易**辨别**。

（《天堂蒜薹之歌》，90）

"嗓音尖上拔尖"涉及"听觉即触觉"（Sound as Touch）、"听觉即视觉"（Sound as Sight）的感觉转换即通感隐喻，话语声音变成了可触摸、看到的有"尖"的三维物体。"尖上拔尖"对这一概念作了进一步拓展，使其超越了常规。这为后面的隐喻打好了基础。动词"辨别"的对象一般为具体物件，辨别话语声音则基于概念隐喻"话语（声音）为实物"。显然，这一隐喻因为前面的铺垫显得顺理成章。因为话语声音"与众不同"的尖与高，所以才"很容易辨别"。下例与之相似：

6）哪里来的小子，说**大话**也不怕**闪断舌头**！

（《丰乳肥臀》，199）

"大话"的概念基础依然是"话语即物体",具体的三维物件才有尺寸和重量。所谓大话即"虚夸的话"(《现代汉语词典》,357)根据日常经验,一般而言,物体越大,分量越重。这一隐喻为下个隐喻打下了概念基础。我们有基本概念"言语器官即容器"和"话语即动体",说话即将动体由容器内发送(transfer)出去,这由言语器官完成。舌头为关键的言语器官,是话语加工、发送的主要参与者。话语这个动体大则重,重则可能使舌头不堪重负并损伤。此外,基于转喻"器官行为激活言辞行为"(Activity of Organ for Speech Activity)(Jing-Schimdt,2008:251),舌头运动意味着发声说话。所以,"大话"是原因,"闪断舌头"是结果。然而,常识告诉我们,舌头是不会因为说话而闪断的。所以,这个结果也是隐喻,这是对常规概念的创造性修饰,以器官意外伤害映射意想不到的惩罚。这句话中威胁的意味即产生于此。

2.3.2.2

前面的隐喻建立在后面隐喻之上,其概念关系为 $\dfrac{A}{B}$ 与上例相反。

7) 李武……**拣起**因为训斥刘老大而**丢掉的话头**,说……

(《檀香刑》,51)

以"话语为具体物品"为基础,话语这个物件还有头有尾,话头为话语开始部分,话尾为结束部分,基于此概念,第一个语言表征"拣起"(话头)指重新回到原来的话题,继续中断的议论。第二个隐喻表征"丢掉的话头"表示刚刚开始但停止了的话题。"拣起"基于"丢掉",无中断则无继续,无"丢掉"何言"拣起"?所以,这两个隐喻在时间上一后一先,在逻辑上一果一因。下例情形稍有不同:

8) 她演说成癖了,说着说着就**说热了嘴**,就像**马儿跑热了蹄子**。

(《丰乳肥臀》,310)

第一个隐喻表征"说热了嘴"依据了概念转喻"器官特征激活言语行为特征"(Property of Speech Organ for Property of Speech Activity)(Jing-Schimdt,2008:246),物理性行为(言语器官活动"说")导致了物理性结果(言语器官"嘴"变热)。但"热"不是或不完全是指嘴的温度,莫言的"嘴热"到底意味着什么?我们不甚了了。好在随后的第二个概念投射给了我们提示:"就像马儿跑热了蹄子"。事实上,这个概念表征可以视为第一个概念(嘴热)的源始域,第一个概念则为目标域,两个概念之间存在隐喻投射关系:我们相对熟悉的经验"马儿跑热了蹄子"投射到相对陌生的经验"说热了嘴"。便形成如下投射:马匹的运动器官蹄子→人类的言语器官嘴;奔跑可使马蹄变热→说话可使嘴变热;马蹄热意味运动快速迅猛→嘴热预示话语顺畅流利。这个句子中的两个概念,一方面本身就是隐喻和转喻,一方面又共同形成了更大的隐喻。作为这个大隐喻中的目标域,第一个概念依赖或者通过第二个概念得以明示,达到可及(accessibility)。同时,后者也是对前者的概念拓展。

2.3.3 综合型

有些隐喻复合体概念结构更为复杂,既有同一层次排列的,又有上下层级组合的。既有序列型,又含叠加型。这种复合体可进一步分为三种情形,1)同一概念支持多个概念,概念结构上层为序列型;2)多个概念支持同一概念,下层为序列型;3)多个概念支持多个概念,上下层都有概念序列。现分而述之:

2.3.3.1

多个概念基于同一概念,序列概念在上。其意义关系如图所示:
A1　A2　A3　　下例的隐喻基础只有一个,但她向上衍生出多个隐喻分支:
　　　A

> 9) 他**大吹大擂**着县太爷的一切,从言谈到举止,从兴趣到嗜好,最后,谈话的**高潮**便在大老爷的胡须上展开。

(《檀香刑》,50)

"大吹大擂"源于两个并列的概念隐喻:"言辞行为即吹奏乐器"和"言辞行为即击鼓","大"隐喻性地表示夸张。其后的"高潮"也与音乐相关,表示乐曲最精彩和重要部分。此处投射到话语域,谈话的高潮便是话语的最关键和引人入胜之处。所以,这些概念都共同基于一个隐喻,即"言辞为音乐"(Speech as Music)。下例类似,但概念基础发生了变化:

> 10) 马大童生道:"算了算了,李武兄,古人**清谈当酒,畅谈作肉**,您就给我们多**讲点钱大老爷和衙门里的事情**,就算我们**吃了大荤了**!"

(《檀香刑》,51)

其中的概念基础为基本隐喻"言辞即食品",她在此句话中能产性很强,派生出三个隐喻:"清谈即酒","畅谈即肉","衙门逸事即大荤"。前两个概念隐喻与语言隐喻即概念隐喻的语言表征少有的一致。三个隐喻分支都对基本隐喻作了创造性修饰。

2.3.3.2

一个概念基于多个概念,序列型概念在下层[5],即如:　　A
　　　　　　　　　　　　　　　　　　　　　　　　　　A1　A2　A3

11）鞭炮声**驱散了**西门闹不能生育的**谣言**……但旧**谣言刚破，新流言产生**，西门闹出圈肥冲撞了太岁的事，一夜间**传遍了**高密东北乡十八个村镇。

（《生死疲劳》,6）

"驱散了……谣言"意味着"言辞是移动的实体"（Speech as Moving Object），是可以聚拢、也可以散开的具体物品。而且，言辞有"新"有"旧"，可以打破，也可以生产（"旧谣言刚破，新流言产生"）。这些概念分别基于隐喻"言辞即实物","言辞即易碎品","言辞即产品"。"传遍了"表示言语的移动靠自我驱动（self-propelled），似乎并无外力参与（Vanparys，1995），而且，言语的移动并无固定路径和明确方位（movement without a destination），却可能向每个方向运动，覆盖大片区域（Semino，2005：45）。这些处于底层的概念全都为一个复合体结构上层的隐喻奠定了基础，即"言辞即实物"。下面的多个隐喻同时也指向另一个常见隐喻：

12）我心酸楚，我**百口莫辩**，因为他们不允许我**争辩**，**斗地主**，**砸狗头**，**砍高草**，**拔**大毛，欲加之罪何患无辞。我们会让你**死**得心服口服的。

（《生死疲劳》,9）

显然，这里所有隐喻的目标域都是言语辩论，其源始域为肢体冲突，从而形成隐喻"争论即肢体冲突"（Argument as Physical Conflict）[6]。"百口莫辩"说明冲突的激烈，在冲突中赢得主动的艰难。同时，这一夸张还基于转喻"言语器官激活言辞行为"（Speech Organ for Speech Activity）。"争辩"以及其后的"**斗地主**，**砸狗头**，**砍高草**，**拔大毛**"无一不是剧烈的肢体动作，无一不涉及激烈的冲突。而其后的"**死**"字（"我们会让你**死**得心服口服的"）无疑将这种冲突上升到性命攸关的高度。这些源始域的不同特质都投射到目标域中，隐喻性地显示了目标域"辩论"的多种特征。

2.3.3.3

多个概念基于多个概念，复合体上下皆为序列，其意义结构为：

A1 A2 A3   B1 B2 B3   C1 C2 C3
  ↓   +   ↓   +   ↓
  A   B   C

13）马洛亚牧师……**嘴里吐出**一句完全高密东北乡化了的**土腔洋词**："万能的主啊……"

（《丰乳肥臀》,4）

此句包含了隐喻"言语器官为容器"（Speech Organ as Container）以及"言辞为实体"。她们处于复合体概念结构底层，其余的概念隐喻都由其生发，处于结构顶层。"嘴里吐出"激活了容器的意象图式（image schema）[7]，意味着人体器官嘴是容器,言辞为动体(trajector),并且经历了由里到外的位置变化。动体的移动是由言者马洛亚牧师所致。其中,"吐出"意味着"说出",它强化了容器概念以及动体的移动。这个意象图式产生了与之相关的概念隐喻:"言语行为即物理行为"(Speech Action as Physical Action),或更准确而言,"言语行为即移动实体"(Speech Action as Moving Entity)。而"土腔洋词"则进一步强化了"言语为实体"的概念,因为,"土"、"洋"作形容词时,分别意为"本地的"、"外国的",首先与具体物件相关(如土产,洋货)。"腔"与"词"表述言辞行为的不同侧面:方式与内容。"土腔"与"洋词"形成对比(antithesis):本地的腔调与外国的言辞。与此相关的另一对比是,言者马洛亚牧师的主动与被动。言辞行为是牧师主动实施的("嘴里吐出"),但情急之下,他的洋词没有配以洋腔,却伴以"高密东北乡化了的土腔"。其不由自主、或无意识的被动之态可见一斑。这个隐喻复合体的概念结构如下:

言辞为动体　　言语行为即移动实体
言语器官为容器　　言辞为实体

图1 "土腔洋词"的概念结构

下例段落中的概念结构更为复杂。其水平和垂直方向的隐喻都多达四个,远远超过大多数复合体:

14) 一声终于忍不住的**嚎叫**从她的**嘴巴里冲出来,飞出窗棂**,起起伏伏地逍遥在大街小巷,与司马亭的喊叫**交织**在一起,拧起一股绳,**宛若一条蛇,钻进**那个身材高大、哈着腰、垂着红毛大脑袋、耳朵眼里生出两撮白毛的瑞典籍牧师马洛亚的**耳朵**。

(《丰乳肥臀》,3)

产妇"她"难产的这段描述,展示了一个完整的言辞行为过程:其发源地、传递线路及目的地,涉及多个隐喻及其认知过程。交际两端各有一容器隐喻,都基于"言语器官为容器"这个概念,其语言表征分别为"从她的嘴巴里冲出来"、"钻进……耳朵";"嚎叫"从一个容器(嘴)到另一个容器(耳朵)的转移(transfer)意味着交际的完成。信息传递过程则牵扯较复杂、多变的认知概念。首先,言语信息的每一次传递都同时建立在两个概念隐喻之上:"言辞为移动的实体"和"言辞行为为剧烈的物理性行为"(Speech Activity as Violent Physical Action),其语言表达为"冲出来"、"飞出"、"钻进"等。不同传递阶段"嚎叫"所依据的概念不断变化,因此产生了一系列不同意象:先为快速移动的实体("冲出来"),而后变为飞行物或飞鸟("飞出"),随即又变幻成绳索("交织"、"拧成一股绳"),最终,幻化成蛇("宛若一条蛇")。此外,飞行物或飞鸟的意象与另外一个隐喻"房屋为容器"("飞出窗棂")纠缠在一起。

这个言语交际的内容是"嚎叫",嚎叫与声音(sound)或听觉相连。如上所述,在交际过程中,这一声音转换成了多个不同的三维实体,而实体与触觉(touch)相关。这意味着在交际过程中,与上述多个概念投射同时并行的,还有一种特殊隐喻——通感隐喻(synesthetic metaphor),即"不同感知域(sensory domain)之间的映射"(Yu, 2003:20),确切地说,还涉及由源始域即触觉域向目标域即听觉域的映射。通过这种映射产生的隐喻"听觉为触觉",使得无形的、飘忽不定的声音变成了有型的、有质感的三维实体,不易感知变为易于感知,还平添了多个意象。

下图是完成"嚎叫"这一言辞行为所依赖的隐喻复合体示意图。其中,纵向而言,左右两端的容器隐喻表示交际的起点和终点,中间部分代表信息传递过程。横向而言,中间部分顶部,从左至右,示意信息传播过程中言语概念或意象变化顺序,其下端是三个支持传递过程的概念隐喻,她们共同为信息传递提供了概念支撑。这里,既有对基本隐喻的创造性拓展和修饰,又有大量综合:

言语是移动实体→言语是飞行物→言语是绳索→言语是蛇

嘴是容器　　　　　　言语是实体　　　　　　耳朵是容器

言辞行为为剧烈的物理性行为

听觉为触觉

图2 "嚎叫"隐喻复合体概念构成

另外,"嚎叫"似乎只有声音,没有言辞内容,但实际上,她含有丰富的语篇信息。嚎叫由"她的嘴"出发,以牧师的耳朵为终点,将"她"与牧师联系起来,确切地说,将"她"的分娩与牧师关联起来,暗示他们之间不同寻常的关系。

3. 结论

隐喻的规约性不是任意的,具有经验理据(Lakoff & Johnson, 1980; Gibbs, 1994)。许多隐喻的源始域与我们最基本的生存经验相关。我们的讨论表明,言辞行为隐喻复合体也不例外,她们大多源自最基本的身体经验,是对基本隐喻加工的结果。其中占突出位置的隐喻有"言辞为具体物品"、"言语器官即容器"、"言辞行为即物理行为"等。转喻在言辞行为复合体中的作用随处可见,涉及到人体器官时尤为如此。身体/物理行为与我们的日常生活紧密相伴,每天都不可避免,有关她们的经验是人类作为生物存在的明证,所以,她们的概念化效果既强大又具有预测性。此外,隐喻不仅仅给言辞行为提供概念通道,她还在构建言辞行为的主观经验,透露对于言辞行为的态度和评价。

　　言辞隐喻复合体是对于简单、基本隐喻拓展、修饰、尤其综合的结果,其概念结构有时呈序列型,有时为叠加型,也可能两者兼而有之。她之所以超越了日常隐喻,是因为通过两次、甚至三次或更多的水平和垂直方向的概念投射,以及与对比等其它修辞方式的结合,产生丰富、浓缩的意象,刺激受众多种感觉、唤醒多种经验。莫言对言语行为隐喻的创新性运用可见一斑。在某种程度上,正由于此,文学语言才不同于日常语言,莫言才成为语言大师。当然,由于语料容积、隐喻识别主观性等因素,我们的讨论还不是穷尽性(exhaustive)的,还需要进一步完善与修正。

注释

1. 此处转喻的定义不同于 Lakoff 和 Turner 等人上世纪九十年代以前转喻的"标准理论"或"主导理论"(standard or dominant theory),而是在综合 K. U. Panther 和 A. Barcelona 等欧洲大陆学者的研究成果基础上得出的。详情请参阅 Panther & Radden (1999),Barcelona (2003)。

2. 言辞行为隐喻,国外文献目前还没有统一的表述,主要有 Linguistic behavior metaphor (Simon, 1995);Linguistic action metaphor (Goossens, 1995);Speech activity/spoken communication metaphor (Semino, 2005);Verbal behavior metaphor (Jing-Schmidt, 2008). 言辞行为转喻亦如此。我们采用 Speech activity,因为她与 Speech act 相近,显示了她与言语行为学说的联系与区别。

3. 按照认知语言学界的惯例,英语中的概念隐喻、转喻和意象图式用小一号的大写字母表示,以区别于原型用法,如:GOOD IS UP,CONTAINER 等。汉字无大小写之别,所以,本文汉语的隐喻、转喻和意象图式表征使用粗体字。例句中的语言隐喻也用粗体强调,例句后括号中给出作品名称,其后数字表示引文页码。

4. 我们有意淡化了修辞学意义上隐喻与明喻(simile)的区别。修辞学强调语言表达,辞格分类依照的是语言形式。而认知或概念隐喻侧重概念化。明喻虽然比隐喻多了"如"、"若"、"像"等字眼,但认知机制相同,同样是简单域向复杂域的概念投射。徐盛桓(2009:4)也认为,隐喻包含了传统修辞学中的明喻和暗喻。

5. 据 Kovecses,普世性(Universal)隐喻构成了特定文化(culture-specific)隐喻的顶层(统领性)(overarching)或下层(支持性)(underlying)经验。我们由此推出,就概念结构而言,某些基本隐喻既可处于其它隐喻之上,也可在其下。

6. 有学者认为 Lakoff & Johnson 的"争论即战争"的所谓战争隐喻值得商榷。首先,有组织的、国家间的武装冲突并非大众都有的切身经验,用她作源始域并非最佳。而肢体冲突充斥于人类生活,是人们幼儿时期就可感知的经验,其概念结构清晰,易于被大众理解(Richardt, 2005:134)。本文采用肢体冲突这一个更可及(more accessible)的源始域。

7. 意象图式指源于人们身体长期与外部世界互动而产生的简单和基本的认知结构,包括 **UP-DOWN**,**OVER-UNDER**,**IN-OUT** 等方位关系(Ungerer & Schmid, 1996/2001: 108),描述的是动体(trajector)沿垂直坐标相对于陆标(landmark)的位移和运动。

References

Barcelona, A. 2000. Introduction: The cognitive theory of metaphor and metonymy. In A. Barcelona (ed.). *Metaphor and Metonymy at the Crossroads*. Berlin: Mouton de Gruyter.

Barcelona, A. 2003. Metonymy in cognitive linguistics: An analysis and a few modest proposals. In Cuyckens, H. et al. (eds.). *Motivation in Language: Studies in Honor of Günter Radden*. Amsterdam: Benjamins.

Cameron, L. 2003. *Metaphor in Educational Discourse*. London: Continuum.

Gibbs, R. W. 1994. *The Poetics of Mind: Figurative Thought, Language, and Understanding*. Cambridge: Cambridge University Press.

Goossens, L. 1995. Metaphtonymy: The interaction of metaphor and metonymy in expressions for linguistic action, in Goossens et al. (eds.).

Goossens, L. et al. (eds.). 1995. *By Word of Mouth: Metaphor, Metonymy and Linguistic Action in a Cognitive Perspective*. Amsterdam: John Benjamins.

Jing-Schmidt, Z. 2008. Much mouth much tongue: Chinese metonymies and metaphors of verbal behaviour. *Cognitive Linguistics*, 19(2): 241−82.

Kovecses, Z. 2005. *Metaphor in Culture: Universality and Variation*. Cambridge: Cambridge University Press.

Lakoff, G. & M. Johnson. 1980. *Metaphors We Live By*. Chicago: University of Chicago Press.

Lakoff, G. & M. Turner. 1989. *More than Cool Reason: A Field Guide to Poetic Metaphor*. Chicago: University of Chicago Press.

Panther, K. U. & G. Radden (eds.). 1999. *Metonymy in Language and Thought*. Amsterdam: John Benjamins.

Reddy, M. 1979. The conduit metaphor. In A. Ortony (ed.). *Metaphor and Thought*. Cambridge: Cambridge University Press.

Richardt, S. 2005. *Metaphor in Languages for Special Purposes*. Frankfurt: Peter Lang.

Semino, E. 2005. The metaphorical construction of complex domains: The case of speech activity in English. *Metaphor and Symbol*, 20 (1): 35−70.

Semino, E. 2006. A corpus-based study of metaphors for speech activity in British English. In S. T. Gries & A. Stefanowitsch (eds.). *Corpora in Cognitive Linguistics: Conceptual Metaphors*. Amsterdam: John Benjamins.

Simon, V. A. M. 1995. Assessing linguistic behaviour: A study of value judgments. In Goossens et al. (eds.).

Ungerer, F. & H. J. Schmid. 1996/2001. *An Introduction to Cognitive Linguistics*. London：Addison Wesley Longman Ltd. 北京：外语教学与研究出版社.

Vanparys, J. 1995. A survey of metalinguistic metaphors. In Goossens, L. et al. (eds.). 1-34.

Wang, D. D. 2000. The literary world of Mo Yan. *World Literature Today*, 74 (3)：487-494.

Yu, N. 2003. Synesthetic metaphor：A cognitive perspective. *Journal of Literary Semantics*, 32：19-34.

Yu, N. 2011. A decompositional approach to metaphorical compound analysis：The case of a TV commercial. *Metaphor and Symbol*, 26(4)：243-259.

莫　言. 2012.《莫言作品集》. http://www.aitxt.com/simple/?t9728.html. 2015 年 10 月 10 日读取.

徐盛桓. 2009. "外延内涵传承说：转喻机理新论".《外国语》(3)：2—9.

张　雁. 2012. "从物理行为到言语行为：嘱咐类动词的产生".《中国语文》(1)：3—16.

中国社会科学院语言研究室词典编辑室.《现代汉语词典》(汉英双语版). 北京：外语教学与研究出版社.

Conceptual Integration and Rewriting of the Madwoman in *Wide Sargasso Sea*

Liang Xiaohui Yang Tianlun (**University of International Relations, Beijing**)

Abstract: The late 20th century witnessed in English literature the popularity of novels of rewriting history from different perspectives. *Wide Sargasso Sea*, as one of the examples, rewrites the classical English novel *Jane Eyre*. Jean Rhys, a female English writer born in Dominica, writes back the story of "the madwoman in the attic", Rochester's first wife, and demonstrates the process that the woman has gradually been driven mad. This paper adopts Conceptual Integration Theory to show that, the integration of the clashing mental spaces on the part of the reader, based upon the images of contradictory senses about "home", "dream", and "identity", can reveal layer by layer how the author portrays the heroine's mental experience on the one hand and the mystery of craziness of this "madwoman" on the other.

Key words: Conceptual Integration Theory; *Wide Sargasso Sea*; rewriting

1. Introduction

The late 20th century witnessed in English literature the popularity of novels of rewriting history from different perspectives. Hutcheon (1988) terms them as "historiographic metafiction", as can be typically seen in works like Fowles' *The French Lieutenant's Woman* and Peter Ackroyd's *Chatterton*, with the postmodern rethinking and re-interpretation of history involved.

On the other hand, a group of writers from the former colonial possessions have rewritten British classical novels, challenging not exactly the interpretations of historical events and phenomena as the prototypical historiographic metafiction does, but the historical sentiments and conceptions as embodied in literary canons. The new novels include among others Jean Rhys' *Wide Sargasso Sea*, rewriting Brontë's *Jane Eyre*. From the technique of stream of consciousness the novel adopts, some critics believe that *Wide Sargasso Sea* forms an intertextual relation with *Jane Eyre* and challenges the textual and ideological construction of the classical novel, so it should be taken as another example of Hutcheon's historiographic metafiction (Adjarian, 1995: 203; Macri, 2000: i; Kimmey, 2005: 114; Widdowson, 2006: 496).

In *Wide Sargasso Sea*, Jean Rhys, a female English writer born in Dominica, writes back the story of "the madwoman in the attic", Rochester's first wife Bertha in *Jane Eyre*, and demonstrates how the woman, a white Creole heiress originally named Antoinette, is being driven mad by her husband and the people around her. The novel consists of three parts, describing successively Antoinette's childhood, marriage, and her final miserable experience of being relocated to England and confined in an attic by her husband. While it is Jane Eyre the title heroine and Rochester who tell the madwoman's story in *Jane Eyre*, depriving the madwoman the privilege of speaking for herself, the story in *Wide Sargasso Sea* is for the most part narrated by this madwoman herself, except in Part Two where she and Rochester rotate the task of narration. The new novel in this way demonstrates how the madwoman suffers under the dual pressures of colonialism and patriarchalism in the 19th century, which is concealed in the original novel by Jane Eyre's narration.

Most previous criticisms abroad on this novel focus on two aspects. On the one hand, feminists as represented by Sandra Gilbert and Susan Gubar base their research on feminist psychological analysis and claim that the heroine Bertha is the evil id of Jane Eyre (Gilbert & Gubar, 1979). On the other hand, critics based on HomiBhabha and Spivak's postcolonial approach observe that, while the 19th century British culture is crystallized in classical fiction like *Jane Eyre*, *Wide Sargasso Sea* challenges the hegemony of British culture by rewriting the canonical novel *Jane Eyre* (Spivak, 1985). Along the latter line, many researches are done both home and abroad. Tiffin (1978) and Huebener (2010) discuss the colonial domination and the cultural clashes in *Wide Sargasso Sea*. Alaussen (1993), Nixon (1994) and Adjarian (1995) disclose the reconstruction and transformation of Bertha from "the other" in

Jane Eyre to "the self" in *Wide Sargasso Sea* by the change of point of view in the colonial context. Most Chinese criticisms also stress the identity reconstruction of the heroine in the colonial context, as can be found in the articles by Zhang (2006), Cao (1998) and He & Ou (2002).

Most previous studies have discussed the reconstruction of the heroine's identity in the colonial context from the content basis. Few criticisms have approached the linguistic forms of the novel for the characterization of the heroine. In fact, the linguistic forms are particularly outstanding in that the author has heavily resorted to sentences with contradictory senses for the creation of the new aspect of the heroine and for the demonstration of the process of her madness. Readers in their turn need to integrate in their mental mechanism the conflicting images contained in the contradictory sentences for the interpretation of the text and the characterization of the heroine. The theory of Conceptual Integration in Cognitive Poetics provides an appropriate tool for this interpreting process.

This paper adopts Conceptual Integration Theory to disclose that the integration of the clashing mental spaces built upon the contradictory sentences on the part of the reader, i.e., mental spaces established on the images with contradictory senses about "home", "dream" and "identity", can reveal layer by layer how the author portrays the heroine's mental experience on the one hand and the mystery of craziness of this "madwoman" on the other.

2. Conceptual Integration and Conflicts in Conception

The theory of Conceptual Integration is initiated by Fauconnier & Turner (1998/2002) based upon the theory of mental spaces, "small conceptual packets constructed as we think and talk, for purposes of local understanding and action" (Fauconnier, 1985: 16-22; Fauconnier & Turner, 2002: 40). A conceptual integration network is a dynamic construct resulting from the interaction between different mental spaces and ending in the creation of a blended space. Thus the network involves four existent mental spaces, including two input spaces respectively playing the role of the source domain and the target domain, a generic space where the two inputs meet, and a blended space in which they are systematically integrated with "emergent structure" of its own (Fauconnier & Turner, 1998: 135), as shown in Figure 1:

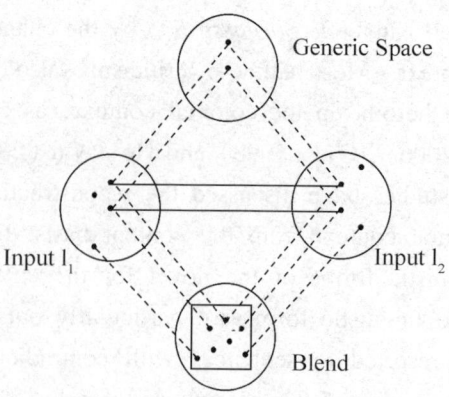

Figure 1

(Fauconnier & Turner, 1998: 143)

According to the types of input spaces and their relationship, Fauconnier & Turner (1998/2002) classify the networks of blended spaces into four types: simplex, mirror networks, single-scope networks and double-scope networks.

In simplex networks, the relevant part of the frame in one input is projected with its roles, and the elements from the other input are projected as values of those roles in the blend. No clashes exist between the two frames.

A mirror network is an integration network in which all spaces — inputs, generic and blend — share an organizing frame. No clashes occur between the inputs at the level of organizing frame. But there will be clashes at more specific levels below the frame level.

Single-scope networks are the prototype of conventional source-target metaphors. It offers a visible type of conceptual clash, since the inputs have different frames. The clash is produced as the frame of the blended space is organized by only one of the input spaces, the framing input.

A double-scope network has inputs with different organizing frames as well as an organizing frame for the blend, which includes completely conflicting parts of the elements of input frames, so the blended space has emergent structure of particular type, inspiring rich and innovative imagination.

It is particularly put forward by Fauconnier & Turner (2002: 249-261) that human identity established in people's mind results from the integration of mental spaces and frames. The language in literary works provides a clue to the conceptual structure of mental spaces of readers when they attempt to understand the works and the characterization. As revealed by the theory of Conceptual Integration, an emergent structure will take shape in the blended space when two or more mental spaces are integrated, and this structure plays a major role in the interpretation of the works being read.

3. Conflicting Images and Integration

In *Wide Sargasso Sea*, the characterization of Antoinette is mainly achieved by the manner of her first-person narration, which, with abundant contradictory sentences, demonstrates her confusions over the home, the relationship between dream and reality, and also her own identity. The conflicting images contained in the contradictory sentences, by which clashing mental spaces are generated, create profound implications beyond the images themselves, thereby unfolding the mental process of how Antoinette goes crazy.

3. 1 Home and Integration

As narrated by Antoinette in the first part of the novel, which describes her childhood experience, the girl after her father's death lives with her mother and brother in the Coulibri Garden. She develops a conflicting mentality towards the garden, which is embodied in the following contradictory sentences:

(1) Our garden was **large and beautiful** as that **garden in the Bible** — the tree of life grew there. **But it had gone wild**. The paths were **overgrown** and a smell of **dead** flowers mixed with the **fresh living** smell. Underneath the tree ferns, tall as forest tree ferns, the light was green. Orchids flourished out of reach or for some reason not to be touched. One was **snaky** looking, another like an **octopus** with long thin brown tentacles bare of leaves hanging from a twisted root. Twice a year the octopus orchid flowered — then not an inch of tentacle showed. It was abell-shaped mass of white, mauve, deep purples, **wonderful** to see. The scent was very **sweet** and strong. I never went near it. All Coulibri Estate had **gone wild** like the garden, gone to bush. No more slavery — why should anybody work? This never saddened me. I did not remember the place when it was **prosperous**. (Rhys, 1966: 10 – 11; hereafter, the title of the

novel and page references to *Wide Sargasso Sea* refer to this edition; the boldface is ours.)

In Antoinette's eyes, the Garden of Coulibri is as large and beautiful as the Garden of Eden, but it is at the same time wild and dead, so much so that even orchids in the garden are associated with scary animals like snake and octopus.

As indicated in Table 1, the conflicting sentences about the garden constitute a mirror network in which two input spaces with different ingredients, the generic space, and the blended space all share the same organizing frame — the garden, with the inputs acting as mirror images of each other. Therefore, there are no clashes between the inputs at the level of organizing frame. But clashes break out between ingredients of the two input spaces.

Table 1

Space	Input Space I1	Input Space I2	Generic Space	Blended Space
Subject	Eden-like Coulibri	Hell-like Coulibri	Garden	living place with contradictory senses
Feature	large and beautiful	gone wild; overgrown; dead	large and beautiful; gone wild	homeless

Based on this mirror network, one input space depicts Coulibri as Eden-like, the other as hell-like, in result readers will conjure up one image of garden with contradictory senses in the blended space about Antoinette's home. And the image of garden with contradictory senses will leave an impression on readers that the garden is illusionary and seems not exist. It suggests that one day Antoinette would be homeless.

Similarly, Antoinette holds a complex feeling towards another refuge of hers, the convent where she stays alone after her mother falls apart for the tragic death of her son. The following paragraph shows how Antoinette feels about the convent:

(2) Everything was **brightness**, or **dark**. The wall, the **blazing colours** of the flowers in the garden, the nuns' habits were **bright**, but their veils, the Crucifix hanging from their waists, the **shadow** of the trees, were **black**.

That was how it was, **light and dark**, **sun and shadow**, **Heaven and Hell**, for one of the nuns knew all about **Hell** and who does not? But another one knew about **Heaven** and the attributes of **the blessed**, of which the least is **transcendent beauty**.

(Wide Sargasso Sea, 34)

Table 2

Space	Input Space I1	Input Space I2	Generic Space	Blended Space
Subject	bright place	dark place	living place	living place with contradictory senses
Feature	brightness; blazing colors; heaven; the blessed; transcendent beauty	dark; shadow; hell	bright; dark	homeless

As shown by Table 2, when the conflicting images of the convent disturb Antoinette, another mirror network with internal conflicts is formed by two structurally similar inputs. As a result, the emergent structure is produced in the blended space for the living place with contradictory senses. Therefore, it is implied that the convent is also illusionary and Antoinette will lose every one of her refuges at last.

The blended image of homelessness is created and never fades away even after Antoinette gets married to Rochester. She is supposed to enjoy a peaceful and tranquil life with her husband in the small garden in the Windward Islands, a gift from her mother, which fascinates her a great deal in the first place. But finally after her husband tries to tease a girl servant, she begins to struggle with her own conflicting feelings about this lovely place.

(3) "If my father, my real father, was alive you wouldn't come back here in a hurry after he'd finished with you. If he was alive. Do you know what you've done to me? It's not the girl, not the girl. But **I love this place** and **you have made into a place I hate**. I used to think that if everything else went out of my life I would **still have this**, and now **you have spoilt it**. It's just somewhere else where I have been unhappy, and all the other things are nothing to what has happened here. **I hate it** now like I hate you and before I died I will show you how much I hate you."

(Wide Sargasso Sea, 88−89)

Table 3

Space	Input Space I1	Input Space I2	Generic Space	Blended Space
Subject	lovely place	hateful place	living place	living place with contradictory senses
Attitude	I love this place	you have made into a place I hate; you have spoilt it	I love this place; I hate this place	homeless

In the passage above, input spaces develop into a mirror network with an emergent structure in the blended space, creating an image of contradictory senses for their home, as illustrated in Table 3.

Ironically, even Rochester finds Antoinette's home is possessed with an image of contradictory senses. He says:

(4) I **hated** the mountains and the hills, the rivers and the rain. I **hated** the sunsets of whatever colour, I **hated its beauty and its magic and the secret** I would never know. I hated **its indifference** and the **cruelty** which was part of its loveliness. Above all I hated her. For she belonged to the **magic and the loveliness**. She had left me thirsty and all my life would be thirst and longing for what I had lost before I found it.

(*Wide Sargasso Sea*, 103)

Table 4

Space	Input Space I1	Input Space I2	Generic Space	Blended Space
Subject	lovely place	hateful place	living place	living place with contradictory senses
Feature	its beauty and its magic and the secret	its indifference; cruelty	its beauty; cruelty	no fixed home

Again in Rochester's response a living place of contradictory images is established as shown by Table 4, implying a home without any security or fixed location.

The contradictory sentences about the living places create an effect that Antoinette keeps changing her abode and could never enjoy a home with safety and stability. Even at her own home she has a feeling of homelessness.

3. 2 Reality/Dream and Integration

Antoinette suffers from the unstable state of mind, and in the meantime she begins to mistake reality for her dream and vice versa. She dreams about moving to England where she can get rid of her unstable feeling. However, even England is an image with contradictory senses.

(5) "Is it true," she said, "that **England is like a dream**? Because one of my friends who married an Englishman wrote and told me so. She said this place London is like **a cold dark dream** sometimes. I want to wake up."

"Well," I answered annoyed, "that is precisely how **your beautiful island** seems to me, quite **unreal and like a dream**."

"But how can rivers and mountains and the sea be unreal?"

"And how can millions of people, their houses and their streets be unreal?"

"More easily," she said, "much more easily. **Yes a big city must be like a dream**."

(*Wide Sargasso Sea*, 47-48)

Table 5

Input Space I1	Input Space I2	Generic Space	Blended Space
dream	England	real or unreal things	nonexistent England

Table 5 illustrates a single-scope network. Input Space I1 "dream" is projected to Input Space I2 "England". But England is a real place and to project dream to this real place creates a sense in the emergent structure that England does not exist for this woman.

On the other hand, some examples show that Bertha often takes what happens in her dreams as real things. For instance,

(6) That was the third time I had my dream, and it ended. I know now that the flight of steps leads to this room where I lie watching the woman asleep with her head on her arms. In my dream I waited till she began to snore, then I got up, took the keys and let myself out with a candle in my hand. It was easier this time than ever before and I walked as though I were flying.

At last I was in the hall where a lamp was burning. [...]

(*Wide Sargasso Sea*, 111-113)

Antoinette's narration of this dream is organized in disorder. When she walks out of the room she has just lighted, she arrives suddenly in Aunt Cora's room where she sees trees outside and the shadows of their leaves on the ground. She also notices the candles, which she hates so much that she beats down all of them except one that sets fire to the thin curtain behind the red one. As the fire spreads, she bursts out laughing and walks out into the hall with a candle. Here she sees a ghost, a woman with dishevelled hair. The ghost is in fact a reflection of herself. She drops the candle, which sets the room on fire. Similar scenarios are narrated in *Jane Eyre*, but from the perspective of Jane Eyre.

It's excusable, for she had a hard life of it: but still it was dangerous; for when Mrs. Poole was fast asleep, after the gin and water, the mad lady, who was as cunning as a witch, would take the keys out of her pocket, let herself out of her chamber, and go roaming about the house, doing any wild mischief that came into her head. They say she had nearly burnt her husband in his bed once: but I don't know about that. However, on this night, she set fire first to the hangings of the room next to her own, and then she got down to a lower story, and made her way to the chamber that had been the governess's — (she was like as if she knew somehow how matters had gone on, and had a spite at her) — and she kindled the bed there; but there was nobody sleeping in it, fortunately. [...]

> "And then they called out to him that she was on the roof, where she was standing, waving her arms, above the battlements, and shouting out till they could hear her a mile off: I saw her and heard her with my own eyes. She was a big woman, and had long black hair: we could see it streaming against the flames as she stood. I witnessed, and several more witnessed, Mr. Rochester ascend through the sky-light on to the roof; we heard him call 'Bertha!' We saw him approach her; and then, ma'am, she yelled and gave a spring, and the next minute she lay smashed on the pavement."
>
> (Brontë, 1980: 432–433)

It could be found that *Wide Sargasso Sea* refers heavily to *Jane Eyre* in terms of the details of Bertha's final result. By means of intertexuality with *Jane Eyre*, the new novel tries to lead its readers to the conclusion that Antoinette's last dream passes for real, though it is described in the form of a dream.

Table 6

Input Space I1	Input Space I2	Generic Space	Blended Space
reality	dream	unreal or real things	real dream

Here as shown by Table 6 a double-scope network is formed. The two input spaces clash with each other fiercely both at the level of frames and that of the ingredients. In the emergent structure, the image of a seemingly real dream is created, an image inspiring rich imagination, indicating that Antoinette is no longer capable of distinguishing between the real and the dreamed — she is turning mad.

3. 3 Identity and Integration

Haunted by the contradictory images about her location and perplexity over reality and dream, Antoinette is overwhelmed by a strong sense of homelessness and insecurity. Worse still, as a white Creole, she is laughed at, poured ridicule upon and excluded from both the white and the black communities. She is taken as a nigger by the pure white people from Europe, while the local black people look down upon her since she as one of them has white skin. The pressures from the both sides push her to the margin, which explain why she is bewildered by her identity in the latter part of the story. For examples,

(7) "Keep them then, you **cheating nigger**," I said, for I was tired, and the water I had swallowed made me feel sick. "I can get more if I want to," That's not what she hear, she said. She hear all we poor like beggar. We ate salt fish — no money for fresh fish. That old house so leaky, you run with calabash to catch water when it rain. Plenty white people in Jamaica. **Real white people**, they got gold money. They **didn't look at us**, nobody see them come near us. Old time white people nothing but **white nigger** now, and black nigger better than **white nigger**.

(*Wide Sargasso Sea*, 14)

(8) So I looked away from her at my favourite picture, "The Miller's Daughter", a lovely English girl with brown curls and blue eyes and a dress slipping off her shoulders. Then I looked across the white tablecloth and the vase of yellow roses at Mr. Mason, so sure of himself, so without a doubt English. And at my mother, so without a doubt **not English**, **but no white nigger either**. Not my mother. Never had been. Never could be.

(*Wide Sargasso Sea*, 21)

Table 7

Input Space I1	Input Space I2	Generic Space	Blended Space
black people in Jamaica	real white people	people living in their own territory	cheating nigger; white nigger; not English, but no white nigger either; the black Englishman; Creole of pure English descent; not English or European (no clear identity)

Here in Table 7 a mirror network is built up again, with one input space for the Dominica black people, and the other input space for European white people. The generic space could be extracted for people living in their own territory. The input frames are similar and produce no conflicts, but the elements in the frames are conflicting, presenting an identity of contradictory senses for the heroine. She is called a white nigger, neither black nor pure white, one without any clear identity. In the emergent structure, her identity, ambiguous as it goes, is built upon those conflicting elements that do not belong to her. She knows not who she is or where she belongs to. She often sinks into sorrowful thoughts as follows:

(9) "It was a song about **a white cockroach. That's me**. That's what they call all of us who were here before their own people in Africa sold them to the slave traders. And I've heard English women call us **white niggers**. So between you **I often wonder who I am and where is my country and where do I belong and why was I ever born at all**. Will you go now please. I must dress like Christophine said."

(*Wide Sargasso Sea*, 61)

Besides the pressure from outside, her state of mind is worsened by her husband's arrogance and tyranny. After marrying him, she is even deprived of her real name by Rochester, who calls her "Bertha" without her consent and thus confuses her even further over her own identity.

(10) "Don't laugh like that, **Bertha**."
"**My name is not Bertha**; why do you call me Bertha?"
"Because it is a name I'm particularly fond of. **I think of you as Bertha**."
"**It doesn't matter**," she said.

(*Wide Sargasso Sea*, 81)

(11) "Certainly I will, **my dear Bertha**."

"**Not Bertha tonight**," she said.

"Of course, on this of all nights, **you must be Bertha**."

"**As you wish**," she said.

(*Wide Sargasso Sea*, 82)

From the conversation above, it is obvious that Rochester names his wife Bertha merely out of his own pleasure. He decides that Antoinette must be called Bertha without taking into consideration Antoinette's own feelings. As for Antoinette, she refuses to be called Bertha at first but succumbs to her husband in the end. For the woman's identity, clashing images are again produced about her name, hence her identity.

Table 8

Input Space I1	Input Space I2	Generic Space	Blended Space
Bertha	Antoinette	the girl's name	Bertha & Antoinette (spilt personality)

In the emergent structure of the mirror network shown in Table 8, the heroine has two names representing totally different identities at the same time. In consequence, her perplexity grows greater, leading her to schizophrenia step by step.

Antoinette does not want her husband to give her the new name Bertha. After Rochester starts to call her Bertha, Antoinette stops cherishing any hope to have his heart again. For her, names are of extremely great importance. Forced to accept this new name, she begins to talk about herself as if she was another person.

(12) Names matter, like when he wouldn't call me Antoinette, **and I saw Antoinette drifting out of the window with her scents, her pretty clothes and her looking-glass**.

(*Wide Sargasso Sea*, 106)

Table 9

Input Space I1	Input Space I2	Generic Space	Blended Space
narrating self Antoinette	experiencing self Antoinette-Bertha	the girl herself	the narrator saw Antoinette disappear

Here we find a mirror network for the split selves of Bertha. Firstly "I" splits into two roles. On the one hand we have the narrating-self Antoinette, as she knows of course that Antoinette has just been given a new name Bertha and she is still sitting there, for only a reflective narrator can see the experiencing character. On the other hand we find the experiencing-self Antoinette, who assumes that Antoinette is drifting away after being given a new name, since only the experiencing character does not know the truth that Antoinette is still there. In the blended space the two roles are integrated so that a new peculiar scene occurs in the emergent structure that Antoinette is watching herself disappear. This scene implies that Bertha has already presented signs of schizophrenia.

Indications of Antoinette's becoming mentally insane are constantly shown thereafter. Locked in the attic where there is no mirror, Antoinette does not know what she looks like, so she recalls the days when she looked herself in the mirror. However, the girl in the mirror seems to be both herself and somebody else.

(13) I remember watching myself brush my hair and how my eyes looked back at me. **The girl I saw was myself yet not quite myself.**

(*Wide Sargasso Sea*, 107)

The "I" in "I remember" is Antoinette's narrating-self, who remembers her experiencing-self combing her hair ("watching myself brush my hair"), and her experiencing-self is watched in return by her image reflected in the mirror ("how my eyes looked back at me"). In this light, the "I" is split into three selves, a narrating one, an experiencing one and one in the mirror. Therefore, two interpretations may be given to the sentence "The girl I saw was myself yet not quite myself". On the one hand, "the girl" refers to the mirror image watched by the experiencing self; on the other hand, "the girl" represents the experiencing-self observed by the image in the mirror. The integration of the two perspectives is summarized in Table 10.

Table 10

Input Space I1	Input Space I2	Generic Space	Blended Space
experiencing self looks at the mirror image (the girl)	the mirror image looks at the experiencing self (the girl)	the self looks at the self	the self is not the self (split personality)

Since the mirror image and the experiencing-self exist in different conceptual levels, two inputs with their distinctive frames are integrated into a double-scope network, a type with the most strong clashes. In the blended space, we can find an emergent structure where the self is not the self, indicating that Antoinette has already fallen into schizophrenia.

Based upon the previous analysis, we may find that living at a home which provides no security but contradictory senses, with no explicit identity except some puzzling monikers, Bertha is gradually driven to the brink of madness and cannot tell the real from the unreal. Thus she finally becomes schizophrenic.

4. Conclusion

When Rhys writes back the classical novel *Jane Eyre*, she resorts to abundant contradictory sentences in recreating the heroine Bertha. The theory of Conceptual Integration, especially the features of emergent structure in the blended spaces of different types of networks, can be found to provide insights into how readers interpret the text and comprehend the characterization of this novel by integrating conflicting images in their mental mechanism.

References

Adjarian, M. M. 1995. Between and beyond boundaries in *Wide Sargasso Sea*. *College Literature*, 22 (1): 59–93.

Alaussen, M. 1993. Jean Rhys's construction of blackness as escape from white femininity in *Wide Sargasso Sea. Ariel*, 24 (2): 65–82.

Brontë, C. 1980. *Jane Eyre*. Oxford: Oxford University Press.

Emery, M. L. 1990. *Jean Rhys at "World's End": Novels of Colonial and Sexual Exile*. Austin: University of Texas Press.

Fauconnier, G. 1985. *Mental Spaces*. Cambridge, USA: The MIT Press.

Fauconnier, G. & M. Turner. 1998. Conceptual integration networks. *Cognitive Science*, 22 (2): 133–187.

Fauconnier, G. & M. Turner. 2002. *The Way We Think*. New York: Basic Books.

Gilbert, S. & S. Gubar. 1979. *The Madwoman in the Attic*. New Haven: Yale University Press.

Huebener, P. 2010. Metaphor and madness as postcolonial sites in novels by Jean Rhys and Tayeb Salih. *Mosaic*, 43 (4): 19–34.

Hutcheon, L. 1988. *A Poetics of Postmodernism: History, Theory, Fiction*. New York & London: Routledge.

Jukic, T. 2000. From worlds to words and the other way around: The Victorian inheritance in the postmodern British novel. *Costerus*: 77-88.

Kimmey, D. 2005. Women, fire, and dangerous things: Metatextuality and the politics of reading in Jean Rhys's *Wide Sargasso Sea*. *Women's Studies: An Inter-disciplinary Journal*, 34 (2): 113-131.

Macri, L. 2000. *Revising the Story: A Rhetorical Perspective on Revisionary Fiction by Women Writers*. Maryland: University of Maryland.

Nixon, N. 1994. *Wide Sargasso Sea* and Jean Rhys's interrogation of the "Nature Wholly Alien" in *Jane Eyre*. *Essays in Literature*, 21 (2): 267.

Rhys, J. 1966. *Wide Sargasso Sea*. New York: W.W. Norton & Company.

Spivak, G. C. 1985. Three women's texts and a critique of imperialism. *Critical Inquiry*, 12 (1): 234-261.

Tiffin, H. 1978. Mirror and mask: Colonial motifs in the novels of Jean Rhys. *World Literature Written in English*, 17 (1): 328-341.

Widdowson, P. 2006. "Writing back": Contemporary re-visionary fiction. *Textual Practice*, 20 (3): 491-507.

曹　莉(Cao, L.). 1998. "简论《茫茫藻海》男女主人公的自我建构".《外国文学评论》(1): 54—59.

何昌邑、区　林(He, C. & L. Ou.). 2002. "边缘女性生存：谁是《简·爱》中的疯女人——《茫茫藻海》的底蕴".《四川外语学院学报》(3): 42—45.

张德明(Zhang, D.). 2006. "《藻海无边》的身份意识与叙事策略".《外国文学研究》(3): 77—83.

Metaphor and Narrative: A Cognitive Poetics of Space in *Absalom, Absalom!*

Pang Yuhou   (**National Research Center for Foreign Language Education**)

Abstract: Metaphor is one of the basic ways of human's understanding the world. Narrative reflects man's being in and thinking about the world. It is a complex cognitive process. This study rethinks cognitive metaphor theory from a discourse perspective and examines the functions of metaphor in narrative with particular reference to spatial representation in William Faulkner's novel *Absalom, Absalom!*. This article argues that metaphor like metonymy is an important mode of narrative construction.

Key words: metaphor; narrative; space; *Absalom, Absalom!*

1. Introduction

In cognitive linguistics, metaphor is considered one of the basic ways of human's understanding the world. Narrative also reflects man's being in and thinking about the world. It is a universal cultural fact. Barthes (1977: 79) claims that "narrative is present in every age, in every place, in every society; it begins with the very history of mankind and there nowhere is nor has been a people without narrative … narrative is international, transhistorical, transcultural: it is simply there, like life itself". However, narrative is a complex cognitive process. To what extent is metaphor involved in the process of narrative production or comprehension? Or what is the role of metaphor in narrative? We argue that metaphor like metonymy is an important way of narrative construction.

To illustrate the function of metaphor in narrative, let's take the following American folktale as an example:

An old man and his son were working their corn patch back in the hills when they heard an awful noise coming up the road besides the creek. "Jumping frog skins!" said the boy. "Whatta think it be, Pa?"

"I don't know," the father said, "but I'm going to git my muzzle loader."

The old man got his gun and ran down the road. When he saw the Model T Ford coming toward him he fired away. The driver slammed on his brakes, jumped out, and ran for his life. When the old man returned to his corn patch, the boy asked, "Did you kill the varmint, Pa?"

"Nope," grumbled the old man. "Wish I had. But I did make the varmit turn loose of the man he had swallowed."

The VARMINT metaphor plays a central role in the narrative. First, it is an important rhetorical strategy for the writer to achieve a humorous effect. It is due to the metaphor that the narrative can be read as a joke in which the Model T Ford is mistaken by the father and son as a varmint. Second, the metaphor reflects the father and son's mind style, i.e. their ignorance of the modern car. It is a tool for characterization. Third, the metaphor is thematically related. It reveals the conflicts between the agricultural world and the industrialized world. Finally, the metaphor also functions structurally by extending throughout the text.

Traditional metaphor theory simply takes it as a rhetoric technique and underestimates its role in narrative. Cognitive metaphor theory regards metaphor as cross-domain mapping and sheds light on the working mechanism of metaphor in narrative (Lakoff & Johnson, 1980; Lakoff, 1987). However, it is largely sentence-based (Werth, 1999). This study will rethink cognitive metaphor theory from a discourse perspective and examine the functionality of metaphor in narrative with particular reference to spatial representation in William Faulkner's novel *Absalom, Absalom!* .

2. Cognitive Metaphor Theory: A Discourse Perspective

Differing from traditional metaphor theory which takes metaphor as a mere language phenomenon, cognitive metaphor theory regards it as a conceptual construct. It refers to the phenomenon of projecting or mapping the conceptual structure of the source domain onto that of the target domain (Lakoff & Johnson, 1980). This provides a new way of rethinking the functions of metaphor in narrative. However, there are some problems with cognitive metaphor theory.

The first one is the distinction of conventional and poetic metaphors. In general, conventional metaphors are considered dead and dull, and commonly used in everyday language; by contrast, poetic metaphors are fresh, vivid and original, and normally used in literary discourse. Cognitive metaphor theorists have shown much greater interest in the so-called dead or conventional metaphors. They seem reluctant to explore the poetic effects of literary metaphor, and claim that conceptual metaphors are underlying both conventional and poetic metaphors (Lakoff & Turner, 1989). Lakoff & Johnson (1980/2003: 251) point out that "new metaphorical ideas — that is, new ways of organizing and understanding experience — arise from the combinations of simpler conceptual metaphors to form complex ones." The second problem is about the linguistic realization of metaphors. Cognitive metaphor theorists mainly concentrate on the conceptual structuring of metaphors and seldom pay attention to their linguistic realization. In recent years, the situation has taken changes. Just as Crisp (2003: 105) says, "there has been a return to language, not in the sense of denying metaphor's conceptual nature, but rather out of the belief that having established that conceptual nature we need to pay more attention to the details of its expression."

The third problem is concerned with linguistic materials. Cognitive linguists normally concentrate on a collection of local examples of specific metaphors trying to identify the conceptual metaphors underlying them. The data are largely restricted to the lexical or sentential level (Werth, 1994, 1999; Stockwell, 2002). The examples are usually isolated, selective and non-authentic. As a result, the theory is inadequate to account for the workings of metaphor in larger linguistic units such as texts. The last one is the ideologies of metaphor. Lakoff & Johnson (1980: 159) have suggested that metaphoric and metonymic concepts structure not just our language but our thoughts, attitudes, and actions — they "play a central role in the construction of social and political reality". Despite this, the critical power of conceptual metaphor theory is far from satisfactory because of its failure to pay enough attention to such social-ideological factors as class, gender and race. In this respect, cognitive linguists may benefit a lot from critical discourse analysis

(Stockwell, 2001).

Considering the above, we argue for a discourse-based approach to cognitive metaphor analysis. It has several advantages. Firstly, while accepting the fundamental role of conceptual metaphors, this approach lays great emphasis on stylistically prominent metaphors in a text, either conventional or poetic. Black (2006: 102) writes: "Metaphor is a scalar phenomenon: there are dead metaphors in common use ('a dead duck'), which requires no special interpretive effort, through fairly conventional metaphors, to the original creations of speakers or writers." Stockwell (2002: 108) has made a similar distinction between expressive and explanatory metaphors — "Expressive (often poetic) metaphors tend to have low clarity but a high degree of richness, whereas explanatory (often scientific) metaphors tend not to be very rich but are very clear." Explanatory metaphors are often constitutive metaphors.

While acknowledging that the basic machinery and constraints of literary (or composed) and everyday metaphors are the same, Werth (1994, 1999) believes that there exist real differences between them. He argues that the phenomenon of "double vision" is a significant difference between poetic and ordinary-language metaphors —"there are many cases where the metaphor is used simply to make the expression more striking, and still others where using a metaphor allows the topic to be viewed simultaneously from more than a single perspective (my double-vision cases). Metaphor in such cases is much more a question of poetic choice, then, rather than being forced on the producer because of the poverty of the language." (Werth, 1999: 318) We agree with Werth that poetic metaphors can create special poetic effects. The employment of poetic metaphor is not only characteristic of a writer's style but also indicative of his or her imagination and creativity. By contrast, conventional metaphors are usually not stylistically prominent in literary discourse.

Werth's idea of double vision about poetic metaphor is supported by the findings of blending theory (Fauconnier, 1997; Fauconnier & Turner, 2002). Four types of mental space have been identified: input space 1 (the source space), input space 2 (the target space), generic space and blended space. The blended space, among others, is an emergent structure which combines elements from both source and target domains to form a new creative construct. Blending is considered to play a key role in cross-space metaphorical mappings.

Secondly, a discourse-based analysis of metaphor naturally lays great emphasis on the linguistic representation of metaphor. A distinction is often drawn between explicit and implicit metaphors, or between visible and invisible metaphors (Goatly, 1997: 39 – 40; Stockwell, 2002: 107 – 108). The explicitness or visibility of metaphor is to a large extent related to the surface realization of metaphor. It is a stylistic matter. The linguistic expressions are the only direct evidence that we can rely upon for the identification, analysis and interpretation of metaphors. Any metaphorical interpretation must be based on a close linguistic analysis of a text or texts. However, the metaphoricity of metaphors varies. It's a matter of degree or a cline. Goatly (1997: 38) has distinguished five clines of metaphoricity: degrees of approximation (or similarity), conventionality, marking, contradictoriness and explicitness. In terms of explicitness, simile is one of the most explicitly expressed while allegory is among the most implicitly expressed. Crisp (2003: 106) thinks that allegory and symbol can activate metaphorical concepts without metaphorical language, for instance, Bunyan's *The Pilgrim's Progress* — they "continuously activate a cross-domain mapping without overtly referring to its target domain". Stockwell (2002: 107) also says: "It matters quite a lot for literary interpretation whether the metaphor is visible or invisible, since the latter requires greater creative input on the part of the reader. Where there is greater potential for creative interpretation, of course there is also greater potential for ambiguity."

Thirdly, only on the level of discourse can we have a fuller and deeper understanding of the nature and function of metaphor. Besides contexts of situation and culture, the interpretation of metaphorical meanings is heavily dependent on co-text. This is especially true of literary discourse. Moreover, metaphorical structuring may operate on the global level of discourse. Goatly (1997: 163) says: "Metaphor can be used, consciously or subliminally, to structure the development of a text, as the organizing principle which gives the text a lexical cohesion." He claims: "It is possible, of course, to regard a literary narrative as one whole extended metaphor" (ibid.: 164). Similarly, Stockwell (2002: 111) states that "when certain conceptual metaphors occur repeatedly throughout a text, often at pivotal moments and often in the form of thematically significant extended metaphor, these can be termed megametaphors". And he further explains: "Megametaphor is a conceptual feature that runs throughout a text and can contribute to the reader's sense of the general meaning or 'gist' of a work and its significance. Specific realizations of the numerous metaphors that occur in the text and that accumulate into the sense of a megametaphor are, by contrast, micrometaphors." (ibid.)

The notion of megametaphor is originally put forward by Werth (1999). It refers to the "accumulation of different metaphors clustering around a single broad frame which gives this text its incredible power" (Werth, 1999: 319). He says: "It is not enough to say, therefore, that metaphors simply cluster. The fact that metaphors can also be sustained, as a kind of 'undercurrent', over an extended text allows extremely subtle conceptual effects to be achieved. I will refer to the sustained metaphorical undercurrents ... as megametaphors." (ibid.: 323) From a text-world perspective, Werth (1999: 324) suggests that the megametaphors "bring together the metaphors in a text into an overarching structure, just as the function-advancing propositions in a world indirectly reveal the 'macrostructure' of the text". Gavins (2007: 152) also thinks that "broadening the focus of analysis beyond the sentence-level phenomena of the micro-metaphors contained in the text to the examination of the discourse-level phenomenon of extended megametaphor allows the true sophistication of the emergent structure of the blended world to be uncovered".

Last but not least, metaphors are not value-free; they are imbued with social-cultural or ideological meanings. Either the metaphors themselves or the choices of metaphors in discourse are value-laden. Fairclough (1992: 194) rightly points out: "Metaphors are not just superficial stylistic adornments of discourse. When we signify things through one metaphor rather than another, we are constructing our reality in one way rather than another. Metaphors structure the way we think and the way we act, and our systems of knowledge and belief, in a pervasive and fundamental way." More clearly, Goatly (1997) states that all metaphors probably have an ideological substratum of which one is often unaware. He thus proposes that "[t]o narrow this epistemological and ontological perspective to an ideological one, we need to concentrate on the ways in which metaphors are used to construct reality as a means of maintaining or challenging power relations in society". (Goatly, 1997: 155)

3. Metaphor and Narrative

The function of metaphor in narrative has been sporadically touched upon by some narratologists and stylisticians. When talking about the rhetoric of description, for instance, Bal (1997: 42 – 43) has identified six types of description in narrative texts: the referential, encyclopedic description, the referential-rhetorical description, metaphoric metonymy, the systematized metaphor, the metonymic metaphor, and the series of metaphors. Obviously, metaphor is considered one of the most important devices of description. More importantly, Bal seems to notice the working mechanisms of extended metaphors on a stretch of text, especially the complementarity of metaphor and metonymy in narrative.

Metaphor is also an important tool for characterization. Fludernik (2009) discusses the narratological relevance of metaphor in the context of narrativity. Metaphor is considered to be located in the category of voice. Specifically, metaphors may occur in the narrator's discourse, the thoughts of characters, or the remarks of the main protagonist. She discovers that "some novelists are very adept at employing simile for the purpose of characterization or of describing a situation in a memorable phrase that echoes throughout the text" (ibid.: 76). Differing from her, Stylisticians have paid particular attention to the role of metaphor in characterization in terms of mind style. According to Fowler (1996: 214), the notion of mind style can be applied to an author, a narrator or a character. However, most studies have applied cognitive metaphor theory to the analysis of the mind style of characters. (e.g. Black, 1993; Semino & Swindlehurst, 1996; Semino, 2002)

Narratologists have noticed the structuring role of metaphor in narrative too. Fludernik (2014/2010: 351) points out: "Metaphor in narrative has been discussed in stylistics in two ways. On the one hand, it has been contrasted with metonymy in the wake of Roman Jakobson's distinction between these two tropes as basic cognitive approaches rooted in similarity and continuity. [...] On the other hand, narratologists have been concerned primarily with the question of who is responsible for specific metaphors in narrative: the narrator, the character, or even the (implied) author?" In her opinion, an attributional analysis of metaphor is not fruitful because positing a narratorial voice is extremely difficult in some cases. She contends that metaphor and metonymy are interbraided in narrative, and calls for (historical) studies of the overall function and impact of metaphor in narratives.

In fact, Fludernik (2009) has already noted that metaphors may transcend their micro-context and become relevant for the entire work. They become the structuring principle of the work and thus a strategy employed by the implied author. The metaphors may assume narratological importance because they create, on the linguistic level of the whole text, powerful and all-embracing structures which not only feature in the discourse but are also crucial to the overall symbolism of the work, operating at the level of the story (plot and setting) as well. She states, "The point at issue here is the significance of this for narrative theory. On the one hand, macro-structural metaphors in texts can be seen as clues to the nature of the implied author (and so to that of the whole text as a construct). Most of the features that are located at this level are to do with story and plot; character grouping, focalization through one character, etc., if we take the relationship of the narrator to the characters into account, however, we begin to bring in the level of style." (Fludernik, 2009: 74)

4. Metaphor and Spatial Representation in *Absalom, Absalom!*

In this section, we shall demonstrate the function of metaphor in narrative with particular reference to spatial representations in *Absalom, Absalom!*. Space is one of the fundamental components in narrative. Compared with temporality, however, the role of space in narrative has long been undervalued. Friedman (2008: 192−193) observes: "Space in narrative poetics is often present as the 'description' that interrupts the flow of temporality or as the 'setting' that functions as static background for the plot, or as the 'scene' in which the narrative events unfold in time." In recent years, there is a "spatial turn" in many disciplines such as sociology, geography, cultural studies and cognitive science. Narrative theorists have begun to rethink the nature and role of space in narrative.

Buchholz & Jahn (2008: 552) said: "At its most basic level, narrative space is the environment in which story-internal characters move about and live." Notably, Chatman (1978: 96) has drawn a distinction between discourse space and story space. The former refers to the place or space in which the narrator stays and tells a story, and the latter is the place or space in which the characters live and act. This distinction is relative but useful for the analysis of complex multi-level narratives. In our opinion, narrative space is a social-cognitive construct as well as a linguistic (or semiotic) construct. It is not only a "lived space" but also a "social space" (Lefebvre, 1991). It is closely related with such social-ideological factors as gender, race and class and it is a product and producer of power relations (Foucault, 1984). William Faulkner is one of the greatest writers who are deeply conscious of the role of space as well as metaphor in the art of fiction.

4. 1　Metaphor, Discourse Space and Atmospheric Style

Thomas Sutpen is the pivotal figure of the fictional narrative. However, he is absent (long dead) when his story is told. He is the "empty center". The tragic story of the Sutpens is told or retold by four narrators: Miss Rosa Coldfield, Mr. Compson, Quentin Compson, and Quentin's Canadian roommate at Harvard, Shreve McCannon. The narrating acts are performed in three discourse spaces: Miss Coldfield's house, Mr. Compson's house and Quentin's dormitory room. These spaces are largely described by an extradiegetic narrator, which are subject to a metaphorical reading.

　　The most well-known description of Miss Coldfield's house as a discourse space is given at the very beginning, i.e. the first paragraph of Chapter I. It is one of the most frequently-quoted parts in the novel, which goes as follows:

> From a little after two o'clock until almost sundown of the long still hot weary dead September afternoon they sat in what Miss Coldfield still called the office because her father had called it that — a dim hot airless room with the blinds all closed and fastened for forty-three summers because when she was a girl someone had believed that light and moving air carried heat and that dark was always cooler, and which (as the sun shone fuller and fuller on that side of the house) became latticed with yellow slashes full of dust motes which Quentin thought of as being flecks of the dead old dried paint itself blown inward from the scaling blinds as wind might have blown them. There was a wistaria vine blooming for the second time that summer on a wooden trellis before one window, into which sparrows came now and then in random gusts, making a dry vivid dusty sound before going away. (AA: 5)

It is a room in Miss Coldfield's house — the "office" called by her father and herself. According to Bal (1997), senses (sight, hearing, touch and smell) are especially involved in the perceptual representation of space in the story. A variety of senses has been employed for describing the surroundings of the room. First of all, a general impression of the discourse space is given by the expression "the long still hot weary dead September afternoon". Superficially, the expression indicates the climatic atmosphere of the afternoon when Sutpen went to visit Miss Coldfield. The head word "afternoon" is modified with redundant adjectives: "long", "still", "hot", "weary" and "dead". Most of these adjectives can be read literally. However, the adjective "dead" brings about the effect of defamiliarization. It appears again in the expression "the dead old dried paint". The word "dead" is a clue for the reader to do a similar metaphorical reading of other related expressions.

The so-called office is described as "a dim hot airless room with the blinds all closed and fastened for forty-three summers because [...] someone had believed that light and moving air carried heat and that dark was always cooler, and which [...] became latticed with yellow slashes full of dust motes". The expressions about dimness or darkness easily evoke a basic metaphor in the mind of the reader: DEATH IS DARKNESS (and the opposite is LIFE IS LIGHT). Moreover, the modifiers "dried" ("the dead old dried paint") and "dry" ("a dry vivid dusty sound") can also be interpreted as a synonym of "dead" according to the basic conceptual metaphor DEATH IS LOSS OF FLUID (the opposite is LIFE IS A FLUID). So the airless dark room can be understood metaphorically as a tomb. Thus the spatial description creates a deathlike atmosphere, which is characteristic of Gothic style. This dull gloomy atmosphere is consistent with the main Sutpen story.

Besides darkness and dryness, another important attribute of the discourse space is hotness. It is expressed either overtly or covertly by the following phrases or clauses: "the long still hot weary dead September afternoon", "a dim hot airless room with the blinds all closed and fastened", "light and moving air carried heat", "dark was always cooler", "the sun shone fuller and fuller on that side of the house", "random gusts" and so on. Besides, the expressions about dryness ("the dead old dried paint", "a dry vivid dusty sound") also indicate hotness. Metonymically, the place where one lives can stand for its inhabitant. That is, the properties of space can indicate the identity or personality of a character closely related to it. Rimmon-Kenan (1983: 66) calls these "trait-connoting metonymies". All the above expressions point to the basic metaphor ANGER IS HEAT. This undercurrent is symbolic of Miss Coldfield's state of outrage, which comes from her hatred for Thomas Sutpen and her father Mr. Coldfield. Her fury has a great impact on her narration, which is highly emotional and subjective.

The basic conceptual metaphors such as DEATH IS DARKNESS and ANGER IS HEAT and the poetic metaphors such as the TOMB metaphor are all extended metaphors or megametaphors in *Absalom, Absalom!*. Together with such basic metaphors as DEATH IS COLD and DEATH IS NIGHT, these megametaphors are operating on stretches of texts representing other discourse spaces. For instance,

> At first, in bed in the dark, it seemed colder than ever, as if there had been some puny quality of faint heat in the single light bulb before Shreve turned it off and that now the iron and impregnable dark had become one with the iron and icelike bedclothing lying upon the flesh slacked and thin-clad for sleeping. Then the darkness seemed to breathe, to flow back; the window which Shreve had opened became visible against the faintly unearthly glow of the outer snow as, forced by the weight of the darkness, the blood surged and ran warmer, warmer. (*AA*: 296)

This is Quentin's dormitory room at Harvard. Apparently, darkness is overwhelmingly overshadowing the discourse space, which can be displayed by the following expressions: "in the dark", "the iron and impregnable dark", "the darkness seemed to breathe, to flow back" and "the weight of the darkness". We argue that a sense of death is created in the above situation and other similar situations by virtue of the basic metaphor DEATH IS DARKNESS together with the DEATH IS COLD metaphor. Thus, a right atmosphere is created for the telling of the main story of the Sutpens, especially the deaths of Thomas Sutpen, Charles Bon, Henry and other characters. Besides, these metaphors also indicate the confusion and desperation of Quentin himself, a character narrator, who is one of the main characters in Faulkner's another well-known work *The Sound and the Fury*. He commits suicide five months after.

4. 2　Metaphor, Story Space and Character Relations

In *Absalom, Absalom!*, (story) spaces plays a significant role in characterization and their representation is stylistically related to metaphors. The metaphors are usually attributed to the character-narrators such as Miss Coldfield and Mr. Compson. Their narration is deeply colored by the relationship in which they stand to Thomas Sutpen or other characters and by their own personalities and emotional involvement. Thus the metaphors may not only show the traits of a character or character relations in terms of gender, race and class but also reveal the narrator's relationship with the character. Berger (2000: 3−4) observes: "Many characters who inhabit the worlds of Southern stories also inhabit houses like the House of Usher, which seems to me a prototype for architectural metaphor in American Literature, that are built on the faulty foundation of a patriarchal ordering system which objectifies, silences and entombs the other. [...] For Faulkner, Warren and Morrison otherness can be inscribed not only in terms of gender, but also in terms of race and class, and along several other dividing lines." This is true of the houses in *Absalom, Absalom!*.

First of all, the house is a significant feminine space dominated by male power. In *Absalom, Absalom!*, the Sutpen house is the most important patriarchal space in which female characters such as Ellen Coldfield (wife of Thomas Sutpen) and Miss Rosa Coldfield (Ellen's younger sister) suffer a lot. For instance, after Ellen's marriage, "the aunt had taught Miss Rosa to look upon her sister as a woman who had vanished, not only out of the family and the house but out of life too, into an edifice like Bluebeard's" (*AA*: 49). The Sutpen house is taken metaphorically as "an edifice like Bluebeard's"; correspondingly, Thomas Sutpen is Bluebeard and Ellen a victim. Another description of Ellen's status is as follows:

> ' Often twice and sometimes three times a week the two of them came to town and into the house — the foolish unreal voluble preserved woman now six years absent from the world — the woman who had quitted home and kin on a flood of tears and in a shadowy miasmic region something like the bitter purlieus of Styx had produced two children and then rose like the swamp-hatched butterfly, unimpeded by weight of stomach and all the heavy organs of suffering and experience, into a perennial bright vacuum of arrested sun [...] ' (*AA*: 57)

Similarly, the place where Sutpen lives is described metaphorically as " a shadowy miasmic region something like the bitter purlieus of Styx ". More importantly, a new metaphor is introduced: ELLEN IS A BUTTERFLY ("produced two children and then rose like the swamp-hatched butterfly"). A sharp contrast exists between the image of Styx and the image of the butterfly. The BUTTERFLY metaphor is extended throughout Chapter III. Bockting (1995: 216 −217) says: "This repetition of images emphasizes the 'emptiness' of Ellen Sutpen, and illustrates the generalization about women in Chapter II. Ellen, then, exemplifies Mr. Compson's characteristically negative view of women." The extended BUTTERFLY and BLUEBEARD metaphors suggest the domination of Sutpen over Ellen.

Moreover, the BUTTERFLY metaphor is frequently combined with the image of the darkened room. It is a typical feminine space in Faulkner's fiction. To exemplify,

> 'So she didn't even see Ellen anymore. Apparently Ellen had now served her purpose, completed the bright pointless noon and afternoon of the butterfly's summer and vanished, perhaps not out of Jefferson, but out of her sister's life any way, to be seen but the one time more dying in bed in a darkened room in the house on which fateful mischance had already laid its hand to the extent of scattering the black foundation on which it had been erected and removing its two male mainstays, husband and son — the one into the risk and danger of battle, the other apparently into oblivion.' (AA: 64)

In connection with the extended BUTTERFLY metaphor, a set of basic metaphors are used here, including PURPOSES ARE DESTINATIONS, DEATH IS GOING TO A FINAL DESTINATION, LIFETIME IS A DAY and LIFETIME IS A YEAR. The expression "to serve one's purpose" means "coming nearer to death", which is the combination of the basic metaphors PURPOSES ARE DESTINATIONS and DEATH IS GOING TO A FINAL DESTINATION. The words "noon" and "afternoon" refer to the prime and late stages of one's life respectively, and the summer corresponds to the prime time of one's life. Underlying them is the basic metaphors LIFETIME IS A DAY and LIFETIME IS A YEAR. Therefore, Mr. Compson probably suggests that Ellen's life is degenerating. The darkened room is like a coffin or tomb or "the shell, the (so I thought) cocoon-casket marriage-bed of youth and grief" (AA: 112) in Miss Coldfield's words. It is symbolic of death (i.e. DEATH IS DARKNESS). Hence, the darkened room is a symbol of power — male dominance and the Sutpen house is a patriarchal structuration of man's systems.

However, differing from Ellen (the BUTTERFLY metaphor), Miss Coldfield is Cassandra-like, who is taught by the aunt to look up on the brother-in-law as "Bluebeard" or "an ogre" — "There was an ogre of my childhood which before my birth removed my only sister to its grim ogre-bourne and produced two half phantom children" (*AA*: 137). More importantly, she takes Sutpen (and Mr. Coldfield, her father) as an "embattled foe", an "adversary", or the "second party to an armistice" (*AA*: 52−53). The WAR metaphor is a megametaphor extended through the whole narrative text. Her victory is symbolically won by her busting down the door barred by Clytie (the half-blood daughter of Sutpen) in the Sutpen house and breaking into the darkened room where Henry (son of Sutpen) lay dying.

Space is also an important domain of racial discrimination. An example is found with Etienne Bon, son of Charles Bon who himself is son of Sutpen with half black blood:

> ' And your grandfather never knew if it was Clytie who ... waited for the day, the moment, to come, the hour when the little boy would be an orphan, and so went herself to fetch him; or if it was Judith who ... sent Clytie for him that winter, that December of 1871 — Clytie ... who had found him, hunted him down, in a French city and brought him away ... Yet he made no resistance, returning quietly and docilely to that decaying house which he had seen one time ... He crossed that strange threshold, that irrevocable demarcation, not led, not dragged, but driven and herded by that stern implacable presence, into that gaunt and barren household ... the child lying there between them unasleep in some hiatus of passive and hopeless despair aware of this, aware of the woman on the bed whose every look and action toward him, whose every touch of the capable hands seemed at the moment of touching his body to lose all warmth and become imbued with cold implacable antipathy, and the woman on the pallet upon whom he had already come to look as might some delicate talonless and fangless wild beast crouched in its cage in some hopeless and desperate similitude of ferocity look upon the human creature who feeds it [...] ' (*AA*: 161−163)

Here the metaphorical representation of space is metonymically related to the animal metaphor on the blacks. A basic metaphor PEOPLE ARE ANIMALS (or rather THE BLACKS ARE BEASTS) is underlying this stretch of text. There is also a micrometaphor LOOKING FOR A PERSON IS HUNTING DOWN AN ANIMAL. It is demonstrated by a series of metonymically related expressions such as "hunted ... down", "returning quietly and docilely", "not led, not dragged, but driven and herded", and "some delicate talonless and fangless wild beast crouched in its cage". Clearly, these expressions all fall into the domain of animal hunting. The child is treated as a wild beast; correspondingly, the house is like a cage for him. Thus the Sutpen house is not only a space of class struggle but also a space of racial discrimination.

The Sutpen house may be a dominated space of class as well. The following example is about the Sutpens' coming to church for the first time:

> ' It was as though the sister whom I had never laid eyes on, who before I was born had vanished into the stronghold of an ogre or a djinn, was now to return through a dispensation of one day only, to the world which she had quitted [...] now and at last this ogre or djinn had agreed for the sake of the wife and the children to come to church, to permit them at least to approach the vicinity of salvation, to at least give Ellen one chance to struggle with him for those children's souls on a battleground where she could be supported not only by Heaven but by her own family and people of her own kind [...] ' (*AA*: 18)

It is told by Miss Coldfield. The Sutpen house (or Sutpen's Hundred, the plantation) is called " the stronghold of an ogre or a djinn", which is metonymically connected with the OGRE/DJINN metaphor for Thomas Sutpen. The STRONGHOLD metaphor is in contrast to the world which Ellen formerly belonged to or to the church, the " vicinity of salvation", which is metaphorically understood as a " battleground where she could be supported not only by Heaven but by her own family and people of her own kind". The spatial metaphors (STRONGHOLD and BATTLEGROUND) show the oppression of the newly-rising plantation owner and the opposition of the middle-class whites. They also show Miss Coldfield's superiority over Sutpen who is considered rude or uncivilized —" He wasn't a gentleman. He wasn't even a gentleman." (*AA*: 11)

Miss Coldfield's middle-class superiority is also displayed by the BEAST metaphor for Wash Jones, a poor white man who once served Thomas Sutpen. The following excerpt is a discourse presented by Miss Coldfield:

> *I had only to lock the house and take my place in the buggy and traverse those twelve miles which I had not done since Ellen died, beside that brute who until Ellen died was not even permitted to approach the house from the front ... that brute who appeared to believe that he had served and performed his appointed end by yelling of blood and pistols in the street before my house [...]* (*AA*: 111)

It is a scene in which Wash Jones comes to the door of Miss Coldfield's house informing her of Charles Bon's death. Wash Jones is taken as a " brute" or an animal. So he is not permitted to approach the Sutpen house from the front and even considered it too rude to stand in the street before Miss Coldfield's house yelling. Clearly, the BEAST metaphor in connection with the spatial practice of the character indicates the prejudice of the middle/upper-class whites against the poor whites.

In addition, metaphor can be structurally projected on the global level of narrative. The DARK HOUSE metaphor is an extended metaphor in *Absalom, Absalom!* , which is operating on the macrostructure of the narrative. It plays a crucial role for both plot and theme. To a certain extent, the whole Sutpen legend is a spatial story about a dark house: the building of the big Sutpen house, the living in it, and ultimately the burning down of it. It is symbolic of the rise and fall of the Sutpen family. Berger (2000: 26) recognizes the symbolic significance of house in Faulkner's novels — "Faulkner clearly represents familial and social relationships relative to the metaphor of the house, and spatially within the house." The house of Sutpen is built not with dwelling but with owning. Its existence depends on the exploitation and later on the exclusion of the other (other gender, race and class). This destabilized foundation accounts for the collapse of the house, symbolizing the failure of individuals, families and even the South.

5. Conclusion

This study has investigated the functions of metaphor in narrative, particularly in spatial representations in Faulkner's *Absalom, Absalom!* . It shows that metaphor is a prominent stylistic device in narrative fiction. It plays an important role for atmospheric creation, characterization, plot structuring and thematic development. Metaphor together with metonymy is a basic mode of narrative construction. Fludernik (2014: 362) states: "Metaphors are therefore not merely ornaments or rare rhetorical flourishes; they crucially model the narrative discourse and are inextricably knotted together with the semiotics of the text. Hence, a poetics of fiction ignores metaphor only at its peril." The study has also shown that space is an active narrative component closely connected with characters, events, plot and theme. Spatiality like temporality is a constitutive factor for narrativity.

References

Bal, M. 1997. *Narratology: An Introduction to the Theory of Narrative.* Toronto: University of Toronto Press.

Barthes, R. 1977. *Image, Music, Text.* New York: Hill and Wang.

Berger, A. E. 2000. Dark Houses: Navigating Space and Negotiating Silence in the Novels of Faulkner, Warren and Morrison. University of North Texas.

Black, E. 1993. Metaphor, simile and cognition in Golding's *The Inheritors. Language and Literature*, 2 (1): 37–48.

Black, E. 2006. *Pragmatic Stylistics.* Edinburgh: Edinburgh University Press.

Bockting, I. 1995. *Character and Personality in the Novels of William Faulkner.* Lanham, Maryland: University Press of America.

Buchholz, S. & M. Jahn. 2008. Space in narrative. In D. Herman, M. Jahn & M.-L. Ryan (eds.) *Routledge Encyclopedia of Narrative Theory.* London and New York: Routledge.

Chatman, S. 1978. *Story and Discourse.* Ithaca: Cornell University Press.

Crisp, P. 2003. Conceptual metaphor and its expressions. In J. Gavins & G. Steen (eds.) *Cognitive Poetics in Practice.* London and New York: Routledge.

Fairclough, N. 1992. *Discourse and Social Change.* Cambridge: Polity Press.

Fauconnier, G. 1997. *Mappings in Thought and Language.* Cambridge: Cambridge University Press.

Fauconnier, G. & M. Turner. 2002. *The Way We Think.* New York: Basic Books.

Faulkner, W. 1971/1936. *Absalom, Absalom!* . New York: Penguin Books.

Fludernik, M. 2009. *An Introduction to Narratology.* London and New York: Routledge.

Fludernik, M. 2010/2014. Narrative and metaphor. In Dan McIntyre and Beatrix Busse (eds.) *Language and Style.* Beijing: Peking University Press.

Foucault, M. 1984. Space, knowledge, and power. In P. Rabinow (ed.) *The Foucault Reader.* New York: Pantheon Books.

Friedman, S. S. 2008. Spatial poetics and Arundhati Roy's *The God of Small Things.* In J. Phelan & P. J. Rabinowitz (eds.) *A Companion to Narrative Theory.* Malden & Oxford: Blackwell.

Gavins, J. 2007. *Text World Theory: An Introduction.* Edinburgh: Edinburgh University Press.

Goatly, A. 1997. *The Language of Metaphors.* London and New York: Routledge.

Lakoff, G. 1987. *Women, Fire and Dangerous Things.* Chicago: University of Chicago Press.

Lakoff, G. & M. Johnson. 1980/2003. *Metaphors We Live By.* Chicago: University of Chicago Press.

Lakoff, G. & M. Turner. 1989. *More than Cool Reason.* Chicago and London: University of Chicago Press.

Lefebvre, H. 1991. *The Production of Space*. Oxford, UK & Cambridge, USA: Blackwell.

Rimmon-Kenan, S. 1983. *Narrative Fiction: Contemporary Poetics*. London and New York: Methuen.

Semino, E. 2002. A cognitive stylistic approach to mind style in narrative fiction. In E. Semino & J. Culpeper (eds.) *Cognitive Stylistics: Language and Cognition in Text Analysis*. Amsterdam/Philadelphia: John Benjamins.

Semino, E. & K. Swindlehurst. 1996. Metaphor and mind style in Ken Kesey's *One Flew Over the Cuckoo's Nest. Style*, 30 (1): 143-166.

Stockwell, P. 2001. Towards a critical cognitive linguistics?. In A. Combrink & I. Biermann (eds.) *Poetics, Linguistics and History*. Potchefstroom: Potchefstroom University Press, 510-528.

Stockwell, P. 2002. *Cognitive Poetics: An Introduction*. London and New York: Routledge.

Werth, P. 1994. Extended metaphor: A text-world account. *Language and Literature*, 3 (2): 79-103.

Werth, P. 1999. *Text Worlds: Representing Conceptual Space in Discourse*. London: Longman.

Metaphors in *Mara and Dann: An Adventure*

Guo Jian Yu Hua   (**University of Chinese Academy of Sciences**)

Abstract: *Mara and Dann: An Adventure* is a representative work of British female novelist Doris Lessing, who won the Nobel Prize in 2007, and it was introduced into China at the same year. In this novel which has been regarded as one of her few works with strong features of scientific fiction, she revealed the theme of story with provocative and stimulating notion of the future human world and the merits and demerits of modern technology. With the description of the future African country in a thousand years, Lessing warns people that they should stop fighting endless arguments about the abstract concept and change to show concern about the basic requirements for the people which include environment, food, shelters, freedom and relationship between people. This study tends to analyze the language features of the novel with combination of cognitive metaphor. The analysis will focus on three questions: 1. What metaphors did Doris Lessing use to depict the disasters of environmental problems facing the human world? 2. How did Lessing portray the future world which might be destroyed by the "advanced modern technology"? To investigate the answer to the first question, the study finds that the author applies a large number of metaphors to refer to the destructive changes of environment which would decrease the living standard and quality of life, and if the situation continues in an unstoppable way, the human world might be destroyed one day. To find the answer to the second question, the study finds that Lessing illustrates vividly her points with very interesting and insightful images. With full application of metaphorical devices, she modifies the world with her long female experience, with "skepticism, fire and visionary power" and she "has subjected a divided civilization to scrutiny".

Key words: *Mara and Dann: An Adventure*; Doris Lessing; metaphors

1. Introduction

Mara and Dann: An Adventure (*Mara and Dann* in the following) was written in 1999 by Doris Lessing, undoubtedly one of the most influential contemporary writers and a British prolific writer who won the Nobel Prize for Literature in 2007 at the age of 88. Lessing was described by Swedish Academy as "that epicist of the female experience, who with skepticism, fire and visionary power has subjected a divided civilization to scrutiny". Her series of works cover a wide range of varieties such as novels, dramas, autobiography, non-fictions and poetry and the themes she touches involve racial discrimination, women's status, ecological issues, and other social issues.

Her eventful personal life, especially her early childhood in the southern part of Africa has a great impact on her works. Her several marital experiences and her engagement with Communism and Sufism contribute a lot to her unique perception, enchanting imagination and boundless inspiration which are reflected in her works.

Lessing is widely viewed as a writer with time spirit. She plunges herself into multifarious themes of social concerns and continuously updates her mind to assimilate new blood (Yu Haining, 2012). Since the 1970s, the ecological environment of the whole world has become worse. Doris Lessing starts to show her concern about the relationship between the ecological environment and human society which conveys her eco-consciousness. *Mara and Dann* is viewed as a science fiction story set in Ifrica, aphysical and spiritual wasteland thousands of years in the future, when people suffer from lots of natural disasters, like famine, drought, heat and attack from aggressive large animals. The two main characters are Mara and Dann, who are seven and four years old respectively. They were born in a head of the Monhond people and in the fight against Rock people, their parents are killed and they are taken care of by Maima who live in Rock village. They lead a very miserable life, most of the time they don't have enough water to drink and enough food to eat, they don't have good shelter either. Having learnt from other people the North is a paradise, they decide to take the journey to the North and indeed, it takes them years of struggling and they have to survive a series of hazardous adventures, and finally they get to the promising land and a happy life as expected at the beginning of the story.

2. Metaphor in the Novel

The author applies a large number of metaphors to pushing the story forward and illustrate her worries about our human's fate in the present and future world.

"A quintessential example of what distinguished her from so many of her contemporaries, women as well as men. She again addressed some of the ideas and concerns that have preoccupied her in other novels: the value of story-telling, the fragility of civilization, and characters who are strong and ingenious enough to survive disruption and sea changes in their lives." (Chettle, 1999)

Lakoff & Johnson develop the cognitive metaphor theory by publishing a masterpiece *Metaphors We Live By* in 1980. Lakoff & Johnson argue that "the essence of metaphor is understanding and experiencing one kind of thing in terms of another" and cognitive metaphor is "a cross domain mapping in the conceptual system". (1980: 5)

In cognitive metaphor theory, there are two domains, i.e. source domain and target domain. The mapping between the two domains is unidirectional (Evans & Green, 2006). It could be illustrated in the following figure.

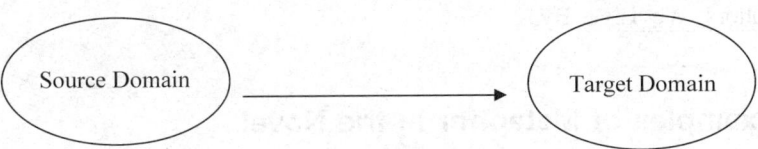

Examples in *Mara and Dann*:

Source Domain	Target Domain
Ugly face: identical	Clone technology which might destroy world
Rock: primitive village	Civilization destroyed, people's living standard decreased
North: long journey	Promising land, which is rich in natural resources
Flying machine: plane	little natural resource left

Cognitive metaphor exists deeply in human being's thought and behavior, and usually it is demonstrated in the language. As Lakoff asserts, "the locus of metaphor is not in language at all, but in the way we conceptualize one mental domain in terms of another. The general theory of metaphor is given by characterizing such cross-domain mappings. In the process, everyday abstract concepts like time, state, change, causation, and purpose also turn out to be metaphorical." (Lakoff & Johnson, 1980: 5)

Concluded from the above explanation, the domains in cognitive metaphor theory are "highly stable knowledge structures" and the core in this theory is "mapping the conventional patterns entrenched in conceptual structure" (Evans & Green, 2006: 295). Therefore, it has been seen that metaphors, especially conventional metaphors, could be construed with cognitive metaphor theory.

As a consequence, metaphor is not seen just as a linguistic phenomenon. *Oxford Concise Dictionary of Linguistics* defines metaphor as "a general pattern in which one domain is systematically conceived and spoken of in terms of another". Metaphor is seen as fundamental cognitive ability that allows us to talk and think about abstract concepts and phenomena.

The Linguistic Society of America has remarked that the most recent linguistic approach to literature is that of cognitive metaphor, which claims that metaphor is not a mode of language, but a mode of thought. Metaphors project structures from source domains of schematized bodily or enculturated experience into abstract target domains. (http://en. wikipedia. org/wiki/ Metaphors_We_Live_By).

3. Examples of Metaphor in the Novel

3. 1 "Face", "Ifrica", "North"

Doris Lessing applies many deviant and abnormal phenomena to satirizing the disastrous results which might be brought by some kinds of modern technology through the description of the ugly people with the same identities and same looking as "Every face was the same, identical, with lumpy noses, long thin mouths, pale eyes under yellow brows, broad foreheads make lower still because of the frizzy brush above" (p. 61), Lessing presents a picture of a society to her readers which one day might become backward and chaotic by applying clone technology — people with same face, same stupid ideas. Another example worth mentioning, Lessing sets her story in "Ifrica", which conveys metaphorical sense, sounding and spelling like "Africa", where she was born, grew up and has deep feelings for. Ifirca or Africa is the place getting the environmental problems like draught, flood, or insects disasters which make Lessing worry a great deal. Therefore, in the novel Mara and Dann decided to go to "the North", and it became their lifelong pursuit. "The North" is not only referred to as a place in the north area, but a metaphor contains many meanings — the ideal place or the promising land with water, trees, fertile land and nice weather, a place full of milk and honey. Lessing employs many metaphors in her novel which describe the concrete images the readers could imagine, associate and have respondence with her. In 1980, Lakoff & Johnson closely examined a collection of basic conceptual metaphors, including LOVE IS A JOURNEY; LIFE IS A JOURNEY; SOCIAL ORGANIZATIONS ARE PLANTS; LOVE IS WAR in their work: *Metaphors We Live By*. These short sentences invoke certain assumptions about concrete experience and requires the reader or listener to apply them to the preceding abstract concepts of love or organizing in order to understand the sentence in which the conceptual metaphor is used.

3. 2 Metaphors of "Rock", "Flying Machine"

In the primitive world, rock may be taken as something very important, people use rock as weapons, as living materials, like containers, the materials to build houses. But in the modern society, rock is no longer a basic material to support people's life. The author describes the village as Rock village, and the houses where people live are made of rock, including rock beds, rock couches. Through the use of rock, she gives a sharp contrast image against the one of the modern world. Lessing implies the life might be thousands of years later, if people fail to protect the present world, they will live a similar life — nothing left, just rocks. She uses the flying machines as another example to show if we waste our natural resources, then our later generation probably have nothing to use, especially may be short of oil. The story describes that people have to push and pull the flying machines and they have to be fuelled with sugar energy, which is to satirize the modern people who now are laboring on the digging out the natural resources to the most, and one day the world may become arid and barren without any valuable resources.

3. 3　The Metaphor from the Bible

Doris Lessing uses the plot of the Bible and biblical characters as the prototype of her stories.

"Mara", the name of the girl in the story, is a Biblical baby name, which means: bitter and bitterness.

In Exodus 15: 23−25 (Douay-Rheims 1899 American Edition (DRA)), when Israeli came into the place, they are very thirsty, but they could not drink the water of Mara, because it was bitter, that's why the place was named "Mara", which means, bitterness.

The author uses the name to imply that Mara has suffered a great deal of bitterness in the way of escaping from the enemies in the story. Mara is the elder sister in the family, when she and her brother are dispelled from her home, she is only 7 years old, but she takes the responsibility to look after her little brother who is only 4. When her brother grows up and follows the people to go to the North, she stays and takes care of the old lady Daima who used to look after the sister and brother. In the following years, she has encountered a series of troubles, for example, her enemies who want to catch her and kill her; some of her tribe people want to get hold of her to have babies and restore their former royal family. She escaped and realized that this kind of life is not what she pursues. She also tries to avoid falling in love with her brother, etc. Eventually, she comes to the promising land with her strong will. Mara, the metaphorical meaning Lessing tries to convey is that Mara is the symbol of a woman possesses strong will and could overcome the difficulties one after another even faced with evil fate.

The story is about an adventure which is basically established on the plot of *Book of Exodus*. According to the story, Moses was born in a time when his people, the Children of Israel, were increasing in numbers and the Egyptian Pharaoh was worried that they might help Egypt's enemies. Moses' Hebrew mother, Jochebed, hid him when the Pharaoh ordered all newborn Hebrew boys to be killed, and the child was adopted as a foundling by the Egyptian royal family. After killing an Egyptian slavemaster, Moses fled across the Red Sea to Midian, where he encountered the God of Israel in the form of a "burning bush". God sent Moses back to Egypt to request the release of the Israelites. Finally, Moses led the Exodus of the Israelites out of Egypt and across the Red Sea, after which they based themselves at Mount Sinai, where Moses received the Ten Commandments. After 40 years of wandering in the desert, Moses died within sight of the Promised Land (http://en.wikipedia.org/wiki/Moses).

Mara and Dann: An Adventure is just like a different version of the immigration of the people from a very depressing land to the promising land. The South is just like Egypt, where Mara and Dann suffer a lot from the death of their parents, famine, drought, the hatred of Rock people and other people. They hear the North is the place they would have enough water, food, nice climate, and other necessities, which is similar to Sinai — the hometown of Israelites. But both the journeys of Israelites and Mara and Dann are not smooth at all. They encounter numerous obstacles and difficulties but finally get to the destination. Moses is guided by God as the head of the Exodus and he helps his people who have strong belief in God and follow Ten Commandments instructed by God; while in the novel, Lessing uses the Bible story to design the development of Mara and Dann's long journey. In some parts, Lessing is critical of some people who do not have any belief. When Dann grows up to be a strong-willed and talented man, many people still don't trust him and they have different opinions upon how to face the challenge. Lessing points out if the group of people has no leader, do not have sense of obeying authority, then the life would be chaos; that is why people cannot succeed in their work, because they are self-centered and selfish, and they fight for their own benefit. But in the Bible, when some people take more share of the food, God punish them by making the food turn rotten. Then people learn to be self-disciplined. Lessing points out that people need to change their bad habits and hope they could be disciplined and united in their search of spiritual life along with the material life.

4. Conclusion

Lessing applies "rock", "flying machines", identical face of the villagers, and even the name of the protagonist "Mara", and the "North" as metaphors to show her worries that people might suffer a lot from the destruction of our own. The whole novel is a kind of warning system, warning people if they continue their pursuing of the material life with "highly developed technology" while ignoring the relationship and good communication between each other, if they don't increase the sense of protecting the natural environment, the modern civilization will be destroyed.

References

Buell, L. 2009. *The Future of Environmental Criticism: Environmental Crisis and Literary Imagination* (Vol. 52). John Wiley & Sons.

Chettle, J. E.1999. Lessons in survival. Washington: The world & I, (14): 239–247.

Crater, T. L. 2004. Temporal temptations in Lessing's *Mara and Dann*: Arriving at the present moment. *Journal of Evolutionary Psychology*, 25 (3–4): 190.

Doris, L. 1999. *Mara and Dann: An Adventure*. New York: HarperCollins Publishers, Inc.

Edward, B. 1999. *Review of Mara and Dann: An Adventure*. Harper Flamingo: HarperCollins.

Evans, V. & M. Green. 2006. *Cognitive Linguistics: An Introduction*. Edinburgh: Edinburgh University Press.

Lakoff, G. & M. Johnson. 1980. *Metaphors We Live By*. Chicago: University of Chicago Press.

Wine and Metaphor: Stylistic Choices within an Institutional Framework

Allison Creed (University of Southern Queensland)

Abstract: In the contemporary era, style is recognised as a significant feature of everyday language communication. Stylistic choices communicate meaning, attitude and emotion to an audience. This is no less true of the creative language used to talk and write about wine. Wine discourse is rich in metaphorical expressions. As a stylistic device, metaphor interfaces with figurative meaning construction mechanisms to evoke and construe images and emotions, and to elicit sensory perceptions and sensations of an aesthetic product. The language domain of wine is organised by an institutional framework reflected in the genre of wine reviews that are short, persuasive texts used by wine critics to convey their appraisal and appreciation of wine. In this paper I will consider the relationship between text structures, functions, and processes of metaphor in the genre of wine reviews given that meaning is situated in larger contexts of understanding. I present initial findings from a doctoral research project, using a cognitive linguistic theoretical and methodological framework of analysis, which examines the heuristic potential of Australian wine reviews across the cultural and linguistic borders of Australia and China. The paper concludes by highlighting the challenge of intercultural communication for wine education and business development.

Key words: wine; metaphor; stylistic choice; institutional framework

The theme of the conference — new advances in stylistic studies in the new century — is approached in this paper through the topic of wine and metaphor. The paper addresses key topics of the conference: generic structure, language variation, education, and comparative studies. An emerging challenge for stylistic studies, and for wine promotion and education, is intercultural communication. The paper is a stimulus for a discussion of the opportunities and challenges for researchers across academic disciplines, languages, theoretical, cross disciplinary and comparative stylistics studies.

Wine Reviews

Wine is made, marketed, sold, evaluated, described and ultimately consumed with undiminishing enthusiasm across the globe. But wine is more than a simple beverage. Wine is an expression of its place and the wine maker who brings it to life; it is a combination of earth and weather conditions, vineyard and grape variety; it has a cultural and historical background and a language of its own. Today, wine and language are enmeshed with European social, cultural and linguistic traditions: so too is the institutional framework of wine reviews where the stylistic choices of wine critics are writ large.

For the wine industry, educators and enthusiasts, wine reviews form a sensory bridge by providing a conceptual framework for wine communication. Wine reviews are a short, persuasive text used by wine critics for analytical and imaginative purposes. They begin with technical information followed by the description and evaluation of wine components, sensations and possibly affective responses of the taster and conclude with an overall rating of the wine and the reviewer's name (e.g., see Figure 1).

For many people, however, the mystique of wine coupled with the choice of language used to talk about it induces anxiety and uncertainty that restrains people's discovery, experience and enjoyment of wine. This is because wine reviews, like all genres, are situated in larger contexts of understanding. They are located not simply in textual conventions but within a blended relationship between text, industry, audience, and historical background. Furthermore, how we categorise and organise the world around us is dependent on our speech community which is "codified in the patterns of our language" (Bennett, 2013: 157).

There is the potential to build research collaborations in regards to the

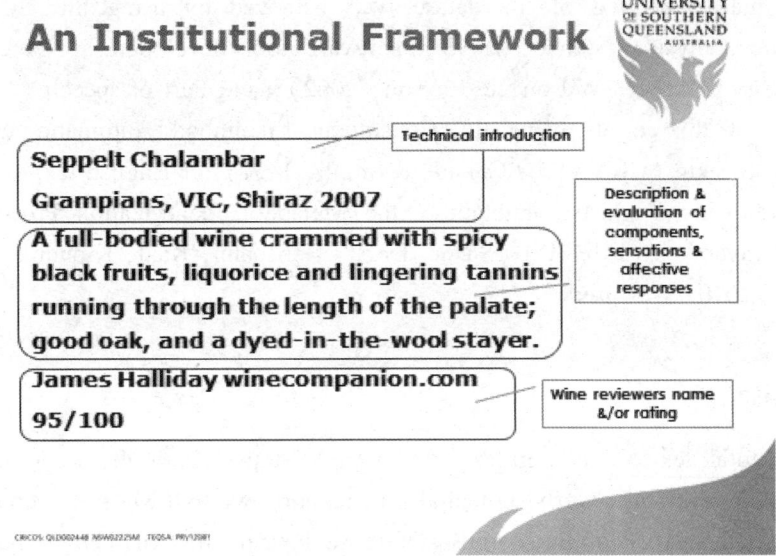

Figure 1   A wine review

structure and usage of genre across cultures particularly in the study of metaphor meaning and variation through the lens of intercultural communication.

Current Research

In the genre of wine reviews, metaphor is a frequent and often deliberate stylistic choice used to spark an audience's imagination and make them a more active text participant (Caballero & Suárez-Toste, 2008). The significance and frequency of occurrence of metaphoric language in Australian wine reviews was the focus of Study 1 for my current research project at the University of Southern Queensland using a cognitive linguistic theoretical framework and methodology.

Method

Data sources and materials

The corpus was a small, selective sample of wine reviews in publically accessible publications from individual Australian wine critics appraising Australian red and white wines exported to China.

Instruments and procedure

Semantic tagging of the dataset was achieved by using the UCREL semantic analysis system (USAS) software tool developed at Lancaster University (Archer, Wilson, & Rayson, 2002), and Part-of-speech (POS) tagging of the corpus using the Constituent Likelihood Automatic Word-tagging System (CLAWS) (Garside & Smith, 1997) for English text.

Following linguistic annotation, the Metaphor Identification Procedure Vrije Universiteit (MIPVU) (Steen, Dorst, Herrmann, Kaal, Krennmayr, & Pasma, 2010) was used.

Results

Of the total lexical units in the data sample drawn from the POS noun, adjective, verb and adverb, potentially metaphoric words (MRW) accounted for more than 10% of the corpus. Of those lexical units marked as having anthropomorphic potential (AMRW), their occurrence was over a third of all MRW; thus making them a significant feature in this representative sample.

Discussion

The findings of this study identify metaphor as a frequent feature of Australian wine reviews and particularly the conceptualisation of wine through anthropomorphic metaphor arising from this situated context. Metaphor appears as a stylistic devise to convey and elicit a physically embodied, sensory and emotive experience in the audience. As Lakoff & Johnson (1980) point out, metaphors provide "a way of partially communicating unshared experiences, and it is the natural structure of our experience that makes this possible" (p. 225). However, although people conceptualise metaphoric expressions similarly across languages and cultures, variation is evident (Kövecses, 2005).

Language variation and meaning conceptualisation are significant given the global interest in wine appreciation and education, particularly in China. Furthermore, how metaphor is understood and why there is variation in understanding across social and cultural environments is of particular relevance for teaching and learning about language in terms of intercultural communication. As with students studying a new academic discipline, discourse domain or a second or foreign language, explicit instruction in language use and function and an awareness of meaning motivation and constraints can be beneficial (Boers & Lindstromberg, 2008). Understanding the influence of stylistic choices on the consumer's conceptualisation of a wine is therefore important pedagogically (Caballero & Suárez-Toste, 2008).

To conclude, advances in stylistic studies in the new century are facilitating a deeper exploration of language use and meaning motivation or constraints particularly in situated contexts. In terms of intercultural communication this research highlights the need to consider meaning in terms of "variation from what? varied by whom? for what purpose? in what context of use?" (Stockwell, 2005: 746). Therefore, the language used in wine writing and the stylistic choices made pose a powerful influence on their audience. Given the established wine trade between Australia and China and the rapid and continuing development of China's own wine industry, intercultural communication is an emerging challenge for wine education and business development.

References

Archer, D., A. Wilson, & P. Rayson. 2002. Introduction to the USAS category system. Benedict project report.

Bennett, M. 2013. *Basic Concepts of Intercultural Communication: Paradigms, Principles, & Practices.* Boston, MA: Intercultural Press.

Boers, F. & S. Lindstromberg. (eds.). 2008. *Applications of Cognitive Linguistics.* Berlin, Germany: Mouton de Gruyter.

Caballero, R. & E. Suárez-Toste. E. 2008. Translating the senses: Teaching the metaphors in winespeak. *Applications of Cognitive Linguistics*, 6: 241.

Garside, R. & N. Smith. 1997. A hybrid grammatical tagger: CLAWS4. In R. Garside, G. Leech, and A. McEnery (eds.) *Corpus Annotation: Linguistic Information from Computer Text Corpora* (102–121). London, UK: Longman.

Kövecses, Z. 2005. *Metaphor in Culture: Universality and Variation.* New York, NY: Oxford University Press.

Lakoff, G. & M. Johnson. 1980. *Metaphors We Live By.* Chicago, IL: University of Chicago Press.

Steen, G. J., A. G. Dorst, J. B. Herrmann, A. A. Kaal, T. Krennmayr, & T. Pasma. 2010. *A Method for Linguistic Metaphor Identification: From MIP to MIPVU* (Vol. 14). Amsterdam, The Netherlands: John Benjamins Publishing.

Stockwell, P. 2006. Language and literature: Stylistics. In B. Aarts & A. McMahon (eds.), *The Handbook of English Linguistics.* pp. 742–758.

从认知隐喻的视角分析《到十九号房间》中苏珊的思维风格

于 华 郭 建 （中国科学院大学）

Mind Style of Susan in *To Room Nineteen* from Perspective of Cognitive Metaphor

Yu Hua Guo Jian （**University of Chinese Academy of Sciences**）

摘 要：短篇小说《到十九号房间》反映了作者多丽丝·莱辛的女性主义视角,反映了在社会上处于弱势地位的女性为寻求自我、争取独立自由而做出的反抗和付出的代价。本文基于认知文体学理论,结合概念隐喻理论,从蛇的隐喻对小说女主人公苏珊的思维风格文体分析,从而引导读者更好地把握和理解作品的主题。

关键词：《到十九号房间》；隐喻；思维风格；蛇

Abstract：Doris Lessing's short story *To Room Nineteen* reflects women's struggle and sacrifice in the male-dominated society and culture. Susan, a middle-aged full-time housewife from an affluent middle-class family, is the main character in this short novel. Based on cognitive stylistics theory, the paper made an analysis of repetitive metaphors of "snake" in *To Room Nineteen* from the perspective of cognitive metaphor theory in order to reveal Susan's characteristic mind style. This analysis could help literary readers to construct and interpret Susan's mental world and understand the theme of the short story well.

Key words：*To Room Nineteen*；metaphor；mind style；snake

多丽丝·莱辛是一位多产的英国作家，2007 年获得诺贝尔文学奖。短篇小说《到十九号房间》(*To Room Nineteen*)最初发表在 1963 年出版的短篇小说合集《一个男人和两个女人》中。小说描写了女主人公苏珊作为家庭主妇的生活，以及她在经历了精神崩溃和思维混乱等痛苦的挣扎后自杀的悲剧。国内对《十九号房间》的研究主要集中在文学评论方面，多在女权主义等方面做文章(杜鹃，2009；王媛，2014)。本文将运用认知隐喻理论来分析《到十九号房间》中苏珊的思维风格，从而探索这篇短篇小说的主题意义。

1. 思维风格研究和隐喻研究的发展

Fowler 于 1997 年将"思维风格"定义为："一致的结构选择，把呈现的世界按照这样或者那样的方式进行切分，由此给人以特定世界观的印象。"(Fowler, 1997)思维风格是"呈现个体精神世界的独特的语言表达"。思维风格这一概念可以用来分析小说作者、叙事者和人物。例如，在分析小说时，小说的语言类型(包括小说作者所使用的词汇、句法特征和及物性)与小说人物的世界观或认知局限联系在一起。

Leech & Short 在《小说文体论：英语小说的语言学入门》一书中，进一步阐释了思维风格，认为"思维风格是人物理解、认知虚构世界的独特方式"(Leech & Short, 1981)，并将"思维风格"划入文体，单列一章。Leech & Short 提出思维风格是文本的固有属性，归属于作者、叙事者和人物。Leech & Short 把不同类型的思维风格，排成了一个级阶：从"自然的和非人工的"到"非正统的"，即从正常到非正常的排列。他们的分析主要集中在非正常思维风格上。在分析方法上，Leech & Short 建立了一个以语言学为基础的分析模式，包括整体结构、词汇、语法和语篇四个因素(刘世生，2002)。

认知语言学的发展为思维风格这一概念的研究提供了新的角度。文体学家 Semino & Swindlehurst 认为思维风格与个体的"认知习惯、能力和缺陷相关"(Semino & Swindlehurst, 1996)，主要是"个人的或者认知的"。与传统的思维风格分析不同的是，她们关注的是隐喻、认知和思维风格的关系。

Lakoff & Johnson 在 1980 年出版的《我们赖以生存的隐喻》一书中首次提出概念隐喻理论。Lakoff & Johnson 认为隐喻将"一个概念域(源域)映射到另一个概念域(目的域)"(Lakoff & Johnson, 1980)，是形成人类概念系统的主要认知手段。概念隐喻理论研究的对象分为常规隐喻和非常规隐喻，其中常规隐喻与特定的文化相联系，体现了某个语言群体所共有的世界观，而非常规隐喻的使用则"反映出个性化的认知习惯，是个人了解、谈论世界的独特方式,即独特的思维风格"(束定芳,2003)。

认知语言学认为隐喻体现了个体感知和认知的视角。因此将概念隐喻与思维风格理论结合起来,可以从认知文体的角度分析揭示人物的思维风格,从而为理解和欣赏文学文体提供新的视角和方法。本文主要从《到十九号房间》中"蛇"的隐喻来分析苏珊的思维风格。

2. "蛇"在西方文学作品中的原始喻体和内涵

根据《圣经·旧约》的《创世纪》,蛇引诱夏娃和亚当偷吃禁果——智慧果,让他们拥有了分辨善恶的能力,打破了上帝所创造的无忧无虑的伊甸园生活方式,这是上帝所不允许的。因此,上帝对蛇说:"你既做了这事,就必受诅咒,比一切的牲畜野兽更甚。你必用肚子行走,终身吃土。"(中国基督教协会,1989)在希伯来与基督文化中,蛇是引诱人类堕落的始作俑者,是撒旦的化身,是被咒骂的对象,是野心、邪恶和诱惑的代表。在《圣经·新约》的《马太福音》中,上帝指责那邪恶之人:"毒蛇的种类! 你们既是恶人,怎能说出好话来呢?"(中国基督教协会,1989)在《新约全书》的《启示录》中,一条大红龙要吃掉"身披日头,脚踏月亮,头戴十二星皇冠"的女人所生的儿子,"大龙就是那古蛇,名叫魔鬼,又叫撒旦,是迷惑天下的。"(中国基督教协会,1989)

在希腊神话中,有时,蛇是英雄成长道路上的一道关卡或难以逾越的险境,最伟大的半神赫拉克勒斯就多次与蛇狭路相逢。有时,蛇也会出现在平静的生活中破坏人们的幸福:如果没有毒蛇的出现,俄耳浦斯与欧律狄刻的爱情会是圆满甜蜜的。

中世纪、文艺复兴时期和古典主义时期的许多文学作品中,蛇的意象多少都带有《圣经》的烙印,离不开撒旦这个原型。例如,莎士比亚的悲剧《麦克白》里,麦克白夫人用"在花瓣底下却有一条毒蛇潜伏"来描述麦克白心中的恶(胡续冬,2011)。二十世纪的西方文学中也出现了很多蛇的意象,例如,在康拉德的《诺斯托罗莫》中"蛇"象征了完美世界与堕落世界;艾丽斯·沃克在《紫色》中以"蛇"来比喻一个黑人女性梅里迪安;托尼·莫里森的小说《秀拉》的主人公秀拉眉宇间就有一枚既像玫瑰又像响尾蛇的胎记,秀拉本人则被认为是罪恶和不幸的根源(李葛送,2008)。

3.《到十九号房间》中"蛇"的隐喻与苏珊的思维风格

短篇小说《到十九号房间》的开头为我们描绘了一幅西方现代社会中常见

而又典型的婚姻生活图景:苏珊和马修均来自中产阶层,聪明理智,有着体面的工作和丰厚的收入;婚后,苏珊为养育四个子女辞退了工作,甘当一名家庭主妇;一家人居住在环境优雅的花园洋房里,保姆和家庭教师定时来提供服务。所有的这一切似乎很完美,然而当孩子们渐渐长大、可以独立地去学校接受教育之后,家庭主妇苏珊的内心发生了极大的变化。孤独和寂寞,再加上马修的一夜情给她的打击,让苏珊对美满的婚姻产生了怀疑。他人羡慕的大房子成了禁锢自由的枷锁。她的精神开始空虚,忙忙碌碌送完孩子去学校后,她回到花园洋房,却发现这里没有真正属于她自己的空间。从阁楼上的"妈妈的房间"到独自旅游,一次又一次,她渴望寻找安静的空间来获得精神上的慰藉和解脱。最终苏珊在廉价旅馆中的十九号房间里找到了她的自我空间。然而,丈夫马修的怀疑和窥探,导致了她的绝望。为寻求解脱,苏珊在十九号房间打开煤气自杀了(Lessing, 1980)。

小说中多次出现蛇的意象。作品中蛇的隐喻与苏珊内心世界的挣扎相关联。首先,在开头部分描绘完苏珊和马修一家幸福美满的生活之后,作者笔锋一转,写道:"他们的生活好像是一条咬住自己尾巴的蛇。"令人胆战心寒的蛇与之前描绘的宁静而甜蜜的画面形成了鲜明的对比,预示着祸害、不幸与悲剧。如同希腊神话的毒蛇或巨蟒一样,蛇在作品中的突然显现,预示着在苏珊平静的生活中,某种力量将要破坏她的幸福和她的生活。接着,一天马修向苏珊坦白了自己的一次一夜情。尽管苏珊表面上原谅了马修,但她难以释怀,她的心理在这一事件后开始发生巨大的变化。一天,苏珊在自家花园中出现幻觉,将风中树枝的影子错以为是一条摆动的、扭曲的蛇,她的精神非常紧张,时刻在提防着、躲避着一种无形的威胁和恐惧。"蛇"在这里隐喻了苏珊心里的恐惧,是她压抑、紧张的内心世界的外化(黎林,2008)。

另外,这部作品在营造蛇的意象时手法独特,将蛇的意象从形状、颜色和声音等不同的方面进行解构,以蛇的某个特征代替整体,使得蛇的意象及其隐喻贯穿整篇小说。苏珊家门前的那条河在苏珊的眼里是"深棕色的缓缓流动的",在形状、颜色和行动的方式上均好似一条深色的缓缓前行的蛇。一种无形的威胁在慢慢地、无声地向苏珊逼近,此时的苏珊开始感觉到精神上的空虚和迷惘了。渐渐地,苏珊开始感觉到家中的花园里有个魔鬼在威胁着她。在她精神迷茫或恍惚时,她甚至感到自己能够亲眼看到这个魔鬼:他的面庞赤红,一头黄毛,身着红色的外套。夸张的色彩,警戒色一样的颜色组合,好似一条花哨的毒蛇,可怕而又危险,邪恶而又难以抵挡。此时的苏珊几近精神崩溃。在作品中,作者以阳性第三人称单数(he)来指代那个邪恶的魔鬼,即蛇。可以说,通过人称代词的使用,蛇的隐喻更明显了——它意味着男权社会给女性带来的无形的控制、压力和恐惧。在这之后,苏珊和马修在卧室里对话时习惯性地一遍遍地梳着头发。梳子划过头发时产生静电,发出"嘶嘶嘶"(hiss, hiss, hiss)的声音,好像蛇在嘶嘶地吐着信子,在向她发出进攻前的警告,此时的苏珊貌似理智、冷静,实则完全崩溃。她心中的那个"魔鬼"离她越来越近,完全控制住了她,随时会将她吞噬。小说的结尾部分,苏珊打开煤气,煤气泄漏时也发出"嘶嘶嘶"的声音。最后苏珊在平静之中结束了自己的生命。

在这部作品中,蛇隐喻了男权社会,而蜗牛则隐喻了身处弱势的女性。小说结尾部分,苏珊将自己想象成一只蜗牛,试图将自己缩进十九号房间里,就像一只探出了脑袋的蜗牛想重新缩回壳里。在男权社会中,女性不可避免地成为社会中被男性控制或统治的对象。凶恶的蛇代表了在社会中处于强势地位的男性,以及他们给女性带来的威胁,而软弱的蜗牛则代表了处于弱势地位的女性。苏珊与丈夫马修的关系,或者说在男权社会中女性与男性之间的关系,就像是蜗牛与蛇的关系,蜗牛的命运自然是不幸的、悲剧的。

4. 结语

思维风格是文体的一个重要方面,认知文体学的研究关注概念隐喻与个人心理的关系。本文尝试性地通过对《到十九号房间》中女主人公苏珊思维风格的认知分析,发现小说中蛇的隐喻与苏珊压抑、紧张、空虚、迷惘的精神状态相关联。通过思维风格的隐喻分析,读者可以走进苏珊的内心世界,从而更好地理解男权社会中女性为寻求独立自由所付出的努力和代价。

参考文献

Fowler, R. 1997. *Linguistics and the Novel*. London: Methuen.

Lakoff, G. & M. Johnson. 1980. *Metaphors We Live By*. Chicago: University of Chicago Press.

Leech, G. & M. Short. 1981. *Style in Fiction: A Linguistic Introduction to English Fictional Prose*. London: Longman.

Lessing, D. 1980. *Stories*. New York: Vintage Books. pp. 396-428.

Semino, E. & K. Swindlehurst. 1996. Metaphor and mind style in Ken Kesey's *One Flew Over the Cuckoo's Nest. Style*, 30 (1): 147.

杜　鹃. 2009. 从《到十九号房间》看多丽丝·莱辛的女性意识.《长春师范学院学报:人

文社会科学版》(4):140—142.

胡续冬.2011.细读玛丽·奥利弗的《蛇》.《语文建设》(1):58—60.

李葛送.2008.《圣经》影响下的文学艺术中蛇意象探源.《湖州师范学院学报》(4):69—72.

黎　林.2008.《到十九号房间》的意象研究.《天津外国语学院学报》(5):58—64.

刘世生.2002.文学文体学:理论与方法.《外语教学与研究》(3):194—197.

束定芳.2003.隐喻学研究.上海:上海外语教育出版社.

王　嫄.2014.《到十九号房间》的生态女性主义解读.《安徽工业大学学报(社会科学版)》(2):61—62.

中国基督教协会.1989.圣经(英文新标准修订版).中国基督教协会,创世纪:4.

中国基督教协会.1989.圣经(英文新标准修订版).中国基督教协会,马太福音:12.

中国基督教协会.1989.圣经(英文新标准修订版).中国基督教协会,启示录:12.

Readers' Reconstruction of Persse's Characterization under Schema Theory[*]

Li Limin　(**Northwest University of Politics and Law**)

Abstract：Persse is a character in David Lodge's masterpiece *Small World*, most of the studies hold that Persse is the protagonist and the narrative speed in the novel is governed by his actions. However, by revealing readers' construing processes of Persse's characterization with the help of scheme theory and the prototype of Percival, the paper finds that Persse is the hero in the semantic level; he is the pursuer, the saver but not the real hero in the structural level. The ironic effect is achieved during the processes of reconstructing Persse's characterization.

Key words：schema theory；reader；Parzival；Persse；characterization

1. Introduction

Schema theory is an important idea in cognitive stylistics which derives primarily from psychology and artificial intelligence. "A schema (plural 'schemata') is a cognitive structure which provides information about our understanding of generic entities, events and situations, and in so doing helps to scaffold our mental understanding of the world" (Emmott, Alxander, & Marszalek, 2014：268). Since the 1920s, it has become firmly established in applied linguistics and discourse analysis. Stylisticians and researchers in related fields such as narratology have used these findings from psychology and artificial intelligence in many different ways. One of the important

---

　* 本论文系教育部项目"认知诗学视阈下《小世界》中浪漫传奇的原型研究"的阶段性成果。

applications is to literature. Different from those regarding literature as a social discourse, Guy Cook (1994: 191) holds that literature is a discourse deviation. During the process of understanding, writers, readers and characters all experience schema preserving, schema reinforcing, schema disrupting and schema refreshing (includes schema destroying, schema constructing, and schema connecting).

"Schema theory is important not only because it explains a central mechanism by which all reading takes place, but also because ' special effects ' can be created by an author through the subversion, exploitation, alteration, or violation of a reader's schema knowledge" (Emmott, Alxander, & Marszalek, 2014: 268). This article shows how the text could violate readers' existent schemata knowledge of Percival and reconstruct a new Persse. Actually, there are more than hundreds of papers and dissertations studies on *Small World*, and less than five articles discuss the character Persse. In her paper "On the Myth Archetype in *Small World*" (2013), Wang Xia asserts that Persse is the Holy Grail knight from exploring the connotative meaning of Persse's name. In her article " On the ' Anti-romance ' Elements in *Small World*" (2008), Ma Daozhen holds that Persse's question activates Kingfisher's academic talents; Persse is the hero in *Small World*. However, with the help of scheme theory and the prototype of Percival, the paper finds that Persse is the hero in the semantic level; he is the pursuer, the saver, but not the real hero in the structural level.

2. Studies on Characterization under Schema Theory

Until now, a few scholars use schema theory to analyze characters in literary works. Among them, Jonathan Culpeper is a rather influential one. In one of his papers " A Cognitive Approach to Characterization: Katherina in Shakespeare's *The Taming of the Shrew*", Culpeper analyzes Katherina from the social schemata and concludes that the protagonist "Katherina is not simply a shrew, or an inconsistent character, or a typical character of a farce" (2000: 291). In his latest paper " Reflections on a Cognitive Stylistic Approach to Characterization" (2009), Culpeper proposes a general theory of characterization which is suitable to all genres.

What's more, in Culpeper's "A Cognitive Approach to Characterization", he holds that schema theory is going to be flourished in social cognition, and it is always related to the notion of "cognitive stereotypes". Stereotype is different from prototype, stereotype equals to the most representative member of a prototypical category. On the contrary, Emmott (2003: 295 – 321) focuses on minor characters, especially those in detective fictions. She states the importance of minor characters in stories by analyzing their representatives of social institutions or general public. These studies on literary characterization under the Schema theory obtain new findings because of the new perspective and methodology.

3. Dynamic Construction of Schemata Model in Characterization

To understand authors' implications from wording, readers need to consult their appropriate generic knowledge from schemata. This process is called filling gaps. In David Lodge's masterpiece *Small World*, nearly all characters' prototypes can be found in classical romance. Thus, readers have to extrapolate details either not mentioned at all in the novel or not fully specified. Moreover, when readers' "knowledge of typical text structure" conflict with "text-specific knowledge of a particular fictional world" (Emmott, 1994: 21), different schemata need to be readjusted. In this section, we try to make clear the working mechanism of the schema theory on literary texts.

Peter Stockwell and Guy Cook have different viewpoints on schema theory, especially when it is applied to literature. Cook manages to make the schema theory explain the linguistic and text-structural deviations. Cook emphases the importance of schema refreshment and cognitive change in literary discourse, and the schema refreshment includes schema destroying, schema constructing, and schema connecting. In addition, Cook claims that "the quality of refreshment is reader-dependent" (1994: 192) and the major function of a discourse is to "effect a change in the schemata of their readers" (1994: 191).

Stockwell has different division of sub-schemata compared with Cook. Stockwell argues that the "most everyday discourse is schema preserving" (2002: 79). Literary schemata are higher-level conceptual structures that organize readers' way of reading when they are in the literary context. Stockwell points out that a literary text needs three schemata to operate: "world schemas, text schemas, and language schemas" (2002: 80).

As long as this section deals with schemata model in characterization, for the analysis of characters in text by schema theory, people always regard that characters are guided by schemata. They will provide a scaffolding for incoming character information once they are activated. Moreover, schemata allow readers to make further knowledge-based inferences, and flesh-out readers' impressions of character. The complexity and indeterminacy of characters can be shown through the process. This is like what Michael Toolan (1988) "refers to as the 'iceberg' phenomenon in characterization: the idea that the words of a text are the observable part of a character impression, and beyond them lies the unobservable but inferable and large part" (Culpeper, 2002: 263).

Both Cook and Stockwell make great contribution to the schema theory, but if their models are used to analyze characters in literary texts, they are not as dynamic as characters. The model of "dynamic reconstructions of characterization schemata" is based on Cook's "discourse effects on schemata"; it is improved by stating that the schemata are not static in human's mind. It is a recycling circle. It has three big entries: schema preserving, schema disrupting, and schema reestablishing. In the first stage of schema preserving, the schema adding has two sub-branches. One goes to schema reinforcement when the schema adding does not interrupt the main characterization of a person. When the schema adding is so tremendous that it threatens the main feature of a person, the schema interruption will occur. In the schema interruption stage, the partially disrupted characterization and the new information in the novel form the schema construction stage, but the total disruption goes to another stage-schema re-establishment. The schema re-establishment stage will have the same developing processes as schema preserving, schema reinforcement, schema interruption.

The schema preserving goes to schema disrupting when the additional elements are numerable to change the characterization of the schema. In the schema disrupting process, readers need to destroy the pre-existent schema, construct a new schema from new textual knowledge, and make connections with the pre-existent schema. The refreshed schema to some extent is a new schema, and it can be called the schema re-establishing. A new schema

Constructing Characterization in Literary Text

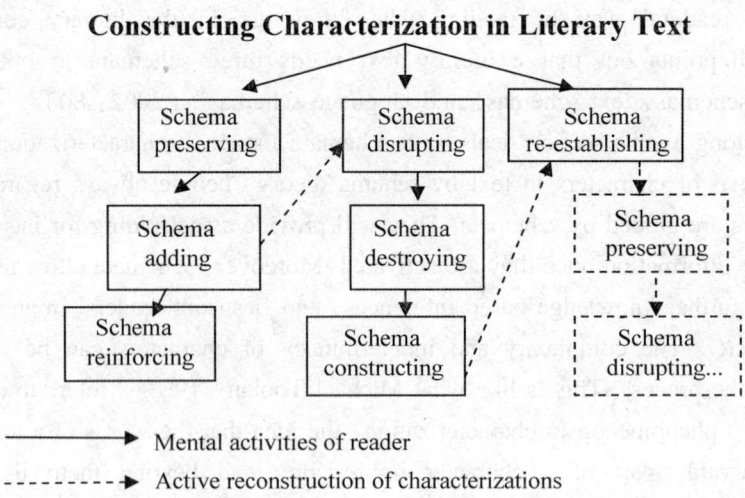

Figure 1.1 **Dynamic Reconstructions of Characterization Schemata (Li Limin)**

establishes, and readers preserve the schema in their mind. When reading happens, the dynamic schemata operate in readers' mind. Bearing these character archetypes in mind, reader will reconstruct the characterization of the characters in *Small World*.

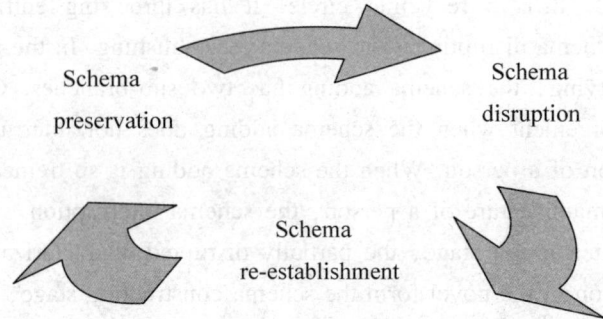

Figure 1.2 **Schema Circle (Li Limin)**

4. Prototypical Characterization of Persse

Persse in *Small World* is depicted according to *Parzival*, a romance written by Chretien de Troyes around 1180. Parzival is the Grail knight or one of the Grail knights in numerous medieval and modern stories of the Grail quest. His natural prowess leads him to Arthur's court. He is the perfect knight and ideal hero, encompassing purity and strength, holiness and courage in his quest for the Holy Grail.

Parzival has a mysterious birth like many other heroes. There are many versions of Parzival's birth. One version is that he has a noble birth in Robert de Boron; his father is stated to be either King Pellinore or another worthy knight. His mother is usually unnamed but plays a significant role in the stories. His sister is the bearer of the Holy Grail, she is sometimes named Dindrane. Other versions mainly state that he has an unknown father, and his leaving of his mother causes his mother's death. The mysterious birth of Parzival is one characterization of him.

Parzival is also an innocent fool. Like a Germanic name Persifal, "Persi" means innocent, and "fal" means fool. When Perzival leaves the wilderness and enters into the society, he is as pure as a white board. He has no father, no manor, no fame, no gentility, and has little idea about knighthood.

Most significantly, Parzival is a developing hero in both Chretien's and Wolfram's treatments. In Book V of Wolfram, Parzival says of one of the clownish actions of his youth, "May I suffer shame and scorn forever in this life and the next if this lady did do anything amiss when I snatched her brooch from her and took her golden ring as well. I was a fool then, not a man, and not yet grown to wisdom" (Scholes & Kellogg, 1966: 168). This sort of speech represents a revolution in romance characterization. He cannot resist the temptation from the ladies and fails his holy task at the beginning. But he realizes his faults and in the future pursuing, he regains the virtue and finally achieves his goal.

Above all, Parzival in the Grail Legend is handsome, innocent, powerful, gentle, and can resist different kinds of temptations. In order to find the Grail and cure the King and save his kingdom, he steps into the self-improving journey. All the evil traits that cursed by the Christianity should be overcome in order to fulfill a knight dream.

5. Readers' Construction of the Prototype of Persse

When reading a novel, the first thing for a reader to do is to construct a space for a story to develop, in that space, characters, plot and situations are gradually looming as the narrative goes. The same is true to *Small World*.

Because the subtitle of the novel — an academic romance — has already activated readers' schemata of the classic romance, and Persse is the first character that has been narrated by the author who requires readers to construct his image first. Persse might be a knight in the novel, readers may have that guess. In order to inform readers that Persse is a derivative character who comes from the classic romance, Lodge contrives a dialogue between Persse and Angelica by discussing the meaning of his name. Their discussions about Persse's name may intrigue readers' pre-existent schema about the Holy Grail and his knights.

1. "Hallo, what's your name?"...
   "**Persse McGarrigle** — from Limerick," he eagerly replied.
   "Persse? Is that short for **Percival**?"
   ...
   "It's a variant of '**Pearce**'." He spelled it out for her.
   "Oh, like in *Finnegans Wake*! The Ballad of Persse O'Reilley."
   "Exactly so. **Persse**, **Pearce**, **Pierce** — I wouldn't be surprised if they were not all related to **Percival. Percival**, *per se*, as Joyce might have said," he added, and was rewarded with another dazzling smile.
   "What about **McGarrigle**?"
   "It's an old Irish name that means '**Son of Super-valour**'."

   (*Small World*: 10)

Angelica provides several possibilities for the name Persse through several sentences. Actually, in *Small World*, Angelica is depicted as an expert in romance, and the derivations of Persse are quite familiar to her. Through her mouth, the background information about the character can be clearly drawn.

Angelica reviews all figures who share the same given name with Persse in literature history, like in medieval romance, *King Arthur and His Knights, Parzival*, and James Joyce's works, and finds that "Persse" is a knight in all these literary works. The same pronunciation of words with different spellings like "Persse, Pearce, Pierce" provides various possibilities for the interpretation of his name. Will he still be a knight in *Small World*?

According to the schema theory, when people read literary texts, they presumably activate their knowledge of the activities normally associated with filling in the gaps and making the narrative coherent; the "normally associated" contextual information in this dialogue is the family name.

"McGarrigle" has the similar pronunciation with "Grail" in Grail Legend. Moreover, the family name "McGarrigle" is an Irish name which means "a man of super-power".

From the name of Persse McGarrigle, readers can construct that the character Persse is derived from *Parzival* and expect that his deeds might be the same as in the Grail Legend. More importantly, readers can experience schema preservation through the construction of the meaning of "Persse". According to Persse's family name, he is powerful; and the name "Persse" itself reminds readers that he might be a modern knight in the novel; and Persse himself cannot explain his name properly and fully reinforces readers' schemata about Parzival's mysterious birth. All in all, readers experience schema preserving, schema adding, and schema reinforcing stages in constructing the meaning of Persse's name.

6. Readers' Reconstruction of Persse's Characterizations under Schema Theory

We presume that readers in the article are familiar with the genre of romance, and they have abstracted the prototypical attributes of Parzival: a handsome, innocent, vigorous, strong-willed, faithful and great young knight who brilliantly achieves his great deeds of finding the Holy Grail and saving the country and the king. After connecting the knowledge of Persse in the novel with Parzival in the classic romance, it is time to check that whether Persse's characterizations in the novel confirm to readers' schemata of Percival's or not.

6.1 Schema Preserving

Small World describes a group of scholars who exchange great thoughts by attending different conferences all over the world. Their pursuing goals are various except true knowledge. If the modern literary critical circle is a new waste land, scholars are the knights and the one who pursues the truth is the real hero. The Rummidge conference is Persse's first academic meeting in life, and he is really a green hand. During his conversation with conference veteran Morris Zapp, Persse announces that he wants to "improve himself" and see what is in and what is out in the literary world.

2. That's why I've come to this conference. **To improve myself. To find out**

what's going on in the great world of ideas. Who's in, who's out, and all that.

(*Small World*: 15)

Persse wants to arm himself with ideas. If Persse is the modern knight, then the searching of great ideas equals to quest the Holy Grail. Both Parzival in the classic romance and Persse in *Small World* are pursuing something really precious, their actions preserve the pre-existent schemata of readers'.

6. 2 Schema Disrupting

Generally speaking, knights appeared in medieval literature were gentle, decent, and handsome, and schema disrupting means to destroy the existing schemata. In this entry, it includes schema destroying and schema constructing. The following description of Persse's appearance may lead to readers' schemata disruption of Parzival in the classic romance.

> 3. Before he got back into bed he switched on the lamp above his sink, and stared **critically at his reflection** in the mirror. He saw **a white, round, freckled face, snub nose, pale blue eyes, and a mop of red curly hair**. "I wouldn't say you were handsome, exactly," he murmured. "**But I've seen uglier mugs.**"

(*Small World*: 14)

The word "critically" implies the tone of the description. Then the negative words like "freckled face", "snub nose", "pale blue eyes" and "a mop of red curly hair" are used to portray Persse. This profile is really not handsome, to some extent, it is rather ugly. Even Persse himself is not satisfied with his appearance, and he himself even uses "uglier mugs" to define his face. A man comes from a noteless college with a common family background and an ordinary face, but a heroic name. The above description gives readers a chance to destroy their pre-existent schemata, as long as schema disruption consists of schema destroying and schema constructing, it is not the right time to construct a new character schemata for Persse.

Then the novel describes that Persse exclaims that he is in love. His love to Angelica made him determined to find Angelica even if he needs to travel the world. The journey of pursuing truth suddenly shifts into pursuing love. Grail-searching becomes girl-searching. Schema-destroying and schema-construing take place at the same time. Different from the classic romance's Grail-quest, *Small World* tells readers a story of girl-quest. This mental activity can also be regarded as schema re-establishing, since the main theme of Persse's life becomes searching for Angelica.

Schema re-establishing refers to the new information of a novel totally interrupts readers' pre-existent knowledge about something. When Persse's goal is changed, Parzival's schemata collapse in readers' mind. Because his motive changes, no matter whether he will find the Holy Grail or not, he is no longer the real hero. At that time, readers' schemata about Parzival need to be re-established according to the text-specific knowledge of *Small World*.

The entry schema-preserving encompasses schema-adding and schema-reinforcing. When the schemata add so tremendously, they might change the pre-existent schemata and go to schema-disrupting. When Persse confesses his love toward Angelica, he stresses the pre-marriage virginity on both sides, although it is disdained by Angelica. However, it is a proof to say that Persse is a pure and innocent man in the semantic level.

4. "**I don't mind if you're not a virgin**," said Persse. He added, "**Of course, I'd prefer it if you were.**" ...

"**God forbid it's either**," said Persse, blushing, "**for I'm a virgin myself.**"

"Are you?" Angelica looked at him with interest. "But nowadays people usually sleep together before they get married. Or so I understand."

"**It's against my principles**," said Persse. "But if you promised to marry me eventually, I might stretch a point."

(*Small Wold*: 39–40)

In *Parzival*, innocent belongs to Parzival. But in *Small World*, Persse asks other's innocence (pre-marriage virginity of Angelica). It seems like they have the same theme of purity, but different emphases shows different values and characterizations. If readers have a vague picture that Persse is not the same as Parzival when they find Persse pursues girl, now their guess becomes fact. On the semantic level, Lodge successfully depicts a man who believes in God and always goes to the chapel to purify his soul, but on the structural level, Persse is not pure. Readers experience schemata disruption and re-establishment in this period.

6.3 Schema Adding, Schema Disrupting and Schema Re-establishing

But the pleasure of reading lies in authors conspiracy and readers revealing. In order to give readers an illusion that Persse is Parzival, Lodge intentionally adds more similar plot.

5. This conclusion, however, only pitchforked Persse into another dilemma. Angelica might be inviting him to become her lover, but she would not allow him to make her his bride, not in the immediate future anyway, **so a contingency had to be thought of**, ... he set his features **grimly** and set off **in search of a chemist's shop**.

(Small World: 46-47)

This is the description of Persse receiving Angelica's invitation to go to her room at night. Thinking of staying one night with Angelica, Persse senses that he needs to take some contingent action for the sake of Angelica from Persse's perspective. Persse does not want to make Angelica pregnant, like his cousin Bernadette. So he decides to find a chemist's shop to buy some condoms.

In *Parzival*, there was one episode which narrated Parzival did not resist beauties temptations and told lies to the king. In *Small World*, Persse's action tells readers that his deed does not accord with his words. He believes in pre-marriage virginity, if Angelica's invitation is a test, Persse surely fails to be a decent knight. When desires govern sensibility, goal is disappearing simultaneously. This episode to some extent confuses the readers. Readers, on the one hand, believe that Persse is not Parzival and has no connection with hero; on the other, they doubt that Persse is Parzival. So, it can be seen as schema-adding and schema-disrupting.

This doubt or suspense lasts to the end of the novel. Persse attends the MLA conference because he heard Angelica will attend the meeting. By chance, after hearing the speeches of different literary theories, such as Structuralism, Deconstructionism, and Neo-Marxism, etc., Persse cannot help asking a question.

6. Persse was aware of himself, **as if he were quite another person**, **getting to his feet and stepping into the aisle and up to a microphone placed directly under the platform**. "I have a question for all the members of the panel," he said. ...

(Small World: 319)

Although scholars have different opinions towards the function of literary criticism, and Arthur Kingfisher, the academic authority, is also puzzled whose statement is right, Persse's question saves everything. When he is asking the question, he feels he is "another person", bravely "getting to his feet and stepping into the aisle and up to a microphone placed directly under the platform". His question is vital because the question cures Kingfisher's impotency in sexuality and in academic creation. The recovery of Kingfisher implies the vitality of the whole academic world. It is like the right question in *Parzival*, which cures the injured Fish-king and saves his kingdom. From this angle, Persse is a decent knight and hero. This specific-text information makes readers experience schemata-adding.

But after a second thought, readers may find that Persse coincidentally asks the question and cures everything. His action is aimless and unintentional; the question is a by-product of searching the girl. Persse's searching is structurally governed by Angelica, without Angelica's passion towards academy and knowledge, Persse will not attend so many academic conferences and of course will not ask the question. Following this logic, readers may experience schema-disrupting and schema re-establishing. Persse is not the real hero, on the contrary, Angelica is.

7. Conclusion

Unlike the prototype of Parzival as a developing character, Persse in *Small World* is rather flat and un-developing. The novel finishes its narrative with Persse starts another round of girl-searching. By projecting Parzival's characterization on Persse, readers gradually reconstruct Persse's characterization through schema-reinforcement, schema-adding, schema-disruption and schema re-establishment. Through the analyses, this article concludes that Persse is only the hero on the semantic level, and his characterization of innocence is substituted by secular social values. His saving of the academic circle is an accidental action, and the underlying action motivation is Angelica, so Angelica is the real hero on the structural level. During readers' reconstruction of Persse's characterizations, they must experience various conflicts between holy and secular, Grail and girl, classic romance canon and modern parody of romance, etc., these conflicts are the main cause of achieving irony.

References

Cook, G. 1994. *Discourse and Literature*. Oxford: Oxford University Press.

Culpeper, J. 2000. A cognitive approach to characterization: Katherina in Shakespeare's *The Taming of the Shrew*. *Language and Literature* 9 (4): 291–316.

Culpeper, J. 2009. Reflections on a Cognitive Stylistic Approach to Characterization. In G. Brone, J. Vandaele (eds.). Applications of Cognitive Linguistics *Cognitive Poetics: Goals, Gains and Gaps*. Berlin, DEU: Mouton de Gruyter, pp. 125–159.

Emmott, C. 1994. *Narrative Comprehension: A Discourse Perspective*. Oxford: Oxford University Press.

Emmott, C. 2003. Constructing social space: Sociocognitive factors in the interpretation of character relations. In D. Herman (ed.). *Narrative Theory and the Cognitive Sciences*. Stanford: CSLI Publications.

Emmott, C., M. Alxander, & A. Marszalek. 2014. Schema theory in stylistics. In M. Burke (ed.). *The Routledge Handbook of Stylistics*. Abingdon: Routledge. pp. 268–283.

Lodge, D. 1984. *Small World: An Academic Romance*. England: Penguin Books.

Scholes, R. & R. Kellogg. 1966. *The Nature of Narrative*. New York: Oxford University Press.

Semino, E. & J. Culpeper. 2002. *Cognitive Stylistics: Language and Cognition in Text Analysis*. Amsterdam: John Benjamins.

Stockwell, P. 2002. *Cognitive Poetics: An Introduction*. London: Routledge.

马道珍. 2008.《小世界》中的"反罗曼司"元素.《扬州职业大学学报》(4):9—12.

汪 霞. 2013. 浅析《小世界》中的神话原型.《湖北第二师范学院学报》(12):17—20;57.

Part III Literary Stylistics

A Discourse Analysis of D. H. Lawrence's *The Prussian Officer*

Lv Zhongshe　(**Tsinghua University**)

Abstract: D. H. Lawrence (1885–1930) from Eastwood, Nottinghamshire, is regarded as one of the most influential writers of the twentieth century, who is known for both novels (*The Rainbow, Sons and Lovers, Women in Love* and *Lady Chatterley's Lover*) and short stories (*Odour of Chrysanthemums, The Virgin and the Gypsy, The Prussian Officer* and *Rocking-Horse Winner*). This study analyzes *The Prussian Officer* (1914) by combining Chatman's (1978) narrative theory and Short's (1996) discourse structure of fictional prose. The findings are, although the orderly murdered his Captain, readers tend to sympathize with him and regard him as the real victim, considering the mistreatment he got from the Captain, which has been achieved by DISCOURSE, that is, how the story has been told.

Key words: discourse; narrative; setting; character; murder

1. Introduction

D. H. Lawrence (1885 – 1930) from Eastwood, Nottinghamshire, UK, is regarded as one of the most influential writers of the twentieth century, who is known for both novels (*The Rainbow, Sons and Lovers, Women in Love* and *Lady Chatterley's Lover*) and short stories (*Odour of Chrysanthemums, The Virgin and the Gypsy, The Prussian Officer* and *Rocking-Horse Winner*).

　　The Prussian Officer was first published in 1914 in Lawrence's collection entitled: *The Prussian Officer and Other Stories*. *The Prussian Officer* sounds like a war story, which is partially true. Instead of a physical war, it is about a psychological war between an officer and an orderly. The officer, who is jealous, cruel and arrogant, wants to conquer and manipulate the orderly. Though from a Prussian aristocrat family, the officer has not achieved much in his career or in his personal life. It is true that he is an expert in riding horses, but to domineer over soldiers is totally different. Having been sexually repressed, he got jealous of his orderly's falling in love, of his youth and vigor. Therefore, the officer began to provoke and torture the orderly both physically and mentally. The orderly tries everything he can to avoid direct conflict with the officer. However, the more he tries, the more furious and irritated the officer becomes. Finally, the conflict between the two soldiers reaches the climax in which the orderly murdered his officer out of the long-time tense, repression and hatred.

This study analyzes *The Prussian Officer* by combining Chatman's (1978) narrative theory and Short's (1996) discourse structure of fictional prose. Chatman's narrative consists of story content and discourse expression. Story content refers to form of content and substance of content, while discourse expression refers to form of expression and substance of expression. Short's (1996) opinion about points of view in discourse structure helps us to better understand why the story has been told in the way it is, which is the writer's rebellishment through discourse. The findings are: though the orderly committed crime by murdering the captain, readers tend to sympathize with him and regard him as the real victim, considering the mistreatment he got from the Captain, which has been achieved by the writers' discourse, that is, the way Lawrence delineates his story.

2. Literature Review

The short story is a modern form of literature, in which a writer presents real, ordinary events in rich and concise description of a scene, characters and a sequence of happenings. Those descriptions are so vivid that readers often develop a kind of illusion that they are actually there, and that they see and feel as much as the characters do (Kennedy & Gioia, 2002). Different from fables and fairytales, scenes, characters, happenings and even speeches/ thoughts in short stories all sound real and meaningful. The comprehensive diagram for the structure of a narrative text proposed by Chatman (1978: 26) and the discourse structure of fictional prose by Short (1996) render some significance in our reading and appreciating short stories.

2. 1　Structuralist Theory on Narrative

As early as 1980, Chatman (1978: 26) proposed a comprehensive diagram for the structure of a narrative text:

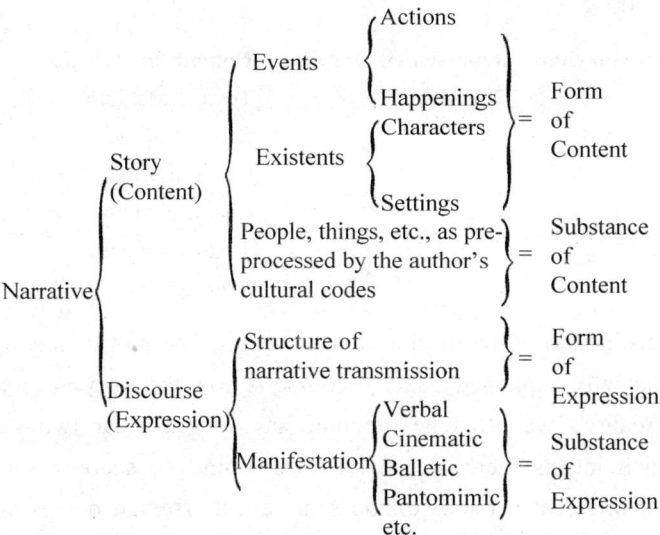

As is shown in this diagram, a narrative is composed of two elements: Story and Discourse. Story is the content of a narrative, which is actually what has happened, who has been involved and where the events took place; while discourse are the ways in which the writer has chosen to tell the story. Discourse is the writer's subjective expression to communicate with his/her readers about how the story takes place. "Discourse looks at the artistic and individualized working with and around the genres, the conventions, the basic story patterns, in the distinctive styles, voices or manners of different authors" (Toolan, 1992: 10). This explains why some stories are highly valued, while some are not, because different writers can achieve different effects through different discourses or expressions when they choose to tell the same story. There is a vast variety of discourses concerning how a narrative is developed, elaborated and delineated, which not only imprints an individual author (Simpson, 2004: 18), but also affects how a reader interprets the narrative. Chatman (1978) realizes the fundamental role of "Structure of narrative transmission" or "form of expression" (See the above diagram) in narrative.

Short (1996: 256) uses the term "the discourse structure" and highlights its function by stating that discourse structure is essential, because it is the way the writer influences, if not decides, how the reader understands the story.

2. 2　Discourse Structure

Simpson uses the following to illustrate the structure of a narrative discourse (Simpson, 2004: 20):

Abstract storyline	Represented storyline	Domain in stylistics
Plot	Discourse	Textual Medium
		Sociolinguisitc code
		Characterization 1 actions and events
		Characterization 2 points of views
		Textual structure
		Intertextuality

There is a distinction between plot and discourse. The plot of a story refers to "what has actually happened" and discourse is how the story is "represented" or told. In reality, we often hear people say "let us hear two sides of the story", which means there are various viewpoints to account for the same happening or different versions of the same event. Human beings are inclined to represent or tell the happenings with their own comments, opinions, attitudes and even assumptions, summarized as "evaluation" by Labov (1972) or "value-laden expressions" by Short (1996). Consequently this evaluation results in great impacts upon hearers' understanding of the happening. This is the same case in reading literature. As Short (1996: 257) states at least three levels of discourse are needed to understand the basic discourse structure of a novel or a short story: the highest level is between novelist and reader, the second level is between narrator and narratee and the basic level is between characters, as is shown in the following diagram.

　　The following diagram indicates that there are several different points of views, that is to say, several possible ways of presenting the same story.

　　However, no matter how many linguistic indications of viewpoints there are, they are all expressed by the writer/author through discourse. Actually it is the writer/author who guides, affects or even manipulates the readers' interpretation of what they are reading through his/her choice of discourse and these choices have a profound impact on the way literary works, such as novels and short stories are structured and understood (Simpson, 2004:22).

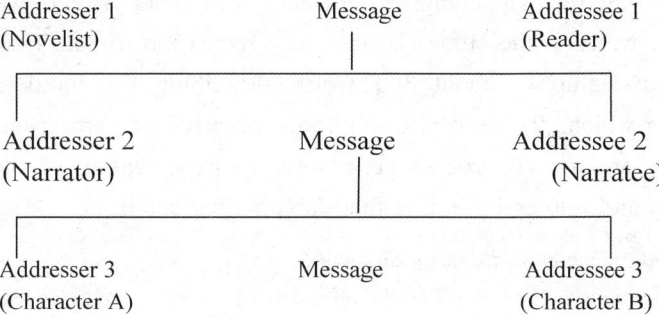

Addresser 1   Message   Addressee 1
(Novelist)   (Reader)

Addresser 2   Message   Addressee 2
(Narrator)   (Narratee)

Addresser 3   Message   Addressee 3
(Character A)   (Character B)

3. A Discourse Analysis of Lawrence's *The Prussian Officer*

This section is going to analyze the particular language employed by Lawrence in describing the events and existents of the short story. According to Leech (2008: 55), "The study of style is essentially the study of variation in the use of language." *The Prussian Officer* has been chosen to demonstrate that a close examination of the language of the short story leads to a deeper and better understanding and appreciation of the story.

3. 1 Detailed Analysis of Story in *The Prussian Officer*

Story includes Events and Existents. In *The Prussian Officer*, story is sketched like the following:

Story:
- **Events: Actions and Happenings**

  Actions: the orderly murdered the Captain

  Happenings: the Captain tortured or mistreated his orderly both physically and psychologically
- **Existents: Characters and Settings**

  Characters: the Captain and his orderly

  Settings: military marching

3.1.1 Events in Story

This section will analyze the language used by Lawrence in describing events, which are the murdering of the Captain and the orderly's mistreatment from the Captain.

3.1.1.1 Actions: The Murdering of the Captain

Compared with the happenings (delineated with over 3,200 words), the murdering, which is the climax of the story seems too trivial. There are only two short paragraphs, about 300 words describing the murdering of the Captain. Of which, 27 verbs referring to the orderly as a participant in the role of actor, 7 are mental process verbs describing perception of the orderly's observation and impression rather than his physical action:

> The orderly watched the lid of the mug ...
> And then he (the orderly) saw the thin, strong throat of the elder man ...
> Then, with a start, he noticed the nostrils ...
> He had hated the face of the Captain.

Only 3 verbs are transitive. Here the orderly is the actor or the doer of the action.

> ... the orderly, with serious, earnest young face, and underlip between his teeth, had got his knee in the officer's chest and was pressing the chin backward over the further edge of the tree-stump.
> ... he shoved back the head of the other man ...

Interesting enough, there are 11 verbs or participles in which the orderly is affected either in passive voice or as the recipient, rather than the doer of action:

> ... as if he were fascinated.
> Heavy convulsions shook the body of the officer, frightening and horrifying the young soldier.
> Yet it pleased him, too, to repress them.
> It pleased him to keep his hands pressing back the chin ...
> It shocked and distressed him.
> It represented more than the thing which had kicked and bullied him.
> He was afraid to look at the eyes.
> In his heart he was satisfied.

All the above examples illustrate clearly the passiveness in the orderly's role as a murderer, which suggests that the murder is not long planned, and that it is only a result of long suppression that bursts automatically and ultimately.

3.1.1.2 Happenings: The Orderly's Mistreatment from the Captain

Lawrence puts lots of efforts (over 3,200 words) to develop the plot, i.e.

what has actually happened between the Captain and the orderly before the final action — murder — takes place. The Captain has bullied his orderly out of jealousy and his own depression and frustration. The following table presents all the happenings:

Table 1　Causes and effects of the happenings

Happenings	Causes	Responses	Effects
1	*Once, when a bottle of wine had gone over, and the red gushed out on to the tablecloth ...*	*The officer had started up with an oath, and his eyes, bluey like fire, had held those of the confused youth for a moment.*	*And from that time an undiscovered feeling had held between the two men. Henceforward the orderly was afraid of really meeting his master. ... the soldier wanted to be left alone, in his neutrality as servant, but he performed his duty.*
2	No reason, only *the influence of the young soldier's being, and his certain zest irritated the officer.*	*The Captain gave him sharp orders, took up as much of his time as possible. Sometimes he flew into a rage with the young soldier, and bullied him.*	*The Captain could not regain his neutrality of feeling towards his orderly. Nor could he leave the man alone.*
3	No reason, but *a scar on the orderly's left thumb ...*	*He became harsh and cruelly bullying, using contempt and satire.*	
4	No reason at all.	*Once he flung a heavy military glove into the young soldier's face.*	*The orderly tried to serve the officer as if the latter were an abstract authority and not a man, to avoid personal contact, even definite hate; but the officer seemed to be going irritably insane, and the youth was deeply frightened.*

(to be continued)

Happenings	Causes	Responses	Effects
5	*The orderly had a girl friend.*	*The Captain perceived it, and was mad with irritation.*	*He kept the young man engaged all the evenings long, and took pleasure in the dark look that came on the orderly's face.*
6	No reason. *The fellow was too exasperating.*	*At last he slung the end of a belt in his servant's face.*	*When he saw the youth start back, the pain-tears in his eyes and the blood on his mouth, he had felt at once a thrill of deep pleasure and of shame.*
7	The orderly was in a hurry.	The Captain occupied all his evenings out of jealousy for his having a girl friend.	
8	*The orderly had a piece of pencil in his ear.*	*The orderly was pitched forward by a kick ... he was kicked heavily again, and again ... and a kick came heavily against the orderly's thigh.*	*The Captain's heart gave a pang, as of pleasure ... The smile came into the blue eyes ... The young soldier was gone, looking old, and walking heavily ... Deep inside the Captain was the intense gratification of his passion ... he successfully refused remembrance. He refused the event of the past night ...*

No matter how well the orderly performed his duty, the Captain kept torturing him both physically and mentally. Naturally the orderly felt frustrated and hated the Captain:

- *when he thought of the kicks, he went sick, and when he thought of the threat of more kicking …, his heart went hot and faint, and he panted, remembering the one that had come … He felt vacant, and wasted … He got to bed at last, and slept inert, relaxed … a dead night of stupefaction shot through with gleams of anguish.*
- *He only wished it would stay night, so that he could lie still, covered up by the darkness …*
- *He felt lost, and dazed, and helpless.*
- *And he went away, feeling as if he himself were coming to pieces, disintegrated … he felt as if he must shut his eyes — as if he must shut his eyes on everything. It was only the long agony of marching with a parched throat that filled him with one single, sleep-heavy intention: to save himself.*

Those happenings lay good foundation for the readers to understand the reasons why the orderly murdered his master. The sole purpose of the murder is to save himself!

3.1.2　Characters and Settings

This section discusses what characters and settings contribute to the plot.

3.1.2.1　A Sharp Contrast between the Captain and the Orderly

There are only two characters in the story; the Captain and the orderly. Neither of them has a name. Nevertheless, Lawrence succeeds in exposing the subtle changes of the emotional relationship between the Captain and the orderly by using simple nouns or noun phrases. In the initial stage, both the Prussian officer and the orderly are introduced with neutral nouns as "the Captain" or the "officer", and "the orderly" or "the soldier". Some changes have taken place gradually. The neutral relationship has changed into a kind of ownership indicated by "his officer", "his orderly"; "the master" and "the servant". Later "young", "youth", "younger" and "elder" are used to show the contrast between the two men. The description of the two characters forms a sharp contrast between the two characters. The following table lists all the differences between the two, including their age, family background information, physical appearance, personal characters, other soldiers' opinion about the Captain and the first impression between the Captain and the orderly.

Table 2 A sharp contrast between the two characters

Brief Summary	The Captain: handsome, cold and haughty; though from an aristocrat family, he is basically a loser.	The Orderly: young and energetic; active and friendly.
Age	*about forty*	*about twenty-two*
Family Background	*from a Prussian aristocrat family, mother being a Polish Countess*	*from a peasant's family*
Career	*had ruined his prospects in the Army, and remained an infantry Captain, for gambling too much …*	*had just joined the Army*
Marital Status	*had never married*	*had a girl friend*
Physical Appearance	*handsome, finely knit figure, reddish-brown, stiff hair, short moustache, a full and brutal mouth, rugged face, thin cheek, blue eyes, with long, fine hands and cultivated movements*	*medium height, well built, had strong, heavy limbs, swarthy, with a soft, black, young moustache; warm and young, had firmly marked eyebrows over dark, expressionless eyes, brown, shapely peasant's hand, strong young shoulders, strong, easy young figure*
Personal Characters	*a gentleman with irritable tension, a man who fights with life; eyes were always flashing with cold fire; haughty and overbearing, a man of passionate temper, always kept himself suppressed, always on the point of breaking out, kept himself hard to the idea of the service*	*seemed never to have thought, only to have received life direct through his senses; acted straight from instinct; blind, instinctive sureness of movement by nature, he was active and had many friends*
Other Soldiers' Opinion	*merely impersonal, though a devil when roused; on the whole, they feared him, but had no great aversion from him. They accepted him as the inevitable.*	*had many friends*
First Impression between the Captain and the Orderly	*cold and just and indifferent: he did not fuss over trifles … his servant knew practically nothing about him, except just what orders he would give, and how he wanted them obeyed*	*young, vigorous, unconscious presence … like a warm flame, so free and self-contained, … the blind, instinctive sureness of movement of the young solider*

This table provides very vivid pictures of the Captain and the soldier, their physical looks as well as their personalities as if they were practically standing in front of us. With those descriptions in mind, it is not difficult for us to understand why the Captain gets jealous of the orderly for his youth, vigor, warmth, innocence, confidence and many other positive personalities. For the Captain those were all gone. He is neither content with his career nor with his personal life, but there is nothing he can do to change the situation. Since he has always kept himself suppressed, he is always on the point of breaking out. Although the orderly like other soldiers did not have great aversion from the Captain, and had tried to accomplish his order and duty all the time, the Captain still got irritated by the orderly simply because of his own long time tense and repression. Gradually they have developed a very strange relationship between themselves: they hate each other, but at the same time they rely on each other. Subconsciously they started a psychological war between themselves:

- *"The orderly felt he was connected with that figure (the Captain): ... he followed it like a shadow, mute and inevitable and damned by it. And the officer was always aware of ... the march of his orderly among the men."*
- *He knew his servant would soon be free, and would be glad. As yet, the soldier had held himself off from the elder man. The Captain grew madly irritable. He could not rest when the soldier was away, and when he was present, he glared at him with tormented eyes.*
- *But he did not want to faint — he did not want anybody to know. No one should ever know.* (The orderly tries to hide his sufferings from other soldiers out of dignity.) *It was between him and the Captain. There were only the two people in the world now — himself and the Captain.*
- *The Captain sat on horseback, watching. He needed to see his orderly.*
- *The orderly must move under the presence of the figure of the horseman.*

The adjectives or noun phrase that are used to depict the Captain and the orderly are called value-laden expressions (See 3.2.1) , which imprint the individuality and personality of the two. First, the Captain, having served in the army for too long, his characters has been inhumanly twisted. Though born of a Prussian aristocrat, well educated, or cultured, he has not achieved as much as he expected. He has remained as an infantry Captain. "*He had never married: his position did not allow of it, and no woman had ever moved him to it.*" To some extent he is a complete loser. This personality of the Captain is one of the key elements which stimulate the development of the conflict between the Captain and the orderly. The second character, the orderly, is young and warm, very innocent. "*He had firmly marked eyebrows over dark, expressionless eyes, that seemed never to have thought, only to have received life direct through his senses, and acted straight from instinct.*" The orderly performed his duty well, but the Captain kept torturing him physically and mentally. Naturally the orderly felt frustrated and despaired, "*He felt lost, and dazed, and helpless ...*", "*And he went away, feeling as if he himself were coming to pieces, disintegrated ... It was only the long agony of marching with a parched throat that filled him with one single, sleep-heavy intention: to save himself.*" Nothing is wrong when one tries to save himself. There is no doubt that the orderly is just the victim of the Captain's inhumanly twisted character.

Furthermore, the expressions concerned to represent the innermost thoughts and feelings of the two reveals the shifts in feeling, relationship and the stream of consciousness of the two males. They start from a neutral officer-solider relationship (The orderly like other soldiers *did not have great aversion from the Captain, though the latter is cold, indifferent and impersonal, and even a devil when roused*); develop into an owner-servant relation (*The elder man was sullenly angry. His servant avoided him. And the next day he had to use all his will-power to avoid seeing the scarred thumb. He wanted to get hold of it and — A hot flame ran in his blood*); and finally get into hatred-dependent relationship. "*It left him rather blank and wondering. Some of his natural completeness in himself was gone, a little uneasiness took its place. And from that time an undiscovered feeling had held between the two men.*"... "*The orderly felt he was connected with that figure (the Captain): ... he followed it like a shadow, mute and inevitable and damned by it. And the officer was always aware of ... the march of his orderly among the men*". Consequently the discourse or "the stylistic flourish" (Simpson, 2008) help the readers to form their opinion and attitudes towards the two characters and the cause of the orderly's murdering the Captain.

3.1.2.2 Military Settings

Lawrence is particularly good at using settings to symbolize what he intends. Like what he did in *Odour of Chrysanthemums* (Nash, 1991: 101-122), he has arranged the settings of *The Prussian Officer* in symmetry: the story begins and ends with the military march.

The Prussian Officer starts with:

> *"They had marched more than thirty kilometres since dawn, along the **white**, **hot** road where occasional thickets of trees threw a moment of shade, then out into the **glare** again. On either hand, the valley, wide and shallow, **glittered with heat**; **dark** green patches of rye, **pale** young corn, fallow and meadow and **black** pine woods spread in a **dull**, **hot** diagram under a **glistening** sky. But right in front the mountains ranged across, **pale** blue and very **still**, **snow gleaming** gently out of the **deep** atmosphere. And towards the mountains, on and on, the regiment marched between the rye fields and the meadows, between the scraggy fruit trees set regularly on either side the high road. The **burnished**, **dark** green rye threw off a **suffocating heat**, the mountains drew gradually nearer and more distinct. While the feet of the soldiers grew **hotter**, sweat ran through their hair under their helmets, and their knapsacks could **burn** no more in contact with their shoulders, but seemed instead to give off a **cold**, prickly sensation."* (173 words)

This first paragraph tells us "who, when, where and what". The soldiers (who) had been marching (what) since dawn (when) in a wide shallow valley (where) and it was burning hot (environment). Marching is boring and exhausting, plus soldiers are exposed to the extreme heat of the sun. It is not difficult for the readers to imagine how agitated soldiers can become. Besides, many epithets (See bolded words in the first paragraph) (Also see 3.2.1), like "*dark*", "*pale*", "*still*", "*deep*", "*cold*", "*scraggy*", and "*black*", and reinforced epithets such as "*hot-heat-hotter-burn-suffocating; white-glitter-glare-glistening-snow; dark-black-pale-still-cold*" contribute not only to a battle field background but also to a very strong sense of repression and frustration which almost comes to the breaking point. Readers easily taste death through those words. Halliday (2014: 376) stated that Epithet indicates some quality of the subset, which may be an objective property of the thing itself (experiential); or it may be an expression of the speaker's subjective attitude towards it (interpersonal). This setting helps the reader understand the characters' depressed emotion with a "*suffocating*", "*breathless*", *and* "*deathly*" air around them, from environmental coloring to human response. Both the Captain and the orderly were driven crazy physically as well as mentally: physically by the "*suffocating*", "*breathless*" air; while mentally by their depression and frustration, which proves that Lawrence often externalizes the relationships of his characters with the outside world, particularly the world of nature (Lu, 2008: 390).

3. 2　Detailed Analysis of Discourse: Points of Views

According to Short (1996: 257-279), there is narrator, either first person or third person, and other linguistic indications of viewpoints summarized below:

a. Schema-oriented language

b. Value-laden expressions

c. Given-new information

d. Characters' thoughts or perception

e. Social deixis

f. The sequencing and organization of actions and events to indicate viewpoint

g. Ideological viewpoint

Because of the limitation of paper length, this analysis will only focus on three aspects, third-person narrator, value-laden expressions and characters' thought presentation.

3.2.1　Value-Laden Expressions

One of the main features of Lawrence's *The Prussian Officer* is the intended use of adjectives, adverbs and noun phrases. They are termed as Epithets by Halliday (2014), evaluation by Labov (1972) and value-laden expressions to indicate viewpoint by choosing what to describe and how it is described (Short, 1996). Most of the value-laden expressions in the short story focus on narration of the settings as well as description of the contrast personality of the officer and the orderly.

For instance:

> *Nothing, however, could give him back his living place in* **the hot**, **bright morning**. *He felt like a gap among it all. Whereas the Captain was* **prouder**, **overriding**. *A* **hot flash** *went through the* **young servant**'s *body. The Captain was* **firmer and prouder** *with life, he himself was* **empty as a shadow**. *Again the flash went through him, dazing him out. But his heart ran* **a little firmer**.
>
> *The air was too scented, it gave* **no breath**. *All the lush greenstuff seemed to be issuing its sap, till the air was* **deathly**, **sickly** *with the smell of greenness ...*
>
> *And just at his feet, below the knoll, was a* **darkish** *bog, where globe flowers*

*stood **breathless** still on their slim stalks.. And some of the **pale** gold bubbles were burst, and a **broken** fragment hung in the air.*

*Gradually the officer had become aware of his servant's **young**, **vigorous**, **unconscious** presence about him. He could not get away from the sense of the youth's person, while he was in attendance. It was like a **warm flame** upon the **older** man's **tense**, **rigid** body, that had become almost **unliving**, **fixed**. There was something so **free and self-contained** about him, and something in the **young fellow**'s movement, that made the officer aware of him.*

*He had a scar on his left thumb, a deep seam going across the knuckle. The officer had long suffered from it, and wanted to do something to it. Still it was there, **ugly and brutal** on the **young**, **brown** hand.*

*But the officer seemed to be going **irritably insane**, and **the youth was deeply frightened**.*

*The **young** soldier was gone, **looking old**, **and walking heavily**.*

Those value-laden expressions well illustrate Lawrence's emotional embellishment in depicting the setting for the atmosphere of the murder and contrast individuality and personality of the Captain and the orderly (also see 3.1.2).

3.2.2　Third Person Narrator

The characters in *The Prussian Office* are introduced by a third-person narrator in an external omniscient voice, who used "he" to refer to the orderly, and "the Captain" to the officer, which sounds distant and objective. However if we look at the following sentences portraying the orderly, we would change our mind.

"He (the orderly) walked on and on in silence … he had determined not to limp. It had made him sick to take the first steps … he had compressed his breath, and the cold drops of sweat had stood on his forehead. But he had walked it off. What were they after all but bruises! … with suppressing the pain, and holding himself in. There seemed no air when he breathed. But he walked almost lightly."

Words like *"walked on in silence"* , *"determined not to limp"* , *"he walked it off"* , *"What were they after all but bruises!"* , *"holding himself in"* , *"walked almost lightly"* indicate that the orderly has been seriously suffering from pain and bruises, but he tries to hide it and walk with pride and dignity. The image of a very brave soldier or even a hero is presented to us, the reader.

Subconsciously we sympathize with the orderly, taking on the attitude produced by the author through the language he employed. This proves that "Authors do tend to use third person narrations to narrate attitudes with which they sympathize" (Short, 1996: 258). The following paragraph tells us the author's attitude towards the Captain:

> *He (the Captain) knew his servant would soon be free, and would be glad. As yet, the soldier had held himself off from the elder man. The Captain grew madly irritable. He could not rest when the soldier was away, and when he was present, he glared at him with tormented eyes. He hated those fine, black brows over the unmeaning, dark eyes, he was infuriated by the free movement of the handsome limbs, which no military discipline could make stiff. And he became harsh and cruelly bullying, using contempt and satire. The young soldier only grew more mute and expressionless.*

Through the words " *madly irritable* ", " *with tormented eyes* ", " *hated* ", " *infuriated* ", " *became harsh and cruelly, using contempt and satire* ", etc., a mean, horrible monster is depicted to us.

The whole story is narrated in the third person which makes the reader feel that the author, being " external to the action of the story " (Simpson, 2004: 27), is describing things objectively, i. e. as it is or as it actually happens. However this is not necessarily the case. This analysis shows how a story can be subjectively manipulated in the third-person narrator and how much readers can be influenced by the fact that the narrator or the author actually praises the orderly for his dignity and sympathizes with the orderly for his suffering from the jealous, cruel and evil Captain.

3.2.3 Characters' Thought Presentation (TP)

Another discourse feature of Lawrence's *The Prussian Officer* is its plenty use of thought presentation, 16.5% in total (129 out of 780 sentences), because novelists or short story writers can manipulate the representation of the mental activities and different types of thoughts of their characters (Short, 1996). If we could divide the story into four parts (a. description of settings, characters and happenings; b. the murdering of the Captain; c. the orderly's conscious in and out after the murdering; and d. the orderly was found three hours after the murdering), all the thought presentations appear in the first three sections. There are four types of thought presentation used in the story, namely: free indirect thought (FIT), narrative report of thought acts (NRTA), indirect thought (IT), and free direct thought (FDT). The functions of those different types of thought presentations are summarized in the following table:

Table 3　Functions of different TPs

Functions / Type of PT	Development of the plot	Revealing the characters' relationship	Revealing characters' personality	Setting for the atmosphere	Total
NRTA	6	2	8		16
FIT	20	15	43	4	82
IT	10	7	12	1	30
FDT				1	1
Total	36	24	63	6	129

For examples:

> *"He could now walk almost without pain. At the start,* **he had determined not to** **limp** *(NRTA). It had made him sick to take the first steps, and during the first mile or so, he had compressed his breath, and the cold drops of sweat had stood on his forehead. But he had walked it off.* **What were they after all but bruises!** *(FIT). He had looked at them, as he …"*

It is the orderly who had made up his mind not to limp, therefore the sentence is an NRTA. The second thought presentation is ended with an exclamatory mark, which sounds like the orderly is talking to himself in the mind. So it is an FIT. Those two thought presentations depict the young orderly's personality: strong-willed, tough, and not showing any sign of weakness. This kind of personality is very important for the development of the plot, especially for the conflict between the orderly and the officer. The orderly has been long bullied and mistreated by the Captain for ridiculous reasons or even for no reasons as is shown in Table 1. The long time mistreatment finally leads him to kill the officer. At the very beginning of the story, Lawrence made use of these two cases of TP to provide readers with a vivid image of the orderly.

The flowing indirect thought presentations describe the desperate situation of the orderly, which helps developing the plot. The orderly has no place to hide and nowhere to escape to, and he is going to break out.

"The orderly felt he was connected with that figure moving so suddenly on horseback"... *"... he felt he must get away"*...
"His instinct warned him that he must not think"...
"He only wished it would stay night, so that he could lie still, covered up by the darkness"...
"And then, he thought, it was impossible"...

The only free direct thought presentation appears in the setting for the murder of the Captain to set up the atmosphere for the murdering. When sheep huddle together, danger is coming.

"Why should the sheep huddle together under this fierce sun?"

The most distinctive function of such a big percentage of thought presentation used in this story is to reveal the individuality and personality of the characters, and to develop the relationship or conflict, to be exact, between the two men. These two functions are mainly fulfilled through the presentation of FIT and partly through the presentation of IT and NRTA. FIT is also the most important way to reveal the characters' relationship and to set the atmosphere. The only appearance of FDT serves only one function: to set up the atmosphere (also see Lv & Zhu, 2006). Lawrence was concerned to find ways of describing the deepest experiences of his characters. He once wrote that the human personality was like an iceberg with the major part of it under the surface. "His art attempts to capture the submerged parts of the self and to develop forms and techniques in the novel which render those intensive experiences. To this end readers have to abandon conventional understandings of 'plot' and 'character' and immerse themselves in the total pattern of rhythm, episodic structure and poetic symbolism which is the experience of reading his fictional work." (Carter, 1994)

The above analysis has confirmed Toolan's (1980) statement that narrator's discourse or linguistic choices imply his/her detached preference, stereotype and prejudiced judgments, which definitely affects the readers' interpretation.

4. Conclusion

This paper has tried to analyze D. H. Lawrence's short story *The Prussian*

Officer by combining Chatman's comprehensive diagram for the structure of a narrative and Short's discourse structure for fictions. The analysis focuses on events (actions and happenings) and existents (characters and settings) on story level and third person narrator, valued-laden expressions and characters' thought presentation on discourse level. The findings prove the fact that writers do try to influence their readers' interpretation and understanding of what they read by manipulating discourse, which refers to how the story is told. Lawrence's preferred choice of linguistic forms results in the "victim" image of the orderly and the Captain's twisted character for which he is doomed to be murdered. As far as the orderly is concerned, it is quite natural for him to burst out after long time suffering from both mental and physical mistreatment from the Captain. Lawrence's skillful narration, particularly, his special use of epithets or value-laden expressions succeeds in imposing his emotional attitude and biased judgment to the reader who feel sympathized for the orderly though he committed the crime of murdering the Captain. The linguistic details contribute to the interpretation of literary works, and Lawrence's selection of those linguistic features is of literary significance in understanding the conflict between the Captain and the orderly in *The Prussian Officer*.

References

Carter, R. 1994. *The Modern Novel to 1939*. Handouts to ELILS course students in Nottingham University.

Chatman, S. 1978. *Story and Discourse: Narrative Structure in Fiction and Film*. Ithaca & London: Cornell University Press.

Halliday, M. A. K. 2014. *Halliday's Introduction to Functional Grammar* (4th Ed.). London: Routledge.

Kennedy, X. J. & D. Gioia. 2002. *Literature: An Introduction to Fiction, Poetry, and Drama* (8th Ed.). New York: Longman.

Labov, W. 1972. *Language in the Inner City*. Philadelphia: University of Pennsylvania University Press.

Leech, G. 2008. *Language in Literature: Style and Foregrounding*. London: Pearson Longman.

Lv, Z. 2008. Systemic functional grammar applied in the stylistic analysis of D. H. Lawrence's *The Prussian Officer*. In C. Wu, C. Matthiessen, & M. Herke (eds.). *Proceedings of ISFC 35: Voices Around the World*. Sydney: 35 ISFC Organizing Committee (390−395).

Nash, W. 1991. On a Passage from Lawrence's "Odour of Chrysanthemums". In R. Carter (ed.). *Language and Literature: An Introductory Reader in Stylistics*. London: George Allen & Unwin Ltd.

Short, M. 1996. *Exploring the Language of Poems, Plays and Prose*. London: Longman.

Simpson, P. 2004. *Stylistics*. London: Routledge.

Toolan, M. 1980. Discourse style makes viewpoint: The example of Carver's narrator in "Cathedral". In E. Traugoot & M. L. Pratt (eds.). *Linguistics for Students of Literature*. New York: Harcourt Brace Jovanovich.

Toolan, M. J. 1992. *Narrative: A Critical Linguistic Introduction*. London: Routledge.

吕中舌、朱 燕(Lv, Z. & Y. Zhu.). 2006. 从心理描写分析《普鲁士军官》中人物的刻画. 《外语教学》,(1):79—82.

The Phonological Rhetoric and Poetical Texture in *Ulysses*

Wu Xianyou （Chongqing Normal University）
Liu Kang （Sichuan Institute of Arts and Sciences）

Abstract: The phonological figures in *Ulysses* have been the weakest aspect in Joycean studies, calling for a systematic scrutiny. From a cognitive phonological perspective, this article aims at a brief survey of those phonological figures in *Ulysses* and illustrate how much phonological figures have contributed to the poetic texture of the novel. Taking as the point of departure the phonological figures in *Ulysses*, by means of a revised model of phonological figures by Plett, this article explores some 15 phonological figures concerning phonemic deviations and phonemic enforcement, and their stylistic effects. These figures have contributed much to the musicality and playfulness, and also to the textual cohesion and coherence of the novel, and in some contexts they may produce synaesthesia in the reader's mind and carry an obvious interpersonal function. Moreover, they have played an important part in the linguistic poeticity of the novel.

Key words: *Ulysses*; phonological figures; stylistic effects; poetical texture

1. Introduction

Phonological figures or schemes, refer to those phonemic patternings which can produce particular sound effects in readers. In terms of rhetorical studies in *Ulysses*, some essential findings have been made by quite a few Joycean scholars such as S. Gilbert (1952), D. Gifford & R. J. Seidman (1988), K. Wales (1992), J. Barger (2001), and others, who seem to rejoice in rhetorical figures at lexical and syntactical levels, of a specific episode, say, "Aeolus", but tend to overlook phonological schemes. But it is a pity that there is no sufficient study of its musicality and poeticity. As we know, one common feature of these two aspects lies in its unusual rhythmic sound patterns and its aesthetic effects, which largely derive from phonological figures, such as assonance, alliteration, rhyme, meter, repetition, and so on. Phonological figures which are inadequately studied, we argue, provide a good angle of vision to understand the poetic texture of the novel. From a cognitive phonological perspective, this article aims at a brief survey of those phonological figures in *Ulysses* and illustrate how much phonological figures have contributed to the poetic texture of the novel.

2. Plett's Model of Phonological Figures

In this section, we shall make a preliminary study of phonological figures by employing H. F. Plett's rhetorical model (1985).

Plett has made a thorough study of classic and modern rhetoric. According to the three dimensions of syntactics (relation: sign — sign), pragmatics (relation: sign — sender/recipient) and semantics (relation: sign — reality), Plett has offered a systematic and practical model of rhetorical figures. He divides rhetorical figures into two basic linguistic types: linguistic levels and linguistic operations or deviations. Linguistic levels refer to the six linguistic aspects: phonological, morphological, syntactic, textological, semantic and graphemic. The linguistic operations consist of two types of rules, one violating the accepted linguistic norm and the other enforcing the primary norm. The former are also known as rhetorical licences, anomalies, metaboles or simply deviations (anti-grammatical forms), the latter as equivalences, restrictions or isotopes (syn-grammatical forms). The rule-violating operations or deviations are carried out by such specific methods as addition, subtraction, substitution and permutation of language signs; the rule-enforcing operations mainly deal with their repetitions. According to these two basic linguistic types, the corresponding figures are constructed at different linguistic levels. For convenience's sake, we are only interested in phonological figures of various subclassifications. Here is the stemma:

Stemma of Phonological Figures

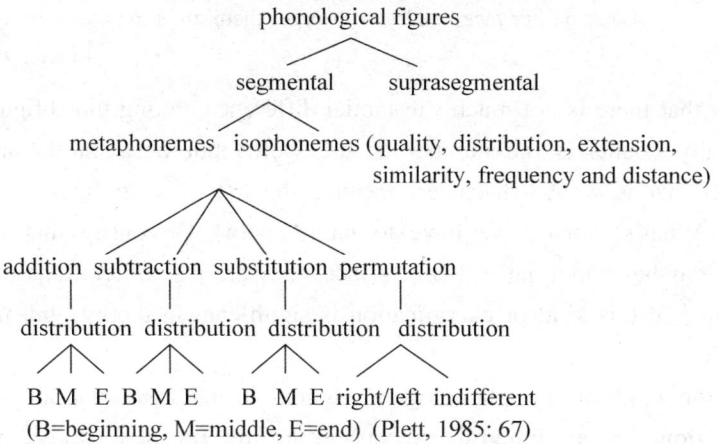

phonological figures

segmental　　suprasegmental

metaphonemes　isophonemes (quality, distribution, extension, similarity, frequency and distance)

addition　subtraction　substitution　permutation

distribution　distribution　distribution　distribution

B M　E B M E　　B M E　right/left indifferent
(B=beginning, M=middle, E=end) (Plett, 1985: 67)

As shown in the above diagram, phonological figures can be divided into two broad categories: segmental and suprasegmental. The former refers to phonological figures at phonemic level and the latter to those derived from such prosodic elements as pitch, range, stress, loudness, pause, speed, rhythm and quality. For the sake of space, we shall only discuss the first category of phonological figures.

The segmental category in turn can be divided into two kinds: metaphonemes and isophonemes. The former refer to those phonological figures deriving from rule-violating operations in metaphonemes and the latter stand for those resulting from the rule-enforcing operations in isophonemes as a result of phonological quality, distribution, extension, similarity, frequency, distance and so on. Plett's model is comprehensive and systematic, but as "all grammar leaks", so does Plett's model. His obvious blemish is that the model is excessively detailed and overlapping. One example will suffice. Look at the last two kinds of phonological figures he listed:

(16) Frequency: single or multiple repetition of phonemes, e.g. at the beginning of a word:

A *cr*uel *cr*afty *Cr*ocodile (Spencer)

(17) Distance: insertion of words between the representatives of phonological equivalence:

a) $A^X B^X$: A *c*oryphée, *c*ovetous of applause (T. E. Hulme)

b) $A^X BC^X$: The Court and Country (Breton)

c) $A^X BC^X DEFG^X HIJ^X KL$:

If to her share some *f*emale errors *f*all,

Look on her *f*ace, and you'll *f*orget them all. (Pope)

(Plett, 1985: 69)

It seems that there is not much substantial difference among those figures, and what really counts is the number of the words put between the alliterated words. If that is what "distance" means, the list of such figures would be endless. What's worse, we have to name them! Obviously that is Plett's headache as he cannot name them. In fact, they are just alliterations with some variations. So this kind of classification is significant in theory, but not much in practice.

In the case of the phonological figures in *Ulysses*, not all of Plett's classifications are meaningful. According to my practical study, we shall discuss 7 figures at metaphonemic level and 4 at isophonemic level, and add 4 more unusual phonological figures to the list.

3. Three Categories of Phonological Figures in *Ulysses*

3. 1 Phonological Figures of Metaphonemes

Phonological figures of metaphonemes are made by various kinds of rule-violating operations such as addition, subtraction, substitution and permutation at the front, middle and end of a word. But in our analysis, we find that subtraction has much in common with permutation, so we will make no further distinction between them. Generally, there are 7 kinds of such phonological figures.

(1) **Prosthesis**: addition of sound or syllable to the beginning of the word. Prosthesis is a special kind of phonological figure and it is rarely seen even in poems or songs. It is mainly used for rhythmic purpose. For example:

Do *p*take some *p*tarmigan. (8: 223)

But wait *a*while. (10: 305)

A sail! A veil *a*wave upon the waves. (11: 329)

Lenehan, small eyes *a*hunger on her humming, bust *a*humming, tugged Blazes Boylan's elbowsleeve. (11: 342)

(2) **Epenthesis**: intercalation of a vowel in a word. Such a figure is rarely found even in classic poetry and it is typical of Joyce's style.

Seabloom, grease*a*bloom viewed last words. (11: 375)

— A — sudden — at-the-moment — though — from — lingering — illness — often — previously

— expect*orat*ed — demise, Lenehan said. (7: 181) ("expect*orat*ed" for "expected"; "expectorate" is also a euphemism for "to spit")

(3) **Aphaeresis**: the omission of the one or more letters at the beginning or end of a word by the apostrope ('). Such a figure is seen not only in poems or songs, but also in our daily writing for rhythmic or humorous effects. Look at the following examples:

— But alas, '*twas* idle dreaming ... (11: 353)

Si sang' *Twas* rank and fame: in Ned Lambert's '*twas*. (11: 357)

'*Tis* the last rose of summer Dollard left Bloom felt wind would round inside. (11: 372)

His image, wandering, he met. I mine. I met a fool *i'* the forest. (9: 256)

(4) **Syncope**: loss of sounds in the interior of a word with or without the sign ('). The first example below is a typical syncope showing loss of sounds at the front, middle and end of words. Syncope is one obvious feature of everyday speech, and in *Ulysses* it frequently occurs in characters' monologues, suggesting the flow of thought and the oral feature of the text. Here are some examples:

... fanned by gentlest zephyrs *tho'* quarrelling with the stony obstacles ... or '*neath* the shadows cast *o'er* its pensive bosom by the overarching leafage of the giants of the forests. (7: 157) (*tho'* for *though*, '*neath* for *beneath*, *o'er* for *over*)

Are you off? *Yrfmstbyes. Blmstup.* O'er ryehigh blue. Bloom stood up. (11: 370). (*Yrfmstbyes* is really hard to decipher and possibly it is the narrator's cliché. The letters "oo" in "Bloom" and "ood" in "stood" are omitted.)

(5) **Apocope**: the loss of one or more sounds from the end of a word, as in Modern English *sing* from Middle English *singen*. Apocope is pervasive in *Ulysses* and it is largely used in a character's interior monologue to suggest urgency or inarticulacy. It is the most faithful representation of a character's speech. Sometimes, a humorous effect or intimacy is expected in certain contexts. Look at the following examples:

He doesn't hear it. *Nannan.* Iron nerves. (7: 152) (*Nannan* for *Nannetti*)

Indiges. (8: 199) (*indiges* for *indigestion*)

Best value in *Dub*. (11: 349)

Bloom dipped, *Bloo mur*: dear sir. Dear Henry wrote: dear Mady. Got you *lett* and *flow*.

Hell did I put? Some *pock* or *oth*. It is *utterl imposs*. Underline *imposs*. To write today. (11: 360) (The original words: *Bloom murmurs, letter and flower, pocket or other, utterly impossible, impossible*)

(6) **Antisthecon**: substitution of one sound, syllable, or letter at the beginning, in the middle or at the end of a word for another, frequently to accomplish a pun. Such a figure is rare even in classic poems and it fully reveals the playfulness of language. For examples:

quotatoes (8: 201) (instead of "*potatoes*")
the Antient Concert Rooms (11: 114, instead of "ancient")

(7) **Anagram**: a word or phrase formed by reordering the letters of another word or phrase, which can bring about pleasure or humorous effect to people, e.g. "emit" to "mite", "lived" to "devil". Anagrams can be made in several ways. 1) One-word anagrams (where a single word is anagrammed into another single word) are sometimes referred to by wordplay specialists as transpositions. For example, "orchestra" is a transposition of "carthorse". 2) Some anagrams are created by perfectly reversing the order of the letters. Examples include "Naomi"→ "I moan", "Evian"→ "Naïve". 3) There are even anagrams which do not involve any rearranging of the sequence of letters at all: merely the insertion or deletion of spaces. Here are two good examples: "Psychotherapist" → "Psycho, the rapist" and "The IRS" → "Theirs!" Anagrams are popular with ordinary people, particularly children. Let us see two examples in *Ulysses*. "— Hush, Lenehan said. I hear *feetstoops*". (7: 162) A humorous effect is easily achieved when Lenehan used "feetstoops" instead of "footsteps". By the way, "feetstoops" is also a euphemism. A typical example is found in Episode 17 when Bloom plays with his own name:

What anagrams had he made on his name in youth?

Leopold Bloom
Ellpodbomool
Molldopeloob
Bollopedoom

Old Ollebo, M. P. (17: 792)

3. 2 Phonological Figures of Isophonemes

Phonological figures of isophonemes are made by rule-enforcing operations or repetition of certain phonemes including such devices as quality, distribution, extension, similarity, frequency and distance. Alliteration, assonance and consonance are derived from distribution of vowels or consonants, while rhyme, reversed rhyme, and pararhyme result from extension.

(8) **Alliteration**: known as "head rhyme" or "initial rhyme", the parallelism or repetition of the initial consonant cluster in stressed syllables in any sequence of neighboring words. The initial consonant letter may consist of zero or 1-3 consonants. Occasionally, alliteration occurs in the middle of the word and this is called internal or hidden alliteration. Internal alliteration is not so striking as at the beginning of the word. Alliteration often appears in poems, proverbs and idiomatic expressions and gives a musical property to the poem as "parallelism of sound is the aspect of poetic language which most obviously relates it to music" (Leech, 2001: 93). Surprisingly enough, alliteration is frequently found in *Ulysses*, which adds to the musical property of the novel. For example:

Dirty Dublin (7: 183)

Joyce borrowed this phrase from the Irish woman writer Lady Sydney Morgan (1780 – 1859). This phrase, succinctly structured, is impressive for two things. One is its striking alliterative sound [d]. This voiced plosive in all three words bears a stressed syllable and a rhythmic feature, and it is both easy to read and to remember, suggesting a decisive unwavering tone. The speeding-up effect is mainly caused by the alliterative stop consonant [d] and two short vowels in the last word. And then, there is its deep implication: Joyce's pet phrase fully reveals his strong ambivalent feelings for his distressed motherland. On the one hand, Joyce cherishes an unwavering love for his motherland; on the other, he bitterly hates her paralysis and provincialism. The "chiming" sound or phonetic bond [d] connects three words by similarity of sound so that "you are made to think of their possible connections" (Leech, 2001: 95), and in this case, the sharp contrast is made. Joyce's ingenious idiom here is similar to Jakobson's classic example "I like Ike". (Jakobson, 1996: 16) *Ulysses* teems with alliterations. More examples:

Memories beset his brooding brain. (1: 19)

*B*elly without *b*lemish, *b*ulging *b*ig, a *b*uckler of taut vellum ... (3: 46)

*P*oor *P*enelope. *P*enelope Rich. (7: 188)

a *r*ugged *r*ough *r*ugheaded kern (9: 265)

*B*eer, *b*eef, *b*usiness, *b*ibles, *b*ulldogs, *b*attleships, *b*uggery and *b*ishops. (14: 556)

(9) **Assonance** or **vowel rhyme**: in prosody, repetition of stressed vowel sounds within words with different end consonants, as in the phrase "quite like". It is unlike rhyme, in which initial consonants differ but both vowel and end-consonant sounds are identical, as in the phrase "quite right". "Assonance not only contributes to musical quality of a literary text, but also to its meaning" (Wang Shouyuan, 2000: 101). Echoic effects can often be conveyed. Consider the following examples:

> H*oa*rse, m*a*sked and *a*rmed, the pl*a*nters' covenant. The black north and tr*ue* bl*ue* bible. (2: 38)
>
> But I old men, penitent, leadfooted, underdarkneath the night: m*ou*th s*ou*th: t*o*mb w*o*mb. (7: 175)
>
> Bl*ew*. Bl*ue* bl*oo*m is on the ... (11: 329)
>
> A s*ai*l! A v*ei*l aw*a*ve upon the w*a*ves. (11: 329)

(10) **Consonance**: correspondence or recurrence of sounds especially in words; specifically recurrence or repetition of consonants at the end of stressed syllables without the similar correspondence of vowels as in the final sounds of "stroke" and "luck". Consonance, similar to assonance, can play a role of rhyme, increasing an internal cohesion of the line, e.g. grea*t*/mea*t*, se*nd*/ ha*nd*.

> ... and ever shall be, wor*ld* withou*t* e*nd*. (3: 62)
>
> A*ll* whee*l*, whir*l*, waltz, twir*l*. (15: 679)

(11) **Rhyme**: as a basic component of verse form, correspondence between rhythmic measures or that of terminal sounds of words or of lines of verse so as to echo one another. Normally the last stressed vowel in the line and all sounds following it make up the rhyming element: this may be a monosyllable known as "masculine rhyme", or two syllables known as "feminine rhyme", e.g. *butter/splutter*, or even three syllables known as "triple rhyme" or "polysyllabic rhyme", e.g. *civility/mobility*. Rhyme is used by http://www. britannica. com/needmorehttp://www. britannica. com/ needmorepoets and occasionally by prose writers to produce sounds appealing

to the reader's senses and to unify and establish a poem's stanzaic form. Almost all the rhymes are expected to be found not only in quoted poems or songs but also in narrative sentences or internal monologues in *Ulysses*. Please look at the following examples:

I am the b*oy* / That can enj*oy*. (1: 10)

She r*ose* and cl*osed* her reading, r*ose* of Castille. Fretted fornlorn, dreamily r*ose*. (11: 340)

Charm*ing*, seasmil*ing* and unanswer*ing* Lydia on Lidwell smiled. (11: 363)

3. 3   Some Unusual Phonological Figures

In addition to the above list of phonological figures, there are some exceptions to Plett's model. Possibly, any other rhetoric models will encounter the same difficulty. Here are 4 additional kinds:

(12) **Onomatopoeia**: use of words to imitate natural sounds. It can be understood in two ways: (1) the use of words formed in imitation of the natural sounds associated with the object or action involved; (2) the recurrence of phonemes in a text unit that suggests certain natural sounds which reinforce the meaning conveyed in that text. "Sirens" contains numerous collections of letters which are not words but typographical representations of sounds. The most memorable may be the "Rrrrrr", "Prrprr," "Fff! Oo. Rrpr." and "Pprrpffrrppffff" (11: 373-376) of Bloom's flatulence at the end of the episode. There are numerous other examples: "Tschink. Tschunk" of clinking glasses (11: 330); "Pwee! Pwee little wee" of a shepherd's pipe (11: 372); the sound of the tram that masks Bloom's gas: "Tram kran kran kran ... Krandlekrankran." (11: 330); the previously discussed "Imperthnthn thnthnthn"; "Hufa! Hufa!" (11: 328). Attridge (1988) calls these fragments "non-lexical onomatopoeia" and argues that onomatopoeia presents itself and is frequently perceived as having an unusually strong intrinsic physical relationship to its object, i.e. of being a non-arbitrary or "motivated" sign — while in fact even non-lexical onomatopoeia depends upon familiarity with a system of signs as much as any word. (p. 136). Consider the following examples:

They bundled their books away, pencils *clanking*, pages *rustling*. (2: 31)

Sllt. Almost human the way it *sllt* to call attention. (7: 154-156)

Rrrpr. Kraa. Kraandl. (11: 330)

With a cock *carracarracarra* cock. *Cockcock.* (11: 364)

(13) **Diaeress**: the separation or resolution of one syllable into two by a mark placed over the second of two adjacent vowels or an intentional extension of a letter, such as co [o] perate, a [e] rial. Diaeress is usually used for emphasis, fun or rhythm, but sometimes for emotional purposes such as annoyance, disgust or anger. Examine the following examples:

> My familiar, after me, calling St*eeeeeeeeee*phen. (1: 24)
> *Co-ome* thou lost one, /*Co-ome* thou dear one. (7: 149)
> ADONAI: D*ooooooooooo*g! (15: 696)
> w*aaaaaaa*lk (11: 370)

(14) **Spoonerism**: an accidental transposition of sounds, usually the initial sounds, of two or more words as in "a *bl*ushing *cr*ow" for "a *cr*ushing *bl*ow". It is a kind of word game like anagram. For examples:

> Quickly he does it. Must require some practice that. mangi*D* kcirta*P* (7: 155)
> — *Cl*amn *d*ever, Lenehan said to Mr O'Madden Burke. (7: 174)
> Substituting Stephen for Bloom *St*oom would have passed ... Substituting Bloom for Stephen *Bl*ephen would have passed ... (16: 798)

(15) **Mimology or contamination**: contamination or influence of some previous sounds or words on later sounds or words. By playing with sounds or words, some humorous effect can be achieved. For examples:

> *Essex*bridge.*Yes* ...*yessex.* (11: 336)
> Her first merciful *lovesoft oftloved* word. (11: 353)
> *Like lady*, *ladylike.* (11: 340)

Some phonological figures, such as alliteration and onomatopoeia and anagram, are pervasive in *Ulysses* while others like metathesis, antisthecon and spoonerism, are few. But it is sufficient enough to illustrate the complexity and intricacy of the phonological figures in *Ulysses*. It is no doubt that we have lost a great deal by almost isolating phonological figures from their contexts. Space permitting, a detailed stylistic analysis would be more significant. To make up for the loss, we shall discuss some typical phonological figures and illustrate their contribution to the tendency towards poeticity in the next section.

4. The Poetical Texture in *Ulysses*

Meighan (1999) holds that phonological figures such as assonance, alliteration, rhyme and repetition, contribute a lot to the poeticity of the text as he points out: "Poeticity generally involves phonological patterning — repetition and variation of some kind of sound-based correspondence. Assonance, alliteration, rhyme, meter and repetition are all examples. Words form relationships and patterns based on their phonology, independent of any syntactic and semantic relationships — and in turn modify those relationships (i.e., phonological connections create semantic ones)." His view is conducive to our understanding of the phonological effects brought about by phonological figures, and of the poeticity of the novel. Let us examine the following examples.

> Between 11 a.m. and noon, Stephen is walking on the beach at Sandymount, his mind going wild. His meditation is like that of a philosopher and his idiolect is that of a poet.
>
> Stephen *c*losed his eyes to hear his boots *cr*ush *cr*ackling *wr*ack and shells. You are walking through it howsomever. I am, a stri*de* at a *time*. A very short space of *time* through a very short *time* of space, Five Six: the *nacheinander*. Exactly: and that is the ineluctable modality of the audible. (3: 45)

This passage is of a "poetical" style. The schematic patterning is extensive on the phonological as well as the syntactical level in quite a few phonological figures such as alliteration, assonance, onomatopoeia and rhyme. These figures are alliteration: "*c*losed", "*cr*ush *cr*ackling *wr*ack"; onomatopoeia: "*cr*ush *cr*ackling *wr*ack"; assonances: "cra*ckling*" and "w*ra*ck", "st*ri*de" and "*ti*me". Abstract expressions like "*nacheinande*" and "the ineluctable modality of the audible" adds to the poetic flavor of the passage. More to the point, the passage has a rhythmic regularity: "a catalectic tetrameter of iambs" (3: 46), which enables it to be written out and scanned as poetry in a quasi-blank-verse meter:

Stephen *c*losed his eyes to hear
His boots *cr*ush *cr*ackling *wr*ack and shells.
You are walking through it howsomever.
I am, a stri*de* at a *time*.
A very short space of *time*

Through a very short *time* of space,

Five Six: the *nacheinander*.

Exactly: and that is the ineluctable

Modality of the audible.

In so doing, Stephen's disposition of a would-be poet is fully displayed and sound play echoes the emotive rhetoric which reflects the sensitive perceptions and sensations of the young artist Stephen. Another example from this episode:

His lips lipped and *m*outhed fleshless lips of air: *m*outh to her w*omb*. O*omb*, allw*omb*ing t*omb*. His *m*outh *m*oulded issuing breath, unspeeched: *ooeeehah*: roar of cataractic planets, globed, blazing, roaring *wayawayawayawayawayaway*. (3: 60)

This passage records well Stephen's mental activity. Let us begin with Joyce's unique narrative technique: shifting point of view from the third-person narration to Stephen's focalization. Seemingly, this passage is narrated from the third-person perspective, but a closer examination will show that the narration is done by both the third-person and Stephen. The beginning parts of both the first and third sentences before the colon are narrated by the third-person and the rest of the passage is Stephen's focalization. The unconscious shifting of perspective among characters is typical of Joyce's feat and it calls for further study. Next, let us examine the phonological figures. They are alliteration: *m*outh (3 times) and *m*oulded; rhyme: t*omb* and w*omb* (including O*omb*, allw*omb*ing); repetition: mouth (3 times), lip (3 times) and onomatopoeia: *ooeeeha* and *wayawayawayawayawayawa* (also imitation of objects, wave-like hair). Next, there is a superfluous use of English consonants: liquid [l] (9 times), bilabial nasal [m] (8 times), sibilant [s], and semi-vowel [w] (8 times). The bilabial [m] and semi-vowel [w], when being produced, have much to do with lip and mouth. "The connection is made not via the ear alone, but through the little understood pathways of empathy and synaesthesia" (Leech, 2001: 97). Incidentally, Andre Topia (1986) has a convincing discussion of the emblematical functions of "lips" in "Siren" and he concludes: "Indeed, it is significant that in a chapter which is under the sign of the voice, the lips should be so omnipresent. They have a double value: they are the place of both sound and utterance and erotic flirtatiousness. They are at the same time the privileged place of romantic, ethereal, idealized figures such as they appear in love songs or heroic ballads — and a part of body associated with erotic caresses, drinking, eating, sensuality in general … They are a basically ambivalent orifice, disembodied *spiritus* and carnal lure" (p. 76-81). So we argue that such words as "lips", "mouth", and "womb" used in the above passage, also play "a double value" as "lips" do in "Sirens". These three words have a phonological aptness to its implied meaning: love or sex. Maybe that is why some scholars such as D. Hayman (1977) and S. Hill (1995) think that Stephen has a masturbation here.

> Listen: a fourworded wavespeech: seesoo, hrss, rsseeiss, oos. In cups of rocks it slops: flop, slop, sap: bounded in barrels. And, spent, its speech ceases. It flows purling, widely flowing, floating foampool, flower unfurling. (3: 62)

Stephen's interior monologue consists of 4 sentences and the rolling waves are turned into rhythmic lines in Stephen's monologue. Four obvious features are revealed in this short passage. (1) A clever use of onomatopoeic words, such as *seesoo*, *hrss*, *rsseeiss*, *oos* and *slops: flop, slop, sap*, appeals much to the ear, suggesting the rolling sounds of the sea. (2) There is an abundant use of phonological figures such as alliteration: *sl*op and *sl*ap, *b*ounded and *b*arrels, *sp*ent and *sp*eechflow, *fl*oating and *fl*ower; rhyme: p*urling* and unf*urling*; assonance: sp*ee*ch and c*ea*ses, r*o*cks and sl*o*ps, fl*o*wing and fl*o*ws, fl*o*ating, f*oa*mpool. Such phonological figures add much to the rhythmic or poetical feature of the passage. (3) "Soft" sounds such as [s] and [f] help to build a vivid image of the running water. The fricatives [s] and [f] are used 20 and 8 times respectively. Abercrombie (1965) tended to attribute some onomatopoeic effects to English consonants on such dimensions as "hardness"/"softness", "thinness"/"sonority" (p. 16 - 25), and Leech (2001) listed classes of English consonants impressionistically on a scale of increasing hardness (p. 98). Such sounds as [l], [s] and [m] are typical of Leech's "soft" sounds, which are effective here in depicting the running water by providing a phonetic correlate of their continuing, fluctuating motion: something we can feel and see as well as hear. (4) The last sentence is a good dynamic imitation of the water flowing far away: as the sentence becomes longer and longer, the force of the running water becomes weaker and weaker. Then what's Stephen thinking about? At first glance, it seems he is describing the waves of the sea as the word "wavespeech" is very tricky. Imagine all those onomatopoeic words and "soft" sounds we have examined. In fact, he is describing his act of urinating at the holes of rocks! The water "flows purling, widely flowing, floating foampool, flower unfurling" all the way from the higher place until it dies away. Please enjoy the Chinese version. By the way, it is very subjective and impressionistic for D. Hayman (1977) and S. Hill (1995) this time to think that Stephen has a masturbation here.

> A sail! A veil awave upon the waves. (11: 323)

This line is highly poetical with a few phonological figures and a remarkable rhythmic patterning. These phonological figures are: assonance of long vowel [ei] in "sail, veil, awave, waves"; triple repetition in "A sail! A veil, awave ...". What's striking in this short line is its regular iambic pattern: | x / | x / | x / | x / | x / | . Such a pattern, appealing to both sight and hearing, is particularly appropriate to give a vivid picture of a small sail rising and falling rhythmically in the sea according to the regular vibrations of the waves. Possibly, Joyce intends to imply the significance of a peaceful relationship between man and nature. What's more, this poetical line also predicts a storm of a musical performance at the bar in this episode. For Joyce, rhythm is fundamental not only to poems but also to all artistic works as he explains: "Rhythm is the first formal esthetic relation of part to part in any esthetic whole or of an esthetic whole to its part or parts or of any part to the esthetic whole of which it is a part." (A Portrait, 1996: 187)

> Miss Kennedy sauntered sadly from bright light, twining a loose hair behind an ear. Sauntering sadly, gold no more, she twisted twined a hair. Sadly she twined in sauntering gold hair behind a curving ear. (11: 331)

This is one of the most interesting sentences in the novel both in sounds and syntax. It seems that this limited linguistic material could be rearranged indefinitely. The linear progress of the sentence is arrested by phonic structures based on repetitions, sound echoes, symmetries and permutations, which fully reveal the playfulness of language. Four words ("sauntered", "sadly", "twining" and "hair") appear in all three sentences and seem that they are likely to be recombined again and again. Now let us focus our attention to the first sentence — the basic one. Phonologically, the first sentence employs such figures as alliteration: "sauntered" and "sadly" (repeated twice); rhyme:

"bright" and "light"; consonance: "*s*auntere*d*, gol*d*, twiste*d*, tw*i*ne*d* and behin*d*"; assonance: "l*i*ght", "tw*i*ning/tw*i*ned", "br*i*ght" and "beh*i*nd"; off-rhyme: "hair" and "ear". So the poetic effect is accentuated by these phonological figures. Syntactically, the initial sentence is varied and repeated twice, providing further poeticity and playfulness of the three lines. The repetitions serve no narrative function nor provide any new information; the text succumbs to the Siren's call of sound and dallies with language for its own sake. Citing this passage as an example, Dermot Kelly (1988) argues: "... in 'Sirens' and 'Scylla and Charybdis', the narrative seems to have been read in an echo chamber. The book's tendency to quote itself becomes a mania ... materials from the omniscient narration, the dialogue and the interior monologue are reiterated either in corrupt forms or in bizarre new contexts." (p. 15)

5. Conclusion

From a cognitive phonological perspective, this article aims at a brief survey of those phonological figures in *Ulysses* and illustrate how much phonological figures have contributed to the poetic texture of the novel. Taking as the point of departure the phonological figures in *Ulysses*, by means of a revised model of phonological figures by Plett, this article explores some 15 phonological figures concerning phonemic deviations and phonemic enforcement, and their stylistic effects. These figures have contributed much to the musicality and playfulness, and also to the textual cohesion and coherence of the novel, and in some contexts they may produce synaesthesiain the reader's mind and carry an obvious interpersonal function. Moreover, they have played an important part in the linguistic poeticity of the novel. My study shows that phonological figures such as alliteration, assonance, consonance and other sound echoes, are the effective devices responsible for the poeticity of the novel which characterizes not only the internal monologues but also the narrative sentences. Reading *Ulysses*, especially aloud, is to take a tour through many possible uses of sounds and songs. On the way, you are sure to be totally enchanted by the melody of a song, by the cadence of a poem and the gracefulness of a piece of prose. But it is important to know that music for Joyce carries special implications: music is not only a natural revelation of one's true feelings, but also an effective way to enrich the novel genre. By these expressive sounds and songs, Joyce tries to make the best of language's sounds, to imbue a sense of rhythm, place, object and motion in the reader or more accurately the listener, giving words many more values than those ascribed to them in dictionaries; through them, Joyce is seeking to extend the limits of language, so as to achieve the special effects of musicality, playfulness and expressiveness of language. "Language moves to the foreground and narrative, never fully abandoned, to the background. On one level this is done through lyricism; Joyce as well as anyone employs the poeticity and euphony of language to create esthetic pleasure through sound." (Meighan, 1999)

References

Abercrombie, D. 1965. *Studies in Phonetics and Linguistics*. London: Methuen.

Attridge, D. 1988. *Peculiar Language: Literature as Difference from the Renaissance to James Joyce*. Ithaca: Cornell University Press.

Gifford, D. & R. J. Seidman. 1988. *Ulysses Annotated*. Berkeley: University of California Press.

Gilbert, S. 1931/1952. *James Joyce's Ulysses: A Study*. New York: Alfred A. Knopf.

Hayman, D.1977. Stephen on the rocks. *James Joyce Quarterly*, 14 (1): 5–16.

Hill, S. 1995. *His Cheeks Were a Flame: Masturbation, Sexual Frustration and Artistic Failure in Joyce's Portrait of Stephen Dedalus*. Canada: Carleton University of ottawa.

Jakobson, R. 1996. Concluding statements: Linguistics and poetics. In J. J. Weber (ed.), *The Stylistics Reader*. London: Arnold.

Joyce, J. 1996. *Ulysses*. Nanjing: Yilin Press.

Joyce, J. 1996. *A Portrait of the Artist as a Young Man*. Nanjing: Yilin Press.

Kelly, D. 1988. *Narrative Strategies in Joyce's Ulysses*. Ann Arbor: UMI Research Press.

Leech, G. N. 2001. *A Linguistic Guide to English Poetry*. Peking: Foreign Language Teaching and Research Press.

Meighan, M. 1999. Words? Music? No, It's What's Behind: The Language of "Sirens" and "Eumaeus" in James Joyce's *Ulysses*. http://home. earthlink. net/~ mdmeighan/ thesis. html, accessed 20/05/2014.

Plett, H. F. 1985. Rhetoric. In Teun A. van Dijk (ed.), *Discourse and Literature*. Amsterdam: John Benjamins Publishing Company.

Sultan, S. 1987. *Eliot, Joyce and Company*. New York: Oxford University Press.

Topia, A. 1986. "Sirens": The emblematic vibration. In Beja, M. & P. Herring (eds.), *James Joyce — The Centennial Symposium*. Urbana & Chicago: University of Illinois Press.

Wales, K. 1992. *The Language of James Joyce*. Houndmills: MacMillan Education Ltd.

Wang Shouyuan. 2000. *An English Stylistics Coursebook*. Jinan: Shandong Education Press.

Repression and Redemption in " In Between the Sheets" : A Psychoanalytic Approach

Cao Jinmei　(Tsinghua University)

Abstract: "In Between the Sheets" is a representative work of McEwan in the era of "Ian Macabre". With the development of story, taboo topics such as pedophilia, homosexuality, and incestuous urge are brought to light one by one in the tepid narration. Is this really a pornographic story as many readers and researchers think? If not, what underlies such heterodox desires? To answer these two questions will be helpful to go into the psychology of the characters, understand their behaviors and then interpret the deep meanings hidden under the apparent absurdity and pornography of the plot. This article, taking the whole story "In Between the Sheets" as analytical data, resorting to a psychoanalytic approach, especially those parts relating to dreams and the unconscious, explores the characters' repressed desires and the process of their self-redemption, hoping to dig up the positive implication of the story.

Key words: desire; repression; redemption; unconscious; dream

1. Introduction

Ian McEwan is one of those writers who can always attract the attention and be taken seriously within and without academia. On the one hand, most of his writings grace the bestseller lists and are welcome among popular readers. On the other, he is enthusiastically commented and studied by critics and scholars. But the opinions about him and his writings are widely divergent. The admirers acclaim him as one of " the decade's better writers", one of " the more important writers of his generation" (Slay, 1991: 5) , one of the "key writers who fashioned an ethical vision for the ' post-consensus ' period " (Head, 2007: 2) and some even entitle him the British "National Author". By contrast, the abominators usually bombard his subject matters, especially those haunting his early works, such as incest, sado-masochism, rape, pornography and so on. In their eyes, such themes are grotesque and disturbing, repugnant and repulsive. Based on such an impression, they fasten McEwan a nickname "Ian Macabre" (Groes, 2009: 1).

"In Between the Sheets" under analysis is an early representative story of McEwan included in his eponymous anthology *In Between the Sheets* (1978). Although narrated by a third-person narrator, it actually presents the perspective of the central character, a divorced writer. The story revolves around the character's preoccupation before and during the visit of his fourteen-year-old daughter who decides to stay with him temporarily. This is a typical "literature of shock". In it, indelicate, heterodox, even taboo topics, such as waste of every kind, formlessness, incestuous impulse, pedophilia, and homosexuality, are touched upon. When reading the story, we cannot help thinking: What's the father's thoughts toward his daughter? How does he think of the relationship between the two girls? What lies behind his dream? What does his return to the paternal role mean? With these questions in mind, the author tries to use a psychoanalytic approach to explore the protagonist's psychology and behavior, hoping to dig out the positive meaning underlying this disputed short novel.

2. Boisterous McEwan Study and Unheeded "In Between the Sheets"

Never being short of commentators and researchers, McEwan has become even hotter these years with the accumulation of works. In the West, there are 19 published monographs, more than 10 Ph. D. dissertations, about 35 book sections and 46 major journal articles devoted to the discussion of McEwan. Studies in China are also on the rise. There are 1 Ph. D. dissertation, 48 M. A. theses, and 43 journal articles on McEwan. In addition, there are 8 books that devote either one chapter or one section of a chapter to McEwan.

Much early criticism on McEwan belongs to moral criticism and mainly concerns the shocking themes such as sex, violence and perversion in his fiction. Some orthodox critics label him as "pornographer", "dirty", "chronicler" of "snot and pimples" (Haffenden, 1985: 173). More understanding critics accept his writings and try to excavate the underlying values. For instance, Hermione Lee (1978: 86−87) claims McEwan as a master of "the power to shock". Jeannette Baxter (2009: 15) takes the conscious desublimation as a "hallmark" of McEwan's early works. Kiernan Ryan (1999: 204) suggests that these shocking elements may stem from an "unnerving honesty about the secret ubiquity of depravity and its seductive appeal".

As time goes, more and more varied perspectives and methods are taken to investigate McEwan's works. Adam Mars-Jones, Angela Roger, and Earl Ingersoll fall into the feminist group. They explore the narrative voice, women figures in *The Child in Time*, *Black Dogs* and *Amsterdam* respectively. Christina Byrnes, Judith Seaboyer and Elizabeth Wallace resort to psychoanalytical methods proposed by Freud and Lacan to make enlightening interpretations of McEwan's individual texts. David Malcolm, Judith Seaboyer, Elke D'Hoker, Nick Bentley and Michael Ross get inspiration from genre criticism and try to clarify the genre adscription of McEwan's works including *Atonement*, *Saturday* and some previous long fictions. There are also a lot of excellent studies based on structuralism (e.g. Earl G. Ingersoll, Richard Pedot), cultural studies (e.g. Hossein Payandeh), family systems theory (e.g. Colleen M. Hennessey), spatial theory (e.g. Robert E. Kohn) and neo-Darwinism (e.g. Jonathan Greenberg, James M. Mellard). Studies from narratological perspective are plentiful as well: taking *Atonement* as an object, Brian Finney explores the metafictional elements; James Harold and Peter Mathew analyze the narrative voice, structure, and the multiple perspectives; James Phelan talks about narrative judgment.

Taking McEwan study on the whole as a reference, studies on "In Between the Sheets" are pathetically meager. As the title story of the anthology, it is undoubtedly attached great importance to by the author himself. And it assuredly helps form the McEwan style in his early career. But maybe because of the limit of its length, and maybe because it is not as shocking as his other contemporaneous stories, "In Between the Sheets" hasn't got deserving attention from the critics. In the literature available, there is no complete study devoted to it, only some sporadic comments scattered here and there. David Malcolm, Jack Slay Jr. and some other critics, when mentioning "In Between the Sheets", pay more attention to the plot and the father-daughter relationship in the story. Dominic Head (2007: 44) takes the story as "the most powerful piece" in the collection, but his analysis also stops at the father's wrestling with the closeness between paternal and erotic love for his pubescent, visiting daughter. After a close reading, it is not difficult to find that "In Between the Sheets" is far from being pornographic as the title appears to be. Instead, according to the author of this article, it can even be claimed as the most serious and human piece in the whole collection. Thus, a thorough re-analysis of the story is necessary and significant, which will not only make up the insufficiency in the study of McEwan's early creation, but also be instructive for readers to realize the philosophical and social implications beneath the absurd and awkward behaviors of characters in the postmodernist novels. In view of the present research status, the author of this article tries to make a thorough exploration of the story from the psychoanalytical perspective.

3. Feasibility and Efficacity of Psychoanalytic Approach

Like a black wizard, McEwan is good at accessing the most ulterior point of reader's heart. In his early creation, McEwan tries various devices to reveal the "psychological and emotional disturbances beneath an ordered social veneer" (Bradbury, 2004: 217). Among them, psychoanalysis is one that McEwan consciously embraces in his works. As far as McEwan is concerned, psychoanalysis is "a structure for understanding the self and the world" (Groes, 2009: 8). David Malcolm has noticed this and summarized McEwan's writing career as such: it shows a broadening of concerns from "the hermetically and luridly psychopathological world of the early fiction" to "a new maturity in his examination of social issues and his endorsement of the possibilities of redemption" in his later work (Malcolm, 2002: 7). Christina Byrnes expresses similar opinion. For her, to fully understand the mysteries enveloping McEwan's works, the sensible way is to resort to psychodynamic methods. Because these methods can not only "shed light on the more obscure aspects of the mind" but also provide a language that makes it possible to "think and write about the hidden processes that explain the irrational and bizarre" (Byrnes, 2002: 2). To support her viewpoint, Byrnes, with the method, analyzes many of McEwan's works.

Psychoanalytic criticism is the literary criticism which adopts concept, method, and form from the tradition of psychoanalysis originated by Sigmund Freud to analyze and interpret texts. Like psychoanalysis itself, this critical endeavor seeks evidence of unresolved emotions, psychological conflicts, guilt, ambivalences, and so forth embedded in literary works. Since open to other critical groups, psychoanalytic criticism now has gained great critical vitality and developed into a rich and heterogeneous interpretive tradition.

The most fundamental concept of psychoanalysis is the notion of the unconscious mind as a reservoir for repressed memories of traumatic events which continuously influence conscious thought and behavior. According to Freud, the conscious and the unconscious are two sides of the same coin — psyche. The unconscious is like a storehouse. It receives and stores hidden desires, ambitions, fears, passions, guilt, and irrational thoughts. And encouraged by its hidden desires and repressed wishes, the unconscious keeps on provoking the conscious. Dreams and parapraxes are the most common way that the unconscious expresses itself. When the repressed feelings or ideas cannot be adequately released, the ego must act and block any outward responses, thus internal conflict produced. Human psyche is very contradictory and intriguing. In order to bury all the conflict in the unconscious, we usually develop defenses such as: selective perception, selective memory, denial, displacement, projection, regression, fear of intimacy, and fear of death, among others.

Dream is privileged in Freud's metapsychology. Interpreting them has become a useful method in psychoanalysis. According to Freud (1961: 608), dreams are "the royal road to a knowledge of unconscious activities of the mind". In *The Interpretation of Dreams*, he argues that dreams originate from repressed desire. When the repressed desire is aroused by a recent experience, the unconscious wish recalls the previous memory. Thus, the unconscious wish needs to be satisfied with an illusory fulfillment at both the effects of recent experiences and a recollection of the distant repression. What matters in this process is the illusory representation of the repressed wish. The representation is different from the original one because the repressed desire has to seek for a fulfillment under the influence of censorship; hence the dream. Freud (1961: 160) assumes that "a dream is a fulfillment of a wish", but its illusory representation is distorted, because it aims to be defensive and subversive for the sake of censorship and the primary impulse, respectively. In the process of absorbing from or being allied with other areas, psychoanalytic criticism has developed many new theories, but overall, it still relies heavily on Freud's theories and practices concerning the development of human personality and the underlying motivations of individual actions.

Since psychoanalytic criticism investigates literary text by means of analyzing the mechanisms of human psyche, it is perfectly appropriate to understand McEwan's frequent portrayal of sexual desires, traumatized childhood, and psychopathic characters, which occupy particular significance in his early works. In the following part, we will resort to the key concepts and opinions in psychoanalysis, by means of analyzing the repressed desires of the main characters and the process of their self-redemption, to achieve a better understanding of McEwan's anatomy of human soul and appreciation of his style in that period of time.

4. Repression and Redemption: A Psychoanalytic Interpretation

Although we have mentioned that "In Between the Sheet" is not as pornographic as the title indicates, sex still occupies a kernel and decisive position in the story. So our discussion unfolds around this sensitive topic. Sex has long been a taboo topic which is closely related with pornography. Sontag is among the first group of scholars who take literary pornography seriously and justify its position in arts. For her, literary pornography is "a minor but interesting modality or convention within the arts" (Sontag, 2002: 35). The power of it can be measured by "the originality, thoroughness, authenticity, and power of that deranged consciousness itself" (Sontag, 2002: 94). McEwan, in his works, makes serious use of sex and makes it a valid method to elaborate on extreme forms of human consciousness, a sharp scalpel to anatomize the human soul. Terence Winch appreciates McEwan's way of dealing with sex. According to him, sex in McEwan's works is "an invitation not to love, but to violence. It is a weapon used to exert power over others, to possess and objectify them. Love becomes an infantile and destructive force, a source of humiliation" (Winch, 1979: 1). Barry Yourgrau in his review of the collection shows an analogous standpoint: McEwan "illuminates the genuine, anguished perplexities of the heart, the grimy desperations of the groin" (Yourgrau, 1979: 88). In one word, to understand McEwan's delicate thought and unique style, sex is a well-suited and meritorious breakthrough point.

"In Between the Sheets" begins with the dream of the male protagonist, Stephen Cooke. In Freud's opinion, dream is the distorted representation of one's repressed desire. So the process of interpreting a dream is the way to penetrate into the deepest recesses of one's psychology. Cooke is a divorcee. At night, he has an erotic dream and welcomes a long lost orgasm. The story seems enveloped in a shroud of eroticism from the beginning. But McEwan holds back the development of the story along this line skillfully. Except the sketchy introduction, he does not allow the narrator to mention anything about the content of that dream. However, this vaguely mentioned sentence provides some basic information about the protagonist: he is lonely, depressive and thirst for love and, at the same time, it successfully arouses the readers' interest in further reading. Just as readers do, Cooke also wants to dig out the reason for his orgasm, because he has long confessed and been considered as an impotent. The dream is the condension and release of his suppressed desire and internal conflict, which is explained explicitly in a book he later reads, "An emission during a dream indicates the sexual nature of the whole dream, however obscure and unlikely the contents are. Dreams culminating in emission may reveal the object of the dreamer's desire as well as his inner conflicts. An orgasm cannot lie" (McEwan, 1979: 85). So what recalls his libido becomes an important clue for readers to grasp the psychology and behavior of this character. Cooke himself also wants to make clear, but the details about the dream are lost in memory. He can only remember that it concerns the café, the girl and the coffee machine. All are so common and no tantalizing at all. How can they arouse his sexual desire?

Recent experience can usually become a trigger of something hidden. From the second paragraph on, the third-person narrator flashes back to what happened on the preceding day — Cooke's appointment with his ex-wife. Can this experience be the stimulus? At the beginning of the retrospect, the narrator succinctly delineates the relationship between the ex-couple. The imbalance of power is striking distinct. Firstly, the habitual late-coming of the woman continues even after they divorced. As usual, she is late again this time, which seems to tell readers that, no matter during the marriage or after, she is accustomed to consuming the protagonist's love and being miserly with her respect for him. Secondly, they have different requirements for the level of the appointment place, which may also be the reflection of their requirement for the quality of life. "She disliked cheap cafés." So before she comes into the poor meeting place chosen by Cooke, she would like to make sure that Cooke has been there. Such a behavior further estranges their relationship. Cooke is evidently clear about his ex-wife's habit, and has been accustomed to catering to her in and out of marriage. When noticing her observing, to reassure her, he "moved his chair to give her a more complete view of his face" (McEwan, 1979: 78). Thirdly, she is the absolute controller of the whole meeting. She severely criticizes Cooke's choice of a poor meeting place; she mercilessly jeered at Cooke's weakness; she resolvedly vetoed Cooke's suggestion for spending a few days with their daughter. Cooke, in contrast, is a weaker and fawner. When the ex-wife criticizes his poor taste, he "smiled indulgently". Seeing she swabs her mouth with tissues, he requests her to give him a piece. Such an ordinary thing also becomes the ex-wife's teasing target. When she makes fun of whether he wants to use the tissue to wipe tears, Cooke only makes a weak retort by arguing that he only wants to blow his nose. Up to this time, Cooke behaves tolerantly and restrainedly although he occupies a disadvantageous position all the way. But when the ex-wife takes the place of her daughter to refuse his invitation, he is irritated and begins to defend his dignity bravely. His insistence on hearing his daughter's opinion and his banging on the table are the symbols of his revolt. Fourthly, they usually disagree with each other. But this time they reach a rare agreement — objecting to employing child laborer.

The unpleasant appointment is an epitome of their life. The mightiness of the woman and the weakness of the man shown during this meeting, in other words, is the projection of their previous marital relationship. The husband has to stoop to the high-handed control of the wife and in the meanwhile he has to endure her cutting remarks. His dignity as a man suffers from ravage now and then. His true self has to be concealed and repressed.

The second meeting of them offers more evidence for the judgment drawn in the former part. Their lopsided power relationship shows clearly from the very beginning. Cooke comes to ask for the daughter's decision about the visit. When the wife comes to open the door out of his expectation, Cooke is evidently shocked. There appears a temporary aphasia and he only squeezes a few words out at last, "Is ... is Miranda there?" The ex-wife continues her usual haughty posture, "She had the advantage of three concrete steps and she glared down at him, waiting for him to speak." Maybe the ex-wife is not the one after his own heart, but the ambiance of family is what he aspires after. He chooses to neglect her attitude. When he steps into the house he once lived sixteen years, his heart cannot help becoming soft and warm. Immersed in such a mood, the room becomes "comfortable, unchanging". The grand piano even stirs his desire to play, if possible, he would like to play happily for some time and forget why he comes here. The ex-wife's calling his daughter becomes a pleasant thing in his ear. He goes so far as to imitate the tune back on piano, which brings the woman's taut. But his mood isn't influenced, because the warmth of home makes him intoxicated. Everything goes well up to now. Yet as soon as the ex-wife turns directly to that question related to the daughter, their relationship becomes tense again. Cooke "resigned himself to hostilities". The ex-wife returns to the opinionated state again.

From the above scene, we can see something more clearly. Firstly, as shown in their first meeting, the relationship is still lack of harmony. The ex-wife keeps a usual domineering position and likes to decide all by herself. Her belittlement and contempt for the ex-husband is obvious. Secondly, the marriage life may not be a good memory for Cooke, but the feeling of home still occupies a very important position and jumps out in the due time to incite his desire for the warmth. Unfortunately, his enthusiasm gets quenched by the ex-wife once again.

If we say the former two meetings annotate the ex-couple's past marital relationship through their present performance, the third confrontation undoubtedly offers some new information. This time the ex-couple is on the phone. They are discussing about Charmian, Miranda's friend, who Cooke has met in the former meeting. He amazes at the two girl's queer association and worries about their relationship. Cooke wants to know about his ex-wife's opinion in that matter. But the ex-wife seems to have no such anxiety and thinks that "It's fine by me." Her calmness sets fire to Cooke's self-contempt. He interprets the ex-wife's reaction as her connivance for the daughter's possible unorthodox behavior and her trial and revenge on him. In his mind, she hates him all the time because of "his fearfulness, his passivity", because of "all the wasted hours between the sheets". It takes her many years of marriage to say that hatred out and "the experimentation in his writing, the lack of it in his life" intensifies it (McEwan, 1979: 88). Cooke is so sensitive that the accumulation of his deeply rooted self-contempt and possible impotence ultimately results in this desperate speculation. The explicit physical manifestation and the implicit sexual anxiety become omnipresent elements in Cooke's life, which shows their influence now and then.

Such an inharmonious husband-wife relationship cannot alone become the trigger of Cooke's wet dream. To know more reasons, we have to come back to the details of the dream finally accumulated by Cooke: "His wife was in the café. It was for her that he was buying coffee. A young girl took a cup and held it to the machine. But now *he* was the machine, now *he* filled the cup" (the italics are in the original version) (McEwan, 1979: 87). In the dream, there appear another two important stimuli — a young girl and a coffee machine. The wife appearing in the dream is the initial stimulus for him to take further actions. What he will do is to meet her need. The girl becomes the direct inducement. Dream is the fulfillment of one's wish in an illusory way, in which some unconscious things are stimulated. Analyze this dream in psychoanalytic terms: coffee is the symbol of desire, while to satisfy the wife's desire is Cooke's innermost wish. To achieve that goal, he transforms into powerful coffee machine. The transformation itself symbolizes Cooke's call for an ideal self. The girl to fetch the coffee maybe represents something which he is really interested in and which helps him finally accomplish his wish. To sum up, the dream transmits the following information: first, Cooke's libido is repressed and he has the urge to release it; second, one reason for his repression is the failed performance in sex; third, he expects his powerfulness. Besides these, the dream lets out another piece of information — Cooke seems to have the inclination of pedophilia. This theme gets McEwan a constant bombardment. But in my pinion, just like the topic of sex in general, McEwan is serious and prudent in dealing with pedophilia.

And more importantly, it becomes a crucial juncture for the characters' self-redemption.

To understand this theme better, we have to reexamine Cooke's contact with the small girls appearing in the story. The girl that first comes into our analysis is the waitress of the café. This Italian girl has nothing attractive in appearance, but she succeeds in catching Cooke's eye and his heart. The world one looks is usually what he thinks. Cooke has great attachment to children, in his eyes they are tinted with a trace of maturity. The Italian girl's eyes are "heavy and dull with adult cares". The disgusting snot of her becomes lovely and changes into "silver thread" and "colourless pearl". Her behavior of making coffee miraculously transforms into a sexual hint for repressed Cooke, which directly leads to his wet dream. The second girl that deserves our attention is Charmian. She is a doll-like dwarf, in Cooke's words, a person "belongs by right in a circus or silk-hung brothel serving tea". Such a figure, from the beginning, challenges Cooke's psychology. The great distance in appearance between her and Miranda leads him to doubt their relationship. When she expresses her respect and tells Cooke Miranda's pride in him, her gaze becomes so penetrating that Cooke almost surrenders upon it and confesses to her the innermost secret about his impotence, "I never satisfied my wife in marriage, you see. Her orgasm terrified me." (McEwan, 1979: 86) With their coming for holiday, Charmian's threat to Cooke becomes much clearer. She even tries to shut the door upon him. Cooke is annoyed by her mischief and scoops her into air. He means to lift her high like a child, but he fails, the reason is that "she was heavy, heavy like an adult". The third thing showing Cooke's extra concern for girls is the preparation he makes for the coming of Miranda and Charmian. In order to welcome them, he does a thorough cleaning and tries every means to make the home comfortable. Even those things that they will never notice are not immune. "He raked out gobs of ancient filth from under the kitchen sink, poured dead flies and spiders from the lamp fixtures, boiled fetid dishcloths; he bought a toilet brush and scrubbed the crusty bowel" (McEwan, 1979: 87). The excessive enthusiasm, consideration and diligence he shows for the matter even makes himself suspect that he has really become an old fool.

Putting these three cases together, we can draw a rough conclusion that Cooke's psychology is complex and contradictory toward these small girls:

instinctively, he has an infatuation for them. In his eyes, these immature bodies not only have liveliness of small children, but also have the sexiness of adult; reasonably, he still likes to regard them as children, their purity is the thing he does not want to blaspheme. Cooke's guilty conscience shown before Charmian is in essence an interrogation of his soul. In face of children's naivety, his deepest repression and wound might be exposed. The failure of lifting Charmian up shows his return to the repressed adult world. In social role, Cooke is the father of Miranda, so he has the responsibility to guide the daughter's life. His enmity toward Charmian is an indirect expression of his paternal love. To summarize, Cooke really has a tendency of pedophilia, but he has tried every means to smother the unorthodox desire.

Cooke's sense of insecurities and inadequacies, his sexual performance in the failed marriage, and his pedophile tendency begin to converge and gradually develops into a complex feeling for his daughter. This feeling is not so pure on the whole. When answering his daughter's letter, Cooke transplants his emotion for his wife into it. Or in another word, he regards his daughter as the substitute for his wife, "In effect it was his wife he had addressed." The evil-doers are always milk-livered. To prevent Miranda from being aware of this inappreciable guilt, he sends her thirty pounds rather than the twenty-five pounds she required. But after sending the money, he begins to worry about that the extra five pounds will betray his real intention. So he spends the following two days in writing his daughter another letter for nothing particular. It is evident that Cooke drops into a trap of mood made by himself.

The process of preparing presents for Miranda, once again, reveals his impure thoughts. Firstly, the slogans on the T-shirts he buys for her speak out his heart: "It is Raining in My Heart" shows his struggle in depression; "Still a Virgin" and "Ohio State University", besides mentioning a fact, express a father's expectation. In short, these three slogans reflect the conflict between his incestuous urge and paternal love. Secondly, he buys her a lot of birthday presents and most of them are adult oriented, such as pomander, dice, necklace, silk scarf and cologne. He even plans to buy her some underwear. All these show that he regards Miranda as a woman rather than a fourteen-year-old child. At the same time, he is making efforts to repel the shabby thoughts, which can be seen from his reselecting presents after coming back home. He loathes the sickly excess and condescension of the presents and tries to retrospect "the certainty" with which he has bought them. At last, he decides to send Miranda the five-pound record token only. The choice itself means that his paternal love gets the upper hand in this round.

Cooke's abnormal affection for his daughter also shows itself when he has physical contact with her. The first embrace happens when he comes to inquire whether she would spend holiday together with him. At that time, his feeling for her is almost pure and fatherly, "She felt different to the touch, stronger perhaps. She smelled unfamiliar, she had a private life at last, accountable to no one" (McEwan, 1979: 85). To Cooke, one thing is sure that his daughter has grown up and begun to have her own life. This may stir some envy in his heart. If the daughter is said to be an evidence of his masculinity, her growth, especially the part without his accompaniment, is the mark of his failure which shows the time he is away from family life. The second time is that Miranda rests her head on his shoulder and acts like a spoiled child. Cooke has sensed something different. When hugging her, the carefulness "not to touch her breasts" has revealed his consciousness about her physical development. As they contact more, Cooke's feelings become more ambiguous and more complex. When Charmian and Miranda does the washing, the whisper of the girls and the clatter of the dishes bring Cooke a sense of home and make him soothed. In an instant, the image of Miranda as his daughter becomes blurred, "She moved easily between woman and child." When Miranda shows her contempt for schoolboys, Cooke clearly sees the trace of his wife on her, "Never before had the resemblance between his wife and daughter seemed so strong." The contact before going to bed brings his incestuous urge to the climax. "He squeezed her hand. 'See you in the morning,' he murmured, left her there and hurried in to his study. He sat down, horrified at his erection, elated." (McEwan, 1979: 91) Impotence has partially led to the failure of his marriage and hurt his dignity as a man. It is his deepest psychological wound. Now the sexual impulse comes. Although he realizes that the elation is ignominious and guilty, he is still immersed in the elation it brings and reluctant to withdraw, "But he wanted to sing, he wanted to play his piano, he wanted to go for a walk. He did none of these things. He sat still, staring ahead, thinking of nothing in particular, and waited for the chill excitement to leave his belly." (McEwan, 1979: 91) His long repressed desire gets released once. While he enjoys it, he doesn't lose his head. He is clear that it is a serious matter, not only precarious for himself but also for his daughter. He should be sober and analytical.

The unexpected urge doesn't bring him a good night. He is tortured and seems to hear a mysterious sound now and then. "He could not remember what the sound was, only that he had not liked it." Does he really hear the sound? What's the sound? Why does he dislike it? When the sound is motioned again, everything becomes clear. That is a sound "so forgotten, so utterly familiar" and it forms the "background for all other sounds, the frame of all anxieties. The sound of his wife in, or approaching, orgasm." (McEwan, 1979: 92) Actually Cooke doesn't hear that sound at all. The sound he hears is only his auditory hallucination, put it in another way, it is only his inner voice. Inner voice is a kind of triggered unconscious. The source of Cooke's agony is that he couldn't satisfy his wife. The wife's elated sound has become an impossible fantasy which has haunted him and become a nightmare of his life. When he is on the verge of violating his daughter, the sound appears, which can be said an alarm for Cooke. It warns Cooke that both his repression and desire are because of his ex-wife. No matter what happens, Miranda still is and must be his daughter. The last contact between the father and daughter is the climax and turning point of the whole story. During the night Miranda awakes and in the hallway she confronts Cooke who is totally exposed. It is a weird scene, but there is nothing obscene, instead, something holy. Miranda pays no attention to the father's naked body. She is only a child who needs father's consolation and accompaniment. Cooke is also not ashamed of his naked self. Although such thoughts as "she could be a child or a woman" and "she could be any age" still flash through his mind, his mean desire has been smothered in the face of the daughter's trust and dependence. Paternal concern asserts itself and he patiently gets her to go to sleep. Looking at the peacefully sleeping girl, Cooke also gets sublimed. "She was asleep and almost smiling, and in the pallor of her unturned throat he thought he saw from one bright morning in his childhood a field of dazzling white snow which he, a small boy of eight, had not dared scar with footprints." (McEwan, 1979: 93) Cooke successfully defeats the sexual predator that, in response to his life's lessons in sexual inadequacy, has been growing within him. Thus, the endangered innocence of father and daughter is re-established and his soul gets redeemed (Head, 2007: 44).

The relationship between Miranda and Charmian is another thing that attracts critics' attention. They are usually taken as the representation of homoerotic desire. Really, from the start everything appears a little bit strange. The atmosphere in the room is sappy and subtle. Miranda and Charmian show a very intimate relationship: both are naked; Charmian is caressing Miranda's back. They are listening to the song of The Rolling Stone "Don'cha think there's a place for you in between the sheets?" They are enjoying the moment of being together, "it was all so remote from the aquatic gloom where time had stopped, where Charmian gently drew her nails across her friend's back for her birthday" (McEwan, 1979: 83). Cooke's coming interrupts them, but their pleasure still can be seen, "Their recent laughter seemed concealed in their silence." But according to me, it is only a strategy McEwan uses to create an ambiguous atmosphere. If we take the tone of the whole story into consideration, everything becomes understandable. Cooke is not so normal in psychology and his focus is on his daughter. Charmian's appearance is a challenge to him. Her composure, politeness, keenness and her later behavior of protecting Miranda arouse Cooke's doubt and envy. When he is haunted by the illusory orgasmic cries of his ex-wife, he seems also to hear such sounds coming from his daughter's bedroom. He is so afraid that Miranda and Charmian are lesbians. But when Miranda stands before him because of sleeplessness, when he sees sleeping Charmian, he knows that everything is only his imagination. He returns back to a normal man and a kind father. Maybe Cooke's desire is still partly repressed, but his soul is surely redeemed with the return of paternal concern.

5. Conclusion

"In Between the Sheets" is a story about desire and redemption. The protagonist, Stephen Cooke, because of the failed marriage becomes lonely, with a strong sense of failure and inadequacy. In the process of contact with different girls, he begins to manifest the inclination of pedophilia, and even forms an incestuous impulse for his fourteen-year-old daughter. His daughter may also have the tendency of homosexuality. How can we understand such heterodox phenomena? Are they sinking into depravity or have they fulfilled self-salvation? By means of the methods of psychoanalysis, especially by analyzing Cooke's wet dream and retracing the causes of that dream, we easily go into the innermost psychology of the characters and dig out the real reasons for their behaviors, and thus better understand the macabre world created by McEwan. The source of Cooke's abnormal predilection and occasional gaffes is his inferior position and repressed sexual desire in the failed marriage. The reason for Miranda's possible homosexuality may be the lack of fatherly protection and family love. But fortunately, the father and the daughter don't slip into the abyss of desire. They save themselves and the people loving them in their respective rational ways. Although enwrapped in absurdity and weirdness, "In Between the Sheets" penetrates into the depth of human nature and transmits the hope of self-redemption in a subtle way. That's why the author calls upon the reexamination and reorientation of this profound and classic short story.

References

Baxter, J. 2009. Surrealist encounters in Ian McEwan's early work. In S. Groes (ed.). *Ian McEwan: Contemporary Critical Perspectives*. London: Continuum International Publishing. 13–25.

Bradbury, M (ed.). 2004. *The Modern British Novel*. Beijing: Foreign Language Teaching and Research Press.

Byrnes, C. 2002. *The Work of Ian McEwan: A Psychodynamic Approach*. Nottingham: Paupers' Press.

Freud, S. 1961. *The Interpretation of Dreams* (first part). In J. Strachey (ed.). *The Standard Edition of The Complete Psychological Works of Sigmund Freud* (IV). London: The Hogarth Press.

Freud, S. 1961. *The Interpretation of Dreams* (second part) and *On Dreams*. In J. Strachey (ed.). *The Standard Edition of The Complete Psychological Works Of Sigmund Freud* (V). London: The Hogarth Press.

Groes, S. 2009. A cartography of the contemporary: Mapping newness in the work of Ian McEwan. In S. Groes (ed.). *Ian McEwan: Contemporary Critical Perspectives*. London: Continuum International Publishing. 1–12.

Haffenden, J. 1985. *Novelists in Interview*. London: Methuen.

Head, D. 2007. *Contemporary British Novelists: Ian McEwan*. Manchester & New York: Manchester University Press.

Lee, H. 1978. Shock horror. In *New Statesman*. 20 Jan. (95.2444): 86–87. Rpt. In *Short Story Criticism*. Vol. 106. Detroit: Gale. 86–87.

Malcolm, D. 2002. *Understanding Ian McEwan*. Columbia & South Carolina: University of

South Carolina.

McEwan, I. 1979 (c1978). *In Between the Sheets*. London: Pan Books. 78–93.

Ryan, K. 1999. Sex, violence and complicity: Martin Amis and Ian McEwan. In R. Mengham (ed.). *An Introduction to Contemporary Fiction*. Cambridge: Polity Press. 203–218.

Shen, Xiaohong. 2010. *Ethical Predicaments in Ian McEwan's Major Novels*. Ph.D. Dissertation. Shanghai: Shanghai International Studies University.

Slay, J. Jr. 1991. *A Prevailing Ordinariness: Society and Interpersonal Relationships in the Fiction of Ian McEwan*. Ph.D. Dissertation. Knoxville: The University of Tennessee.

Sontag, S. 2002. The pornographic imagination. In S. Sontag (ed.). *Styles of Radical Will* (c1967). Farrar, New York: Picador USA. 35–73.

Winch, T. 1979. Writing on the razor's edge. *The Washington Post (Book World)*. 5 Aug.: 1.

Yourgrau, B. 1979. Snot, sex, and something new. *The Village Voice*. 27 Aug.: 88.

"Idea-Image" and the Stylistic Dimension of Classical Chinese Fiction

Luo Huaiyu (**Beijing University of Chemical Technology**)

Abstract: In order to legitimize its own status as a literary genre and conform to the Confucian orthodoxy, classical Chinese fiction inherited many features of literariness from poetry and prose essay, of which a major one is the profusion of *yixiang*, or idea-images. This paper traces the theoretical development of idea-image as a literary term, compares with similar uses in Western literary theory, and explores its role in shaping the stylistic dimension of classical Chinese fiction.

Key words: idea-image; stylistic dimention; classical Chinese fiction

Towards the end of their seminal work *Style in Fiction: A Linguistic Introduction to English Fictional Prose,* Leech & Short made the following remark about the possible areas for future research:

> ... there are still aspects of stylistic involvement with novels that we have hardly begun to account for as yet. The stylistic explications of theme and evaluation are the most obvious areas awaiting development.

(Leech & Short, 2007: 304)

If we take a comparative perspective and look across into the world of Chinese literature, what Leech & Short meant by "the stylistic explications of theme and evaluation" might perhaps direct the scholarly attention further to the so-called "idea-image" (*yixiang*, 意象) in classical Chinese fiction, which often serves thematic purposes and conveys authorial values in addition to shaping its aesthetic form. Classical Chinese fiction may be regarded as a melting pot of different generic features, notably those of historiography, poetry, and rhythmical essay. To legitimize its status as a literary genre whilst conforming to the Confucian social orthodoxy, classical Chinese fiction inherited from these other genres certain features of literariness, of which a major one is the profusion of "idea-images". As the term itself indicates, "idea-image" is a state of indivisibility between the "conceptual" and the "perceptual", between the "intangible" and the "concrete". Such a juxtaposition may point to the possibility of deciphering the underlying "theme and evaluation" through stylistic analysis of iconic words. Hence the task of this research, which is to briefly trace the origin and development of "idea-image" in Chinese literary theory, classify the major forms of "idea-image" in classical Chinese fiction, and illustrate its important relevance to, and role in, "theme and evaluation".

1. Origin and Development in Chinese Literary Theory

The earliest discussion of "idea-image" as a literary term can be found in *The Literary Mind and the Carving of Dragons* by Liu Xie (ca. 465−520):

独照之匠,窥意象而运斤;此盖驭文之首术,谋篇之大端。

(Lu & Mou, 1982: 85)

English Translation: The uniquely discerning carpenter wields his axe with his eye to the **idea-image**. This is the foremost technique in directing the course of *wen*, the major point for planning a piece.

(Owen, 1992: 204)

The notion of "idea-image" is highly metaphysical in Liu Xie's theoretical context, so he illustrated it with a vivid example: when an experienced carpenter starts making an artefact, he wields his axe not according to any given object or schema, but follows his "inward eye", whose vision Liu Xie designated as the "idea-image". It is obvious that, according to Liu Xie, "idea-image" stands for the general and predominant idea or design that an author has in mind when he sets his pen to paper.

With the development of Chinese literature, particularly the blossoming of rhymed poetry since the Han Dynasty and its golden age in the Tang and Song Dynasties, the notion began gradually to lose its metaphysical dimension and was concretized as a stylistic feature of good poetry. That is why almost every Tang poetry features the profusion of "idea-images", which are largely unique to the Chinese literary aesthetics. Suffice it to contrast two well-known poems of a similar theme. One is "Autumn Thoughts" by Ma Zhiyuan of the

Yuan Dynasty (a dynasty which bridges the golden age of poetry in the Tang and the Song Dynasties and the heyday of narrative fiction in the Ming and the Qing Dynasties), and the other is "I Wandered Lonely as a Cloud" by the English Romanticist poet William Wordsworth.

Autumn Thoughts [1]

Withered vines, olden tree, ev'ning crows;
Tiny bridge, flowing brook, hamlet homes;
Ancient road, wind from west, bony horse;
The sun is setting,
Broken man, far from home, roams and roams.

(**A Chinese painting based on the poem**)

The poem is composed of a string of different but interrelated "idea-images", almost all static. Even the setting sun cannot be taken as a moving image in this context, but rather an indication of time, a toning of atmosphere, and a transition to the weighty end — the world of the "broken man". With this end line, all the "idea-images" come together to appeal to the reader's heart and mind as a whole, amounting to an experience of the "idea-realm" (*yijing*, 意

---

1   This English version "Autumn Thoughts" was translated by the late Professor Zhao Zhentao of Hunan Normal University. The present author is unable to find a published source when this article is being penned, and the above rendering is recalled from his memory of a version shared by Professor Cao Bo of Hunan Normal University, who is a former student of Professor Zhao's.

境) teeming with the sense of melancholy and forlornness. In English poetry, the importance of images may similarly be felt. However, there seems to be a general tendency where more prominence is given to the persona's consciousness or the actions s/he initiates or experiences, rather than to "frozen" "idea-images" themselves, although there can be exceptions such as in the poems of imagism. In contrast with the foregoing Chinese poem, I have selected a segment of Wordsworth's "I Wandered Lonely as a Cloud":

> I **wandered** lonely as a <u>cloud</u>
> That **floats** on high o'er <u>vales and hills</u>,
> When all at once **I saw** a crowd,
> A host, of <u>golden daffodils</u>;
> Besides the <u>lake</u>, beneath the <u>trees</u>,
> **Fluttering** and **dancing** in the <u>breeze</u>.
>
> (Fergusonet et al., 2005: 801)

Very clearly, Wordsworth's poem is centred on the persona's flowing consciousness. It is the persona's dynamic vision and a temporal progression with narrative potential that directs the reader's literary imagination. The images themselves, such as "cloud", "vales and hills", "golden daffodils", etc. merely denote physical objects in the real world and fulfils mostly the purpose of rhyming.

The reasons for the prevalence of and preference for "idea-images" in classical Chinese literature may be sought further from a more fundamental level of philology and etymology. As is earlier mentioned, traditional Chinese fiction embraced many features of "orthodoxy" from rhymed poetry and the rhythmical essay in order to enhance its own literary legitimacy. But, apart from this inheritance from poetry, a more fundamental reason for the literary significance of "idea-image" must be the particularities of the Chinese language itself, which has no formal markers of tense, number, or case, and is highly paratactic, and the pictographic or ideographic Chinese characters. Simply take the word "天涯" (tianya) in "Autumn Thoughts" for example. Literally, it means "the edge of sky". For metrical foot and meter, it was translated into "far from home" in Zhao's English version. However, even though the basic meaning is shared between "天涯" and "far from home", readers of the Chinese original may still have a subtly different reading experience, because this word, though itself an "idea-image", is constituted by three concrete and smaller "idea-images", namely, "天" (*tian*, heaven), "氵" (a radical in Chinese characters meaning "water"), and "厓" (*ya*, an ideograph for cliff or edge). When the Chinese read this word, they grasp its meaning naturally without having to recall images of its three constitutive elements. However, on the other hand, it is also because of such a linguistic habitus and cultural immersion that they have attached to this word their strong sentiment and rich imagination of far-off people or situations, making it one of the most frequently used in literary diction.

2. "Idea-Image" and the Style of Classical Chinese Fiction

Having delineated the theoretical origin and development of "idea-image" as an important literary term, I shall now discuss in details how it functions to shape the distinct style of classical Chinese fiction. The contribution of "idea-image" to the style of classical Chinese fiction is multifarious and complicated. Yet, based on its textual features in the *Outlaws of the Marsh* and *A Dream of Red Mansions*, I shall classify it into three major forms and functions and analyse how each of them enriches the stylistic dimension of classical Chinese fiction.

a. Rich Implications of "Idea-Image" through Proper Names

In the *Outlaws of the Marsh*, it is very common for important characters to bear nicknames, which usually goes together with their formal names when making the first show. In fact, all the 108 heroes have nicknames that either stand for their striking physical features or their reputations in the world of heroes. For example, Lin Chong is known as "the Panther Head" (豹子头). The "idea-image" contained in his name stimulates imagination in three directions. Firstly, the reader may construct a unique "visual" image of Lin Chong before reading any specific description. Secondly, the fierce image of the panther head naturally agrees with Lin Chong's identity before taking to banditry as an "arms instructor of the Mighty Imperial Guards" (八十万禁军枪棒教头); Thirdly, the brevity in the name "Lin Chong" and the dynamic sense of the given name character "Chong", which means "to dash or charge", echo strongly his alias "the Panther Head", and foreshadow his forthright character as a rebellious combat general. By the same token, Lu Da's alias "the Tattooed Monk" (or, more literally, "the Flowery Monk", 花和尚) implies that he might not be a Buddhist monk by nature. So the truth is that he became a monk just to evade criminal punishment. In addition, the juxtaposition of the word "monk" (和尚) with the word "flower" (花) in his nickname can enhance an effect of comicality during his several encounters with women.

In *A Dream of Red Mansions*, most of the maids' names contain a particular "idea-image". For example, Baoyu's favorite maid has a name with strong aesthetic and symbolic effect. Her full name Hua Xiren (花袭人), a result of Baoyu's improvisation, literally means "(the fragrance of) flowers assails men" (Yang & Yang, 1994: 51). The combination of these three particular characters not only makes a beautiful feminine name both in shape and sounds, but also carries an extraordinary "idea-image": *hua* (flower) *xi* (assail) *ren* (man). In the course of novel reading, such an "idea-image" can expand literary imagination in three dimensions. First, one may visualize through her name a scene of fragrant petals and pretty maids in Grand View Garden (大观园) of the Jias' Mansions. As a result, there seems to be a deeper connection between Xiren and the Jia family apart from her apparent affiliation. Second, the name reveals certain authorial values. By assigning such an unworldly name to this maid through Baoyu's mouth, the author must have wanted to present her differently from the other maids. As it turned out, Xiren was a very devoted and caring maid to the Jias, particularly to Baoyu, her virtue appealing strongly to masters of the Jias' Mansions; on the other hand, however, she was very calculating and perhaps aggressive in dealing with other maids of the household, which often left her jealous or loathed by others. Both aspects well explain the verb "assail" (袭) in her name. Third, the "idea-image" of this name partly reveals Baoyu's intuitive sensitivity for individualities in the ladies and maids around him.

The "idea-image" can also reside in place names. For example, the *Yuanyang Lou* (Duck and Drake Bower, 鸳鸯楼) in the chapter of Wu Song's killing General Zhang in the *Outlaws of the Marsh*. The word *yuanyang* (鸳鸯) stands for "mandarin ducks", with *yuan* (鸳) referring to the male bird and *yang* (鸯) the female bird. In Chinese culture, mandarin ducks are a beautiful symbol of true love and affection between men and women. Therefore, by naming the bower "Duck and Drake", a touch of romance or even licentiousness seems to be haunting the place. Jin Shengtan went further in interpreting this "idea-image". He conjectured that what was implied in this bower's name could be a metaphysics of duality in relation to plot development. He thus commented:

> 鸳鸯楼之立名,我知之矣,殆言得意之事与失意之事相倚相伏,未曾暂离, 喻如鸳鸯二鸟双游也……

(Shi & Jin, 2005: 350)

> About naming the bower Duck and Drake I know well. It must be alluding to the truth that weal and woe either accompany or cloak one another — not for an instant do they part — just like a pair of swimming mandarin ducks.

(Dolston, 1990)

b. "Idea-Image" of Descriptive or Rhetorical Functions

Since traditional Chinese fiction has a general preference for static descriptions of scenes and characters, "idea-images" of this kind abound. The employment of "idea-images" in descriptions can create a sense of beauty between vividness and ambiguity, thus fulfilling the reader's visual and visionary needs at the same time. Probably owing to an immanent process of metaphorization, the "idea-image" in Chinese fiction often goes hand in hand with rhetorical devices. The following example, taken out of a lengthy description of Lu Da's fight with Zheng (or Lord of the West, 镇关西), focalizes the three fatal punches Lu dealt at Zheng and involves three distinct "idea-images" and three figures of speech.

> 扑的只一拳,正打在鼻子上,打得鲜血迸流,鼻子歪在半边,却便似开了个**油酱铺:咸的、酸的、辣的,一发都滚出来。**……提起拳头来,就眼眶际眉梢只一拳,打得眼棱缝裂,乌珠迸出,也似开了个**彩帛铺**的:**红的、黑的、紫的,都绽将出来。**……又只一拳,太阳上正着,却是做了一个**全堂水陆的道场:磬儿、钹儿、铙儿,一齐响。**…… (Shi & Jin, 2005: 37-38)

> He landed a punch on Zheng's nose that flattened it to one side and brought the blood flowing like **the sauces in a condiments shop-salty, sour and spicy** ... He punched the butcher on the eyebrow, splitting the lid so that the eyeball protruded. **Red, black and purple** gore flowed like **swatches of cloth in a draper's shop** ... He struck the butcher a heavy blow on the temple. Zheng's head rang like **the clanging of gongs, bells and cymbals** in a big **memorial service** ...

(Shapiro, 1980: 54-55)

The three "idea-images" in the quoted description are introduced with three similes, namely, the "condiments shop" with all its "sauces", the "draper's shop" with "swatches of cloth", and the "memorial service" with "clanging gongs, bells and cymbals". And then **synaesthesia** is used to strengthen the effect of simile so that Zheng's painful reactions to the three punches are respectively linked to the salty, sour and spicy tastes of sauces in the condiments shop (taste), the red, black and purple colors of cloth in the draper's shop (sight), and the clanging of gongs, bells and cymbals in a big memorial service (sound). Descriptions of these three thrashings are presented in strict **parallelism**, with the effect of the third one compared to "a big memorial service", which also implies the ensuing death of the "Lord of the West".

The advantage of these three "idea-images" is that they are all familiar to everyday Chinese life, so that the reader may find more passion and pleasure reading it. He may also feel more convinced of the effect of Lu Da's fists than if the narrator pried omnisciently into Zheng's inner world and blankly told what he felt to the reader. For, if the psychological activities of Zheng were directly revealed to the reader, the latter would simply be put at the passive receiving end of narrative information; but through using "idea-images" in conjunction with synaesthesia, the reader can construct his own version of the story by activating real-life memories and experiences.

A Dream of Red Mansions marks the most extensive employment of "idea-images" as it reached a new depth in characterization, both physical and psychological, described numerous scenes within the Jias' Mansions, and incorporated a large number of classical poems. Another important feature is that it treated characters from different social strata with very different sets of "idea-images". The two examples below will show how "idea-images" function to deliver sharp contrast between characters' images. The first one is a small segment taken out of a long extravagant description of Wang Xifeng, the smart, charming, and powerful household manager of the Jias' Mansions, to show how, unlike the girls, she was richly dressed and resplendent as a fairy.

······一双丹凤三角眼,两弯柳叶吊梢眉······粉面含春威不露,丹唇未启笑先闻。

(Cao & Gao, 2002: 28)

... She had the almond-shaped eyes of a phoenix, slanting eyebrows as long and drooping as willow leaves ... The springtime charm of her powdered face gave no hint of her latent formidability. And before her crimson lips parted, her laughter rang out.

(Yang & Yang, 1994: 38-39)

It is worth pointing out that, unlike the English translation, the original is all made up of sentences of rigid **antithesis**, with a concentration of uncommon but elegant words portraying her attire, ornaments, and carriage. From this perspective, the presentation of "idea-images" might also be availed by the author to showcase his extraordinary capability of diction and ease of rhetoric. Aside from the apparent use of **simile**s and **metaphor**s, the most salient feature of the quoted segment is the combination of the real (*shi*, 实) and the virtual (*xu*, 虚) in presenting these "idea-images". For example, in presenting the "idea-image" of her eyes, there is a combination of the real "almond-shaped" and the virtual "phoenix"; in depicting the particular shape of her eyebrows, a more concrete image of "willow leaves" is effected; her rosy powdered cheek is matched with the intangible "springtime charm" and "latent formidability"; and, finally, the time gap between the parting of her crimson lips and the ringing of her laughter forms an interesting **hyperbole** that implies Wang's intrusive presence as a powerful lady in the house.

However, when portraying Granny Liu (刘姥姥), the old country woman who claims to be a "distant relative" of the Jias and is received purely formally by Wang Xifeng, the author employed entirely different "idea-images" and skilfully imbedded them into her verbal language to create a sense of jocosity and to exhibit her vulgarity and slickness.

> "嗳,我也是知道艰难的! 但俗语说的,'**瘦死的骆驼比马大**',凭他怎么,你老拔根**寒毛**,比我们的**腰**还粗呢。"

(Cao & Gao, 2002: 71)

> "Ah," she cried, "I know what difficulties are. But 'A **starved camel** is bigger than a **horse**.' No matter how, 'A **hair** from your body is thicker than our **waist**.'"

(Yang & Yang, 1994: 100)

The old granny said the above after Wang had mentioned giving her 20 taels of silver "to be going on with" while also stressing the big difficulties of a big household. Granny Liu, under such a circumstance, felt both gratified by the generous promise and somewhat embarrassed with this last point of Wang's. Hence, she made a pathetic gesture of standing in Wang's shoes and tried to flatter the latter while debasing herself (as contrasted by the disparity between the camel and the horse, the waist and the hair). As a result, the **metaphor**s, **hyperbole**, and **contrast** in the two sets of "idea-images" amount to the most hilarious effect, and the character of Granny Liu suddenly becomes true-to-life.

c. "Idea-Images" of Symbolic or Thematic Functions

The Ming-Qing critic Jin Shengtan had a very keen eye for those iterative "idea-images" in *Outlaws of the Marsh* and thought they had symbolic or thematic functions. He had a habit of recording on the margin the exact numbers of appearance for many symbolic words such as "club" (*shaobang*, 哨棒), when Wu Song was about to cross the tiger-haunted Jingyang Ridge, and "curtain" (*lianzi*, 帘子) in Pan Jinlian and Wu Da's house. He thought of this as a narrative technique and named it "snake in the grass or (discontinuous) chalk line" (Rolston, 1990: 140) (*caoshe huixian*, 草蛇灰线). When a snake is moving through the grass, portions of its body are hidden from view, but looking at its exposed portions one sizes up the whole body. Likewise, when the carpenter is working on a piece of lumber, he plans by drawing discontinuous chalk lines on it. Jin Shengtan commented on the elusiveness and structuralizing effect of such symbols:

> 骤看之,有如无物,及至细寻,其中便有一条线索,拽之通体俱动。
>
> (Shi & Jin, 2005: 4)
>
> Read in haste, there seems to be nothing there, but a closer look reveals a connecting thread (*xiansuo*, 线索) which, if pulled, draws the whole sequence together.
>
> (Rolston, 1990: 141)

Take the "idea-image" of "curtain" for example. Jin Shengtan highlighted sixteen significant repetitions of this "idea-image" between Wu Song's first homecoming, when his sister-in-law Pan Jinlian pulled open the door curtain to greet him, and his second return from an official escort mission, when he raised the door curtain only to see the memorial tablet for his brother. Due to the space allowed here, five significant repetitions out of the sixteen are quoted below to show the basic "connecting thread":

(1) 武松替武大挑了担儿,武大引着武松,转弯抹角,一径望紫石街来。转过两个弯,来到一个茶坊间壁,武大叫一声:"大嫂,开门。"只见**帘子**开处,一个妇人出到**帘子**下,应道:"大哥,怎地半早便归?"

（Shi & Jin, 2005: 261）

Wu Song carried his brother's shoulder-pole and hampers and Wu Da led the way. They wound through several lanes until they came to Purple Stone Street. The house was beside a tea-shop. "Wife, open the door," Wu Da shouted. A bamboo **curtain** was raised, and a woman appeared, "What are you doing home so early?" she asked.

（Shapiro, 1980: 363）

（2） 那妇人独自一个,冷冷清清,立在**帘**儿下等着,只见武松踏着那乱琼碎玉归来。那妇人揭起**帘子**,陪着笑脸迎接道:"叔叔寒冷。"

（Shi & Jin, 2005: 265）

She stood alone by the door **curtain** watching the snow till she saw him (Wu Song) coming through the falling flakes of white jade. She raised the **curtain** and greeted him with a smile. "Cold?"

（Shapiro, 1980: 368）

（3） "……假如你每日卖十扇笼炊饼,你从明日为始,只做五扇笼出去卖。每日迟出早归,不要和人吃酒。归到家里,便下了**帘子**,早闭上门,省了多少是非口舌。……"

（Shi & Jin, 2005: 269）

"... If you sell ten trays of buns a day usually, from tomorrow on don't sell more than five. Leave the house late and come back early. Don't drink with anybody. And when you get home, lower the **curtain** and bolt the door. In that way you'll avoid arguments ..."

（Shapiro, 1980: 373）

（4） 当日武大将次归来,那妇人惯了,自先向门前来叉那**帘子**。自古道:"没巧不成话。"那妇人正手里拿叉竿不牢,失手滑将倒去,不端不正,却好打在那人头巾上。

（Shi & Jin, 2005: 270）

Golden Lotus, expecting her husband home shortly, went to the door with a forked pole to lower the **curtain** over the entrance way. But then something happened. A man was passing by. As the old saying goes: "Without coincidence there would be no story." The pole she was holding slipped and landed right on the man's head.

（Shapiro, 1980: 376）

（5） 且说武松到门前揭起**帘子**,探身入来,见了灵床子,又写"亡夫武大郎之位"七个字,呆了!

（Shi & Jin, 2005: 297）

Wu Song raised the door **curtain** and entered. The first thing he saw was the tablet with the inscription: "In Memory of Wu the Elder, My Departed Husband". Shocked, he stared.

(Shapiro, 1980: 411)

In example (1), the "curtain" was the first object to register in the eye of Wu Song, and that of the reader, even before the heroine herself. Since traditional Chinese women were largely confined to the household, this "curtain" seems to be the thing separating Pan's domestic life and the outside world. Pan's reply to her husband "What are you doing home so early?" sounds typical of a housewife of her class, although, with further reading, we may find it indicative of the unequal power relations between the couple.

Pan Jinlian was more than pleased to know this unexpected brother-in-law was the tiger-beating hero who was made constable of the county. Admiring his handsome figure and manly character, she insisted Wu Song move over so that he could fare better as a bachelor. So Wu Song agreed. Example (2) tells of a snowy evening when Pan Jinlian was expecting Wu Song home instead of her laborious husband. The "curtain" takes on psychological colour this time as if it were witnessing Pan's loneliness and her amorous attachment to Wu Song. Her heart leapt each time she saw him, her smile and care to Wu Song form a sharp contrast to her response to Wu Da in example (1).

With Pan Jinlian more actively flirtatious with him, Wu Song became increasingly averse and alert. He was also concerned about the possible consequences for his poor brother. So, before leaving for a two-month escort mission, he gave advice to his ignorant brother in example (3), including "lowering the curtain and bolting the door" after getting home in the evening to avoid gossip. Now, the "curtain" binds the three people together and carries the plot to a point of transition, where the reader wonders what may happen to the "curtain" next in Wu Song's absence. Then, subsequently in example (4), the "curtain" serves as a medium by which the plot is diverted towards the romantic encounter between Pan Jinlian and her future paramour Ximen Qing. Their fiery adultery became so uncontrollable that it finally led to the calculated joint murder of Wu Da. Hence in example (5), when Wu Song came back, he raised the "curtain" only to see a memorial tablet.

The "curtain" is the obtrusive object in both example (1) and example

(5). However, the situations and emotions are overwhelmingly contrastive. In example (1), Pan Jinlian raised the "curtain" to show Wu Song into the house and he was touched by the warmth of hearth and home, whereas, in example (5), he raised the "curtain" himself and there was nothing to welcome him except the death memorial of his brother. Throughout the story in focus, the "curtain" was the only thing that remained unaffected, bearing witness to all the dramatic happenings. Commonplace as the "curtain" may be, its repeated appearances at key narrative junctures makes it an "idea-image" helping to "string" plot elements into a unified whole. The function of this "idea-image" is exactly what Jin Shengtan described as the "snake in the grass or (discontinuous) chalk line". Besides its part in assisting structuralization, the "curtain" also serves as a foil to Pan Jinlian's changing psychology and emotions, as, symbolically, it may also be seen as the demarcation between seclusion and temptation, ethics and lust.

Chinese fiction is teeming with varieties of "idea-images" which add to its style and meaning. Apart from all the concrete types, there are also those with archetypal significance. One typical example is the "Stone" in *A Dream of Red Mansions* (also known as *The Story of the Stone*). In the beginning chapter of the novel, introduction is made to the "pure translucent Stone" left unused by Nvwa in her sky-mending project. After tempering for aeons, this stone "had acquired spiritual understanding" (Yang & Yang, 1994: 2) and began to lament its unfulfilled fate, until a Buddhist monk and a Taoist priest passed by and agreed to reincarnate it into "a cultured family of official status" (Yang & Yang, 1994: 2) in the "civilized and prosperous realm" (Yang & Yang, 1994: 2). So this "Stone" became Baoyu, the legendary hero who was born into the Jias allegedly with a piece of jade in his mouth. With Baoyu gradually becoming a focus of narration, the archetypal "idea-image" of the "Stone" transformed into three less abstract aspects, namely, the mysterious jade he wears, his name "Baoyu" which means "precious jade", and, more importantly, his unique temperament and his experience of the earthly "dream". And it is precisely such a "dream" that formed the keynote of the novel. From this perspective, therefore, the primary function of this "idea-image" of the "Stone" must have been to orient the novel and its reading towards a deeper and higher reflection on the vanity of earthly life.

3. "Idea-Image" in English Literature: A Comparative Perspective

In English literature, one may also find a rich distribution of evocative images. For example, in *Jane Eyre*, the heroine's name "Eyre" might have suggested the scattered "idea-images" of the "**eye**" and the "fi**re**". But, one may gather that, traditionally, the issue of "idea-image" has rarely been given such emphasis as it has been in Chinese literary criticism. In fact, most of the critical attention to it was brought by the rise of "Imagism" in Anglo-American poetry. Ezra Pound, the major champion of "Imagism", described "Image" in a way that perfectly explained its similarities to, and differences from, the Chinese notion of "idea-image".

> An "Image" is that which presents **an intellectual and emotional complex** in an instant of time ... It is the presentation of such a "complex" instantaneously which gives that **sense of sudden liberation**; that **sense of freedom from time limits and space limits**; that **sense of sudden growth**, which we experience in the presence of the greatest works of art. It is better to present one Image in a lifetime than to produce voluminous works.
>
> (Pound, 1913: 201)

Pound points out the basic commonality that an "Image" represents "an intellectual and emotional complex". From the poem *Autumn Thoughts* to the three forms of "idea-images" that I summarized, all the quoted examples agree with this feature. It is also a shared truth that an "Image" can afford a "sense of freedom from time limits and space limits" because an "idea-image" always tends to decelerate the pace of narration by opening up a window onto a different spatio-temporal dimension. For example, in Lu Da's thrashing of the butcher Zheng, the three synaesthetic "idea-images" describing the effect of Lu's three punches on Zheng bring the reader's imagination into three different spatial experiences. Likewise, the iteration of the "curtain" allows the reader to pause and peer for a short while into Pan Jinlian's and Wu Song's inner world.

However, the "sense of sudden liberation" and the "sense of sudden growth" might be more relevant to the context of poetry. Since "images" in poetry are mostly condensation and configuration of highly emotive factors, they may naturally produce the "sense of sudden growth" and the very sense of liberation may occur to the poet upon his accomplishment of it and to the reader when he feels his own sentiments coalesced to the poem. But in traditional Chinese fiction, the pursuit of "growth" is prioritized over that of "liberation" and even for the former the author manages to build it into a "chronic" process, instead of a "sudden" eruption. This is all explained by the author's own intention or pursuit, which is to design a "masterwork" and "outwit" some of his ordinary readers.

References

Cao, X. & E. Gao. Collated by Yu Pingbo and annotated by Qi Gong. 2002. *Hong Lou Meng*, Beijing: People's Literature Publishing House.

Ferguson, M. et al. 2005. *The Norton Anthology of Poetry*. New York: W. W. Norton & Company, Inc.

Leech, G. & M. Short. 2007. *Style in Fiction: A Linguistic Introduction to English Fictional Prose*. Harlow: Pearson Education Limited.

Lu, K. & S. Mou. 1982. *Wenxin diaolong yizhu* (文心雕龙译注). Jinan: Qilu Press.

Owen, S. 1992. *Readings in Chinese Literary Thought*. Cambridge, MA: Harvard University Press.

Pound, E. 1913. A few don'ts by an Imagiste. *Poetry: A Magazine of Verse*, 1(6). Chicago: Harriet Monroe.

Rolston, D. L. (ed.). 1990. *How to Read the Chinese Novel*. Princeton: Princeton University Press.

Shapiro, S. (Trans.). 1980. Shi, N. & G. Luo. *Outlaws of the Marsh*. Beijing: Foreign Languages Press.

Shi, N. & S. Jin. 2005. Jin Shengtan piping ben shuihu zhuan (金圣叹批评本水浒传). Changsha: Yuelu Publishing House.

Yang, X. & G. Yang. (Trans.). 1994. Cao, X. & E. Gao. *A Dream of Red Mansions*. Beijing: Foreign Languages Press.

乔伊斯的《姉妹们》：磬折形与社会思维

张之俊 （清华大学/中国地质大学）

Joyce's "The Sisters"：Gnomon and Social Minds

Zhang Zhijun （Tsinghua University/China University of Geosciences)

摘　要：乔伊斯的短篇小说《姉妹们》开篇,第一人称小男孩叙述老神父弗
　　　　林病危时提及了"瘫痪"、"磬折形"和"买卖圣职"三个词,其中磬
　　　　折形图形投射出了不完整概念的隐喻视角。以往基于该视角的
　　　　研究侧重于人物的个体不完整性,即个人精神瘫痪。本文将结合
　　　　思维风格概念,运用社会思维理论探讨《姉妹们》人物之间关系的
　　　　不完整性,即群体精神瘫痪,并得出结论:1. 大人的思维世界是不
　　　　可理解的;2. 大人的思维世界是无法摆脱的。因此,从社会思维
　　　　角度可洞察小男孩与大人之间的磬折形关系,进一步揭示精神瘫
　　　　痪这一主题。
关键词：《姉妹们》；磬折形；社会思维；瘫痪

Abstract：The opening paragraph of Joyce's short story "The Sisters"
　　　　　projects a gnomonic perspective of incompleteness in light of the
　　　　　first-person boy narrator's three words：paralysis, gnomon and
　　　　　simony. The previous studies of this gnomonic perspective are
　　　　　slanted towards the paralysis on the individual level. Against this
　　　　　backdrop, the present study aims to explore the gnomonic human
　　　　　relations of incompleteness, i.e. the paralysis on the collective
　　　　　level, by using social minds theory that synthesizes the concept
　　　　　of minds style. It is found that the adults' mental worlds are
　　　　　unreadable and unavoidable. As a result, the gnomonic human

relations are shed light upon through the social minds theory so that the theme of paralysis is enriched through this study.

Key words: "The Sisters"; gnomon; social minds; paralysis

1. 引言

《姉妹们》("The Sisters")是爱尔兰作家乔伊斯短篇小说集《都柏林人》(*Dubliners*, 1914)的开篇之作[1],该篇以小男孩为第一人称叙述者,讲述了这个寄宿在姑妈家的小男孩听到他熟悉的老神父弗林去世的消息,努力想知道其死因,但极力不表现出来。大人总是说着不完整的话,让他摸不着头脑。小男孩的梦境和回忆成为读者了解他和弗林交往的关键。第二天晚上,小男孩和姑妈一同去弗林姐妹的家里探望,同样,在姑妈与弗林姐妹之一伊丽莎谈论弗林时,小男孩还是听得一头雾水。故事最终以伊丽莎的省略句收场。

众多评论家一致认为磬折形(gnomon)[2]为读者勾勒了一个不完整的神秘画面,并与精神瘫痪主题相吻合。Walzl通过对比几个版本,发现《姉妹们》的最终版本里乔伊斯新增了"瘫痪"(paralysis)、"磬折形"和"买卖圣职"(simony)三个词;她认为"《姉妹们》的重新设计对《都柏林人》的主题起到了引言的作用"(1973:74)。磬折形体现的不完整性包括各个感官与行动造成的精神瘫痪(Rice, 1991)、家谱的关系即去掉的平行四边形是小磬折形,代表了小孩,而去掉之前是大磬折形,代表了神父(Albert, 1990)、沉默的作用(Rabaté, 2006)等;以上研究未考虑到这样一个事实:小男孩与其他人物之间的关系也体现了精神瘫痪。Friedrich在谈及gnomon的两个意义即磬折形和日晷[3]的基础上,提出磬折形展现了人物关系的不完整(1957:422),然而他并没有深入下去,这一论点正是本文将要探讨的。Norris将长大后的小男孩定位为叙述者,将小男孩定位为经历者;在此基础上,她将大人(长大后的小男孩)叙述者、读者、小男孩经历者三者的关系扩展到两个姐妹,从而形成一个磬折形的平行四边形(2003:18)。Karrer认为两个姐妹与弗林的关系也是磬折形的关系(1997)。尽管两位评论家都涉及了人物关系,但未通过人物的思维角度来洞察人物之间的磬折形关系。为什么要考虑人物思维呢? Riquelme在探讨乔伊斯作品中叙述者多变的视角时特别指出《都柏林人》展现了人物思维这一现象(1983:99);Beck在分析《都柏林人》中的另一短篇小说《公寓》时,在结尾处指出《都柏林人》的所有短篇小说,"占主导的是人物刻画,特别是通过人物细微的思想意识来描写都柏林人具体的实例和他们瞬间的状态"(1969：157)。然而，Riquelme 和 Beck 关注的是人物个体的思维，并没有把个体的思维与他人的思维联系起来。《都柏林人》醒目地表明该短篇小说集不是关于一个人的，每个人物及他们的关系也体现着精神瘫痪。因此，基于磬折形隐喻视角，有必要探讨小男孩与他人的思维关系，即社会思维关系。由此可预测，在都柏林这样的成长环境中，小男孩长大后将会遭受《都柏林人》中其他主人公的境遇。对人物社会思维关系的剖析能够更加全面地投射出磬折形，展现都柏林社会的集体精神瘫痪。

社会思维理论(Social Minds Theory)的提出者 Alan Palmer 强调，"小说叙事本质上就是展现思维运转方式(mental functioning)"(2010：9)。思维运转方式不仅直接体现在含有思维词语的话语中，还体现在会话中的声音(Gregoriou，2014：165)以及行为或客观叙述(Keen，2014：71)。此外，Palmer 认为，传统文学批评采用了内在论视角(internalist perspective)来看待人物思维：内省性的、孤立的、个人的等属性，属于内在思维(intramental thought)。相反，社会思维理论强调外在论视角(externalist perspective)，强调人物思维之间的社会属性，即公开性的、行为性的、具身性的等，属于交互思维(intermental thought)和集体思维(collective thought)。Palmer 结合内在论视角，将外在论视角引入人物思维研究。Phelan 概括了社会思维理论的核心，即叙事展现了人物思维与外部世界之间以及人物思维之间的关系(2011：319)。Stockwell 在评价社会思维理论时指出，"Palmer 对内在思维和交互思维的区分进一步阐明了 Fowler 的文体学概念'思维风格'(mind-style)"(2011：289)。思维风格指"任何通过独特的语言表征出来的个体思维特征"(Fowler，1977：103)。Fowler 的思维风格概念采用了传统文学批评的内在论视角，如果采用外在论视角，思维风格不仅属于个人，某个群体也有一致的思维风格[4]。

本文将基于磬折形隐喻视角，运用社会思维理论，通过剖析小男孩与大人之间的不同思维风格来反映他们的社会思维关系，从而体现出磬折形人物关系，即群体精神瘫痪。

2. 磬折形隐喻视角

《姊妹们》开篇，乔伊斯就为读者建构了一个隐喻视角。一心想着老神父弗林的病危情形，小男孩自述着：

> 每天夜里，我仰望那窗户时，总是轻声对自己说"瘫痪"一词。这词我听着
> 总觉得奇怪，像是欧几里得几何学里的"磬折形"一词，又像是《教义问答手册》

里"买卖圣职"一词。(1)[5]

Friedrich 提出了瘫痪—磬折形—买卖圣职三元体系(1957:422)。对小男孩而言,瘫痪如此抽象的概念,使他联想起上学时学到的"磬折形",如图1所示的阴影部分:

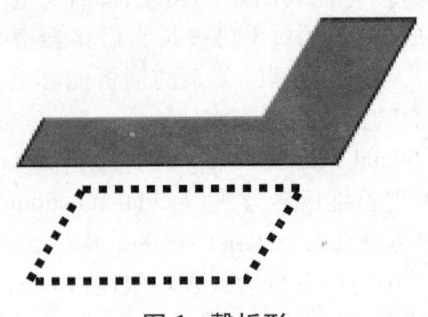

图1. 磬折形

该图形为读者理解《姊妹们》乃至《都柏林人》提供了隐喻视角,即《都柏林人》是不完整的。Friedrich 概括了《姊妹们》中关于磬折形体现的不完整性:老柯特说不完整的话、小男孩记不清梦的结尾、小男孩犹犹豫豫走到墙角那把他常坐的椅子、省略式的结尾、老神父独自一人在忏悔隔间里无人交流、空荡荡的壁炉、打破了的圣杯、无用的圣杯等(1957:423)。这个不完整性还可以扩展下去,如小男孩无父母(文中甚至未提及他的名字)、姐妹之一南妮耳背等。这些都成为都柏林人精神瘫痪的背景,而本文要突出的则是人物之间的社会思维关系,这也体现着磬折形的不完整性。

3. 小男孩与大人的社会思维关系

小男孩与大人的社会思维关系主要体现在:1)小男孩与邻居老柯特、姑父、姑妈之间(发生在姑妈家里),以及小男孩与姑妈、弗林的两个姐妹之间(发生在老神父弗林姐妹的家里);2)小男孩与老神父弗林之间(发生在小男孩的梦境与回忆里)。其中,老柯特、姑父、姑妈和弗林的两个姐妹代表世俗社会,老神父弗林则代表宗教社会。

3.1 小男孩与代表世俗社会大人的社会思维关系

在姑妈家里,晚餐时间,邻居老柯特也在,他和姑父为主要对话者,姑妈偶尔加入,话题围绕着老神父弗林的死。小男孩与大人的接触这样开场:

[1] 我下楼吃饭时,老柯特正坐在炉边抽烟。就在我姑妈给我舀麦片粥时,他

仿佛接着自己前面的谈话似的说道：

"不，我不想说他完全是……但有些奇怪……他是有些不可思议。我来告诉你我的想法……"（2）

选段［1］里，小男孩没下楼之前，老柯特已经聊到老神父弗林的死了。这可以从姑父之后的话得到证实："柯特先生刚刚才告诉了我们。他正好路过那座房子"（2）。然而，小男孩出现之后，老柯特开始采用一种新的说话方式——省略句式。这种省略句的反复使用会让人产生省略式的思维风格，这种思维风格的体现在老柯特的语言中比比皆是：

> ［2］"对这事我有我自己的看法，"他说。"我想这是那些……怪病中的一种。……不过，很难说……"（2）
>
> ［3］"我的意思是，"老柯特说，"那样对孩子不好。我的看法是：让年轻的孩子到处跑跑，与同年龄的年轻孩子们去玩，不要……我说的对不对，杰克？"（3）
>
> ［4］"那样对孩子们有害，"老柯特说，"因为他们的心灵很容易受到影响。孩子们看见那种事情时，你知道，它就会产生效果……"（3）

选段［1］［2］［3］［4］里，没有传达出任何关于弗林死因的信息。很明显，小男孩的出现对老柯特的语言产生了影响：他每次提及弗林死因的时候，都采用了省略句式。此外，选段［1］中表达态度的词"奇怪"、"不可思议"，选段［2］［3］［4］中的指示词"这事"、"那些"、"那样"、"那种"等，都让小男孩和读者无法了解到弗林的死因。在选段［3］中，老柯特避而不谈为什么对小孩不好，反而去寻求姑父杰克的肯定来产生共鸣。姑父的回答"那也是我的原则"（3）表明他与老柯特处在交互思维中，甚至他自己也开始使用老柯特式的省略句式："教育实在是极其细致而广泛……给柯特先生吃点羊腿肉吧"（3）。由此可见，在作品将近两页的对话中，大人在小男孩出现时有意地采用了大人独有的思维风格，这表明大人之间形成了交互思维，而小男孩完全被排除在外。这种省略式的思维风格也体现在姑妈和弗林姐妹之一伊丽莎的对话中。

第二天傍晚，姑妈带着小男孩去"拜访那个居丧之家"（6）。弗林的两个姐妹分别叫伊丽莎和南妮。南妮耳背负责招待，伊丽莎相反很善谈并主持家务。对话只在姑妈和伊丽莎之间进行，小男孩只是倾听者，一言不发。姑妈在询问关于弗林之死及善后工作时，在三处用了省略句式：

> ［5］"他死时……安详吧？"她问。（8）
>
> ［6］"那么一切都……？"（8）
>
> ［7］"真的是那样么？"我姑妈说。"我听到了一些……"（11）

选段[5][6]的省略为委婉用语,选段[7]中姑妈同样采用了大人省略式的思维风格。本来这是个机会来透露到底发生了什么,姑妈的话却戛然而止。姑妈的"一些"究竟是指什么呢?无论如何,伊丽莎能够听懂姑妈的话,因为她们处在交互思维中,这从伊丽莎的反应和回答可以看出:

[8] 伊丽莎点点头。
"那事影响了他的精神,"她说。(11)

显而易见,伊丽莎明白了姑妈的省略,她的动作和语言及后面的解释表明她和姑妈的确处在交互思维中,小男孩则被排除在外。另外,小男孩"犹犹豫豫走到墙角那把我常坐的椅子"(7)、呆在墙角处,这从空间角度更加形象地说明他不在大人的交互思维之中。伊丽莎是关于弗林死因的信息的主要提供者。弗林在世的时候,小男孩常常上门给弗林送鼻烟,有常坐的椅子,所以伊丽莎很清楚小男孩与弗林的关系。每到关键时刻,她也采用了大人特有的省略式思维风格:

[9] "可是我知道他已经走了,再也不会回来了……"(10)
[10] "他一直想做这件事……可怜的詹姆斯!"(11)
[11] "这全是因为他打碎了那只圣杯……那是事情的开始。"(11)
[12] "不过,尽管如此……他们说是那个男孩的过错。"(11)
[13] "还有在那里的另一个神父,拿着灯进去找他……你会怎么想呢?"(12)
[14] "他完全醒着,好像对自己发笑……那时,他们看见那种情形,当然会觉得他出了毛病……"(12)

伊丽莎的话共有七处省略。这种省略句式随着对话的深入为弗林之死陡增神秘色彩。小男孩和读者,不知道究竟发生了什么,而处在交互思维中的姑妈和伊丽莎却彼此心照不宣。选段[9][10]表明人死去不能复生,表达了伊丽莎的遗憾和悲痛。选段[11][12]中当伊丽莎谈到打碎了的圣杯,讲话戛然而止。选段[13]中伊丽莎讲述弗林在忏悔隔间到底怎么了,又是骤然停止。不可思议的是,选段[14]是用省略句式结束了该作品。此外,伊丽莎同之前老柯特一样,关于弗林,也采用了"奇怪"(10)一词,这进一步说明大人的语言是一致的。对于小男孩,大人共有的语言使他们形成了统一的思维风格,他们采用晦涩的语言和省略句将他排除在交互思维之外。代表世俗社会的大人的语言背后体现着都柏林社会里的集体思维,老柯特、姑父、姑妈以及弗林的两个姐妹"有着共同的词汇、句法"(Kershner,1989:31)。面对着"对语言充满想象力的小男孩"(Beck,1969:48),或许大人们在试图规避关于死亡的一切,然而,他们反复使用省略句式及一些陈词滥调反映了集体话语瘫痪,并营造出一种压抑的氛围,正当保护了"统治阶级的话语权"(Kershner,1989:28),进一步展现了世俗社会的群体精神瘫痪。

面对如此压抑的氛围,小男孩的思维风格会是什么样的呢?在姑妈家里的对话中,一开始小男孩就注意到了老柯特的省略句式。"他开始抽起烟斗,吐着烟雾,无疑是在心里整理他的想法"(2)。尽管不知道老柯特在想什么,但小男孩察觉到老柯特有意不让他听懂。全文对话中小男孩说的唯一的两句话都是问句,共四个词。姑父观察到小男孩因为听不懂老柯特的话而"瞪着眼"(2),便说道:

[15] "喂,你的老朋友终于走了,你听了一定会很悲伤。"
　　　"谁?"我问。[6]
　　　"神父弗林。"
　　　"他死了?"(2)

选段[15]中带下划线的两个问句都是小男孩简短的问句。他对老柯特不满,所以"瞪着眼",这被和老柯特处在交互思维中的姑父察觉到了,姑父似乎读懂了他的心思,直接告诉他"你的老朋友(终于)走了"。从作品开篇话题的焦点就集中在弗林上,所以小男孩肯定知道是谁走了,然而他还是问"谁?"以拒绝表现出他对弗林之死的关注。后面的问句"他死了?"直截了当,小男孩并没有像姑父那样采用委婉语"走了",这表明小男孩不想让他人知道他和弗林很熟。这两个简短的问句体现了小男孩表面漠不关心的思维风格。听到弗林的死讯,小男孩意识到别人在观察他对弗林之死的反应,他表面漠不关心的思维风格转而体现在行动上:

[16] 我知道他们在看着我,于是我继续吃饭,好像对这消息漠不关心。(2)
[17] 老柯特看了我一会儿。我觉得他那双又小又亮的黑眼睛在审视我,但我不想让他看出什么,便仍低着头吃饭,不抬眼睛。(3)
[18] 我用麦片粥把嘴填满,生怕自己气得叫喊起来。这个令人讨厌的红鼻子蠢老头子!(4)

选段[16][17][18]中,小男孩面对大人对他的观察,借由吃饭的动作表现出若无其事的样子。其实他对弗林的死有着强烈的求知欲,而且对老柯特的话充满了愤怒。小男孩这种表面上漠不关心但求知的思维风格在晚上睡觉时完全暴露出来:

[19] 虽然我对老柯特把我当作小孩子非常生气,但我还是绞尽脑汁琢磨着他那没说完的话是什么意思。(4)

选段[19]表明小男孩对弗林的死非常感兴趣,他试图努力读懂大人的思维世界,而这一切只能在随后的梦境得以实现,真是日有所思、夜有所梦。因此,思维风格的不同,证明了大人的思维世界对于小男孩来说是无法理解的。

在姑妈和伊丽莎的对话里,小男孩完全是一个旁听者,没有讲任何一句话。Verschueren 指出,"人物在场的一刻他就参与到了会话中,[...]他成为了诠释者"(2000:82)。小男孩虽然一言不发,但他的在场对对话产生了一定影响。对话中强调得更多的是形式,而非内容,每到关键时刻,姑妈和伊丽莎均以省略句结束。之前小男孩对弗林的回忆,特别是梦到了他,都反映出小男孩对弗林的死极其关注。女人们对话的前半段没有展示小男孩任何心理活动。作为第一人称叙述者,他的"消失"表明了他表面上对弗林之死若无其事。这种叙事手法也在《都柏林人》等其他采用第三人称叙述的短篇小说中得到了延续,即叙述者表面上采取漠不关心的态度,却从未远离故事中心,仿佛一直"偷窥"着都柏林人的精神瘫痪世界。对话的后半段,姑妈谈到弗林一生的"不得意"(11),房间里"一片静寂"(11)。这时,小男孩出现了,这说明他在仔细地听,而不像南妮"好像要睡着了似的"(9):

> [20] 小屋里一片静寂,乘此机会,我走近桌子,尝了尝我那杯雪利酒,然后又悄悄地回到我坐的那把椅子。伊丽莎似乎陷入了沉思。我们不无敬意地等着她打破静寂。(11)

选段[20]中,小男孩描述自己的动作为"悄悄",这与他之前的"消失"吻合,体现了他表面上漠不关心的思维风格。对话最后,伊丽莎说到弗林自己藏在小教堂的忏悔隔间里,"他竟然呆在那里,一个人摸黑坐在他的忏悔隔间,完全醒着,好像轻声地对自己发笑"(12)。这时伊丽莎突然停了下来。小男孩表现出了真实反应。"我也侧耳细听;可是整个房间里没有任何声音"(12)。可见,小男孩表面上漠不关心实则十分想了解弗林的死因,文中对小男孩的轻描淡写,表现出他表面漠不关心但求知的思维风格。因此,小男孩的思维风格与大人的思维风格形成了鲜明对比,小男孩虽然表面漠不关心,但渴望知道关于弗林的死因,而大人采用的语言则体现了省略式的思维风格。这再次表明,对于小男孩而言,大人的思维世界是无法理解的。

然而,这些大人的思维世界代表了都柏林人某一阶级的世俗社会思维。这种集体思维对小男孩的成长有着深远的影响,令他始终无法摆脱。Palmer 认为,"小说人物思维运转方式无法抛开它所存在故事世界中的社会和外在环境"(2010:8)。Bakhtin 也强调,"个人的意识只有在与其相适应的意识形态环境中得以实现才能成为意识"(1991:14)。老柯特、姑父、姑妈、伊丽莎和南妮代表了中低下层都柏林人的社会思维,因为他们的集体语言是"爱尔兰式的、中低下层的、跨世纪的、没有受过良好教育的"(Kershner,1989:25)。在伊丽莎与姑妈的对话里,伊丽莎除了有语法错误,还有两处很明显的词语误用,她把 *Freeman's Journal*(《自由人日报》)中的"Journal"说成了"General",把"pneumatic wheels"(胶轮马车)说成了"rheumatic wheels",由此可见伊丽莎的教育程度并不高。伊丽莎与姑妈的对话、老柯特与姑父的对话,"有超过一半的篇幅记录了他们毫无意义的谈话,[...]这样的语言,就是小男孩真实的生活环境,他不得不忍受下去"(25)。小男孩"不得不忍受"意味着他摆脱不了世俗社会思维。当姑妈带着他去弗林的姐妹家探望,南妮带着他们上楼哀悼死者弗林并祈祷时,南妮的"喃喃低语使我分心。我注意到她的裙子在后面笨拙地扣住,布鞋的后跟儿踩得歪倒在一边"(7)。南妮的语言与衣着犹如大人的世俗社会思维,小男孩分心是因为他无法摆脱掉他理解不了的大人思维世界。此外,在老柯特和姑父的对话里,姑父告诉老柯特,小男孩与弗林是"极好的朋友"(2),两个大人便开始讨论如何教育小孩的问题。对于老柯特而言,"我可不喜欢自己的孩子跟那样的人谈得太多"(3),因为"那样对孩子不好。我的看法是,让年轻的孩子到处跑跑,与同年龄的年轻孩子们去玩,不要……"(3)。老柯特还从姑父那寻求一致的观点。姑父表示赞同老柯特:"那也是我的原则"(3)。老柯特所说的,"他们的心灵很容易受到影响"(3)本身就证实孩子无法摆脱大人的思维世界。老柯特只注意到儿童容易受到代表宗教社会思维的弗林们的影响,却未意识到他们所代表的世俗社会思维也影响着儿童的心灵。这种省略式思维风格立竿见影地折射到小男孩的语言上,"我觉得自己到了遥远的地方,在风俗奇异的他乡——大概是在波斯,我想……但我记不起梦的结局了"(6)。小男孩也采用了省略式思维风格,他"已经学会了语言的使用——用以隐藏"(French,1978:448)。正如 Brown 所言,"仿佛每个人都陷入了圆圈的外缘,无法进入圆圈,但又无法完全离开。就像爱尔兰一样,注定被遗落在生命的边缘"(1972:41)。

3.2 小男孩与代表宗教社会大人的社会思维关系

老神父弗林已经死去,小男孩和他的社会思维关系体现在小男孩的梦境和回忆里。Kershner 强调,尽管老神父弗林已经死去,他的声音仍强有力地回荡在故事中(1989:27)。对于小男孩而言,代表世俗社会大人的省略式思维风格不可理解,而代表宗教社会的弗林复杂而神秘的思维风格同样不可理解,这体现在了小男孩的回忆中:

[21] 他的问题使我明白了教会规章制度是多么复杂和难解,而以前我总觉得它们是最简单的条例。(6)

[22] 每当我想到这点时,常常无法回答,或者只是作出一种非常愚蠢的、犹豫含糊的回答,对此他总是微笑,或者点两下头。(6)

选段[21][22]呈现了小男孩对宗教无知的思维风格,相反,弗林却有着复杂而神秘的思维风格。在之前老柯特与姑父的对话中,小男孩几乎是个倾听者,大人采用省略式思维风格将小男孩排除在外;同样,小男孩在回忆与弗林的对话时,虽然自己本身也是对话者,"但是他却常常从宗教对话中被宗教语言所排除在外"(Kershner,1989:27)。可见,小男孩与弗林没有处在交互思维之中。弗林其实也是这种复杂而神秘思维风格的受害者,据伊丽莎说,"这全是因为他打碎了那只圣杯……那是事情的开始"(11)。这种复杂而神秘的思维风格也影响着弗林的两个姐妹。小男孩看到弗林躺在棺材里,"一双大手松松地捧着圣杯"(7)。由此可见,两个姐妹对于圣杯的神圣深信不疑,尽管这是"一只无用的圣杯"(12)。小男孩以前很喜欢听代表世俗社会的老柯特讲故事,"我们刚认识他时,他倒是相当有趣,常常说到劣质酒精和蛇管;可是我很快就讨厌他了,讨厌他那些没完没了的酒厂故事"(2)。小男孩后来与弗林成为朋友,表明小男孩放弃世俗社会而投奔宗教社会,然而代表宗教社会的老神父弗林和代表世俗社会的老柯特都是和 spirit 有关的(Milesi,1997:99),因此,小男孩同样会对宗教失去好感,无法真正进入宗教思维世界。然而,正如他所言,"令我奇怪的是,不论我自己还是天气,似乎都没有哀伤的意思,我甚至还不安地发现有一种获得自由的感觉,仿佛他的死使我摆脱了某种束缚"(5),难道他真可以摆脱掉宗教社会思维吗? 或许小男孩摆脱了弗林本人的思想束缚,但是他无法摆脱弗林所代表的宗教社会的思想束缚。这种束缚出现在小男孩的梦境中:

[23] 在我昏暗的房间里,我想象着又看见了那瘫痪患者阴沉灰白的面孔。我用毯子蒙住脑袋,尽力去想圣诞节的情景。但那张灰白的脸仍然跟着我。它低声嘟哝着;我知道它是在想表白什么事情。我觉得自己的灵魂飘荡到一个令人愉快而邪恶的世界;在那里,我发现那张面孔又在等我。它开始向我忏悔,但我奇怪为什么它不停地微笑,为什么嘴唇上那么多唾沫。可那时我又记起它已经因瘫痪病死了,于是我觉得自己也在无力地微笑,仿佛要宽恕他买卖圣职的罪孽。(4)

梦境中小男孩并未直接描述弗林本人,而是采用了身体部位"面孔"、"脸"、"嘴唇"以及无生命代词"它",表明小男孩极力地想摆脱掉宗教上的束缚。然而他摆脱不了瘫痪了的宗教思维,"那张灰白的脸仍然跟着我","我觉得自己的灵魂飘荡到一个令人愉快而邪恶的世界"，"我发现那张面孔又在等我"。此外，小男孩与弗林的身份转换表现为弗林向小男孩忏悔："它开始向我忏悔"，表明小男孩获得了宗教角色，体会着宗教的复杂与神秘。同时，弗林嘴上的"唾沫"让人想起了老柯特"最后粗鲁地往壁炉里吐了一口痰"（3），可见，世俗社会和宗教社会是如此相似，如此这般压抑的、瘫痪了的生活空间是任何人都逃脱不了的。更讽刺的是，文中反复出现的弗林的"微笑"，也传染给了小男孩："我觉得自己也在无力地微笑"。Milesi 总结到，这种难以抑制的重复，仿佛传染给了所有人物，表明瘫痪了的神父象征着他们内心未承认的痼疾，在乔伊斯关于爱尔兰症候学的刻薄语体创作中，这也成为了精心设计的写作策略，为最终的"幻觉想象"做好铺垫（1997：96）。

诚然，这种思想束缚或宗教社会思维的束缚已经根植到小男孩的语言里面，例如小男孩在讲述弗林抽鼻烟时，红手帕"被鼻烟染得污黑不堪，擦也无济于事"（5），Riquelme 认为，"无济于事"（inefficacious）这个词是成年叙述者所选用的，而不是小男孩经历者的（1983：91）。本文并没有区分成年叙述者和小男孩经历者，但可以肯定的是他们是同一个人。如果小说的语言是成年叙述者所选用的词语，这种正式的用语恰恰表现了宗教对小男孩从小到大的持久影响。其他的词语包括"邪恶的罪人的名字"（maleficent and sinful being）（1）、"买卖圣职"（simony）（1）、"宽恕"（absolve）（4）、"罪孽"（sin）（4）等。显而易见，以弗林为代表的宗教社会思维对小男孩的教导"改变并限制了其认知能力"（Karrer, 1997：55）。

《都柏林人》的其他短篇小说无一例外地展现了宗教社会思维无法摆脱这一事实。《姊妹们》中主人公的处境，预示着《都柏林人》其他主人公的命运。人与人之间的关系，体现在人与人之间的社会思维关系中，小男孩无法理解整个都柏林社会，又无法摆脱笼罩都柏林的社会思维。这种人物之间关系的不完整也是乔伊斯设计磬折形隐喻视角的体现，影射出都柏林社会的群体精神瘫痪。

4. 结语

《姊妹们》开篇小男孩所提及的"瘫痪—磬折形—买卖圣职"三元体系，不仅为《姊妹们》而且为《都柏林人》提供了磬折形隐喻视角，即不完整的图形。这个不完整的图形在传统文学评论中过多地关注人物的个体精神瘫痪。本研究基于磬折形隐喻视角，着重剖析犹如磬折形的人物关系。《姊妹们》中，人物之间的关系体现于人物之间的社会思维关系，即小男孩与代表世俗社会的大人的社会思维关系、小男孩与代表宗教社会的老神父弗林的社会思维关系。借助社会思维理论,并结合思维风格概念,本文发现,对于小男孩而言,大人的思维世界是无法理解的,但又是无法摆脱的。这也从另一角度折射出都柏林乃至爱尔兰社会中人与人之间的磬折形关系,反映了都柏林的群体精神瘫痪,折射出了社会转型期人们在精神上的无所适从。该角度也为《都柏林人》中其他短篇小说如《赛车以后》、《公寓》、《委员会办公室里的常青节》、《圣恩》等进行人物社会思维研究奠定了基础。

注释

1. 《姊妹们》首次于 1904 年单独发表在《爱尔兰家园》(*The Irish Homestead*)杂志上,后经作者几次修改,最终作为《都柏林人》的开篇小说,于 1914 年发表。
2. 从一个平行四边形中去掉另一个平行四边形,剩下的部分为磬折形(Friedrich, 1957: 422)。
3. 尽管该词包含日晷等意义,但在《姊妹们》中,乔伊斯通过小男孩口吻告诉读者该词的含义与欧几里得几何学相关,故笔者遵循该词为磬折形的意义。
4. Fowler 后来用思维风格取代意识形态观,而 Semino & Swindlehurst (1996) 则区分了思维风格与意识形态观,认为思维风格属于个人层面,意识形态观属于群体层面。本文只采用思维风格这一术语来探讨个人层面和群体层面。
5. 本文《姊妹们》中的选段均来自王逢振的译文。下文对本作品的引用只标注页码。
6. 文中下划线部分为笔者标记。

参考文献

Albert, L. 1990. Gnomonology: Joyce's "The Sisters". *James Joyce Quarterly*, 27 (2): 353–364.

Bakhtin, M. M. & P. N. Medvedev. 1991. *The Formal Method in Literary Scholarship: A Critical Introduction to Sociological Poetics*. Baltimore and London: The Johns Hopkins University Press.

Beck, W. 1969. *Joyce's Dubliners: Substance, Vision, and Art*. Durham, N.C.: Duke University Press.

Brown, H. O. 1972. *James Joyce's Early Fiction: The Biogrophy of a Form*. Cleveland & London: The Press of Case Western Reserve University.

Fowler, R. 1977. *Linguistics and the Novel*. London: Methuen.

French, M. 1978. Missing pieces in Joyce's *Dubliners*. *Twentieth Century Literature*, 24 (4): 443–472.

Friedrich, G. 1957. The Gnomonic Clue to James Joyce's *Dubliners*. *Modern Language Notes*, 72 (6): 421–424.

Gregoriou, C. 2014. Voice. In P. Stockwell & S. Whiteley (eds.). *The Cambridge*

Handbook of Stylistics. Cambridge: Cambridge University Press.

Karrer, W. 1997. Gnomon and triangulation: The stories of childhood in *Dubliners*. In M. Power & U. Schneider (eds.). *New Perspectives on Dubliners*. European Joyce Studies 7. Amsterdam: Rodopi.

Keen, S. 2014. *Thomas Hardy's Brains: Psychology, Neurology, and Hardy's Imagination*. Columbus: The Ohio State University Press.

Kershner, R. B. 1989. *Joyce, Bakhtin, and Popular Literature: Chronicles of Disorder*. Chapel Hill and London: The University of North Carolina Press.

Milesi, L. 1997. Joyce's anamorphic mirror in "The Sisters". In M. Power & U. Schneider (eds.). *New Perspectives on Dubliners*. European Joyce Studies 7. Amsterdam: Rodopi.

Norris, M. 2003. *Suspicious Readings of Joyce's Dubliners*. Philadelphia: University of Pennsylvania Press.

Palmer, A. 2010. *Social Minds in the Novel*. Columbus: The Ohio State University Press.

Phelan, J. 2011. Toward a rhetorical perspective on social minds. *Style*, 45 (2): 319–324.

Rabaté, J. 2006. Silences in *Dubliners*. In A. Thacker (ed.). *Dubliners: James Joyce*. New York: Palgrave Macmillan.

Rice, T. J. 1991. The geometry of meaning in *Dubliners*: A euclidian approach. *Style*, 25 (3): 393–405.

Riquelme, J. P. 1983. *Teller and Tale in Joyce's Fiction: Oscillating Perspectives*. Baltimore and London: The Johns Hopkins University Press.

Semino, E. & K. Swindlehurst. 1996. Metaphor and mind style in Ken Kesey's *One Flew Over the Cuckoo's Nest. Style*, 30 (1): 143–166.

Stockwell, P. 2011. Changing minds in narrative. *Style*. 45 (2): 288–291.

Verschueren, J. 2000. *Understanding Pragmatics*. Beijing: Foreign Language Teaching and Research Press.

Walzl, F. L. 1973. Joyce's "The Sisters": A development. *James Joyce Quarterly*, 10 (4): 375–421.

詹姆斯·乔伊斯. 2013.《都柏林人》(王逢振译). 上海:上海译文出版社.

《仓央嘉措情歌》的戏剧化抒情文体

巴　微　（陕西师范大学）

Dramatic Lyrical Style of *The Love Songs* by Tshangyang Gyatsho

Ba Wei　(Shaanxi Normal University)

摘　要：少数民族抒情诗的戏剧性特征常常与民歌传统密切相关。"谐"是藏族民间重要的诗歌种类，它运用四句六音三顿的格律形成鲜明的节奏感以配合且歌且舞的表现形式，这使它有别于书面语诗歌而具备一种戏剧化文体特征。《仓央嘉措情歌》是藏族作家诗与"谐"体民歌结合的典范之作，它一改过去藏族僧侣典雅华丽的"年阿体"风格，借鉴民歌的修辞手法和抒情模式，以对比鲜明、突出对话和简短叙事的方式建构了戏剧化抒情模式，强化了民歌对话与交流的文体功能，通过文人创作极大地提升了"谐"体民歌的审美表达力，成为藏民族传统文化积淀中的重要元素，对藏族诗歌的发展具有深远的影响。

关键词：《仓央嘉措情歌》；"谐"体民歌；戏剧化抒情模式；文体特征

Abstract：Dramatic characteristics of minority lyric is often associated with a folk song's tradition. "Gzhas" is an important style of poetry in the Tibetan folk, its six-syllabol quatrains with a trimetric form highlights rhythm and cooperates the performance singing while dancing. This form sets it apart from writing poetry and has a dramatic stylistic feature. *The Love Songs* by Tshangyang Gyatsho is combined with a model of "gzhas" folk songs and scholar poetry. These songs, different from elegant and gorgeous "nian-a" style of Tibetan monk writing, find expression in the experience of rhetoric and lyrical mode of folk songs. They highlight the dialogue and brief narrative to construct the dramatic lyrical mode, strengthen the folk song's function of dialogue and communication and through literary creation greatly improve the aesthetic power of "gzhas" expression. As an important element in Tibetan traditional culture, *The Love Songs* has far-reaching influence on Tibetan poetry development.

Key words: *The Love Songs* by Tshangyang Gyatsho; "gzhas" folk song; dramatic lyrical model; stylistic feature

  在人类艺术的起源时期,各种艺术形式尚未独立分化,但其共同的精神内核已然形成。缘于此,作为祭祀娱神、歌舞表演的重要形式,诗歌和戏剧在创作和发展中相互借鉴与结合,既形成了诗剧这样的文体范式,也在各种诗歌类型中广泛借用戏剧化元素,其中,抒情诗中戏剧化元素的运用常常成为增强抒情效果的重要手段。在西方以莎翁、华兹华斯为代表的古典主义和浪漫主义诗歌,在中国始自屈原、繁荣于唐宋、并延续至现代的抒情诗传统都普遍存在着对戏剧元素的借鉴与运用。而在少数民族抒情诗中,这种戏剧性特征常常与民歌传统密切相关,突出其对话交流的功能。

  仓央嘉措是清康熙二十二年至四十五年间西藏的宗教领袖,同时又是藏族著名诗人,在民间和宗教领域中都享有极高的地位。在传统藏族文学史中,他创作的诗歌是藏族作家诗的典范,具有极高的艺术价值和丰富的民族文化内涵。与同时期典雅华丽的藏族僧侣诗歌主流相异,仓央嘉措创作的抒情诗在很大程度上源于藏族民歌传统,他充分借鉴了藏族"谐"体民歌形式,建立了戏剧化的抒情模式,极大地提升了"谐"体民歌的审美表达力。他的抒情诗沉淀着藏民族深沉的精神文化内涵,对藏族诗歌的发展具有深远的影响。本文将从叙事性、冲突性、对话性和表演性几个方面来分析仓央嘉措[1]诗歌的戏剧性特征。

---

1 本文中所引仓央嘉措诗歌的藏文原文主要参考青海人民出版社 1980 年整理版,共计 74 首,译者为王沂暖,引自黄颢,吴碧云. 1982.《仓央嘉措及其情歌研究(资料汇编)》. 拉萨:西藏人民出版社.

1. 叙事性

抒情诗侧重于情感表达,但并非完全摒弃叙事要素。新批评代表人物布鲁克斯(Gwendolyn Brooks)在《理解诗歌》(*Understanding Poetry*)中指出:"一切诗歌的表现方式最终都是戏剧性的。事实上,我们说在所有的诗中——即使是在最简单、最浓缩的抒情诗中——我们也会发现某人对某人讲述,而讲述者的言语出自一个具体的情境",因此,"从某种意义上讲,所有的诗都是一部小小的戏剧。"(Brooks, 2004)

抒情诗中的叙事主要是通过构置场景和简短叙事来加以体现的。诺思罗普·弗莱(Northrop Frye)认为:"一首诗的形式与内容的每个细节都有关,不管我们在考察形式时,把它看作静止不变或视其为从作品开头到结尾在运动,都是一回事,就像一首乐曲,不论读它的乐谱还是听它的演奏,也都是一样的。情节是处于动态中的思想,思想则是处于静态中的情节。"(弗莱, 2006)

在仓央嘉措的抒情诗中,叙事性特征主要有两个层面:首先,每一首诗相当于一出简短的情景剧。通过设置特定的场景勾勒个性化情节;其次,整个诗集通过展现完整的爱情历程来隐喻重大的人生主题。在完成单个作品细读的基础上与之拉开审美距离,调整为宏观视角,造成文本解读的层次感。

西藏民歌称为"鲁谐",即"鲁"体民歌和"谐"体民歌。前者的表现形式为只歌不舞,以《米拉日巴道歌》为代表,后者为且歌且舞,以《仓央嘉措情歌》为典范。为配合口传的需要,民歌常常采用简短叙事的形式。如《仓央嘉措情歌》第11首"我和集上的姐姐,结下了三句誓约。却像那花蛇结,自己在地上开裂。";第15首"生机勃发的哈罗花,如果做了供品的话,把我这年少的玉蜂,也带到佛堂里去吧。";第46首"杜鹃鸟来自门隅,带来春天的气息;我和情人见了面,身心也感到快意。";第53首"入夜去会情人,破晓大雪纷扬。保不保密都一样,脚印已留在雪上。"等,这些民歌设置了集市、佛堂、月夜、故乡(门隅)、雪地等场景,并在这些特定场景中进行简短叙事以凸显相应的抒情主题。第11首中的"集市"象征着熙来攘往、瞬息万变的红尘,通过简短叙述"我"与情人在此缔结誓约到誓约在没有外力作用下自解的过程,极力表达了爱情聚散的轻易和无常;第15首中"玉蜂"和"哈罗花"分别指代男女主人公,"佛堂"象征宗教信仰,"做了供品"描述了与女主人公意图投身信仰的愿望相随而来的是男主人公因爱情的缘故决定追随她的信仰;第46首中提及的"门隅"是诗人出生成长的故乡,也是他情感的生发地和归宿地,杜鹃鸟带来的故乡的气息对诗人来说正如同春天的气息,而与情人的相会过程也给"我"带来了勃勃生机,在杜鹃、门隅、情人所构成的这样一个美满和谐的氛围中"我"自然抒发出"身心快意"的感受了。第53首是仓央嘉措诗歌中颇有代表性的一首,也常常被人当作是他不守清规的佐证。仓央嘉措处于清初西藏复杂的政治权力中心,特殊的经历与地位使他长期处于压抑之中,因此他时常更名改姓、乔装打扮,在夜晚到拉萨城中饮酒约会。这首诗描述了抒情主人公夜晚去会情人,破晓时分归来,本来可以悄悄地不为人知,哪知夜里下了大雪,他的脚印留在了雪地上,这样一来即使想要保密也不可能了,因此诗人索性以自嘲和诙谐的口吻说"保不保密都一样",表现出一种顺其自然、洒脱自在的人生态度。

仓央嘉措的诗歌在西藏民间广泛流传,"它不仅被当作歌词毫无顾忌地用在不同场合的各种民间曲调中,广泛传唱,而且各个私塾还把它作为学生练字字帖的内容。特别是以前专门编辑的《情歌集》,由拉萨出版行会雕刻成短条本,书一上市,广大群众争相购买,这是如今老一辈人亲眼所见的事实。"(恰白·次旦平措,1990)相对于藏族文学史上的其他文人诗歌,仓央嘉措诗歌传播的广泛性和持续性一方面源于其文本内容的世俗化、民间化,另一方面也与其通过场景设置和简短叙事的戏剧性抒情模式有直接的关联。

如果将每一首诗看作整体叙事中的一个单元的话,那么《仓央嘉措情歌》就是一部以爱情为线索串联起来的完整戏剧。作为一个年轻僧侣,仓央嘉措也有着与普通人一样对爱情的向往和憧憬,也经历了恋爱的甜蜜、惶惑、离别、坚持、失落甚至背叛,最终更是通过爱情领悟了人生的真相。因此,从整体上以爱情隐喻人生是《仓央嘉措情歌》的基本结构。诗集开篇就以"月"寄寓了爱人、母亲和神灵相重叠的意象:"在那东山顶上,升起了皎洁的月亮。母亲般的情人脸庞,浮现在我的心上。"第3—5首连续抒发对爱人的思念和眷恋,如第3首:"夺我心魂的人儿,若能够厮守到老,仿佛从大海深处,捞上来奇珍异宝。"第6—9首进一步表达了因分离而导致的悲伤和灰心丧气,如第6首"心儿随她去了,夜里无法安眠,白天未能得手,叫我心灰意懒。"以及第8首"茭茭草上的白霜,寒风的使者,就是它俩呀,拆散了花儿和蜂儿。"第10、11、35—38首等表露出爱人的背叛所带来的愤怒和伤心,如第35首"姑娘不是娘生的,怕是桃树上长的,要不然她的爱情,怎比桃花还谢得快呢?"和第37首"野马跑到山上,可用套索捉住;情人一旦变心,神力也拿她不住!"第13—18、23、65首等展现了抒情主人公对爱情和信念的坚持,第30、32和33首则渲染了爱人被偷走和被抢夺之后的失落,最后第47、63和66首统领整个诗集,表达了诗人对人生的领悟:"对于无常和死亡,若不常常观想,纵然聪明盖世,也和傻子一样。"

2. 冲突性

藏族民歌常常运用对比修辞突出事物特征,不但所取意象形成对比,而且诗句前后造成反义以强调主题,给听者造成深刻印象。仓央嘉措诗歌所借鉴的"谐"体民歌就突出地表现出这个特点。"谐"体民歌最早可以追溯到吐蕃时期,是深受藏族人民喜爱的民歌样式,在各大藏区广为流传,其中藏、甘、青及四川的阿坝、巴塘等地称之为"谐",德格地区称之为"古尔姆",云南中甸等地区则称之为"日尔玛"。"谐"的基本结构是两句四行,每句为六音节三顿,仓央嘉措诗歌主要采取的就是这种样式,通常第一、二句与第三、四句分别形成反义,或是前两句与后两句在意思上形成强烈反差。由于这种诗体节奏鲜明,配合歌舞表演时能有效地提升表现力,因此在传播过程中也为其他文体所采纳,如 16 世纪末 17 世纪初的著名藏戏《诺桑王子》中就使用了"谐"体民歌的形式。

《仓央嘉措情歌》第 32 首描述了恋爱中的争斗,"与我相恋的情人,已被人家娶走;心儿被相思折磨,人比黄花瘦。"第 10 首"渡船无心,马头回眸,负心的人啊,一去不回头!"西藏的木船船头一般都安着一个头朝后的木雕马头。前两句以"渡船无心"和"马头回眸"形成反义,为下面慨叹负心人一去不回头造势,语义上既有对比又有引申递进,将人与人的冲突演化为抒情主人公内在自我的冲突,表达了对负心之人既怨恨又不无眷恋的矛盾情绪。再如第 13 首"以手写出的黑黑小字,已被雨水冲消;刻在心头的图画,想擦也不会擦掉!"黑色的小字和心头的图画构成同类递进对比,但写出来的字迹本是醒目的却被雨水抹去了痕迹,而未写出的本来是模糊的图画却在人的心中难以磨灭,因此一、二两句与三、四两句分别形成反义,而一、二与三、四句中的写出—未写出、冲消—铭刻也形成反义,造成这首短诗层次的丰富性和主题的表现力。第 17、18、19、24、25 首等都十分典型地表现了主人公内心中信仰与爱情的冲突,如:"默想的喇嘛尊容,怎么也不显现;没想的情人面庞,却在心头灿烂","如果遂了美人心愿,今生就与佛法绝缘;若到深山幽谷中修行,又辜负了姑娘的芳心。"

仓央嘉措诗歌通过相反事物的对比凸显人与人的冲突和人与自我的冲突,表现了以设置冲突来进行戏剧化抒情的结构特点。

3. 对话性

戏剧与其他叙事文学的重要差异在于戏剧以台词搬演人生。戏剧台词包括独白与对话,而独白实质上也是一种自我对话。兰色姆(Ransom)认为抒情诗和戏剧密不可分,因为抒情诗源于戏剧独白:"抒情诗脱胎于戏剧独白。抒情诗完全可以直抒胸臆般慷慨陈词,但它更喜欢让芸芸众生中的普通一员作为'人物'代言"(兰色姆,2006)。艾略特认为诗的戏剧性对白可分为四种形式,即对他人说话、相互说话、对自己说话和对上帝说话。也就是说,抒情诗中的对话关系在文本中体现为抒情主体与抒情对象、抒情主体与自我、抒情主体与自然等几个方面,除此之外,站在批评者的立场上还可以将诗人与抒情主体甚至于批评者与诗人、批评者与抒情主体的关系一并纳入到对话关系的研究中。仓央嘉措诗歌正是通过抒情主体角色的多重变换体现了层次丰富的对话关系。

例如《仓央嘉措情歌》第44首"初三的月儿弯,银光洒满天;请对我发个誓言,要像十五的月亮那样圆。"其中的"月夜"是仓央嘉措诗歌中频繁出现的时间场景,在开篇第1首中皎洁的月亮就与母亲、情人的形象交相辉映,成为抒情主体内心独白的重要内容。而在第41—43首等中月亮或是作为自然意象构成时间场景,或是作为抒情对象的喻体参与了人与人之间的对话,既包含了人与自然的对话,也成为人与人之间情感交流的媒介与桥梁。在第11、14、23、27首等中,"誓言"多次出现,誓约是恋爱双方对话关系的持续稳固或产生变化的重要情节要素,如第23首"问问心爱的人儿:可愿做终身伴侣?回答说:除非死别,永不生离!"通过情侣间简短的对话显示了深厚稳定的情感关系,交流了彼此坚定不移的主观意愿。再如第56首:"帽子戴在头上,辫子甩在背后。'请慢走','请留步';'心中难过','重逢在即'。"有场景,有人物,有情节,只通过简短对话暗示丰富的情感内容,真是一幕情侣离别的短剧。

除了抒情诗表达中正面的陈述或感叹语气之外,仓央嘉措诗歌还善于以反问句、疑问句、设问句等多种问句的形式展开对话,造成抒情人物阐释的开放化格局,传递出人生经验的复调性,构成抒情主体"声音"的多重立体性。如第23首"问问心爱的人儿:可愿做终身伴侣?回答说:除非死别,永不生离!"通过问答形式对话;第35首"姑娘不是娘生的,怕是桃树上长的,要不然她的爱情,怎比桃花还谢得快呢?"通过设问倒装展开对话;第36首"两小无猜的情侣,莫非是狼的后裔?与我相恋同居,还想逃回山里。"以设问对话;第55首"温香暖玉的姑娘,被锦被所拥抱,莫非虚情假意,骗我少年财宝?"以疑问句展开对话。

以多种问句展开对话使读者由抒情主体自然关注到文本中所潜藏的抒情对象,对对话关系背后所暗示的抒情内容展开遐想。因此,现代诗人卞之琳认为在诗歌的戏剧性叙事对话中,主体常常可以进行角色和声音的置换,形成多声部的复调形式,产生类似于小说一样的众声喧哗的效果。

在此意义上,诗歌绝非仅仅是诗人情感经验的个性化表达,而是具有"非个人化"审美特征的社会话语交流的平台,而这正契合了戏剧的社会功能。

仓央嘉措诗歌的戏剧代言体特征正表明了抒情主体的"非个人化"特征,具有戏拟的功能,所以诗中的"我"可以从多角度来理解,带有变动性,并随之也带来动作性。因此,将诗中的抒情主人公对号入座地理解为是仓央嘉措本人的做法就显得过于局限了,这也是从文体学意义上对诗歌主题的开拓与延伸。

少数民族文学尤其是民间文学总体上有着口头性、集体性、变异性和传承性等本质特征(万建中,2006),这些普遍特征即便是在以个体创作为主导的少数民族作家诗中也有着明显的表征,从文体形式上显示出与汉族作家诗完全不同的风格特色和文化取向。这种差异的生成原因是复杂多重的,我们仅仅从传播形式方面来考察便可初见端倪。"从文学作品传播的形式来看,口头语言传播与书面文字传播历来是文学传播的最主要形式。"(郑土有,2008)与汉族文学以书面文字为主要传播形式相对比,少数民族文学更多依靠口传的形式来延续本民族的文化传统。口传模式不局限于单一的语言传播,传播者往往集创作、传播、表演于一体。口传文学以表演为中心,其"表演和语境,是确认诗歌文本实现过程的重要方面。不同的表演、不同的表演时间和场合、不同的表演者、不同的听众,这些不同都会影响口头诗歌的文本。……口传文学的交流更加依赖于社会语境。"(尹虎彬,2005)诗歌的叙事性、冲突性和对话性则是其传播得以实现的重要因素。少数民族诗歌的存在是动态的,其发生、演变和最终归宿都已超越狭义的文体范畴甚至文学范畴,负载了民族独有的思维模式和审美理想,是不断叠加的民族的记忆与阐释。

仓央嘉措诗歌从叙事性、冲突性和对话性方面实现了抒情诗的戏剧化抒情模式建构,强化了抒情诗交流对话的功能,作为藏族作家诗与"谐"体民歌结合的典范之作,它一改过去藏族僧侣典雅华丽的"年阿体"风格,借鉴民歌的修辞手法和抒情模式,通过文人创作极大地提升了"谐"体民歌的审美表达力,成为藏民族传统文化积淀中的重要元素,对藏族诗歌的发展具有深远的影响。

参考文献

Brooks, C. & R. P. Warren. 2004. Understanding Poetry. 北京:外语教学与研究出版社.

约翰·克罗·兰色姆. 2006.《新批评》(王腊宝、张哲译). 南京:江苏教育出版社.

诺思罗普·弗莱. 2006.《批评的解剖》(陈慧,袁宪军,吴伟仁译,吴持哲校译). 天津:百花文艺出版社.

恰白·次旦平措著,曹晓燕译.1990.谈谈与《仓央嘉措情歌》有关的几个历史事实.《西藏民族学院学报》,(3):81.

万建中.2006.《民间文学引论》.北京:北京大学出版社.

尹虎彬.2005.二十世纪口传文学研究的十个误区.《民族艺术》,(4):86.

郑土有.2008.打通"民间文学""俗文学",构建"口传文学"平台——关于新时期民间文学学科建设的思考.《民族遗产》(第一辑):143.

Part IV   Functional Stylistics

The Multimodal Symbolic Articulation in Illustrated *Shì Shuō Xīn Yǔ* (《世说新语》)

Liu Shisheng　(**Tsinghua University**)
Song Chengfang　(**University of International Business and Economics**)

Abstract： Every illustrated text is a new text. Then how does the new text articulate its theme? This paper tries to give an answer to this interesting question by applying a modified version of Hasan's stylistic model of verbal arts in the analysis of Liu Yiqing's story collection *Shì Shuō Xīn Yǔ* (《世说新语》).

Our analyses show that two factors are important： one is the semiotic foregrounding, that is, patterning of patterns of the multimodal text； the other is the theme articulated by each component. In our tentative analyses, distinctions are made between multimodality as a phenomenon and as a perspective, between general multimodal discourse analysis and multimodal stylistic analysis, and between stylistic enquiries concerning why and how a text means what it does and stylistic analysis of symbolic articulation.

Treating multimodality as a phenomenon, we use texts with illustrations as data to investigate firstly how texts and images interact to make meaning and then how themes are multimodally articulated. Eight ways of illustrating are summarized in the present investigation.

Key words： stylistics； illustrated text； symbolic articulation； multimodality

1. Introduction

Multimodality is a term used both to refer to a phenomenon and to designate a perspective. As a phenomenon, it indicates that some discourses, or a certain type of discourse conventionally or predominately, employ more than one mode to make meaning; Roland Barthes is one of the earliest researchers who investigated the phenomenon (e.g., 1977); and advertisements, the text type examined in Barthes (1977), are the multimodal texts which are firstly and also most extensively examined so far (for example, Myers, 1994; Forceville, 1996; Cook, 2001). As "perspective" is a theoretical notion and a new perspective is usually inspired by accounts of new or once overlooked facts, multimodality as a perspective, in comparison with multimodality as a phenomenon, is a relatively recent proposal, holding that all texts and all communication are bound to be multimodal and mono-modes do not exist (Baldry & Thibault, 2006: 19; Nørgaard, Busse, & Montoro 2010: 30; Nørgaard, 2011: 222; Page, 2010: 4). The designating of multiplicity of semiotic modes in communication by the term underlies the increasing attention paid to modes other than language in texts and the examination of texts produced with the help of new technology (e.g., Piazza, Bednarek, & Rossi, 2011); and the new research angle, in addition to motivating research changes as mentioned above, also sheds fresh light on some semiotic resources discussed in traditional frameworks (e.g., Nørgaard, 2009).

Discourse studies are usually categorized as applied research, as they usually take a certain linguistic framework as their analytical tool and aim to analyze different types of discourse. Studies concerning multimodality are inevitably discourse studies, which can be shown by the favorite term, Multimodal Discourse Analysis (MDA in short), chosen by eminent scholars in this field such as O'Halloran (2011); the reason is that their research object is nothing but discourse. However, multimodality designates something new, that is, other modes in addition to language, which received little or no attention in past studies. Therefore, efforts must be made to devise theoretical framework(s) before it/they can be applied in multimodal discourse analysis.

Ideally speaking, individual theories to account for the working of separate modes or a general theory that can be applied across all modes should be developed independently and originally; and some researchers, for example, Page (2010: 4-5), anticipated the possibility. Nevertheless, as language, as one of the modes, has been far more adequately explored than others, the usual practice in theorizing multimodality builds multimodal frameworks by borrowing or reworking concepts from different schools and various subfields of linguistics. The most influential school of multimodal analysis is the one developed with reference to systemic-functional linguistics. Researchers taking this approach have devised grammars for several modes frequently deployed in communication, such as images (O'Toole, 1994; Kress & van Leeuwen, 2006), sound (van Leeuwen, 1999), hypermedia (Lemke, 2002); and they have drawn discourse semantic systems to analyze multimodal discourse (Martin, Painter, & Unsworth, 2013). They have put forward frameworks to analyze various intersemiotic relationships, for instance, image-text relations (Kress & van Leeuwen, 2006; Martinec & Salway, 2005), language, images and mathematical symbols (Lemke, 1998), and have illustrated how multimodal choices realize contextual variables and construe power and identity (Djonov & Zhao, 2013). O'Halloran (2011) provides a concise but comprehensive introduction to intra-group differences and central theoretical and analytical issues within this approach and a nice illustration of what she calls MDA text analysis. Other approaches to multimodality include, but are not limited to, cognitive linguistics and interactional sociolinguistics. The former one is illustrated by Forceville's (1996) analysis of multimodal metaphor on the basis of conceptual metaphor theory (Lakoff & Johnson, 1980); and the later one includes Norris & Jones' (2005) introduction of mediated discourse analysis, which is founded on interactional sociolinguistics.

Taking as their point of departure the multimodal frameworks developed in the works mentioned above, researchers have analyzed a wide variety of discourse. According to the traditional distinction between ordinary language use and high-valued texts (Halliday, 2002), their endeavors can be divided into two categories: one is general multimodal discourse analysis and the other is multimodal stylistic analysis. Ordinary language uses, sometimes called practices (Kress & van Leeuwen, 2001; O'Halloran, 2011), include both well established and, most of the time, also familiar genres such as advertisements (Barthes, 1977), scientific texts (Lemke, 1998) and mathematics (O'Halloran, 2005) and newly sprung discourses like online chatting, web-logs, and other types of technology-assisted (also driven) communication, with themes ranging from analytical issues and methodological considerations to their generic features and interpersonal functions.

Multimodal stylistic analysis or multimodal stylistics is now considered a new branch of stylistics (Nørgaard, Busse, & Montoro, 2010: 30-34). But multimodal analyses of literary works, which, like the earliest multimodal discourse analyses conducted in Barthes (1977), O'Toole (1994), and Kress & van Leeuwen (2006), also analyze mainly the integration of language and images, as can be found in literary criticism. For instance, Qian Zhongshu, the foremost man of letters in contemporary China, remarks that illustrations to famous poetic lines in the imperial academy during the Song and Ming dynasties embodied the artistic practice and principle which he called "meaning surpassing the image" (意余于象) (Qian, 1998: 29), which is indeed a very insightful observation of image-text relations and a key-to-point summary of a means of explicating themes. Most multimodal stylistic analyses focus on narratives, especially those inherently multimodal ones such as telecinematic discourse (Piazza, Bednarek, & Rossi, 2011), opera (Hutcheon & Hutcheon, 2010), filmed drama, etc., which were familiar to us a long time ago, largely due to the availability of analytical tools, and twenty-first century experimental literature and new media narratives of various kinds, for instance, interactive narratives (Hatton, Mcgurgan, & Wang, 2010), polymorphic fictions (Dena, 2010), and panfictions (Thomas, 2010), probably mainly because of their originality. Their aims have been summarized in Page (2010: 11) as the desire to:

1. Explore the enabling and constraining properties of different combinations of modes in narrative production or reception;
2. Ask how the relationship between narrative and multimodality is influenced by particular contexts;
3. Critique existing definitions of narrative and construct alternatives that take account of the multimodal nature of communication;
4. Expand the transmedial study of narrative to investigate the relationship between medium and mode.

The significance of their studies lies in how they draw people's attentions to audiovisual stories of various kinds and the stories that are based on new technologies that extend far beyond the boundary of classical narrative studies; and that they "mark a paradigm shift away from mode blindness" (Page, 2010: 3). In their multimodal studies of narratives, a wide range of semiotic resources have been analyzed, including, for instance, visual elements, sound, typography, gesture, and haptic resources. However, their research focuses are mainly on the multimodal nature of the text and matters related to production, and they aim to illustrate how to make sense of the story, how additional meaning is created, and how our understanding of a particular narrative text is augmented. That is, their analyses belong more to multimodal discourse analyses of narratives than to stylistic analyses, fulfilling the more immediate goal of stylistic inquiry to show why and how the text means what it does (Halliday, 1983: x; Hasan, 1989: 94−99); but this fails to address the further goal, which characterizes stylistic analysis.

Halliday (1983: x) conceptualizes the further goal as that of showing why the text is valued as it is. Hasan (1989: 94−99) provides a detailed account of the further goal and, more significantly, builds a semiotic model that reflects these two goals of stylistic analysis (Figure 1). According to her, the art of verbal art lies in the symbolic articulation of theme through verbalization.

Taking Hasan's semiotic model of verbal art as the theoretical framework, this paper aims to go further to explore how symbolic articulation mediates between theme and verbalization in multimodal texts. As symbolic articulation, even as far as verbal texts are concerned, is not a fully developed notion (Liu & Song, 2010), the study takes a quantitative approach and makes an attempt to substantiate the notion by generalizing the ways it operates in various cases. The paper consists of five parts. After this introduction, a revised Hasanian semiotic model of verbal art and its key concepts are introduced, and then an account of data chosen and the method used in the analysis is provided. On the basis of the quantitative analysis, it is found that there are as many as eight ways of illustrating, which give rise to four ways of explicating: Compound articulation; Duplicate and Combinational; Inflectional articulation; Assonant and Dissonant.

2. Theoretical Framework

2. 1 Semiotic Model of Multimodal Verbal Art

As it gradually becomes a common sense that figurative and deviant linguistic expressions alone do not define literature, as they are also prevalent in our non-literature use of language (Halliday, 1983: xi; Hasan, 1989: 91-94), stylisticians begin to rethink what constitutes the legitimate object of stylistic analysis or, in other words, what distinguishes stylistic analysis from text analysis in general.

The founders of functional linguistics, as shown above in Halliday (1983) and Hasan (1989), admit that any stylistic analysis is based on the textual understanding, which presupposes knowing the language in which the text examined is written, and starts from the recognition of various (individual) linguistic patterns. They further point out that verbal art resides in the semantic value of linguistic patterns and of patterning of such patterns (Hasan, 1989: 91, 100); and stylistic analysis sets itself apart from text analysis in being concerned with the uniqueness of the text under study (Halliday, 1983: xii) and in studying how themes are construed in language. Hasan (1989: 94-99) puts forwards a semiotic model of verbal art and language (Figure 1), which, on the one hand, accounts for what constitutes verbal art and, on the other hand, explains the relationship between the understanding of a text and its thematic articulation.

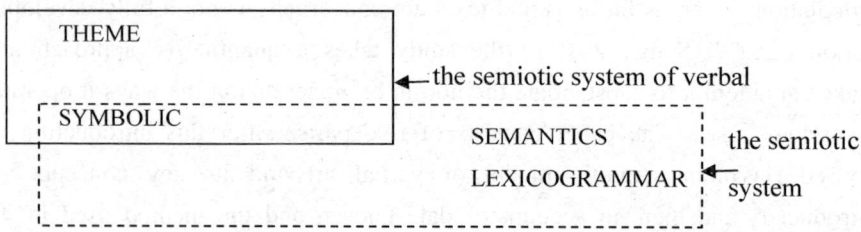

Figure 1   Hasan's semiotic model of verbal art and language (Hasan 1989: 99)

According to Hasan (1989: 96), verbal art can be theorized as a semiotic system, which resembles that of the semiotic model of language as proposed by systemic functional linguistics. As shown in Halliday & Matthiessen (1999: 5), language is a multiple coding system, consisting of three strata (Figure 2):

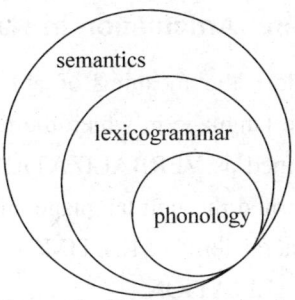

Figure 2　Language strata

The relationship between the strata is that of realization: meaning is realized by lexicogrammar; lexicogrammar is in turn realized by phonology. As far as the semiotic system of verbal art is concerned, at the lowest stratum — that of VERBALIZATION — a literary text is like any other text: a reader knows the meanings encoded in it through knowing the language. And the stratum of theme is "the deepest level of meaning in verbal art" (Hasan, 1989: 97). These two levels interrelate with each other through the stratum of SYMBOLIC ARTICULATION, which functions in the same way in the semiotic system of verbal art as lexicogrammar does in the semiotic system of language. It, like a power generator, turns the meanings of language into signs having a deeper meaning (Hasan, 1989: 98).

　　We contend that this model, with some modification, can be used to account for multimodal art as well, for multimodal texts differ from verbal texts mainly in that they deploy more than one semiotic mode to make meaning. The revised semiotic model of multimodal art and semiotic modes can be presented as Figure 3, and the terms used in it are to be explained in the following sections.

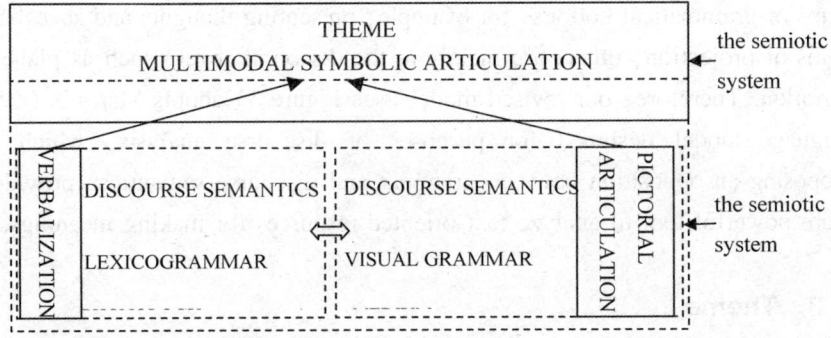

Figure 3　A semiotic model of multimodal art and semiotic modes

2. 2　Multimodal Literal Articulation in Narratives

In Hasan's（1989）model, the meaning of a text which is to be decoded through understanding the language in which the text is written（i.e. the literal meaning of a text）is termed as VERBALIZATION. As the literal meaning of a multimodal text is construed through language and other non-verbal modes as well, we use a more general term, MULTIMODAL LITERAL ARTICULA-TION, to replace VERBALIZATION.

　　This MULTIMODAL LITERAL ARTICULATION has its own features. Zhang & Mu（2012）point out that although words and images realize a single text and they are mostly complementary to each other, each of them makes their own contribution to the meaning of the text. And it is especially the case with illustrated texts（which are to be analyzed in this paper）, in which illustrations are mostly added to verbal texts in a later time. To add this feature into the semiotic model of multimodal art, we separate different articulations according to the mode. As it will be shown below, the multimodal texts to be analyzed in this paper are verbal-pictorial texts; therefore, two types of articulation are identified in Figure 3: VERBALIZATION and PICTORIAL ARTICULATION, with a double-headed arrow drawn between them to show their interaction.

　　In the language model as depicted in Figure 2, which Hasan's（1989）model adopts, the level of semantics is concerned with clause-size meanings. However, in her analyses of short stories, Hasan（1989）, in fact, examined non-structural resources for making meaning like logical relations between clauses and those phenomena which have been studied as narrative techniques and devices. Although some of the phenomena can be equally accounted for in terms of grammatical notions, for example, presenting thoughts and speeches in terms of projection, others are mainly at the discourse level, such as planes of narration. Therefore, our revised model（see Figure 3）adopts Martin's（1992）language model designed for purposes of discourse analysis, which, by proposing an opposition between grammar and discourse semantics, provides a more powerful tool to analyze text-oriented resources for making meanings.

2. 3　Theme

In linguistics, especially the school of systemic functional linguistics, THEME is a well established notion, employed in grammatical analysis to designate "the point of departure of the message" (Halliday, 2004: 64), and it can be identified with reference to some objective linguistic criteria. However, in literary criticism, it refers to "the 'point' of a literary work, its central idea, which we infer from our interpretation of the plot, imagery and symbolism" (Wales, 2001); and it is neither clearly stated in the text nor safely identified by adhering to some textual principles. Hasan (1989: 97, 98) has tried to clarify this notion, on the one hand, by elucidating its nature and, on the other, by explaining how it is inferred from the order of linguistic semiosis:

> The stratum of theme is the deepest level of meaning in verbal art; it is what a text is about when dissociated from the particularities of that text. In its nature, the theme of verbal art is very close to a generalization, which can be viewed as a hypothesis about some aspect of the life of a social man.
>
> (Hasan, 1989: 97)
>
> [...] The stratum of symbolic articulation is where the meanings of language are turned into signs having a deeper meaning. Foregrounding and patterning of patterns play an important role in ascribing the second order meanings (*theme, our note*) to the patterns of the first order meanings (*verbalization, our note*).
>
> (Hasan, 1989: 98)

As for the role foregrounding and patterning of patterns play in giving meaning to meanings, Hasan's (1989: 54, 88, 98) illustrative analyses show that it is metaphor that is central to this process. Hasan (1989) seems to treat the deepest level of meaning and the second order meaning as the same thing. But we contend that they are actually two superficially similar but substantially different notions, which differ from each other in the way that emblematic images in the *Changes* differ from metaphors in the *Songs* as discussed by Qian (1998: 135):

> [...] The emblematic images in the *Changes* remain separate and apart from the meanings associated with them; they guidepost to a meaning (*sign*). The referential imagery and similes in poetry, on the other hand, are inseparable from the meanings they convey. They are the very tracks of the ideas they embody (*icon*). The former can be replaced by other formulations, while the latter do not permit alternation without changing meaning.

That is, the theme characterized as "what a text is about when dissociated from the particularities of that text" and the theme that is ascribable to verbalization are of different orders. In conformation to Hasan's (1989) delineation of semiosis, we can term the former one as the second order theme, and the latter one the first order theme. Using Hasan's (1989: 88) terms, we can define the first order theme as the symbolic particularities of a text and the second order theme as abstraction or generalization over those particularities.

Theme is also sometimes divided into two categories: thematic concept and thematic statement. While the former one refers to "what readers 'think the work is about'", the latter one designates "what the work says about the subject" (Wikipedia). Our contention is that "theme" at each order necessarily consists of both a thematic concept and a thematic statement; and the thematic concept at the two orders should be the same and themes at the two orders probably differ in the degree of generality of their thematic statements.

As the second order theme generalizes over the first order theme, it is somehow separate from patterning in multimodal texts. The main purpose of the present study is, as shown below, to explore multimodal symbolic articulation; therefore, only the first order theme is taken into account in our analysis. Thus, no bother is made to include the two orders in the level of "theme", which also has the effect of simplifying the model and avoiding confusion in analyses as the distinction is hard to maintain in practice.

2.4 Multimodal Symbolic Articulation and Semiotic Foregrounding

According to Hasan (1989: 98), the stratum of SYMBOLIC ARTICULATION in the semiotic model of verbal art is analogous to that of lexico-grammar in the semiotic model of language. Halliday (e.g., 2005) has metaphorically referred to lexico-grammar as the powerhouse of a language; Hasan (1989: 98) likewise, as shown in the above quotation, defines the stratum of symbolic articulation as the place "where the meanings of language are turned into signs having a deeper meaning". Although these two levels have the same function, they differ in the forms in which they exist. Lexico-grammar comprises structural resources for making meaning, while symbolic articulation takes the form of non-structural patterns of foregrounding.

Since the English term "foregrounding" was introduced to the wider public as the translation of the Prague School term, *aktualisace*, by Garvin (Mukarovsky, 1964), it has become one of the key concepts in stylistics. Hasan (1989: 14) holds that foregrounding in terms of linguistic patterns has two bases: repetition and contrast. This is indeed a keen insight, and its modern version is what Simpson (2004) summarizes as two main guises of foregrounding: "foregrounding as 'deviation' from a norm and foregrounding as 'more of the same'".

Foregrounding has, up to now, been a concept used to analyze verbal texts, or, at most, monomodal texts, and foregrounded items are identified through being compared or contrasted with items at the same level and of the same rank. Nevertheless, multimodal texts pose challenges to this notion, as the architecture of a multimodal text consists of several sets of components; and contrast and comparison across modes have to be included in stylisticians' agendas to find out the foregrounding across modes. In fact, studies on intersemiotic relations in multimodal discourse analysis have proposed several terms to account for multimodal construal of meaning in multimodal texts: namely, "resemioticization" (Iedema, 2003: 30), "multiplication of meaning" (Lemke, 1998), "semiotic metaphor" (O'Halloran, 1999a, 1999b) and "translation" (Kress & van Leeuwen, 2006: 78). By analogy with O'Halloran's semiotic metaphor, we propose to analyze the motivated patterning across modes in terms of "semiotic foregrounding". As far as the analysis in this paper is concerned, this means that the level of multimodal symbolic articulation has to take account of three types of foregrounding: verbal foregrounding, visual foregrounding, and semiotic foregrounding.

Concerning the three types of foregrounding, a point has to be made clear here. They are actually of two different categories. Verbal and visual foregroundings are monomodal foregroundings, and they are the results of comparison and contrast of items of the same rank at the same level. Whereas, semiotic foregrounding is a multimodal phenomenon, and comparison and contrast made in this case have to be done with reference to semiotic principles applicable to all semiotic modes under study (cf. Kress & van Leewwen, 2001).

3. Method

3. 1 Data

As it is pointed out in Hasan (1989: 100), "the art of verbal art resides in its symbolic articulation"; the exploration of symbolic articulation is destined to be the primary task of stylistic studies. As the intermediary level of the three-layered semiotic model, the study of multimodal symbolic articulation would be easier if the other two strata are constants or are simple enough to be given a clear account. The illustrated version of Liu Yiqing's *Shì Shuō Xīn Yǔ* published by Zhonghua Book Company in 2007 provides ideal data for such a kind of study.

Shì Shuō Xīn Yǔ, or A New Account of Tales of the World, consists of 36 sections and 1,130 short texts in total. These texts record stories, conversations, and short characterizations of 626 characters who lived in the period that spans from the late years of the Eastern Han Dynasty to the early years of the Liu Song Dynasty. The work is said to hold a special place in historical and cultural studies, because what was kept in it was sometimes also documented elsewhere and thus was regarded as a reliable source of facts regarding to the period, whose official document, *The Book of Jin*, is, however, considered below standard due to the hasty compilation three hundred years or so later (Mather, 1976). Moreover, it is also highly valued as a literary work in literary criticism. Lu (1973: 203) pointed out that the work reports the sayings and narrates the stories in an extremely concise and efficient way, vividly depicting characters, clearly articulating the deepest thoughts, and keeping alive the spirits of the time.

The newly published illustrated version of the work contained all the 36 sections, but it selects only 255 texts out of the whole collection. Although there have been other illustrated versions published recently — for instance, the one published by Shanghai Classics Publishing House, an influential publishing house in China, in 2004 — this version is chosen for analysis for the following two reasons.

Firstly, among the 255 texts, 106 are illustrated with one or two images, and each section also contains one illustration. There are all together 149 illustrations of various kinds, including portrayals, calligraphy, wall paintings, New Year paintings, etc. Therefore, these texts with their illustrations are both quantitatively sufficient and qualitatively adequate for exploring ways of multimodal symbolic articulation.

Secondly, the title of each section makes clear the thematic topic of texts included, and each text is usually three or four lines long and is convenient to analyze in full. These two features fulfill the required conditions of the study mentioned just above and explain why these multimodal texts are regarded as ideal data.

3.2 Analysis

Theoretically speaking, an interpretation of the theme of a text has to be based on an explicit analysis of the text; and the more exhaustive the analysis, the more convincing the interpretation. Martin's (1992) discourse semantics theory presents a powerful tool kit for analyzing verbal texts, and recent developments in multimodal discourse analysis have also put forward "grammars" of other modes to analyze non-verbal meaning-makings (and have devised frameworks to explore intersemiotic relations in multimodal texts). Therefore, we are now equipped with a rich assembly of tools to conduct highly exhaustive analyses of the data: that is, the illustrated texts.

Shì Shuō Xīn Yǔ, originally a collection of verbal texts, is, as mentioned above, clearly structured according to the themes it chooses to articulate, and these themes are, in fact, widely accepted, as the division of 36 sections is adopted in various later versions of this work (e.g., Liu, 2007) and has received no rejection in studies on this work (e.g., Mei, 2004). Whereas, the purpose of this paper is not to verify whether the identification of these themes are reasonable; it aims, instead, to explore how newly created multimodal texts relate to these themes. Departing from this purpose, the analysis in this paper will not take an expected unbiased approach to the data, and will proceed in the following steps.

Visual analyses are conducted first for the following reasons: firstly, images are the added elements which create the new texts; secondly, images, in comparison with verbal texts, are easier to analyze and to classify; thirdly, visual analyses facilitate the understanding of images, which serves as the basis for the forth-coming analyses. Kress & van Leeuwen (2006) have proposed an elaborate grammar for analyzing images with reference to

Systemic Functional Grammar (e.g., Halliday, 2004). Although they (2006) cautiously state that their data are confined to visual text-objects from 'Western' cultures (3) and rightly point out that cultural and semiotic landscapes play important roles in the interpretation of any semiotic mode, of which images are one instance (4, 35–41), the analytical notions we believe are quite universal. Therefore, we will conduct the visual analyses by employing Kress & van Leeuwen's (2006) framework. Figures 4 (1) and 4 (2) provide their system networks for analyzing the ideational component of images; Figures 5 (1) and 5 (2) outline the choices for analyzing interactive meanings and modality, two components of the interpersonal meaning, in images; and Figure 6 reports their concepts for analyzing the composition of an image.

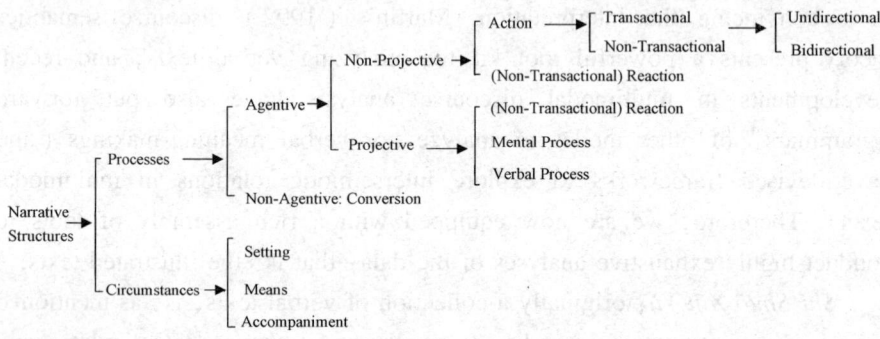

Figure 4(1)　Narrative structure in visual communication (from Kress & van Leeuwen, 2006: 74)

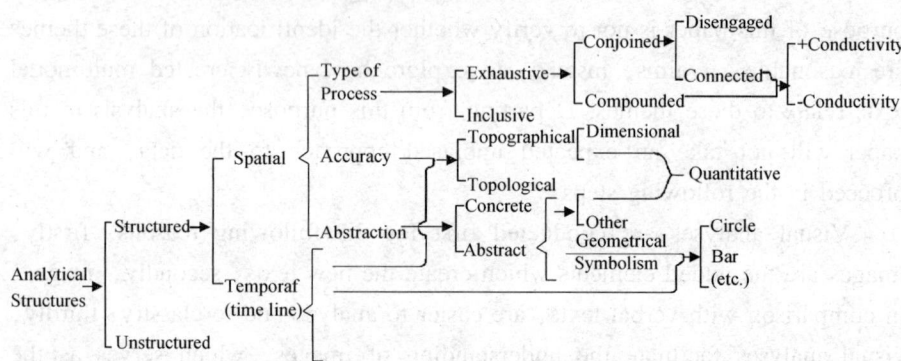

Figure 4(2)　Analytic image structure (from Kress & van Leeuwen, 2006: 104)

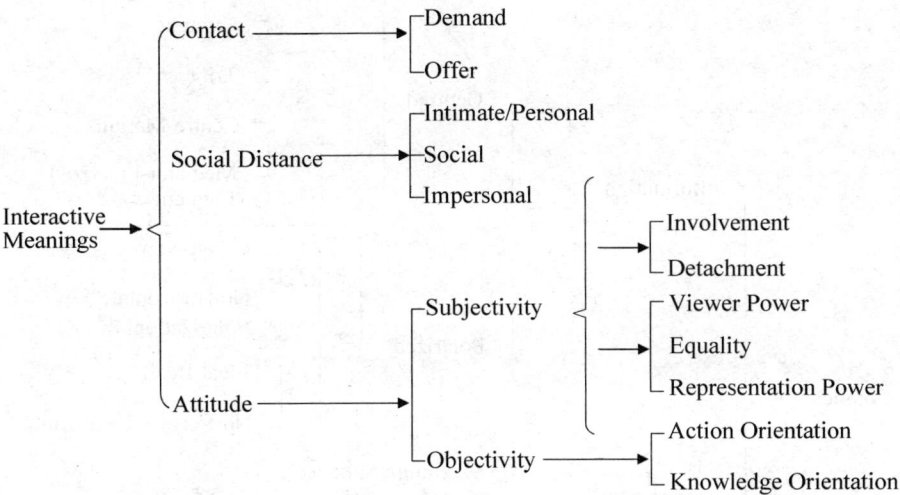

Figure 5(1)   Interactive meanings in images (from Kress & van Leeuwen, 2006: 149)

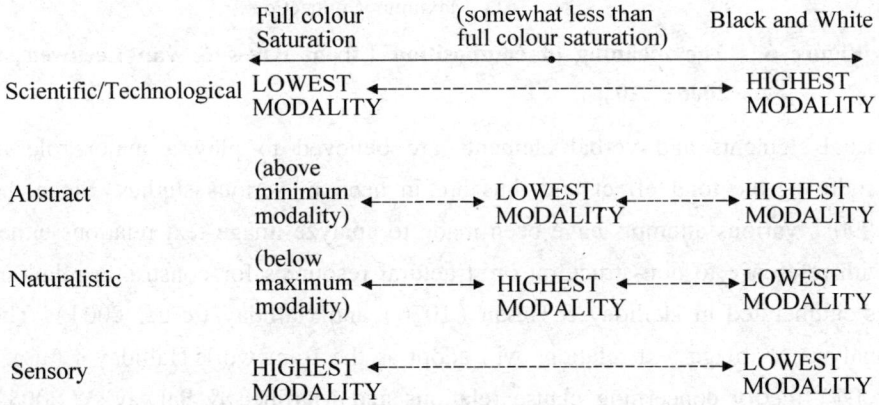

Figure 5 (2)   Modality values of colour saturation in four coding orientations (from Kress & van Leeuwen, 2006: 166)

Afterwards, image-text relations are studied. As it is pointed out by Royce (1998), an illustrated text is not a text in which the visual semiotic and the verbal semiotic simply co-occur and have a simple conjunctional relationship, the relationship between them is synergistic, which means that the newly created piece has "a total effect that is greater than the sum of the individual elements or contributions". The intersemiotic relations between

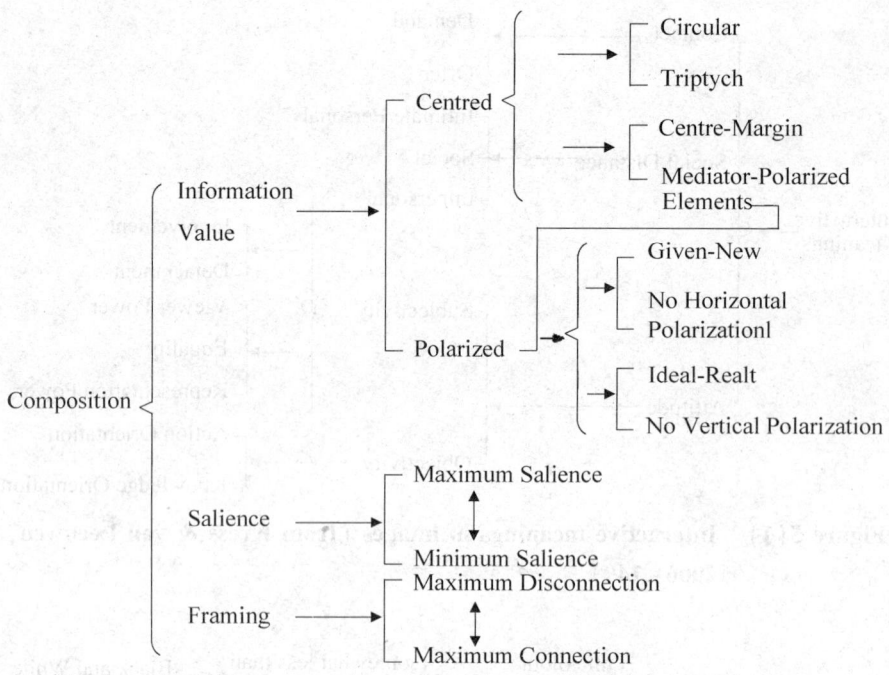

Figure 6   The meaning of composition (from Kress & van Leeuwen, 2006: 210)

visual elements and verbal elements are believed to play a major role in producing the total effect and thus are in need of serious studies. Since the 1990s, various attempts have been made to analyze image-text relations either with reference to non-structural or structural resources for construing relations as enumerated in Halliday & Hasan (1976) and Halliday (e.g., 2004). The analysis of image-text relations will adopt as the framework Halliday's (e.g., 2004) theory concerning clause relations and Martinec & Salway's (2005) system of image-text relations which is based on Halliday's theory for their exhaustiveness and applicability. However, some revisions will be made as narratives have their own principles, such as "part for whole" as discussed in Section 4. Figure 7 presents Martinec & Salway's (2005) proposed network. The analyses in the first two steps, taken together, should produce a summary of various ways in which illustrations are made.

In a multimodal text, despite their contribution to the overall effect, each semiotic mode is said to construe meaning independently as well (Royce, 1998; Zhang & Mu, 2012). Similarly they should also articulate their own

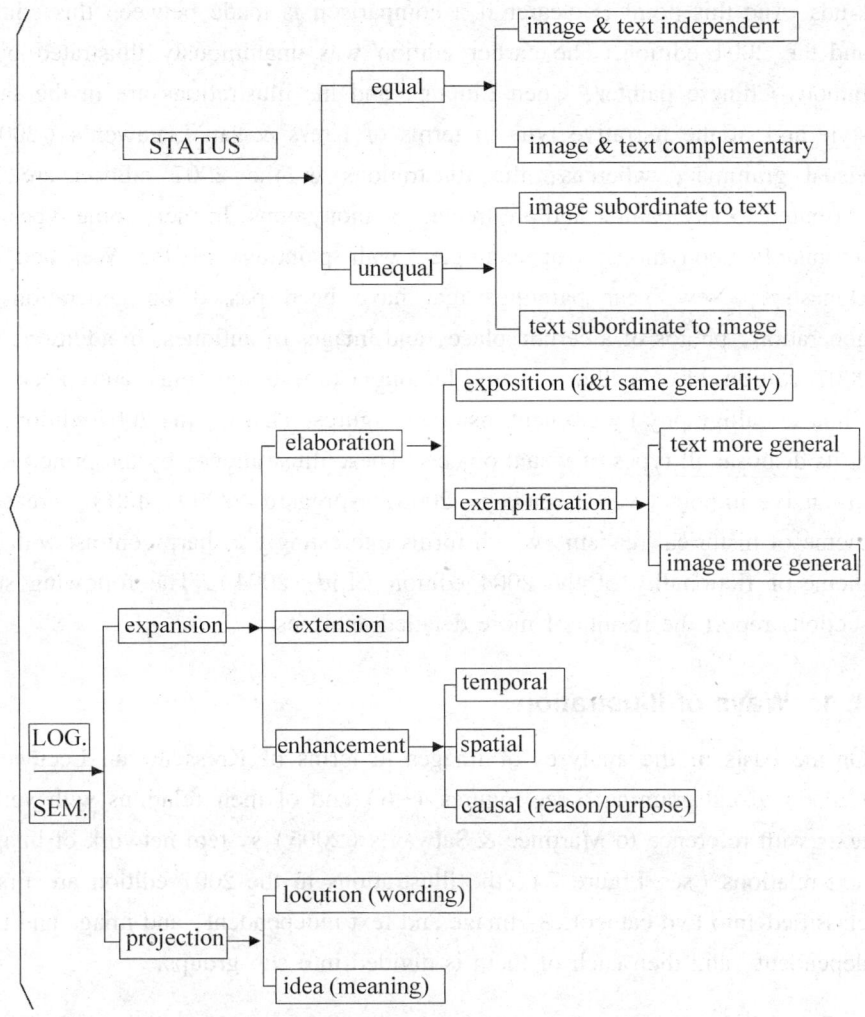

Figure 7 Network for combined status and logico-semantics

themes. Since themes of verbal texts have been identified, the visual articulation of themes is explored in the third step.

On the basis of the above discussions, ways of multimodal symbolic articulation are finally examined.

4. Results

As previously mentioned, illustrations in the 2007 edition are of various kinds. And this point is clearer if a comparison is made between this edition and the 2004 edition. The earlier edition was unanimously illustrated by a famous Chinese painter, Chen Linong, and his illustrations are in the same style and of the narrative type in terms of Kress & van Leeuwen's (2006) visual grammar; whereas, the illustrations in the 2007 edition are not attributed to any painter and are treated as anonymous. In fact, some types are reasonably anonymous, for example, wall paintings of the Wei and Jin Dynasties, New Year paintings that have been passed on generation by generation, photos of a certain place, and images of antiques. In addition, the 2007 edition also includes many famous Chinese paintings and pieces of Chinese calligraphy by eminent historical figures. That is, the 2007 edition has at its disposal all types of visual objects. These illustrations, by the principle of discursive import (van Leeuwen, 2005; Nørgaard, 2009: 438), create a theme of historical realism, which forms interestingly a sharp contrast with the theme of fictionality of the 2004 edition (Liu, 2004). The following sub-sections report the results of more detailed analyses.

4. 1 Ways of Illustration

On the basis of the analyses of images in terms of Kress & van Leeuwen's (2006) visual grammar (see Figures 4-6) and of their relations with verbal texts with reference to Martinec & Salway's (2005) system network of image-text relations (see Figure 7), the illustrations in the 2007 edition are firstly classified into two categories: image and text independent, and image and text dependent, and then each of them is divided into sub-groups.

4.1.1 Image and Text Independent
Image and text independent: exposition

Images involved in this type of relation with texts usually have a narrative structure. For instance, Figure 8, entitled "The elder brother ordering his younger brother, Cao Zhi, to compose a poem", depicts that Cao Zhi (the young man facing the other three) is composing a poem at Court in accordance with his royal brother's (the sitting one) order. Two other persons are in their company (including the half-hidden lady). The following is the multimodal text, which is from Section 4 *Letters and Scholarship* and its illustration:

Example 1

Emperor Wen of Wei (T'ao (*sic.*) P'ei (Cao Pi), r. 220–226) once ordered the Prince of Tung-o (Ts'ao Chih) (Cao Zhi) to pace seven steps and within the duration of time he should compose a poem. If it was not completed in time, heavy penalty would be imposed on Cao Zhi. On the spur of the moment the latter then composed the following poem:

> "Boiled bean are taken to make a soup,
> Strained lentils utilized for stock.
> While stalks beneath the pot are blazing up,
> The beans within the pot are sobbing.
> Originally from the same root grown,
> For one to cook the other, why such haste?"

The emperor looked profoundly ashamed. (Liu, 1976: 126)

Figure 8 **The elder brother ordering his younger brother, Cao Zhi, to compose a poem**

Strictly speaking, the illustration only provides a snapshot of the event. If the strict criteria listed in Martinec & Salway (2005) are applied, the image is just related to part of the verbal texts, because the detailed order, including possible penalty, and the poem itself are not included in the image; consequently, the relation between them is one of "image dependent on text". But such an analysis is weird, especially to a native speaker of Chinese, because other details are like elements that, together with information provided in the illustration, create a "historical gestalt", if we are allowed to create such a term. Mei (2004) identifies "part for whole" as a narrative principle in *Shì Shuō Xīn Yǔ*. We hold that this principle applies equally to visual telling and thus analyze the relation in this case as "independent" concerning STATUS and "exposition" in terms of logico-semantics as they are at the same level of generality.

This type of illustration is the actual practice in the 2004 edition. However, only "Xie An inviting his relatives to compose poems on snow", "Xie An playing Weiqi with others" and another two stories concerning Zhao Jun and Shi Chang belong to this category in the 2007 edition.

Image and text independent: extension

Images of this type are the same as images of the former one and also have a narrative structure, which serves to trigger readers' stored historical knowledge and tells a complete story. This type differs from the former one in that the story is narrated through the image "extending" the verbal one in the sense of "addition" (Halliday, 2004: 378). Here follows three examples from Sections of *Virtuous Conduct* (1), *Speech and Conversation* (4), and *Taunting and Teasing* (25).

Example 2

Wang Hsiang (Wang Xiang) in serving his stepmother, Mme. Chu, was extremely conscientious. There was a plum (*li*) tree in their home whose fruit was exceptionally good, and his stepmother always had him protect it. Once when a storm of wind and rain came to pass, Hsiang embraced the tree, weeping.

On another occasion Hsiang was sleeping on a separate bed when his stepmother herself came over and slashed at him in the dark. As it happened, Hsiang had gotten up to relieve himself, and her vain slashing struck only the bedclothes. After Hsiang returned to the room he realized his stepmother bore him an implacable resentment, and kneeling before her he begged her to end his life. His stepmother then for the first time came to her senses and loved him ever afterward as her own son. (Liu, 1976: 8)

Example 3

When K'ung Jung (Kong Rong) was apprehended those both inside and outside the court were panic-stricken. At that time Jung's elder son was in his ninth year, and the younger in his eighth. The two boys continued, as before,

Figure 9　Wang Xiang breaking ice to catch carp

their game of throwing spikes (*cho-ting*) without the slightest agitation showing in their faces.

Jung said to the officer who had come for him, "I trust the punishment ceases with my own person. May my two sons be spared?"

The sons came forward gravely and said, "Father, would you expect to find any unbroken eggs under an overturned nest?"

In a short while officers came to apprehend them as well. (Liu, 1976: 27)

Figure 10　Liu Bei rescuing Kong Rong at Beihai

Example 4

While Ho Lung (Hao Long) was serving as Huan Wen's aide to the Commandant of the Southern Barbarians (Nan-man) (ca. 345), there was a gathering on the third day of the third month when everyone shall compose poems. Whoever was unable to do so shall pay a forfeit by drinking three cups of wine.

At first Lung was unable to compose anything and paid the forfeit. But after drinking three cups of wine, he seized a brush and wrote the words:

"The *chü-yü* leaps in the clear pool."

Huan Wen asked, "What on earth is a *chü-yü*?"

Lung replied, "The Southern Barbarians call 'fish' *chü-yü*."

Huan asked, "Who ever heard of using the Nan-man language to compose poetry?"

Lung replied, "I came a thousand *li* to serve under Your Excellency's command, and only got to be an aide in the Southern-Barbarian headquarters (Hsiang-yang (Xiangyang), Hupei (Hubei)), so how can I avoid using the Nan-man language?" (Liu, 1976: 414–415)

Figure 11   Gathering at Lan Ting on occasion of the spring purification

In these three examples, each illustration tells a story different from the one narrated in the verbal mode. Figure 9 shows another of Wang Xiang's filial events: His stepmother wanted to eat fish on an icy winter day, so Wang Xiang came to the river and decided to melt the thick ice with his body heat, and finally when he was almost frozen to death he caught some fish which leaped out of the hole under his body. Figure 10 depicts a story about Kong Rong from *Romance of the Three Kingdoms*: when he held his position at Beihai, he was attacked and was in danger; so he pleaded Liu Bei to save him, and Liu Bei agreed and finally sent a troop and helped him get out of trouble. Figure 11 presents a gathering on the third day of the third month at Lan Ting which Wang Xizhi organized and in which a lot of celebrities participated; and it became famous because of the preface Wang Xizhi wrote to the collections of works written by participants from this occasion.

All these three stories, although related to the verbal one in different ways as discussed in the following section, are independent of their verbal company and can stand alone. This way of illustration is a predominant one in the 2007 edition and about 20 multimodal texts take this practice. This dominance maybe results from "intertextuality", a popular phenomenon in literary work.

Image and text independent: enhancement

Different from images in the above two types, the images in this type belong to the category of conceptual representation. Example 5 from Section 9, *Classification According to Excellence*, and Example 6 from Section 26, *Contempt and Insults*, are two illustrations.

Example 5

When P'ang T'ung (Pang Tong) arrived in Wu (in 210), the people of Wu all befriended him. After he had seen Lu Chi (Lu Ji), Ku Shao (Gu Shao), and Ch'ü Tsung (Quan Zong), he made characterizations of them as follows: "Lu Chi might be called an old horse who has the capability for swiftness of foot; Ku Shao might be called an old ox who can carry heavy burdens and travel long distances."

Someone asked P'ang, "According to your characterization, then, is Lu the better of the two?"

P'ang replied, "An old horse, though he may be the finest and swiftest, can carry no more than one man. As for an old ox, though in one day he might travel but a hundred *li*, is his load limited to one man?"

Since no one of the people of Wu raised any objections, (P'ang continued,) "Ch'ü Tsung is a lover of fame and reputation, something like Fan Tzu-chao (Fan Zizhao) of Ju-nan (Ru'nan)." (Liu, 1976: 249)

Example 6

After Fu Huang (Fu Hong) had rebelled against the Later Ch'in (Qin) (384-417) and returned his allegiance to the Chin (Jin) (in 384), the grand tutor, Hsieh An (Xie An), often entertained him. Hung fancied himself to have ability, and in most cases enjoyed getting the better of other people. On one occasion there was no one present who could break him, but it happened that Wang Hui-chih (Wang Huizhi) arrived, and the grand tutor had them converse together. Wang merely stared at him for a long time, then, turning,

said to the grand tutor, "He, too, in the end is no different from the others."
Fu withdrew in great embarrassment. (Liu, 1976: 339-340)

成都武侯祠

Figure 12   Temple for Zhuge Liang (in Chengdu)

前秦"大秦奥兴化年古菓"瓦当

Figure 13   Tiles of the Former Qin

Figure 12 is a photo of the temple that was built to honour Zhuge Liang,
and Figure 13 is a photo of an ancient tile, which was made and used in the
Early Qin dynasty. Neither of them are mentioned in their accompanying
verbal texts; therefore, we analyze the relation between image and text in this
case as independent. In his analysis of typography, van Leeuwen (2005)
mentions that written signs sometimes make meaning through the principle of
discursive import. It seems that the two images can be interpreted as denoting a
symbolic process (Kress & van Leeuwen, 2006: 105-106), in which the two

carriers are identified by means of their spatial and temporal location due to the place and the period from which they as signs originate. That is, Figure 12 makes clear the place in which the story narrated in the verbal text took place, and Figure 13 makes clear the period in which the story narrated in the verbal text happened.

Image and text independent: logical relations free

The above analysis has exhausted all the possibilities of Martinec & Salway's (2005) framework (see Figure 7) as far as the case of "image and text independent" is concerned. Nevertheless, the 2007 edition also contains some multimodal texts in which it is difficult to perceive any relation between the verbal and visual components. Example 7 from Section 1 *Virtuous Conduct* is such a case.

Example 7

After Yin Chung-k'an (Yin Zhongkan) had become governor of Ching Province (Jing Province) (Huan-Hupei) (Hubei), he encountered a shortage of food due to floods. His meals always consisted of five bowls, and there was no extra food beyond what was in the dishes. If a grain of rice fell between the dishes and the mat, he would always pick it up and devour it. Although in doing so he wished to set an example for others, he was also following the true simplicity of his nature. He would often say to his sons and younger brothers, "Don't imagine, because I have accepted office in the present province, that I have given up my usual attitude of earlier days. At present the situation in which we are living is not easy, but 'poverty is the gentlemen's normal state'. Why should he climb out on the branches and lose contact with his roots? You all should preserve this principle!" (Liu, 1976: 19)

Figure 14　Celadon sheep from the Jin Dynasty

Probably the same as the images discussed in the last section, Figure 14 presents another instance in which meaning is created through a symbolic process. The most obvious interpretation is as follows. The carrier is the Celadon sheep of the Jin Dynasty, and as a priceless antique, it has the attributes of the beautiful, the elegant, the ancient, the rare, and so forth. But in the verbal text, neither the carrier nor attributes are mentioned. If the two parts indeed define a coherent text, the relation seems not to be at the logico-semantic level but at a higher level, most likely that of theme, where a sound interpretation is made that Yin Zhongkan's conduct, just like the Celadon sheep, is beautiful, elegant, and of ancient virtue as well. As the analysis conducted so far has been confined to the first level of stylistic analysis as clarified in Section 1 (Halliday, 1983; Hasan, 1989), this type of illustration is referred to as "Image and text independent: logical relations free". And there are, in fact, more cases of this type in the 2007 edition.

4.1.2 Image and Text of Unequal Status

As there are four types of relations when images and texts are of equal status, there also are four types of relations when images and texts are of unequal status.

Image subordinate to text: exposition

This type of illustration is used frequently in the 2007 edition. Martinec & Salway (2005) define "image subordinate to text" as "an image [...] related to part of a verbal text". Example 9 from Section 2 *Speech and Conversation*, Example 10 from Section 1 *Virtuous Conduct*, Example 11 from Section 15 *Self-renewal*, and Example 12 from Section 24 *Rudeness and Contempt* illustrate that the partial relatedness can be encountered in different ways.

Example 8

When Pien Jang (Bian Rang) came for an interview with Yüan Lang (Yuan Lang), he got the order of precedence backward. Yüan remarked, "When the Sage-king Yao summoned the recluse Hsü Yu (Xu You) for an interview, Hsü showed no sign of embarrassment in his face. 'Why are you putting your clothes on topsy-turvy'?"

Pien replied, "Your Excellency has only just arrived at his post, and the moral order of Yao has not yet been displayed. It's only for this reason that your humble servant has 'put his clothes on topsy-turvy'." (Liu, 1976: 25)

Figure 15　Xu You washing ears

Example 9

Kuan Ning (Guan Ning) and Hua Hsin (Hua Xin) were together in the garden hoeing vegetables when they spied a piece of gold in the earth. Kuan went on plying his hoe as though it were no different from a tile or a stone. Hua, seizing it, threw it away.

On another occasion they were sharing a mat reading when someone riding a splendid carriage and wearing a ceremonial cap passed by the gate. Kuan continued to read as before; Hua, putting down his book, went out to look. Kuan cut the mat in two and sat apart, saying, "You're no friend of mine." (Liu, 1976: 7)

Figure 16　Painting of ploughing on tomb bricks (the Wei-Jin Dynasties)

Example 10

When Chou Chu'u (Zhou Chu) was young, his cruel and violent knight-errantry was a source of distress to his fellow villagers. [...] (Liu, 1976: 318)

Example 11

When Hsieh Wan (Xie Wan) went on the northern expedition (against Earlier Yen (Yan) in 358), he constantly demonstrated his superiority by whistling and chanting poems, and never showed any consideration for his officers or men. His elder brother, Hsieh An (Xie An), who highly respected and loved Wan, but sensed that Wan would surely be defeated, accompanied him on the expedition. Very casually he said to Wan, "Since you're the supreme commander, you should invite your generals to banquets now and then to cheer their morale." [...] (Liu, 1976: 397)

Figure 17   Portrait of Zhou Chu

Figure 18   Wall painting of riding and shooting (the Wei-Jin Dynasties)

In Example 8, the verbal passage mentions that Xu You showed no sign of embarrassment in his face when the Sage-king Yao summoned him, and Figure 15 shows that Xu You washed his ears when he was summoned the second time. Although the contents of these two representations are not strictly identical, Figure 15 could be said to tell what is verbally presented in another way. And this is what "exposition" means in Halliday's (2004) theory.

While in Example 9, the first sentence of the verbal passage tells us that the two participants in the story were hoeing vegetables in the garden, but what Figure 16 depicts is that ploughman living in the Wei-Jin Dynasties was ploughing the field. The image illustrates the corresponding textual segment in the sense that hoeing and ploughing are co-subordinates of work in the field. And this example differs from the former one also in that the actor in Figure 16 is neither of the two participants mentioned in the verbal text while the two participants in Figure 15 and in the verbal passage of Example 8 are the same.

Figures 15 and 16 have a narrative structure. Figure 17 presents a symbolic process, in which Zhou Chu is the carrier, and his attributes are "cruel" and "violent" which are verbally given in the first sentence.

Despite some minor differences existing among the above three examples, the illustrations and their verbal counterparts relate to each other in a direct way. Example 11 provides a different case. The verbal text mentions that Xie Wan went on the northern expedition against the Earlier Yan in 358, but Figure 18 is a wall painting of riding and shooting. Obviously riding and shooting are not equal to an expedition, and they are in fact, in Peircean terms, related to each other in an indexical way.

In whatever ways the illustrations make meanings and in whatever ways the illustrations are subordinate to the verbal texts, the illustrations add no new information to the texts at the discourse level; therefore, the logico-sematic relation between image and text is that of exposition.

Text subordinate to image: exposition

As far as the 2007 edition is concerned, illustrations are made 1,800 years later. It seems natural that images are subordinate to texts. But we do find an example that indicates texts can be subordinate to images.

Example 12

When Yin Hao was appointed senior administrator for Yü Liang (Yu Liang), as he was about to set out from the capital (Chien-K'ang) (Jian Kang), Chancellor Wang Tao (Wang Dao) held a gathering in his honour. Huan Wen, Wang Meng, Wang Shu, and Hsieh Shang (Xie Shang) were all present. The chancellor, personally rising and pushing aside the curtains, took his sambar-tail chowry from his girdle and said to Yin, "Today you and I will converse together and analyze principles."

Once they had become engrossed in pure conversation (ch'ing-t'an) (qīngtán) together, they continued until the third watch (midnight). The chancellor and Yin both talked back and forth, while the other worthies hardly participated at all. [...] (Liu, 1976: 103)

Figure 19   Pottery figurine of the literati from the Wei-Jin Dynasties

This example is from Section 4 *Letters and Scholarship*. In Figure 19, two men of letters are conversing intensely, and the story about the pure conversation between Yin Hao and Wang Dao seems to offer an instance of what is depicted in Figure 19. Therefore, we analyze this case of illustration as "text subordinate to image: exposition". And this is the only case of this kind we find in the 2007 edition.

Image subordinate to text: extension

The Dynasty of Wei and the Dynasty of Jin witnessed the birth of many famous calligraphers, including Wang Xizhi and Wang Xianzhi. The 2007 edition uses many famous pieces of calligraphy as illustrations. The following text from Section 3 *Affairs of State* is an example.

Example 13

While Huan Wen was governing Ching (Jing) Province (ca. 345) he wanted very much to have his virtue extend throughout all the area of the Yangtze and Han rivers, and he was therefore ashamed to employ harsh punishments to intimidate his subjects. On one occasion a clerk was being flogged and the rod merely passed over his vermilion robe of office. Wen's son Huan Hsin (Huan Xin), who was young at the time, came in from outside and said, "Just now I passed by the courtroom and saw a clerk being flogged. They were clearing away the cloud roots above and sweeping off the earth footings below." He meant to make fun of the fact that the rod made no contact.

Huan Wen replied, "I'm still sorry it was so severe." (Liu, 1976: 89)

In this example, the contents in the calligraphy are not the main concern and should not be analyzed as a verbal text. This calligraphy, according to van

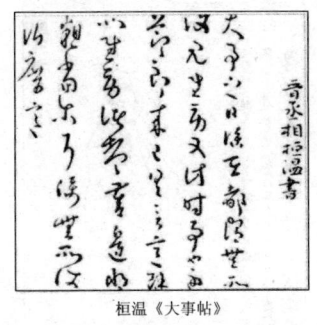

桓温《大事帖》

Figure 20　Huan Wen's calligraphy

Leeuwen（2005）and Nørgaard（2009：438）, can be regarded as an index or the carrier of a symbolic process. On the one hand, it assigns the identity of calligrapher to its writer; and, on the other hand, its own quality indicates the calligrapher's admirable abilities and other prototypical attributes that characterize a calligrapher in Chinese traditional culture such as more elegance, naturalness and restraint. These pieces of information are not included in the verbal text and are something new that is derived from the illustration. Therefore, in terms of logico-semantics, the relation is that of extension.

Image subordinate to clause

In addition to the above ways of illustrating, there is one more type, which is the most regularly used in the book but seems difficult to find a position in Martinec & Salway's（2005）framework. The following 5 examples each represents a sub-type.

Example 14

In the time of Hsieh An（Xie An）many soldiers and camp followers who had deserted or become vagrants had come near the capital and had sneaked in among the boats moored below the southern bank（of the Ch'in-huai River）. Someone wished to make a simultaneous search to round them up, but Hsieh（Xie）would not permit it. He said, "If we didn't make room to accommodate this crowd, how could this be the capital?"（Liu, 1976：90）

Example 15

At the New Year's Assembly（in 317）Emperor Yüan（Yuan）（Ssu-ma Jui（Sima Rui）, r.317-323）drew Chancellor Wang Tao（Wang Dao）by the hand to mount the imperial dais. Wang steadfastly declined, but the emperor drew him the more insistently. Finally Wang said, "If the sun were to shine

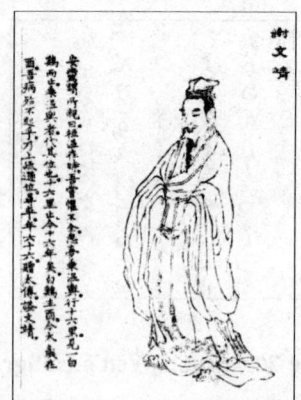

Figure 21   Portrait of Xie An

with exactly the same brilliance as all other things, what would the ministers below have to look up to?" (Liu, 1976: 369)

Figure 22   Portrait of Emperor Yuan

Figure 23   Portrait of Wang Dao

Example 16

When Liu Yüan-chih (Liu Yuanzhi) was young he was recognized by Yin Hao, who praised him to Yü Liang (Yu Liang). The latter was extremely pleased and proceeded to take him on as an assistant. After he had greeted him, he had him sit on a single couch (*tu-t'a*) (*dútà*) while he conversed with him. That day Liu failed conspicuously to come up to expectations, and Yü (Yu), somewhat disappointed, finally named him "Yang Hu's crane".

Previously, Yang Hu (d. 278) had a crane which was skilled at dancing. Once Yang praised it to a guest, but after the guest arrived, when he tried to drive it forward, it made a flurry of feathers but would not dance. This is why Yü Liang compared Liu Yüan-chih to the crane. (Liu, 1976: 419)

Figure 24   Portrait of Yang Hu

Example 17

When the Chin (Jin) Emperor Chien-wen (Jianwen) (Ssu-ma Yü) (Sima Yu) was serving as General Controlling the Army (345 – 361), he would not permit the dust to be brushed off the dais on which he sat. When he saw the tracks where rats had run he looked on them as a thing of beauty. [...] (Liu, 1976: 18)

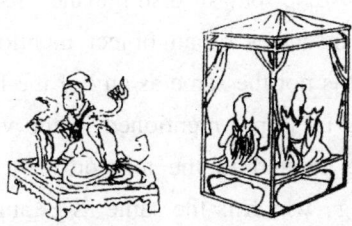

Figure 25   Dais from the Wei-Jin Dynasties

Example 18

When Huan Wen was about to start his punitive expedition against the kingdom of Ch'eng-Han (Chenghan) in Shu (Szechwan (Sichuan), in 347), all the worthies in his administration of Ching (Jing) Province argued that the family of the Ch'eng-Han (Chenghan) ruler, Li Shih (Li Shi), had lived in Shu a long time, and Li had inherited his patrimony through successive generations. Moreover, his territory was situated at the upper reaches of the Yangtze River, and the Three Gorges had never yet been easy to conquer.

It was only Liu T'an (Liu Dan) who said, "That man's certain to be able to conquer Shu. I've observed his gambling habits, and if he's not certain of winning, he won't play." (Liu, 1976: 206)

Figure 26   Armed pottery figurine from the Wei-Jin Dynasties

Figure 21 in Example 14 is the portrait of Xie An, the protagonist in the verbally narrated story. Figures 22 and 23 in Example 15 differ from Figure 21 in that they visually introduce both the protagonist and the antagonist of the verbal story. Figure 24 in Example 16 is different from the above two groups of figure in that what it represents is not a participant in the verbal story at all, but a mentioned figure. Figure 25 in Example 17 shares the differences Figure 24 has with Figures 21 – 23, but it distinguishes itself from Figure 24 by presenting visually two instances of an object mentioned in the verbal text. Figure 26 in Example 18 is not the same as any of the figures discussed above, because what it shows to us is not mentioned in the verbal text and it can be interpreted coherently as related to the text only by means of an indexical mode of making meaning, which is the same as Example 11.

In the above 5 examples, the relation between images and texts are obviously not equal, as these images do not have a narrative structure and they are not related to the whole text. Nor is it that of text-subordinate-to-image, because no deixis can be perceived from text to image (Martinec & Salway, 2005). The only possible interpretation is that images are subordinate to texts. However, according to Martinec & Salway (2005), an image is subordinate, or related, to a text which is more than a clause or a clause complex under the condition that there are some relations between the process(es) in the image and at least one process in the text; otherwise, the image has no relation with the text but some component-cohesive relation with a specific clause.

On the basis of the above discussion, we therefore analyze the relation as image-subordinate-to-clause in general. And it is included in this section just for the convenience of organization. As for the detailed classification in terms of logico-semantics, we contend that although all the images in Examples 14– 18 can be analyzed as having a symbolic process, their contributions to the story development and to the thematic articulation vary greatly as what they depict have different roles in the narrative. The contributions by a protagonist, by an antagonist, by a mentioned person, by a mentioned object, and by an indexically related object should form a declining sequence. So the logico-semantic relation in Examples 14 and 15 can be analyzed as that of extension because attributes assigned to carriers are new pieces of information that could make contributions to the whole text through extending image-related clauses, while the logico-semantic relation in Examples 17 and 18 should be referred to as that of exposition for the reason that the images only visualize relevant objects mentioned or indicated in the text. Example 16, we think, is a fuzzy case, which could be analyzed in either way.

4. 2　Ways of Multimodal Symbolic Articulation

Every illustrated text is a new text. Then how does the new text articulate its theme? Figure 3 shows that this question needs to be answered by taking into account two factors: one is the semiotic foregrounding, that is, patterning of patterns of the multimodal text; the other is the theme articulated by each component.

Semiotic foregrounding, as discussed in Section 2.4, involves comparison and contrast of items of the same nature across modes. The analysis of image-text relations in the above section provides a basis for such a type of comparison and contrast. As image-text relations have been firstly classified according to status relations, multimodal articulation in terms of semiotic foregrounding can be divided into two groups as well. The first group can be termed as compound articulation, by analogy with compound words, just as the verbal text and its illustration, like the components of a compound, can stand alone. The second group can be referred to as inflectional articulation (again a term from morphology) as in this case either the text or the image is independent with the other dependent on it.

As for the second factor, it seems that a preliminary distinction should be made between identical and different examples to account for the thematic contributions of each mode. Consequently, compound articulation can be further classified into duplicate articulation if the themes articulated by the verbal text and the image are identical; and combinational articulation if the themes articulated through the different modes are different from each other. Inflectional articulation can be further divided into assonant articulation if themes of the independent and the dependent components are the same, and dissonant articulation if they are not the same.

4.2.1 Compound Articulation: Duplicate

Reduplication, defined as "the repetition of all or part of the radical element" in Sapir (1921: 79), is prevalent in language. Sapir (1921) lists it as one of the grammatical processes. We use it here to refer to cases in which images and texts are of equal status and articulate the same theme as discussed above. The foregrounding in this case is achieved through repetition.

Examples 1 and 2 are two illustrations. But as the analysis of their logico-semantic image-text relations shows, there are some subtle differences. In Example 1, the verbal text and its corresponding illustration narrate the same story, which shows that Cao Zhi excels in letters; and the duplicate articulation is that of re-articulation. While in Example 2, the verbal text and its illustration, in fact, tell two different stories, which provide two pieces of evidence as to Wang Xiang's filial piety. The principle of quantity iconicity means, more form, more meaning (Hiraga, 1994). If the rhetorical effect is taken into account, the duplicate articulation in Example 2 can be more concisely termed "amplification".

4.2.2　Compound Articulation: Combinational

This category differs from the former one in that themes articulated in each component are different. And the foregrounding of this category results from differences. As "different" can be in various ways, this category, like the former one, is subject to finer distinctions.

Examples 3, 4 and 7 are three different cases of this category. Among them, the difference between the verbally articulated theme and the visually articulated theme in Example 7 is the biggest, as the verbal text is a narrative which reports Yin Zhongkan's virtuous conduct, while the image is a photo of a Celadon sheep from the Jin Dynasty. Our previous analysis has noted that the interpretation of this multimodal text needs to be based on the parallelism between attributes of the Celadon sheep and those of Yin Zhongkan's conduct. That is, the articulation of theme in the multimodal text is through the interaction of two different themes. With reference to Peircean semiotics, we refer to this combinational articulation as metaphorical articulation.

Among the three examples, the difference between differently articulated themes in Example 3 is the smallest, as both the verbal text and the image tell stories about the same person, Kong Rong. Nevertheless, the themes of the two texts are different: the verbal story is about his two sons' unexpected reaction and artful speech in face of his apprehension, while the visual story is about how Liu Bei came to his rescue when he held positions in Beihai. Kong Rong was a great man of letters and was also famous for his righteousness. The two stories, providing two accounts of his miserable life, make us feel sorry for him, which in turn make us admire more his sons' swiftness and keenness in understanding the situation and in giving an artful answer. That is, the visual story facilitates the articulation of the theme in this case, which is, technically speaking, a scaffolding articulation.

Example 4 lies between Example 3 and Example 7, as the verbal text and the image record two events which have no relation with each other but are of the same type: that is, a spring gathering of celebrities. The combinational articulation in this example seems to operate via the principle of analogy. The conversation in the verbal text shows that Hao Long is highly capable in letters, and the illustration helps to establish his status as a celebrity by introducing a famous spring gathering of celebrities in Lan Ting and by inviting readers to conceive the two gatherings as the same. Therefore, this type of articulation can be termed as "analogical articulation".

In addition to the 5 examples discussed above, there are two more examples, Examples 5 and 6, in Section 4.1.1. As they function to provide circumstantial information, they do not contribute a lot to the articulation of the theme.

4.2.3 Inflectional Articulation: Assonant

Different from compound articulation where two voices interact in various ways to explicate the theme, inflectional articulation is a process in which the independent component determines the theme and the dependent component just provides some modification. Assonant articulation refers to cases where the modification is in a positive way. Our analysis shows that the positive modification mostly takes the form of illustrating what is positively evaluated in the verbal text.

The following examples are all subject to this explanation: Examples 8, 9 and 10 in the category of "Image subordinate to text: exposition", Example 12 of the category of "Text subordinate to image: exposition", Example 13 in the category of "Image subordinate to text: extension", and Examples 14 and 15 in the category of "Image subordinate to clause". For instance, Figure 15 in Example 8 depicts the casual manner of Xu You when summoned by Yao, which is an illustration of the noble manner advocated by the verbal text; Figure 16 is a wall painting of ploughing, which is a more admirable profession for a man of letters in comparison with seeking to be rich and being a high ranked official as implicated in the verbal text.

4.2.4 Inflectional Articulation: Dissonant

All the other examples in Section 4.1.2 can be grossly grouped into the category of dissonant articulation, as no such evaluative assonance is perceived in them. For example, Figures 18 and 26 in Examples 11 and 18 indexically depict an expedition, which is secondary to the story as it is the background of the event and which is, moreover, basically evaluation free. They do not make any noticeable contribution to the thematic articulation.

5. Concluding Remarks

Distinctions are made between multimodality as a phenomenon and as a perspective, between general multimodal discourse analysis and multimodal stylistic analysis, and between stylistic enquiries concerning why and how a text means what it does and stylistic analysis of symbolic articulation. Treating multimodality as a phenomenon, this paper uses texts with illustrations as data to investigate firstly how texts and images interact to make meaning and then how themes are multimodally articulated. The investigation finally summarizes eight ways of illustrating and four ways of explicating. A comparison of ways of illustrating and of explicating additionally shows that status relations between images and texts play a more important role than logico-semantics in identifying ways of illustrating; and ways of explicating are, to a certain extent, independent from ways of illustrating, which is perhaps a reflection of the loose relation between theme and discourse semantics as contended by Hasan (1989: 98).

References

Baldry, A. & P. J. Thibault. 2006. *Multimodal Transcription and Text Analysis: A Multimedia Toolkit and Coursebook*. London: Equinox.

Barthes, R. 1977. Rhetoric of the image. In Roland Barthes. *Image-Music-Text*. Essays selected and translated by Stephen Heath, 32–51. London: Fontana Press.

Cook, G. 2001. *The Discourse of Advertising*. London and New York: Routledge.

Dena, C. 2010. Beyond multimedia, narrative, and game: The contributions of multimodality and polymorphic fictions. In R. Page (ed.). *New Perspectives on Narrative and Multimodality*, 183–201. New York and London: Routledge.

Djonov, E. & S. Zhao. (eds.). 2013. *Critical Multimodal Studies of Popular Discourse*. New York and London: Routledge.

Forceville, C. 1996. *Pictorial Metaphor in Advertising*. London and New York: Routledge.

Halliday, M. A. K. 1983. Foreword. In M. Cummings & R. Simmons (eds.). *The Language of Literature: A Stylistic Introduction to the Study of Literature*, vii-xvii. Oxford: Pergamon Press.

Halliday, M. A. K. 2002. *Linguistic Studies of Text and Discourse. Vol. 2 in the Collected Works of M. A. K. Halliday*. Edited by Jonathan Webster. London and New York: Continuum.

Halliday, M. A. K. 2004. *An Introduction to Functional Grammar* (3rd Ed.). Revised by C. M. I. M. Matthiessen. London: Arnold.

Halliday, M. A. K. 2005. On matter and meaning: The two realms of human experience. *Linguistics and the Human Sciences*, 1 (1): 59–82.

Halliday, M. A. K. & R. Hasan. 1976. *Cohesion in English*. Harlow: Longman.

Halliday, M. A. K. & C. M. I. M. Matthiessen. 1999. *Construing Experience Through Meaning: A Language-Based Approach to Cognition*. London and New York: Continuum.

Hasan, R. 1989. *Linguistics, Language, and Verbal Art* (2nd Ed.). Oxford: Oxford University Press.

Hatton, S., M. Mcgurgan, & X. Wang. 2010. Keg party extreme and conversation party: Two multimodal interactive narratives developed for the SMALLab. In R. Page (ed.). *New Perspectives on Narrative and Multimodality*, 202–216. New York and London: Routledge.

Hiraga, M. K. 1994. Diagrams and metaphors: Iconic aspects in language. *Journal of Pragmatics*, 22: 5–21.

Hutcheon, M. & L. Hutcheon. 2010. Opera: Forever and always multimodal. In R. Page (ed.). *New Perspectives on Narrative and Multimodality*, 65 – 77. New York and London: Routledge.

Iedema, R. 2003. Multimodality, resemiotization: Extending the analysis of discourse as multi-semiotic practice. *Visual Communication*, 2(1): 29–57.

Kress, G. & T. van Leeuwen. 2001. *Multimodal Discourse: The Modes and Media of Contemporary Communication*. London and New York: Arnold.

Kress, G. & T. van Leeuwen. 2006. *Reading Images: The Grammar of Visual Design*. London and New York: Routledge.

Lakoff, G. & M. Johnson. 1980. *Metaphors We Live By*. Chicago, IL: University of Chicago Press.

Lemke, J. L. 1998. Multiplying meaning: Visual and verbal semiotics in scientific text. In J. R. Martin & R. Veel (eds.). *Reading Science: Critical and Functional Perspectives on Discourses of Science*, 87–113. London: Routledge.

Lemke, J. L. 2002. Travels in hypermodality. *Visual Communication*, 1 (3): 299–325.

Liu I-ch'ing. 1976. *Shih-shuo Hsin-yü: A New Account of Tales of the World*. Translated with introduction and notes by Richard B. Mather. Minneapolis, MN: University of Minnesota Press.

Liu S. & C. Song. 2010. Functional stylistic studies. *Foreign Language Education*, 31 (6): 14–19.

Liu Y. 2004. *A New Account of Tales of the World with Illustrations*. Illustrated by Chen Linong, translated by Ma Zhaoqian, and with notes by Zhang Wei. Shanghai: Shanghai Classics Publishing House.

Liu Y. 2007. *Shì Shuō Xīn Yǔ* (with illustrations). Beijing: Zhonghua Book Company.

Martin, J. R. 1992. *English Text: System and Structure*. Amsterdam: John Benjamins Publishing Company.

Martin, J. R., C. Painter, & L. Unsworth. 2013. *Reading Visual Narratives*. London: Equinox.

Martinec, R. & A. Salway. 2005. A system for image-text relations in new (and old) media.

Visual Communication, 4 (3): 337–371.

Mather, R. B. 1976. Introduction. In Liu I-ch'ing. *Shih-shuo Hsin-yü: A New Account of Tales of the World*. Translated with introduction and notes by Richard B. Mather. Minneapolis, MN: University of Minnesota Press.

McIntyre, D. 2008. Integrating multimodal analysis and the stylistics of drama. *Language and Literature*, 17 (4): 309.

Mei J. 2004. *Shì Shuō Xīn Yǔ de Yǔyán yǔ Xùshì* [The language and the narration in *Shì Shuō Xīn Yǔ*]. Taipei, Taiwan: Le Jin Books Ltd.

Mukarovsky, J. 1964. Standard language and poetic language. In P. L. Garvin (ed. and trans.) *A Prague School Reader on Esthetics, Literary Structure, and Style*, 17–30. Washington, D.C.: Georgetown University Press.

Myers, G. 1994. *Words in Ads*. London: Edward Arnold.

Norris, S. & R. H. Jones. 2005. *Discourse in Action: Introducing Mediated Discourse Analysis*. Abingdon, Oxon: Routledge.

Nørgaard, N. 2003. *Systemic Functional Linguistics and Literary Analysis: A Hallidayan Approach to Joyce, A Joycean Approach to Halliday*. Odense: University Press of Southern Denmark.

Nørgaard, N. 2009. The Semiotics of typography in literary texts: A multimodal approach. *Orbis Litterarum*, 64 (2): 141–160.

Nørgaard, N. 2010a. Modality. Commitment, truth value and reality claims across modes in multimodal novels. *Journal of Literary Theory*, 4 (1): 63–80.

Nørgaard, N. 2010b. Multimodality: Extending the stylistic tool-kit. In D. McIntyre & B. Busse (eds.). *Language and Style: In honour of Mick Short*, 433–448. New York, NY: Palgrave Macmillan.

Nørgaard, N. 2011. Teaching multimodal stylistics. In L. Jeffries & D. McIntyre (eds.). *Teaching Stylistics*, 221–238. Basingstoke: Palgrave Macmillan.

Nørgaard, N., B. Busse, & R. Montoro. 2010. *Key Terms in Stylistics*. London and New York: Continuum.

O'Halloran, K. L. 1999a. Interdependence, interaction and metaphor in multisemiotic texts. *Social Semiotics*, 9 (3): 317–354.

O'Halloran, K. L. 1999b. Towards a systemic functional analysis of multisemiotic mathematics texts. *Semiotica*, 124 (1/2): 1–30.

O'Halloran, K. L. 2005. *Mathematical Discourse: Language, Symbolism and Visual Images*. London and New York: Continuum.

O'Halloran, K. L. 2011. Multimodal discourse analysis. In K. Hyland & B. Paltridge (eds.). *Companion to Discourse*, 120–137. London and New York: Continuum.

O'Toole, M. 1994. *The Language of Displayed Art*. London: Leicester University Press.

Page, R. 2010. Introduction. In R. Page (ed.). *New Perspectives on Narrative and Multimodality*, 1–13. New York and London: Routledge.

Piazza, R., M. Bednarek, & F. Rossi. 2011. *Telecinematic Discourse: Approaches to the*

Language of Films and Television Series. Amsterdam: John Benjamins Publishing Company.

Qian Z. 1998. *Limited Views: Essays on Ideas and Letters by Qian Zhongshu*. Selected and translated by Ronald Egan. Cambridge (Massachusetts) and London: Harvard University Press.

Royce, T. D. 1998. Synergy on the page: Exploring intersemiotic complementarity in page-based multimodal text. *JASFL Occasional Papers*, 1 (1): 25-50.

Simpson, P. 2004. *Stylistics: A resource book for students*. London and New York: Routledge.

Thomas, B. 2010. Gains and losses? Writing it all down: Fanfiction and multimodality. In R. Page (ed.). *New Perspectives on Narrative and Multimodality*, 142-154. New York and London: Routledge.

van Leeuwen, T. 1999. *Speech, Music, Sound*. Basingstoke: Macmillan.

van Leeuwen, T. 2005. Typographic meaning. *Visual Communication*, 4 (2): 138-143.

Wales, K. 2001. *A Dictionary of Stylistics* (2nd Ed.). Harlow, England: Longman.

Wikipedia. Theme (Narrative). <http://en.wikipedia.org/wiki/Theme_%28narrative%29>

Zhang D. & Z. Mu. 2012. On the theoretical framework of multimodal functional stylistics. *Foreign Language Education*, 33(3): 1-6.

视角逆行、评价隐喻与情感—伦理诉求

——《你还在我身旁》的评价文体效应与解读模型

彭宣维（北京师范大学）

Perspective Retrogression, Appraisal Metaphor and Emotive-Ethic Pursuit

— The Appraisal Stylistic Effects of *You Are Still with Me*

Peng Xuanwei　(Beijing Normal University)

摘　要：文学文本的话语组织涉及经典文体学关注的相关前景化成分，但更有评价主旨引导下的文本整体评价意义建构：前者是网状关系，属于词汇语法范畴；后者是纺锤型模式，由不同评价范畴的累积与终极评价指向两个方向相反的圆锥型意义要素构成。这一过程涉及从评价主旨到文本组织的三种基本话语策略：谋篇视角、人际性语境对比与概念意义投射。为此，作者以当下流行的一首小诗为例，以"作者—文本—读者"一体化解读机制为出发点，演示了评价意义范畴应用于文学文本分析的一种解读效应模式，说明文学文本分析的多层次性，以此揭示文学是以评价为特点、手段和目的的互动性艺术话语行为，文学性就是评价性，超常规经验表述的是心理实在性。这一尝试是个案性质的，但对文体分析、甚至对语篇语言学理论模型的建构具有启示意义。

关键词：文学文本；组织策略；《你还在我身旁》；个案分析；评价主旨；内容平面分层

Abstract：The discoursal organisation of literary text does not go without referring to relevant foregrounding elements that the classical stylistics embraces, but as well it engages the holistic appraisal meaning unit construction under the guidance of the general appraisal motif that lies behind, the former being interwoven into a texture, which is lexicogrammatical in nature, whereas the latter making itself a spindle model that comprises two butt-to-butt joint cones in opposite directions, with one expanding in categorical domains and the other contracting into a point of the ultimate appraisal appeal of the whole text. The whole aesthetic meaning-making process relies on three fundamental discourse strategies from option selections to text organisation: textual perspectivisation, interpersonal contextual comparison and ideational meaning projection. For that purpose of literary stylistic analysis, the paper takes a currently popular little poetic text as an example to illustrate, on the hypothesis of "author-text-reader" being a unity, the view that literary text is multi-layered in appraisal meaning. It aims to argue, not directly though, that literature, whether the theoretical account or practice, is the artistic discourse behaviour in interaction featured with the characteristics, strategies and purposes of appraisal, that literariness is indeed evaluativeness and that extraordinary experience has its due psychological reality. This attempt is case-natured, but it has significant inspiration for all literary stylistic analyses and even text-linguistic model construction.

Key words: literary text; organisational strategy; *You Are Still with Me*; case analysis; appraisal motif; content plane stratify

1. 引言

最近微信朋友圈里很多人在转发一首题为《你还在我身旁》(简称《身旁》)的小诗。这首诗是香港中文大学《独立时代》杂志 2014 年"愿付雁书长思君——微情书大赛"一等奖获奖作品(以下是原作,笔者用拉丁字母为各行标上了序号,以便后文指代使用)。

    a. 瀑布的水逆流而上,
    b. 蒲公英种子从远处飘回,聚成伞的模样,
    c. 太阳从西边升起,落向东方。

d. 子弹退回枪膛,

e. 运动员回到起跑线上,

f. 我交回录取通知书,忘了十年寒窗。

g. 厨房里飘来饭菜的香,

h. 你把我的卷子签好名字,

i. 关掉电视,帮我把书包背上。

j. 你还在我身旁。

类似作品有特定读者群,也受表达空间制约,估计难以进入主流文学视野;但就莘莘学子而言,它确有独特的情感和伦理价值。

本文以此例为立足点,系统阐述一种综合性的文学文本解读模式。这既有演示一种解读路径的初衷,更有一名教育工作者的职责意识[①]。所谓"综合",即一种既涉及作品、更有读者和作者介入的文本分析方法,入口是系统功能语言学视野里的前景化成分,目标是经验世界中的意识形态和价值观念。"评价"指作者寓于文学文本中的主体性与主体间性立场,以隐含读者意识[介入范畴]和叙事强弱口吻[级差等级]为调节手段,抒发情感[情感范畴:意愿、愉悦、满意、安全],评判行为[判断范畴:是否常态、是否有能力、可靠、诚实、真诚、恰当],品评事物[鉴赏范畴:是否冲击或吸引读者;构成是否均衡与复杂;是否有价值]。这在语言学中叫做评价范畴(Appraisal Category),属于系统功能语言学的一个人际意义次类(Martin & White, 2005);将它系统用于文学文本分析则是文体学性质的方法(彭宣维,2015),为功能文体学的一个分支(如 Halliday, 1971; Birch & O'Toole, 1988;张德禄,1998)。

这里涉及三个策略性范畴,在从系统选择到实例化体现过程中发挥调节性策略作用。首先是"视角",为谋篇策略。但在现有系统功能语言学的语篇语法模型中告缺,跟主位化(Thematisation)关系密切,却不属于主位化或信息化甚至衔接范畴;事实上,这是支配相关语篇语义选项进入词汇语法结构关系的一种策略机制,在叙事学中叫做视角化(Perspectivisation),即所述情景和事件的陈述角度(Prince, 1989:31, 71)。其实,作为一个学科的叙事学,它关注的基本议题具有突出的基础性,对语言学理论具有启示和补益作用。鉴于叙事学的出发点是语言交际,跟系统功能语言学在学理上兼容。因此,这里拟采用这一术语,但须做一点范畴化归口处理:根据系统功能语言学的扩展模式(Halliday, 1995/2006),视角化是从系统到实例的过程中采用的一种选择策略,旨在调节相关词汇语法的结构化配置方式。其次是语境性对比:褒扬的同时意味着贬抑,给予意味着接受,提问意味着陈述,敬人则意味着抑己,这是人际性话语策略。最后是投射,是概念性话语策略：说话人或作者的任何言语行为都是他/她思想的投射（彭宣维，2015）。视角化在《身旁》一文中起重要作用。

"评价隐喻"属于语法隐喻的一个次类，指采用带标记的评价意义确立方式。就评价意义的三大子范畴看，行文如果主要是通过纯粹经验意义来确立态度立场的，就属于态度隐喻；文本隐含了说话人或作者强烈的感情态度、行文却是缺乏级差强弱成分的，近似于低调陈述（Understatement），属于级差隐喻；说话人或作者的立场本该鲜明典型，而实际叙述却是平实沉稳、立场不够明确的，则为介入隐喻。这些叙事方式与具有明确评价特征的铭刻性（Inscribed）词汇语法手段相对，在 Martin 等人的理论描述中叫做引发性评价意义（Invoked）：通过其他词汇语法手段临时引发的评价立场。

本文将阐述两个要点：《身旁》所用叙事策略以及相应文体措辞与美学意义层次。具体行文则细分为三个小节进行：1 视角逆行：超常规叙事带来的解读张力，附带涉及语境性对比和投射叙事策略；2 评价隐喻：态度立场的间接体现途径；3 评价内容的可视化描述。最后我们从总体上概述评价文体分析的主导思想。

2. 视角逆行：超常规叙事带来的解读张力

这里涉及语篇性视角、人际性对比和概念性投射三类话语策略，不过相比较而言，视角设计的修辞效果最为突出；其他两类对这里的文本解读虽然也很重要，但不是重点，所以放到之后讨论。

从内容构成看，《身旁》有四个小节，前、后两节既相对独立，又是一个整体，衔接纽带是时空因素。直言之，这里的叙事策略采用了一种不同于常规的聚焦方式：它不是人们常见的倒叙，更不是顺时叙事，后两者均以叙述者时空为立足点呈现叙事者视野里的事件：一者回顾过去，一者着眼于当下或走向未来；而这里采用的是一种时空逆行叙事或视角逆行方法：以叙事者所在的当时作为立足点，叙事者自己沿着事件和时间轨迹逆行，从而回到先前经历过的时空中去。而整个过程又体现出明确的前后时空对比关系。这是一种谋篇策略，也叫管道隐喻（Conduit Metaphor）：人们把时空看作一种流程，可以沿"路"返回，从而回到从前，整个过程将叙事者经历过的事件连缀成一个整体。这种视角化方式可以让常规日常事件，以反常规的叙述途径，创造一种超常规的感知体验，即与社会人在个体发生历程中获得的常规经验相悖，以便实现隐喻性的评价效果（见下一小节）。

文本最后两个小节似乎失去了时空进一步逆行的解读契机；不过，我们仍然可以做逆向理解。我们先从顺时方向看，最后一句陈述自己被父母守候,说明叙事者还小,这自然应该是在入学之前;然后是叙述者上幼儿园大班或小学,因为自己还未到背书包的年龄,毕竟很小;再往后是"我"去上学了,或者晚上看着电视睡着了,之后父母把我打开的电视关上;最后是整个小学、中学阶段:放学回家,我带回考试试卷让家长签字,知道父母已经做好了饭菜在等我。现在把上面的顺序倒过来,就是行文的逆行叙事了。据此,整个行文叙事便都在视角逆行的范围之内了。

把常规社会经验按反常规方式加以重组,这就是众所周知的时空倒流假设。当然,这里没有直接提及时空,而是直观陈述具体事件及其相关事物。它们构成一幅接一幅经验动态画面,这一现象我们在影视作品的倒向放映时见过。但影视作品并没有起始参照点;而我们在这里接触到的是文字媒介,是语义措辞。它们总是提醒读者:我们始终站在当下,以此时此地为出发点,随事件回溯带动时空逆行,从而让读者进入一种非常规时空体验领域,从而给解读制造一种对比张力。人们会因此被吸引,并产生理性诘问:何以可能?

这是一种关于"现在"的观念:过去的经验和经历,一旦为记忆所扑捉,必定为当前调用,不管是听与说,还是阅读写作。从生命的成长历程看,尽管行文当下与孩提时光前后相隔 10 年、20 年,但自己经历的一切,均由记忆加工并呈现到当下,从而提供一个"整体语境"(the context of the whole),这就是大脑记忆的作用(Halliday, 2008: 183, 189;彭宣维,2015)。Halliday 明确指出:"系统有赖于记忆:有赖于每一个说话人铭刻在大脑中的内容,尤其是共享记忆,从而确保一定数量的、切实可行的不同说话人——大脑具有足够的共享基础,连续而无断裂。"(Halliday, 2008, 15;Hjelmslev, 1943/1961: 1)这一跟记忆联通有关的语言事实和社会经验事实,可为事件的逆行叙事提供社会心理基础,为可理解性解读作前提,从而成就"作者—文本—读者"一体化解读机制,因为是作者和前人的外在行为与内在思想共同创造了特定社团的文化与历史。而具有不同社会经历的个体会有不同的编码和解码倾向,从而确立不同的解读立场,甚至相互对立(伽德默尔,1960/2010)。这些一同呈现到当下的相关经验和经历,构成文本解读的外部语境(Hasan, 1995)。至于有悖常理的事件回溯问题,这是文学文本允许的:在叙事世界里,一切反常识的知识均可接受,因为它的目的不在于所述事件和情节本身,而是以此指向"经验和生命的真实质地",是"人类对生活和生命的认识、想象和选择"(李敬泽,2009:59,5)。事实上,由记忆支配的思维活动可以对自身经验进行随意重组,构成一种心理实在(彭宣维,2015)。所以,这种能够引起读者好奇心的叙述方式,不会因为超越常理的经验世界而迫使读者终止阅读。

这种叙事视角是一种底层操作，支配行文"表层"的措辞配置，从而在前景化"层面"呈现出相关行文走向。底层操作是在从语义特征的结构化过程中选择涉及的。不过，是什么促成了这样的选择而非别的选择？这是作者在关注潜在读者可能的社会经历与体验范围时所制定的行文决策。

现在我们转向人际性的语境性对比策略。叙述者陈述的是具有代表性的中国父母对成长中的儿女的关爱行为。因为习以为常，所以儿女们总有一种心安理得的接受心理，一般很少念及这一份恩情，甚至还可能出现一些极端情况，如一味"啃老"。下面这个片段也引自微信，是一位母亲写给儿子的信的开头部分：

> 儿子，今天你又装作若无其事地暗示妈妈，说市中心的房价又在飙升，如果再不行动，或许以后你和女友连一间栖息的小屋都没有。我淡淡地看你一眼，终于没有像你希望的那样，说出"妈妈给你们买"这样的话来。而你，也在尴尬的沉默里，随即气嘟嘟地放下碗筷，甩门出去……你已经25岁了，有一份稳定的工作，有一个需要呵护的女友，还有两位日益老去、需要你照顾的父母，难道这些还不足以让你成熟、让你彻底地离开父母的羽翼、放下啃老的惰性、独自去承担一个成人应该承担的责任吗？记得从很小的时候，你就习惯有事找妈妈。你总是说："妈妈，我的衣服脏了，你帮我洗洗。""妈妈，明天我们去郊游，你帮我收拾好要带的行李。""妈妈，女友想吃老醋茄子，记得下班后给她做。"……

也许叙事者本人也有过类似经历，而一旦完全明白"你"不再"在我身旁"时，前后对比可能让人幡然醒悟。这里的叙述间接地将当前社会中的相关人文诉求关联起来，形成一种反差，从而达到扬此抑彼的用语效果。这里有语境因素的促成作用：倘若缺乏当前这种后现代文化语境，把类似叙述改用文言文前推到明清时代，那将是另一番情形。此外，这种对照让我们看到了行文背后可能存在的两种情感因素：一是后悔、内疚，属于情感中的消极满意范畴；另一个是对亲人的思念，当为情感中具有积极意义的意愿；而它们还会提醒读者回归亲情，学会感恩，主张一种更深层次的可靠性社会评判伦理。

最后，我们来看此文中采用的投射策略。投射，本来指行文中的言说者直接或间接引出的言辞或思想（Halliday，1994：250-273）：言辞性投射如上引文本中加引号的部分；思想性投射如开篇"暗示妈妈，说"后面的内容——虽然这里用了一个"说"字，其实是"儿子"暗示母亲的心理意向，毕竟没有说出来，仍然是思想投射。当然，思想投射通常是一种全知叙事，因为任何人也无法直接进入别人的思维领域去探个究竟。在《身旁》中，叙事者作为行文中的一种角色、以第一人称叙事的方式向叙述对象"你"表达自己的体验和情感,这也是一种投射,一种概念性表征策略。在这里,我们可以把整个文本看作双重投射:言辞和思想,只是缺乏明确的"我说"和"我看见"或"我感觉到"之类的元话语成分。这里有明确的隐含作者介入:他或她将自己的相关心理活动通过文字叙述的方式呈现出来。②

　　总之,文化共同体在促成群体心理时,也为个体造就了分享社会经验的阅读基础,从而成为语义内容跟语境关联的依据。当然,这可能是整个大的社会文化背景,也可能是临时面临的具体情境语境,但前者蕴涵在后者之中,成为支配言语行为的潜在因素。这里有一个潜在的认识论立场,即记忆为我们提供的当前语境。

3. 评价隐喻:态度立场的间接体现途径

上面从整体上分析了叙事策略、尤其是视角效果带来的评价效应;这里拟对上述效果与相关语言成分做出具体关联,并在最后对全文的评价特征成分,无论是隐喻式的还是一致式的,给予总结。

　　我们先看态度隐喻,这在《身旁》中是通过及物性过程(Process of Transitivity)来间接确立的(Halliday,1994)。《身旁》的基调并非直接的情感与伦理诉求,而是以直观陈述的方式展示叙事者的经历、从而达到引发读者相应情感的目的。

　　全文的及物性过程成分一共15个。其中,物质过程成分11个:逆流、飘回、聚成、升起、落向、退回、回到、交回、飘来、关掉、背上,占总数的73.33%。心理过程1个:忘了十年寒窗,占总数的6.67%,但它跟整个行文的情感主旨无关,只是说明时空逆行而阻断所有求学经历的甘苦经历、蹒跚于儿时感知的局部心理体验。另有两个关系过程句:(蒲公英聚)成伞的模样、你还在我身旁,占13.33%;行为过程1个:签(名字),占6.67%。注意,"聚成"是一个复合成分,包含两个及物性特征,"聚"为物质过程特征,"成"为关系过程特征。而以物质过程为主导的文本,追求的自然就是意象效果和直观体验(另见申丹,2009)。

　　在这15个特征中,前面四行涉及的6个成分,即逆流、飘回、聚成、升起、落向、退回,均指向事物,引发鉴赏性态度意义,即反应中的冲击类(Impact of Reaction):所述现象是否抓住了我? 后5行的及物性过程小句确立判断意义:隐含作者不再关注事物,而是人的行为可靠性(Reliability);这些特征成分一共8个:运动员回到起跑线上;我交回录取通知书;忘了十年寒窗;你做好了饭菜等我吃;为我从学校拿回的考试试卷签上名字;在我上学前、或者看着电视入睡后帮我关掉了电视;你总是陪着我,所以我"现在"的感觉是"你还在我身旁"。其中，"忘了"和"寒窗"是两个非常态性（Abnormality）的判断成分：记忆力好坏在这里不是能力问题，"寒窗"也指不寻常的求学经历；"签名"是一个关于行为的可靠特征，而"签"后的"好"是对"签名"结果的圆满性描述，应将"好"表达的平衡构成特征单列；第三行后一句中的"聚成"，跟"签好"一样，也是一个动补结构，但应作整体成分看待："聚"和"成"一起体现完满平衡性。第三节第一句"厨房里飘来饭菜的香"，似乎应该从字面上作物质过程分析，即引发性反应特征；但它间接陈述的是母亲做好饭菜等"我"回家的常态，揭示的是一种潜在的行为特征，宜作可靠性判断成分看。

注意后面的 5 个可靠性成分，都是跟"你"有关的行为，它们构成一个积极的可靠性特征集。即是说，叙述对象"你"始终是我的依靠，无微不至，无处不在。这里虽无明确的判断成分，但特定经历伴随着特定的情感取向，从而促成相关解释。理由很简单：人类的身体构造大致相当，会在同一社会和文化历史背景下经历大致相当的家庭、学校和传媒教育，从而积累有差别的共享经验领域；据此，即便是这样的间接陈述，读者同样可能获得叙述者希望达到的效果：中国父母的可依赖性。

语音也有直接表达评价意义的作用。一方面，押韵模式可以体现"构成"（Composition）意义，从而给人均衡性。类似特征成分全文一共 9 个：（逆流而）上、（模）样、（东）方、（枪）膛、（起跑线）上、（寒）窗、（饭菜的）香、（背）上、（身）旁。它们能营造一种协和、均衡与平稳之感，所以体现的是构成范畴中的平衡义，即音韵效果的和谐一体性。另一方面，这些不断累增的语音效果还有级差调节作用：从第二个押韵的韵脚开始到结束，每个韵脚的出现便会增加一个品质强化特征，这样的特征成分应该是 8 个。它们的相关行文也可以看作一种隐喻式，一种超出常规的标记性前景化体现成分。

或许有人会认为这种押韵方式有些像歌词。其实，从发生学的意义上说，诗和歌本来就是一体的，如《诗经》和《坎特伯雷故事集》以及所有人类文明早些时候产出的文学文本，莫不如此。虽然当代诗歌早已不再主张这种规整的修辞组织技巧，但后现代毕竟是一个多元时代。在如今这个人心不古的大背景下重申这种回归亲情的主张时，采用押韵格式来配伍，毕竟很合拍：年轻人写给年轻人读，无须世故口吻。事实上，我们应该为他们在步入社会之前留下这样一片成长天地，毕竟这是人类的"精神原点"和"生命原点"。

此外，《身旁》的介入和级差方式也带有语法隐喻性质。从介入角度看，整个行文是一种独白式的倾述——一种收缩性主体间性叙述方式：直观陈述自己所"见"、所"闻"、所"感",既没有对话,没有留给读者认可与否的机会;叙述者为"我",叙述对象是"你",很直接。这种主体间性方式可以看作一种断言性(Pronounce)收缩介入:毋容置疑的排他性口吻。从级差角度看,文中有 3 个量化语力成分:"远(处)"(空间)、"十年"和"还(在)"(时间);而叙述过程显得平实沉稳,虽然暗含着的情感催人泪下,但既没有明确的"想念"与"追悔"之类的字眼,也缺乏锐化(Sharpening)甚至柔化(Softening)等明确的强度成分来凸显叙述者的强烈意愿。经验可以补足作者这一创作动机留下的空位,从而在显性事件陈述与隐性思亲意愿之间形成一种动态平衡,在一定程度上回避直接情感诉求带来的直白感。

这里,我们对语法隐喻手段促成的评价特征成分给予小结。隐喻性成分本身是语义性质的,它们在及物性关系结构中与其他相关成分一起构成组合性措辞。这些成分间接体现的是评价语义特征,彼此关联则构成有关评价意义的措辞关系(见图1)。

代表性及物性成分及其指向的态度特征:

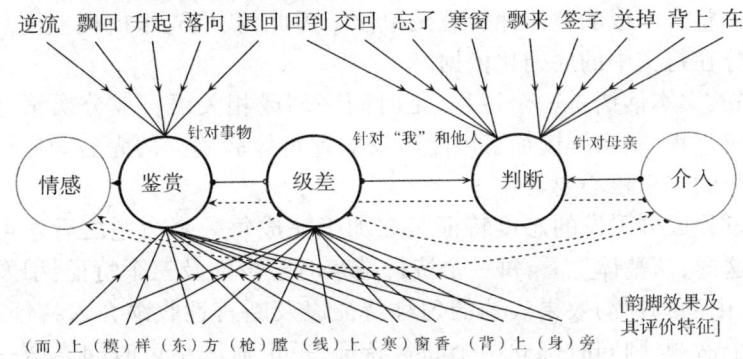

图 1　文本中出现的隐喻性评价特征成分

上面讨论的主要是隐喻性评价成分;现在我们对全文的所有评价成分给予归纳总结,包括尚未提及的非隐喻性成分。这样的成分全文一共53个。

(1) 由及物性过程成分引发的积极冲击性反应成分 5 个:逆流、飘回、升起、落向、退回;

(2) 由及物性过程成分引发的积极可靠性判断成分 5 个:飘来、签(好)名字、关掉、背上、在(母亲);非常态成分 4 个:回到、交回、忘了、寒窗(前三者是引发性的);

(3) 由韵脚带来的协和平衡效果特征 9 个(构成性):(逆流而)上、(模)样、(东)方、(枪)膛、(起跑线)上、(寒)窗、(饭菜的)香、(背)上、(身)旁;

(4) 铭刻性鉴赏成分 3 个:香[积极品质性反应];聚成、(签)好(名字)[积极完满平衡〕；

（5）引发性积极估值鉴赏成分 2 个：录取通知书、饭菜；

（6）由全文 14 个小句的肯定命题确立的断言性收缩特征 14 个；

（7）明确的跨度级差成分 3 个：远处（空间）、十年（时间）、还（时间）；韵脚组织的协和匀称特征 8 个。

需要特别说明的是，这里列出的只是一些关键性词语；事实上，相关评价特征是在整体语句甚至语境中才会产生的，这些只是索引符号而已。

至此，我们通过文字叙述的方式陈述我们对样本的理解；我们还需要考虑由这些前景化成分构成的在线组织特点。

4. 评价内容的可视化描述

按照叶尔姆斯列夫的见解，话语内容涉及形式与实体两个层次；按照笔者的理解，前者是《身旁》一文中所有评价意义特征组织而成的评价措辞，后者是它们整合而成的整体评价意义单位。为此，我们先来梳理上面总结的特征成分在行文中的序列化依据。

首先，文本话语是一个过程，是时间序列或相关语言成分次第加工出现的生成过程，是由解读加工可能涉及的评价体验确立的先后顺序。这是话语组织的一个核心要素。

由过程成分引发的态度特征是在加工完成每一个命题之后才可能获得的。这样，从整体上看，每一个诗行结束时至少涉及三个特征：引发性态度特征、由韵脚押韵效果表达的匀称特征以及断言性收缩介入特征；一行若有两个命题，则同时确立两个断言特征，每个命题结束时即累增一个特征成分，无需等到整个诗行结束，因为到那时又会增加一个新的介入特征。阅读每个诗行的过程中遇到的铭刻性评价成分，则随即进行累积；第一行结束时无所谓韵律效果，要等到第二行结束时、"样"回应第一行结束时的"上"、甚至第三行结束时的"方"才会让第一行末的"上"带上均衡特征，因此，在结束对"样"的加工结束后才会出现"上"的韵律应和效应，所以"上"应在"样"后面。断言顺序放在韵脚特征之后，因为只有在处理完所有其他特征之后才会获得相应的介入体验。沿此，我们对上述 53 个特征成分做如下解读排序（罗马字母顺序为诗行行号，上标为所在诗行的命题序号，○代表韵律的级差增值特征）：（后文在进行可视化描述时逐一使用）

1 逆流、2a、3 远处、4 飘回、5b^1、6 聚成、7（模）样、8（而）上、9○、10b^2、11 升起、12c^1、13 落向、14（东）方、15○、16c^2、17 退回、18（枪）膛、19○、20d、21 回

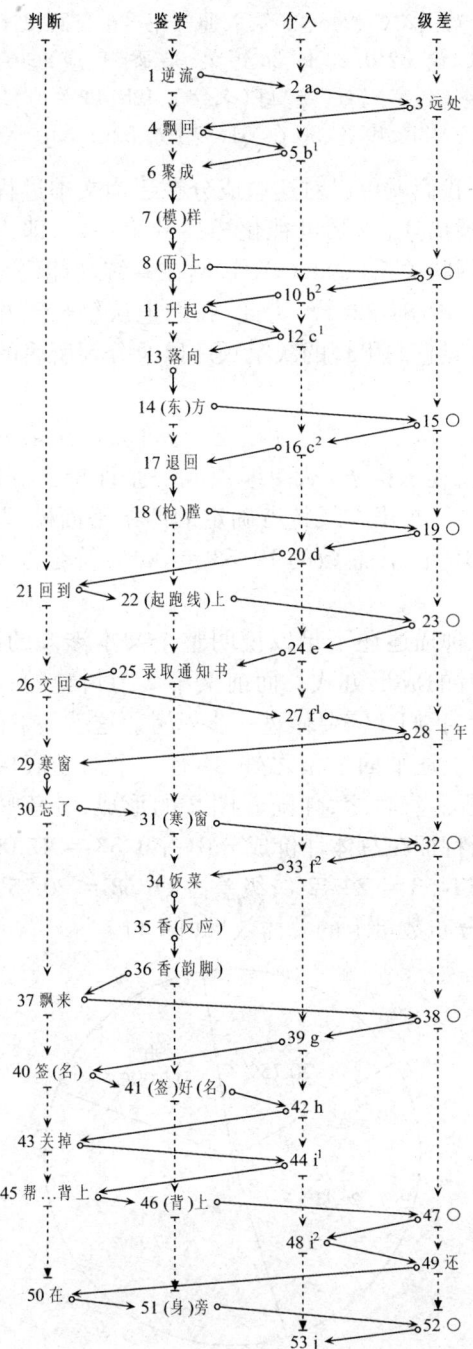

图 2 《身旁》措辞平面模型

到、22（起跑线）上、23○、24e、25 录取通知书、26 交回、27f[1]、28 十年、29 寒窗、30 忘了、31（寒）窗、32○、33 f[2]、34 饭菜、35 香（反应）、36 香（韵脚）、37○、38 飘来、39g、40 签（名字）、41（签）好（名字）、42h、43 关掉、44i[1]、45 帮……背上、46（背）上、47○、48i[2]、49 还、50 在、51（身）旁、52○、53j。

有了上面的准备，我们就可以对这些成分在建构文本过程中涉及的"表层"措辞平面给予直观描述，这是可视化描述的第一步，即由上述前景化特征成分组织而成的网状关系（texture），它们在系统功能语言学中属于词汇语法的范围（Hasan，1978：229）。为此，我们把从《身旁》中梳理出来的所有评价特征成分，按照它们出现的次第顺序以及分别所属的范畴类别，用图 2 的方式描述出来。

从发展走向看，这是一种波动模型：评价叙述次第分呈于不同范畴特征之间，往复穿梭，逐步推进，从而编织成一张评价措辞网，构成评价的词汇语法层面。这是一个由在线特点确定的两维平面模型。注意，全文鉴赏性特征成分一共 19 个，占总数的 19/53 = 36%，符合行文铺陈直观意象的阅读感知。

不过，这样一种描述还不足以说明整个文本涉及的所有评价意义，尤其是深层评价主旨的成形方式。而前文第 2 节讨论的一些内容也没有在该图中体现出来。我们还需要做进一步思考。这就是下面要讨论的内容。

我们发现，在上述平面模型之外，还有一个居于底层的伴随性评价意义单位的生成过程。直言之，伴随着图 2 的形成，各范畴领域的量也随之累增。其中，判断特征在总体评价成分中占 8/53 = 15.09%；鉴赏占 20/53 = 37.74；介入占 14/53 = 26.42%；级差占 11/53 = 20.75%。我们可以直观描写这些成分在分布数量上的总体效果（图 3）。

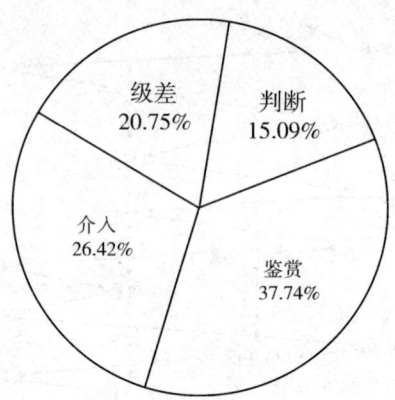

图 3　各类主要范畴随文本过程的累增结果

根据这个最终结果,我们反过来设想一下:这其中的每一个范畴都是从第一个成分开始逐渐累增的。如果把这些范畴的累增过程加入图3中,那么圆面背后就应该是一个不断变大的圆锥模型。可见,图2只是一种依据文本表层延伸的形式描写;图3倒是考虑到了态度、介入和级差之间的并行关系,但毕竟是静态的。我们需要把这两个方面结合起来。于是我们得到图4(a)。

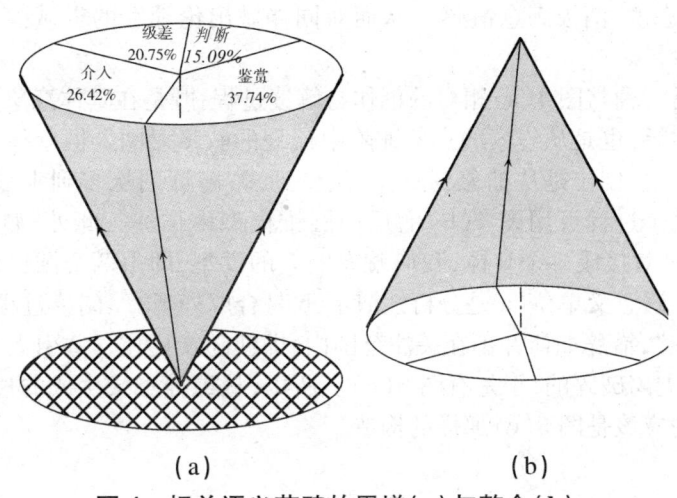

（a）　　　　　　　　　　　　　　（b）

图4　相关语义范畴的累增(a)与整合(b)

对比图2和图4(a)。图2只是二维平面,只关注相关特征次第出现的序列及其在不同范畴之间的交替关联特点,没有考虑态度、介入和级差的并行合取关系,即它们之间是同时进入待选状态的。但图4(a)揭示了态度立场受介入和级差调节的思想。具体而言,《身旁》平实沉稳(级差)而不容忍其他声音(介入)的叙事策略,体现的是叙事者"我"的情感表征方式:寻常周遭(瀑布长流、蒲公英播种、太阳运行)触动了"我"的亲情记忆。总之,级差和介入是为态度意义的确立做策略调节之用的,它们之间不是序列关系。

还有一个与图4(a)累增方向相反的缩减或整合过程。这就是文本在整体评价主旨引导下、通过相应词汇语法手段体现的整个文本的评价意义单位。换言之,我们还需要从整合上看文本话语的组织方式。在《身旁》中,隐含作者采用的是传统修辞策略。第一节是对周围自然事件的重组,看似天马行空,却是一种起兴方式。第二节将叙述对象转向"人",而且有远近之别:先是物"子弹",然后是人"运动员",最后回到叙述者自己身上,从全局看这是承接第一段时光逆行的进一步叙述,更是过渡到行文主旨的中间环节。第三节是转,转向亲人,根据常识应该是母亲,从而进入主体叙述对象,包括"你"为"我"从生活到学习的日常操劳。最后一节是合,以简洁的一行识解体验——"你"并没有离开"我",从而走向叙事者的评价主旨。换言之,也许当事人还没有在生活中熬到"子欲养"的阶段,但从叙述内容看,"亲不待"已成现实③。根据常理,这里便出现了由"你还在我身旁"的思念[态度:积极意愿情感]引发的"你已经不在我身旁"的追悔与遗憾心理[态度:消极满意情感],从而对同伴做出伦理上的告诫:亲情无价,且行且珍惜。

这是一种与图4(a)相对的创作与解读过程:既是在具体意象之外孕育的一种主旨,也是从纷繁的意象铺陈中梳理的叙事意图。但创作与解读过程正好相对:创作是从抽象到具体、从少到多;解读则从多到少、从具体到抽象。这个过程可用图4(b)的反向圆锥模型来描述。此外,如果将图4(a)和(b)对接成一个整体,我们就有图5的模型,即由两个圆锥体合成的纺锤形话语意义单位(a是分析性演示;b是合成外观)。阅读过程往往"得鱼而忘筌",措辞如何并不在关注范围内,即便随文记住一些引人注意的词句,也是支离破碎的,于是有图5(c)。所以,从纯粹意义生成的过程看,我们获得的应该是图5(c)那样的构造。

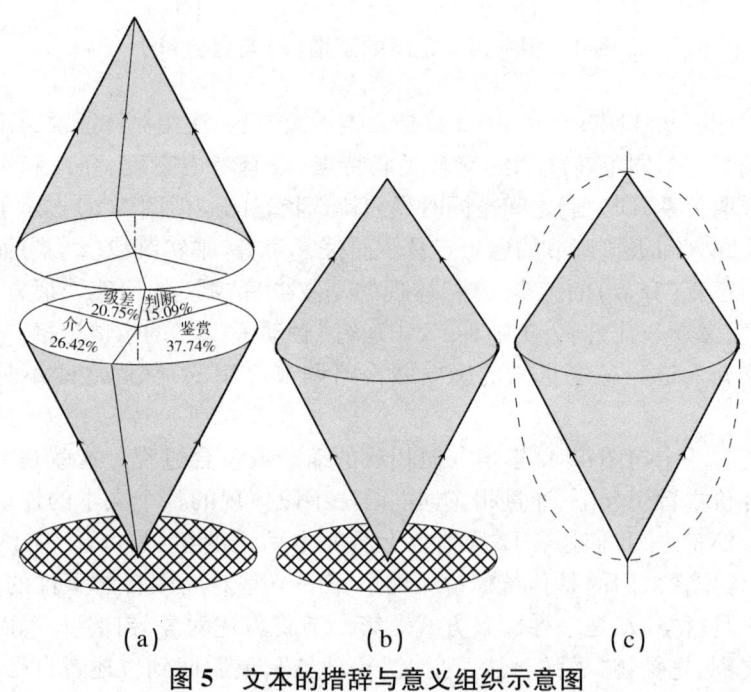

图5 文本的措辞与意义组织示意图

前文在做问题分析时同时涉及到相关评价因素的社交基础,它们是生成整体评价意义单位的必要条件,故在图5(c)的外围加上了一个虚线椭圆,以示一种相互依存特点:评价主旨引导并构建文本的评价意义,而评价意义的建构过程同时意味着创立相应的评价语境:——上下两端的竖向短线表示整体评价意义单位的非封闭性。

再次回顾整个文本。其中存在一个三段论式的行文组织特点:假如时光可以倒流,那么"我"就可以回到过去,跟母亲待在一起;现在"我"用视角逆行的方式"看到了"世事回溯,所以"我"实实在在地感觉到了母亲在"我"身旁的"现实"。这种"自欺欺人"的叙事策略并非实在的自然与社会过程,但也不是为了欺骗读者,而是为了提升一种由情感引发的理性,一种社会评判(Social Judgement)诉求:感念亲情、且行且珍惜吧。这是《身旁》一文积极思念意愿与消极追悔满意指向的终极伦理价值。这是一个由整个网状铺陈平面同时走向纺锤型意义组织的动态生成过程,在模型中用上面的尖端代表。

可见,一个文本的潜在评价主旨并非完全由表层评价成分类别来确定:《身旁》以可靠性判断为明确评价取向,但全文只有4个成分,而且还是引发性的;其他类别的评价成分,包括鉴赏、介入和级差,一并为此服务。而更深层次的情感和伦理诉求(意愿和可靠性)却不曾涉及任何一个前景化评价成分。

5. 结束语

可见,由意义和措辞构成的评价内容平面涉及多个层次的意义建构:①视角组织间接表征的及物性类别,指向②鉴赏和判断——态势性与可靠性,它们一同带来③积极思念意愿与消极满意痛苦,并最终指向④感念亲情的伦理主张。先前的文体学研究并不是没有这些要素,但缺乏一种机制和模型来做明确的分层处理。我们的工作有望使相关研究走向具体和深入。

这里,我们换一个角度来总结本文涉及的基本主导思想:文学,包括创作实践与批评审美,是以评价为特点、手段和目的的互动性艺术话语行为。首先,《身旁》关注的是某种评价主旨:意愿情感和伦理诉求,从而为整个行文赋予突出的立场特点。其次,相关题材极其普通,但叙述过程去凡求新,以视角逆行的方式、用具体意象引发性地凸显情感和判断诉求;同时,鉴于文本延伸空间受限,隐含作者在设计上惜墨如金,小心翼翼地围绕评价主旨给予组织表述。最后,这是一个从"铭刻性及物性过程"、到"引发性鉴赏和判断"、到"思念与追悔情感"、再到"且行且珍惜的伦理诉求"逐层深入的体现过程:文本围绕这一目的展开,并以间接体现的途径点明评价主旨,从而实施以评价为目的的话语策略。作者以对话诉说的方式追求一种互动效应;以字斟句酌的话语修辞构建一个相对独立的时空世界,以此彰显一种精巧的艺术性。可见,文学性就是评价性。

行文中梳理归纳的纺锤型意义组织模式,不只适用于《身旁》,所有文学文本的意识形态和价值观念的形成,均可由此表达;而从整个社会符号系统的角度看,以文学为契机的一切人学、甚至一切人类行为,包括日常生活的与道德修为的,传统理性的与现代、后现代解构的,均以评价意义建构与价值凝聚为终极目的,从而实现思想与行为的增值效应,不管是有规划的还是潜意识的,只是表述和组织方式不同罢了。据此,真正的文学实践自有其潜在的生命价值。

注释

① 最近网络上流传着《百家讲台》某位名人"旗帜鲜明"的帖子,帖子声称其在教育中反对"励志",主张"快乐"成长。看来,这位自称"教书匠"的先生可能真的只有教书匠的认识水平:人的成长过程可能全然快乐? 中国教育存在的问题是"励志"主张带来的吗? 教育讲求方式方法就必须以牺牲励志原则为代价? 这种因噎废食、低级迎合的问题意识,实在让人匪夷所思。

② 试比较下面这种直抒胸臆的行文方式:"苦日子过完了/妈妈却老了/好日子开始了/妈妈却走了/这就是我苦命的妈妈/妈妈健在时/我远游了/我回来时/妈妈却远走了/这就是你不孝的儿子。"同一个题材,相近的内容,不同的表述方式。(http://weibo.com/p/1001593782614140996948? from = page _ 100505 _ profile&wvr = 6&mod = wenzhangmod)

③ 皋鱼对孔子说:"吾失之三矣,少而学,游诸侯,以后吾亲,失之一也;高尚吾志,闲吾事君,失之二也;与友厚而少绝之,失之三也。树欲静而风不止,子欲养而亲不待也。往而不可追者,年也;去而不可见者,亲也。"(《韩诗外传》卷九)

参考文献

Birch, D. & M. O'Toole (eds.). 1988. *Functions of Style*. London & New York: Pinter Publishers.

Prince, G. 1989. *A Dictionary of Narratology*. Lincoln & London: University of Nebraska Press.

Halliday, M. A. K. 1971. Linguistic function and literary style: An inquiry into the language of William Golding' *The Inheritors*. In S. Chatman (ed.) *Literary Style: A Symposium*. London & New York: Oxford University Press. pp. 330−368.

Halliday, M. A. K. 1994. *An Introduction to Functional Grammar* (2nd edition). London:

Arnold.《功能语法导论(第二版)》(彭宣维等译). 北京：外语教学与研究出版社，2010.

Halliday, M. A. K. 1995/2006. Computing meanings：Some reflections on past experience and present prospects. In J. Webster (ed.) *Computational and Quantitative Studies, Volume 6 in the Collected Works of M. A. K. Halliday*. London：Continuum.

Halliday, M. A. K. 2008. *Complementarities in Language*. Beijing：The Commercial Press.

Hasan, R. 1978. Text in the systemic-functional model. In W. U. Dressler (ed.) *Current Trends in Textlinguistics*. Berlin & New York：Walter de Gruyter. pp. 228-246.

Hasan, R.1995. The conception of context in text. In P. H. Fries & M. Gregory (eds.) *Discourse in Society: Systemic Functional Perspective: Meaning and Choice in Language: Studies for Michael Halliday*. Norwood, New Jersey：Ablex. pp. 183-296.

Hjelmslev, L. 1943/1961. *Prolegomena to a Theory of Language*. F. J. Whitfield (trans.). Madison：University of Wisconsin Press.

Martin, J. R. & P. White. 2005. *The Language of Evaluation: Appraisal in English*. Hampshire & New York：Palgrave Macmillan.

伽德默尔著,洪汉鼎译. 1960/2010.《诠释学:真理与方法》. 北京:商务印书馆.

李敬泽. 2009.《为文学申辩》. 北京:作家出版社.

彭宣维. 2015.《评价文体学》. 北京:北京大学出版社.

申　丹. 2009. 休斯《在路上》的及物性系统与深层意义. 载申丹著《叙事、文体与潜文本——重读英美经典短篇小说》. 北京:北京大学出版社.

张德禄. 1998.《功能文体学》. 济南:山东教育出版社.

文学语篇的语言艺术分析框架
——《麦田守望者》的功能文体分析

王竹青 （青岛农业大学） 苗兴伟 （北京师范大学）

An Analytical Framework of Verbal Art in Literary Discourse
— A Functional Stylistic Analysis of *The Catcher in the Rye*

Wang Zhuqing （**Qingdao Agricultural University**）

Miao Xingwei （**Beijing Normal University**）

摘 要：Hasan（1985）提出的语言艺术研究的三层次理论框架为文学语篇的文体分析提供了一个语言学的理论模式。本文以 Hasan 的语言艺术分析框架为理论基础，对小说《麦田守望者》的文体特征进行了分析。本研究从语言结构描述入手，通过具体的语言分析，探讨语言表达如何服务于文学语篇的主题和意象表达，从而为文学语篇的解读提供功能文体学的视角。

关键词：语言艺术；分析框架；文学语篇；功能文体学；《麦田守望者》

Abstract： The three-stratum theoretical framework proposed by Hasan （1985） for the study of verbal art provides a linguistic model for the stylistic analysis of literary discourse. Taking Hasan's model as the theoretical basis, this paper attempts an analysis of the stylistic features of *The Catcher in the Rye*. With the description of linguistic structures as the point of departure, this study focuses on linguistic analysis, aiming to investigate the contribution of linguistic expressions to the literary theme and symbolic articulation, with the hope of providing a functional stylistic perspective for the interpretation of literary discourse.

Key words: verbal art; analytical framework; literary discourse; functional stylistics; *The Catcher in the Rye*

1. 引言

建立在系统功能语言学理论基础之上的功能文体学在文学语篇的研究中，把细致的语言学分析作为解释文本意义的有力工具，把文学文本的形式特征同语言的社会功能相联系，探讨语言表达层的证据如何通过意象表达层的符号表达文学文本深层次的主题，以及这个过程如何运作、运作过程中涉及到的因素有哪些。在功能文体学领域影响最大的是 Halliday 的功能思想和分析方法，而 Hasan(1985)在其基础上发展了前景化理论，提出了语言艺术研究的三层次理论框架，为文学作品分析提供了切实可行的分析框架和分析模式。本文将以 Hasan 提出的语言艺术三个层面为分析框架，对《麦田守望者》的文体特征进行功能文体学分析，从而揭示语言表达与文学作品的主题和意象表达之间的关系，为文学作品的语言学解读提供可资借鉴的理论模式和分析方法。

《麦田守望者》是美国作家塞林格的经典之作，以主人公霍顿自叙的语气讲述了自己被学校开除后在纽约游荡的经历和心灵感受。塞林格运用独特的语言生动细致地描绘了霍顿苦闷彷徨、孤独愤世的精神世界，批判了成人社会的虚伪和做作。本文将依据 Hasan 的语言艺术研究理论框架，分析小说《麦田守望者》的三个层面，即主题、意象表达和语言表达，从语言结构描述入手，分析产生文体效果的客观依据——语言依据，重点是从那些被"前景化"了的语言特征入手，研究语篇的语言文体特点的规律和规则，挖掘作者的语用意图和语言表达的文体效果，领会语言的形式和意义之间的密切联系，围绕小说的语言表达、意象表达和故事的主题对作品进行深层意义的解析。

2. 语言艺术的三个层面

Hasan (1985)认为,文学作品是一种语言艺术(verbal art),而语言艺术可以看作是一个符号系统,其内部设计与语言符号系统的内部设计是相似的。语言是一个由语义层、词汇—语法层和音位层构成的编码系统(Halliday,1985;Halliday & Hasan,1985)。同样,语言艺术也包括三个层面:主题、意象表达和语言表达。语言表达就是运用语言资源表达意义的过程,是最基本的底层,是为主题和意象表达服务的,因此要理解文学作品的主题与意象表达,应该从语言表达出发,通过对语言特征的文体分析来揭示文学作品的主题和意象,也就是说,理解文学语篇中语言表达的意义是理解文学语篇意义的基础。主题是语言艺术作品表达的最深层的意义,是超越了语言表达的具体意义的高度概括,是关于"社会人"生活的某些方面的看法和理论。语言表达和主题是通过意象表达联系在一起的。意象表达由产生主题意义的符号系统构成,前景化和语言模式的组合在这一层面上发挥着至关重要的作用。语言表达层提供"初级意义"(first order meaning),为语篇意义的理解提供基础。而前景化手段和语言模式的共同作用赋予了初级意义更高层次的意义,即"二级意义"(second order meaning)。因此,语言艺术作品中有两个语义层。第一个语义层产生于自然语言这一符号系统的使用,第二个语义层通过初级意义的前景化和重新组合产生于艺术系统。语言艺术作品的特点是,语言模式的组合用来表达第二层语义,语言艺术的技巧存在于意象表达的层面上。

结合 Halliday 的语言模型,Hasan 提出了一个语言艺术的符号系统模型(1985),见图一。

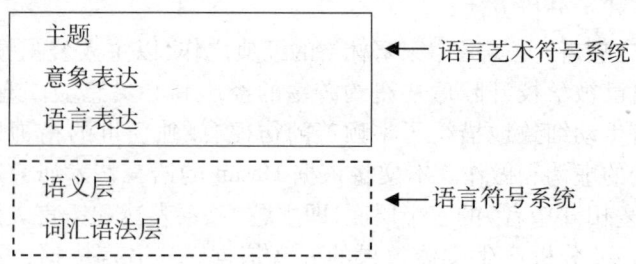

图 1:Hasan 的语言艺术符号系统与语言符号系统的关系

Hasan(1985)认为语言艺术的根本就在于语言艺术的意象表达层。语言艺术作品的特点是语言艺术的技巧存在于意象表达的层面上,语言模式的组合是表达第二层语义的手段。因此她强调语言在文学作品分析中的必要性,提出文学语篇分析应侧重文学作品中的语言功能,语言艺术分析的侧重点在于语言模式的组合,即不同的语言模式如何相互联系,共同为深层主题意义的表达服务。语言的形式与意义之间存在着密切的联系,语法规则和语言结构只是为意义的建构服务,并在具体的语言使用中为特定语类中的语篇建构提供意义潜势。由于语言是建构意义的社会符号系统,通过分析作者选择的语言结构,可以找到语言形式与意义或功能之间的联系,从而阐释文学语篇的意义,以便更好地理解和鉴赏其意义和艺术价值。

3. 语言表达与主题

《麦田守望者》讲述的是一个叫霍顿的 16 岁男孩,因五门功课中四门不及格而被学校开除后,在纽约近两昼夜的流浪经历和内心感受。对霍顿而言,这是心底深处的一种精神体验,也是其孤独的根源所在。两天里,他见了不同的人,并努力与这些人交流,甚至经常靠说谎以求与人沟通、与周围的世界建立联系,然而最终"他没有能力与周围的世界建立真正联系,只好沉湎于内向的幻想"(丹尼尔·贝尔,1989:89)。他感到孤独、沮丧,只有通过谎言和幻想,为自己建构一个虚幻的世界。

塞林格为小说取名 *The Catcher in the Rye*(《麦田守望者》),是因为这是主人公霍顿的理想和追求,他觉得自己有义务去保护和妹妹一样纯真的孩子,在他们即将坠入悬崖时,拉住他们、拯救他们。"我只想当个麦田里的守望者。我知道这有点异想天开,可我真正喜欢干的就是这个"。霍顿的理想源自他对现实世界——成人世界的厌恶和对童年的留恋。在霍顿看来,成人社会就是悬崖、灾难,充满了欲望、虚伪、自负和恐惧。这从他的语言中得到了充分体现。小说语言极度口语化、生活化,看似平常,实则却是有意选择的。其最明显的特征是作者打破了语法的常规惯例,采用了重复这一"过度规则"(overregularity)的文体策略,包括词汇和语法结构的重复。小说中重复的词汇和语法结构前景化程度最突出,增强了语言表达的感染力,突显了小说的语言和人物特色,强调了主人公霍顿的感情色彩和风格,突出了小说的深层主题意义。

本文作者借助 Wordsmith 语料库分析软件对小说高频词汇、词组和句子做了统计,发现小说中有几个突出现象:小说口语化特征明显,俚语使用频繁;贬义词和消极情感词汇出现频率较高;句子结构松散随意,且通过重复加强语义(见表一、表二和表三)。词汇的重复出现从概念意义上是冗余现象,但在人际意义上却具有加强情感的作用,在语篇意义上具有强化信息的作用,词汇的失衡手段产生了生动形象的意象而前景化。而高频率出现的短句和松散句短小精悍、干净利落、直达明快,揭示了主人公霍顿简单、淳朴的个性,达到了很好的文体效果。

表1：高频口语词汇统计表

词汇	次数	频率（每千词）	描写对象
Old	377	5.3	任何人、事，无论是好还是坏
Goddamn	245	3.3	任何人、事，无论是好还是坏
Hell	225	3.0	任何人、事，无论是好还是坏
Guy	170	2.3	指任何人
Damn	125	1.7	任何人、事，无论是好还是坏

通过对统计结果的分析可以看出，小说语言粗俗，俚语和诅咒语使用频率高，如"old"使用频率高达每千词5.3次，"goddamn"每千词3.3次，"hell"每千词3.0次，"guy"每千词2.3次，"damn"每千词1.7次，而且词的意义模糊，不仅诅咒坏人坏事，"甚至在谈论温柔或优美的事物时，他依然使用这些词来加强语气"（李战子，1994：22—25）。霍顿是美国五十年代亚文化青年群体的一员，当时的大学生和高中生言行举止都不合常规，他们使用俚语表明其相同的利益和志趣，透露出对社会现实和世俗成规的强烈不满。而小说中俚语的反复使用起到了反讽作用：霍顿想做麦田守望者，他愤世嫉俗，蔑视成人社会的一切，然而他自己却不能摆脱世俗，就连他的语言都处处体现出当时社会环境的影响，所以他的理想最终也只能是幻想。

在描写成人世界时，作者大量使用贬义词，"phony"及其变体出现80次，频率达到每千词1.1次，"lousy"，"bastard"，"stupid"等词也都频频出现。霍顿所看到的成人世界的一切，包括校长、校友、同学、老师、杂志、电影中的男男女女、交往过的女孩子、霍顿哥哥的前女友、酒吧里的钢琴手、酒吧里的顾客、电梯工、演员、就读于常春藤学校的学生等这些成年人或年轻成人，都是那么的假模假式、虚伪做作。这些词语的反复使用极具讽刺效果，突出了成人世界的虚伪、势利、卑鄙、肮脏和愚蠢，凸显了主人公霍顿对成人世界的厌恶和反叛情绪，同时也使单纯、可爱、心地善良的霍顿感到沮丧、痛苦、叛逆、绝望，所以霍顿悲愤"You never saw so many phonies in all your life"。"depress"，"sorry"，"sad"等表达消极悲伤情感的评价意义的词汇传达了霍顿对成人世界的绝望，在读者心中引起共鸣。

表2：贬义词和消极情感词汇统计表

消极情感词汇	次数	频率（每千词）	描写对象
phony（phone、phonies、phoniest）	80	1.1	学校的校长、为学校投资的校友、同学、老师、杂志故事中的男男女女、交往过的女孩子、霍顿哥哥的前女友、酒吧里的钢琴手、酒吧里的顾客、电梯工、演员、就读于常春藤学校的学生等这些成年人或年轻成人
Lousy	50	0.7	电影、人、性格、牙齿、腿、膝盖、词汇、坟墓等一切
Bastard	49	0.7	学校的校长、为学校投资的校友、同学、就读于常春藤学校的学生、电梯工、楼管员、自己
depress（depressing、depressed）	49	0.7	霍顿对所看到的成人世界的一切人和事的感想
Stupid	44	0.6	成人世界的一切，甚至包括用过的毛巾、穿的袜子、开的车、脚步声、手指、发型、晚会、电影、像乒乓球这样的运动等

荒谬的现实终使他身心疲惫，精神几乎崩溃。去妹妹学校时看到的写在墙上的脏话几乎让他发狂，他要杀了那个写字的人。因此霍顿决定做一个麦田守望者，去保护像妹妹一样天真的孩子们，守护他们的快乐、单纯、真诚、温情与爱，防止他们摔下成人世界的悬崖，防止他们被虚伪、自私的成人社会吞噬。

在句子结构上，塞林格也采用了小句重复来加强文体效果。在叙述过程中，霍顿反复使用"I mean …"，"It/She really is …"等小句来强调自己所表达的意思。如"I mean …"小句重复了158次，既表明他很清楚自己所要说的话，同时又强调了他所要表达的意思。而含"really"的小句结构出现了112次，主要出现在"It/She/He/They really is/are …"结构中，既突出了霍顿与人交流的困难，也让读者看到了霍顿的真诚和真实，这种小句让别人相信他的急切之情溢于言表。小说中重复使用以"boy"开头的感叹句，并以第二人称"you"称呼读者，拉近了与读者的距离，使读者感到身临其境，极易引起读者的共鸣。

表3：高频率重复的小句统计表

语法结构	次 数
I mean …; I don't/didn't mean …	158
以"boy"开头的感叹句	90
I（She，He，It，They）really am/was/do/did/didn't/would/wouldn't/couldn't/had …	44
I don't know.	41
If you（really）want to know the truth …	22

这些小句的反复出现，看似随意、松散，却意义深刻。霍顿看似随意的一问"If you（really）want to know the truth"，却让我们感受到了他的无奈，事实上，在他的世界里很少有人真的想这么做，整个社会，包括父母，都不想去了解真相。所以霍顿说"People never notice it"，"People never notice anything"，"People never think anything is anything really"，"People never believe you"，"He wasn't even listening. He hardly ever listened to you when you said something"，"They never want to discuss anything"。这些重复出现的句子结构凸显了他与社会交流的困难，周围人可怕的冷漠与霍顿为沟通所付出的努力形成强烈对比，纯洁善良的霍顿自觉与社会格格不入，感到了被遗弃和无望的孤独，一度想要放弃努力，逃离社会，装聋作哑，不与任何人进行愚蠢的谈话，只用纸和笔跟人交流。

　　小说中句子结构的重复变化多样，时而变化词语，时而变化结构。这种既有重复又有变化的语言表达避免了单调的重复，增强了语言的感染力，更重要的是它让所强调的意义直指主题。如作者在描写历史老师时这样写到：

　　　（1）He started going into this nodding routine. （2）You never saw anybody nod as much in your life as old Spencer did. （3）You never knew if he was nodding a lot because he was thinking and all, or just because he was a nice old guy that didn't know his ass from his elbow.

（Salinger, 1958：12）

句（2）和（3）重复了"You never …"结构，从逻辑语义关系上来说是句（1）的扩展，内容相同，都是描写老师一个劲儿点头的毛病，但在语义上增加了新的内容：句（2）运用比较结构说明老师点头的毛病绝无仅有，句（3）用两个"because …"的从属句，以因果关系加强语义，表示霍顿对老师一个劲儿点头的毛病反感，他不理解老师一个劲儿点头是表示在动脑筋思考呢，还是由于他只是个挺不错的老家伙,糊涂得都分不清东南西北了。霍顿本希望老师能够为他答疑解惑,然而,透过这段描写我们看到的却是他对老师的失望和对人生的迷茫。福克纳说,霍顿的进退两难是因为没能找到和接受一个真正的导师或引导者来唤醒他对成年人的信任,这个处境在精神上伤害了我们中的许多人,霍顿代我们表达了心中的疑问和我们的需要。

《麦田守望者》的语言特色体现在词汇、语法和意义层次上,"形式是意义的体现"(黄国文,1999:102)。词汇、语法系统在深层主题"促动"下产生意义。小说中大量使用重复词汇和随意松散的语法结构,通过这种违背常规的语言模式突出了霍顿的性格特点,表达霍顿与他眼中的虚假世界的抗争。

4. 语言表达与意象表达

根据《辞海》的解释,意象就是作者用来寄托主观情思的客观物象,是情感的载体,作者把所要表达的情感和对人生的思考用物象呈现出来。意象是文学作品的重要组成部分,具有丰富的表情达意功能。Hasan(1985)认为,语言艺术的技巧存在于意象表达的层面上。

《麦田守望者》的作者塞林格运用明喻、暗喻、暗示和象征等形式,捕捉和表达人物心灵瞬间的震颤,同时又借助意象的重复出现,如鸭子、红色鸭舌帽等,把霍顿的内心体验和感受呈现给读者,成功地刻画了霍顿内心痛苦矛盾的复杂感受、无奈的反抗和对人性美好的渴求。在意象表达上,小说所使用的语言颇为平淡,但是叙述细致,描写形象,取得了很强的艺术效果,与小说的整体结构、人物的发展阶段和情景语境相联系,与小说的主题意义达到了完美的统一。

表 4:意象表达与主题意义的统一

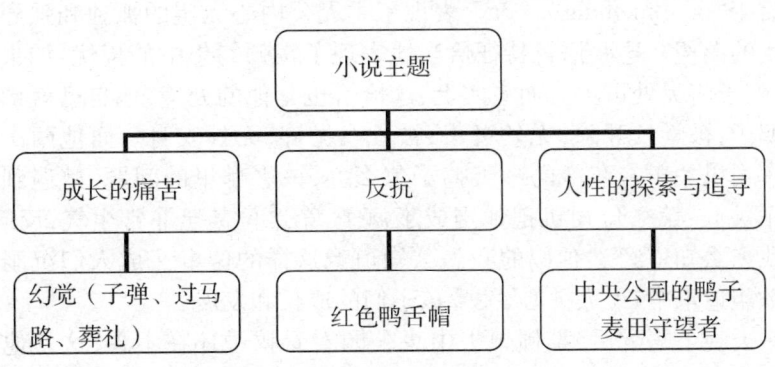

虚伪、自私的成人世界使霍顿非常痛苦，他喝醉酒后幻想自己的心窝中了颗子弹，幻想自己的葬礼，幻想那些虚伪的大人们安葬他并到墓地看他、为他献花，而他却希望能有个聪明人干脆把他的尸体扔在河里什么的，别埋在墓地被死人包围着。而且在每次穿越马路之后，他总会有一种像是失踪了的感觉："每次我要穿过一条街，我的脚才跨下混账的街沿石，我的心里马上有一种感觉，好像我永远到不了街对面。我觉得自己会永远往下走、走、走，谁也再见不到我了。"所以每次要穿过一条街，霍顿就假装跟弟弟艾里说话："艾里，别让我失踪。艾里，别让我失踪。艾里，别让我失踪。劳驾啦，艾里。"等走到街对面，发现自己并没失踪，霍顿就向弟弟道谢。对霍顿来说，温柔善良的弟弟艾里就是爱的化身，霍顿需要的就是爱的拯救。

虽然现实世界使成长中的霍顿感到孤独寂寞、寒冷痛苦、厌恶一切，但他并没有放弃对人性美好的渴求。他也试图反抗，用那顶有一个很长、很长的鸭舌的红色帽子向成人世界示威。霍顿最喜欢的戴帽子的方式是把鸭舌转到脑后，他知道这样戴十分粗俗，"可我喜欢这样戴。我这么戴了看上去挺美"，"我就喜欢这么戴"，"这顶帽子的确让我心里得意"。当阿克莱告诉他这是顶人们打鹿时候戴的帽子时，霍顿说"这是顶打人时候戴的帽子"，"我戴了它拿枪打人"。语言简洁，但色彩鲜明，极具形象性，生动展示了霍顿叛逆的个性和内心世界。霍顿有时候也把那顶帽子的鸭舌转到前面戴，"算是换个花样"，有时也脱掉那顶帽子，不让自己有任何形迹可疑的地方。正如霍顿所说，"我那顶帽子在某些部分的确给我挡住了不少雨，可我依旧淋得像只落汤鸡。不过我并不在乎。"

小说中霍顿对中央公园里鸭子的找寻暗示了他对人性的探索与追寻。霍顿得知被学校开除后去跟老师斯宾塞先生道别，他一边跟老师胡扯，一边竟想起了中央公园里的鸭子。这部分描写中出现了几次文体转换，从现在时到过去时，游离于现实与幻想之间。而复杂的"主句+从句"的排比结构"I was wondering …"、虚拟结构限定条件句"If it would be …"、随意的句子后缀"or something"、"or"，表现了主人公内心无望的孤独和强烈的逃避现实的渴望。这些语言特征恰当地表现了霍顿幻想中的担忧：如果湖水结冰，鸭子将无处可去。而事实上，这恰恰也是他的处境，他自己就像那无助的鸭子：被学校开除，无处可去；被社会抛弃，无处安身。而他两次追问出租车司机关于在寒冷的冬天鸭子怎么办、该去哪里的问题，遭遇到的都是漠不关心：第一位司机把他当成了疯子，第二位甚至非常生气，反问"他妈的我怎么知道？"、"他妈的我怎么知道像这样的傻事？"成人们沉溺于自己的欲望追求中，无人关心、关爱孩子们的成长和发展。

一天晚上喝醉后，霍顿想去中央公园看看鸭子还在不在，这是他最后一次找寻鸭子。在这一部分描写中,作者的语言非常简单,然而却蕴涵丰富的意象,且主题意义深厚。漆黑一片的中央公园物化了霍顿心里的迷茫。尽管小时候经常去那里滑旱冰、对中央公园熟悉得就像自己的手背一样,然而霍顿却费了非常大的劲才找到那浅水湖。他越往前走,四周围也越黑、越阴森可怕("I kept walking and walking, and it kept getting darker and darker and spookier and spookier." (Salinger, 1958))。霍顿马上要步入成人社会,然而成人世界的种种令他非常失望,他迷茫地在黑暗中寻求人性的美好。霍顿"围着这个混账的湖绕了他妈的整整一周——事实上,我还险些儿掉进湖里——可我连一只鸭子也没看见"。就像他找不到鸭子一样,霍顿也看不到人生的希望。霍顿坐在公园长椅上冷得浑身发抖,头发都结成一块块冰了。他的心也发冷,还以为自己要死于肺炎了。他想到了死去的弟弟艾里,想到下雨时人们可以躲到车里,而艾里却不能,感到悲伤不已。最后想起了妹妹菲比,霍顿才鼓足了勇气活下来,走出公园,回到家里。妹妹是纯真、真诚和真爱的象征,妹妹的美好与成人的丑陋形成强烈对照。妹妹的世界是天堂,而成人的世界是悬崖,因此他情愿做麦田守望者,守望那份真挚的情感和美好的希望。

5. 结语

系统功能语言学视文体为"选择",认为文体是受一定的情景语境的"促动"在语言系统中进行选择的结果。任何选择都是有意义的,选择就是意义。Hasan(1985)提出的语言艺术三个层面的分析框架,以语言为切入点,运用语言学手段阐释文学作品的意义,通过对小说中前景化程度最高的词汇语法系统的分析,帮助我们更好地理解文学作品的主题,领会语言的形式和意义之间的密切联系和语言使用原则——选择就是意义。

参考文献

Halliday, M. A. K. 1978. *Language as Social Semiotic: The Social Interpretation of Language and Meaning*. London: Edward Arnold.

Halliday, M. A. K. 1971. Linguistic function and literary style: An inquiry into the language of William Golding's *The Inheritors*. In S. Chatman (ed.), *Literary Style: A Symposium*. Oxford: Oxford University Press.

Halliday, M. A. K. 1985/2004. *An Introduction to Functional Grammar*. London: Edward Arnold.

Hasan, R. 1985. *Linguistics, Language and Verbal Art*. Victoria: Deakin University Press.

Hasan, R. 2012.《语言学、语言与语言艺术》. 北京:世界图书出版公司.

Salinger, J. D. 1958. *The Catcher in the Rye*. England: Penguin Books Ltd.

丹尼尔·贝尔. 1989.《资本主义文化矛盾》(赵一凡、蒲隆、任晓晋译). 北京:三联书店.

黄国文. 1999.《英语语言问题研究》. 广州:中山大学出版社.

李战子. 1994.《麦田的守望者》口语特色分析.《外语研究》,4:22—25.

申 丹. 2000. 西方现代文体学百年发展历程.《外语教学与研究》,1:22—28.

张德禄. 1998.《功能文体学》. 济南:山东教育出版社.

张德禄. 1999. 韩礼德功能文体学理论述评.《外语教学与研究》,1:43—48.

张德禄. 2005.《语言的功能与文体》. 北京:高等教育出版社.

Part V   Pragma-stylistics

Stage Directions as an Object for Stylistic Analysis of Drama

Li Huadong　(Hangzhou Dianzi University)

Abstract：　So far, most stylisticians of drama seem to have excluded stage directions from their studies. Even when stage directions came into the horizon of dramatic stylisticians, they were only considered as indicators of the complicated writer-reader relationship. The exclusion of stage directions as an object for stylistic study is probably caused by the fact that these scholars consider the dialogue as the dramatic language proper and stage directions as acts or performance, which is beyond the study of language. This paper, however, will argue that stage directions are an important component of the dramatic text, therefore should be included in stylistics of drama. Moreover, it will argue that stage directions do not just reveal the writer-reader relationship, but also contributes to the aesthetic values of drama. This paper will first discuss some theoretical preliminaries relevant to this argument, then show by deletion test and substitution test that stage directions are indispensable for drama interpretation.

Key words：stage directions; stylistics of drama; writer-reader relationship; aesthetic value

1. Introduction

Stylistics of drama is a relatively new interdisciplinary area of study[①]. It applies various linguistic theories to the dramatic text in order to find out how the aesthetic values of the drama are achieved through the use of language.

Among the linguistic theories adopted, pragmatics and discourse analysis are the most fruitful ones[2]. The combination of pragmatics, a discipline of linguistics aimed at discovering how inference is achieved through the use of language, and discourse analysis, particularly that of conversation analysis, has successfully explained how the aesthetic properties such as characterization, power relationship, plot development and theme construction have been achieved through the playwright's composition of the dialogue.

However, a problem that concerns the object of study exists within stylistics of drama: most stylisticians have excluded stage directions from their studies[3]. Even when stage directions came into the horizon of dramatic stylisticians (e.g., Feng, 2002), they were only considered as indicators of the complicated writer-reader relationship. The exclusion of stage directions as an object for stylistic study is probably caused by the fact that these scholars consider the dialogue as the dramatic language proper and stage directions as acts or performance, which is beyond the study of language.

In this paper, however, I will argue that stage directions are an important component of the dramatic text, therefore should be included in stylistics of drama. Moreover, I will argue that stage directions do not just reveal the writer-reader relationship, as was discussed by Feng & Shen (2001). More importantly, it contributes to the aesthetic values of drama. I will first discuss some theoretical preliminaries relevant to this argument. Then, I will show by deletion test and substitution test that stage directions are indispensable for drama interpretation.

2. Stage Directions as an Important Object for Stylistic Analysis

A dramatic text is noticeably composed of two parts: the dialogue and stage directions. They are visually differentiable as they are in different fonts and placed in different positions. The dialogue always comes after the name of the characters and usually constitutes the main body of a play[4]. The stage directions are either in the beginning of a play or of a scene, or in the brackets in the main body of the dramatic text.

Actually the above theoretical discussion has already indicated in theory why stage directions are important for a drama, and therefore for drama stylistics. I have already established a method of "reading the text while imagining the performance" or "visualized discourse analysis". In order to do this I have to rely not only on the dialogue but also on stage directions because the aesthetic value (the inference or message) is not achieved solely through the dialogue but through the combination and interaction of the dialogue and stage directions. I have also expanded the speech act theory and found that both speech and act share the common feature of being signs conveying inference or implications. Both speech and act are influenced by the dialogue and stage directions. These four concepts are all "goal-driven" in that they are all triggered and restrained by the inference or communicative goals.

It is necessary here to make a comparison and contrast between drama and other genres of literary discourses. For example, if we compare and contrast between drama and fiction, we will find that the stage directions in drama are very much like the narration of fiction. In doing a stylistic analysis of fiction, we normally consider the narration as an important object for analysis, although a fiction usually contains dialogue which deserves the stylistician's attention as well. Likewise, even though the main mean of expression in drama is the dialogue, we cannot simply ignore the stage directions, the narrative part of the drama. For another example, if we compare and contrast between drama and poetry, we will find that poems normally include narrations as well, some also include dialogue. Of course, we also admit that the poetic language is marked more considerably with features of sound and images. But we cannot simply ignore that some poems also feature the narration. Likewise, we cannot disregard the stage directions as an important component of the drama as well, although some plays are also marked with poetic features of sound and images that normally appear in the poetry. In this sense, as will be discussed in the conclusion of this book, the theory of pragma-stylistics of drama put forward in the present study also has implications for analysis of other genres of discourses.

To elicit the importance of stage directions for drama and drama stylistics, I will do some experiments by the procedure of deletion and substitution here. Substitution is often used in phonology and morphology to determine the phonemes and morphemes of a language. In phonology this is done by substituting one sound for another to see whether the substitution results in a change of meaning. Here, I also try to delete the stage directions and substitute them to see if this results in a change of meaning or inference. I do this not to differentiate the minimal unit in dramatic text, but to check the contribution of stage directions to drama.

I selected a famous play, namely, Henrik Ibsen's *A Doll's House*, as the source of my sample because it is considered representative or prototypical. I selected the lines in the beginning part of Act I out of two reasons: One is that I do not have to explain what has happened prior to these lines, the other is that when reading these lines the reader will not be affected in interpreting the play by the context of language, i.e., what occurred prior to these lines.

The following example is taken from Henrik Ibsen's *A Doll's House*, the beginning of Act I.

(5)

> (*SCENE.* — *A room furnished comfortably and tastefully, but not extravagantly. At the back, a door to the right leads to the entrance-hall, another to the left leads to Helmer's study. Between the doors stands a piano. In the middle of the left-hand wall is a door, and beyond it a window. Near the window are a round table, arm-chairs and a small sofa. In the right-hand wall, at the farther end, another door; and on the same side, nearer the footlights, a stove, two easy chairs and a rocking-chair; between the stove and the door, a small table. Engravings on the walls; a cabinet with china and other small objects; a small book-case with well-bound books. The floors are carpeted, and a fire burns in the stove. It is winter.*
>
> *A bell rings in the hall; shortly afterwards the door is heard to open. Enter Nora, humming a tune and in high spirits. She is in outdoor dress and carries a number of parcels; these she lays on the table to the right. She leaves the outer door open after her, and through it is seen a porter who is carrying a Christmas Tree and a basket, which he gives to the maid who has opened the door.*)

Nora.   Hide the Christmas Tree carefully, Helen. Be sure the children do not see it till this evening, when it is dressed. (*To the porter, taking out her purse.*) How much?

Porter.   Six pence.

Nora.   There is a shilling. No, keep the change. (*The porter thanks her, and goes out. Nora shuts the door. She is laughing to herself, as she takes off her hat and coat. She takes a packet of macaroons from her pocket and eats one or two; then goes cautiously to her husband's door and listens.*) Yes, he is in. (*Still humming, she goes to the table on the right.*)

Helmer. (*calls out from his room*) Is that my little lark twittering out there?

Nora. (*busy opening some of the parcels*) Yes, it is!

Helmer. Is it my little squirrel bustling about?

Nora. Yes!

Helmer. When did my squirrel come home?

Nora. Just now. (*Puts the bag of macaroons into her pocket and wipes her mouth.*) Come in here, Torvald, and see what I have bought.

Helmer. Don't disturb me. (*A little later, he opens the door and looks into the room, pen in hand.*) Bought, did you say? All these things? Has my little spendthrift been wasting money again?

...

Henrik Ibsen, *A Doll's House*, **Act I**

An act conventionally begins with the stage directions for the scene. If we are able to "visualize" the discourse, we will be able to form a picture of the scene in our mind from the first paragraph of the stage directions. A reader who is trained in the basics of fine arts will be able to draw a sketch out of the stage directions. Even though most readers are not trained artists, given the chance of viewing the stage design, they are likely to be able to identify which parts or features of it are not "in correspondence" with the stage directions. For example, if we look closely at such a picture of the stage design (Picture 1), we will be able to tell after careful scrutiny that there are certain things which are not in accordance with the above stage directions, as listed in Table 1.

Picture 1: *A Doll's House*, Act 1, Stage Design, February 1984 (Source: http://www.lib.ndsu.nodak.edu/archives/exhibitions/donlarew/DollsHouse.html)

Table 1: **The differences between the stage directions and stage design of**
A Doll's House

Stage directions	Stage design
A room furnished comfortably and tastefully, but not extravagantly.	The room may be furnished a little extravagantly.
At the back, a door to the right leads to the entrance-hall, ...	The entrance hall seems to be in the middle rather than "to the right" of the stage, and there is not a door that "leads to" it.
Between the doors stands a piano.	The piano is not standing between the entrance door and the study door. It has been put to the left.
In the middle of the left-hand wall is a door, and beyond it a window.	There is no window.
Near the window are a round table, arm-chairs and a small sofa.	The round table has been placed in the center, rather than in the left. There are no arm-chairs or a small sofa near the round table. Rather, two dinner chairs have been placed around it.
In the right-hand wall, at the farther end, another door; and on the same side, nearer the footlights, a stove, two easy chairs and a rocking-chair; ...	Only one rather than "two" easy chairs have been placed near the stove.
between the stove and the door, a small table	There is no "small table between the stove and the door".
a cabinet with china and other small objects	There is no "cabinet with china and other small objects".
a small book-case with well-bound books	There is no "small book-case with well-bound books".
	There are other decorations not mentioned in the stage directions, like two statues on wooden stands, lamps on the wall, tablecloth, etc.

I am not trying to downgrade the value of the work stage designers do. In fact, stage designers are usually good at keeping the balance: while they try to be as loyal to the stage directions as possible, they have to change certain things to make the stage more suitable for the performance. For example, the position of the round table in the center rather than in the left has been a preferable change since much of the performance has taken place around it.

What I am trying to say is that the stage directions of the scene setting play an important role, even though some of them will be subject to change by stage designers. They enable the reader (stylisticians included) to visualize the stage setting, which helps to create a context for the story and to build the character as well. In this sample, we will tell from the information of the stage directions that the characters are typical bourgeois.

Paragraph Two of the stage directions describes the routine homecoming of a middle-class housewife from shopping. Her status of being the housewife is further indicated in the scene in which the MAID opens the door and the PORTER gives the MAID the load of goods. The shopping was apparently a happy experience, since Nora is "*humming a tune*" and "*in high spirits*". From the mentioning of a Christmas Tree, we know that this is the festival season, and the things Nora bought might include some Christmas gifts or decorations.

So far, I have already inferred from the stage directions the context of the story and the status of one of the characters, Nora. The context here not only refers to that of situation, but also to that of culture. These are all contributions of the stage directions in the beginning part of the play (some people [e.g., Feng, 2002: 107–110] name this part of stage directions stage directive, as being distinct from performance instructions).

Then I will move to the dialogue part. In between the dialogues, there are stage directions too. These stage directions serve as performance instructions. Some of them refer to whom the speech is addressed to (*e.g.*, *To the porter …*), what act the dialogue is supposed to perform (*e.g.*, *… taking out her purse*), what mood the character is in (*e.g.*, *… Nora … is laughing to herself, as she takes off her hat and coat. She takes a packet of* macaroons *from her pocket and eats one or two;…*), paralinguistic features (e.g., (Helmer) *calls out from his room*; (Nora) *busy opening some of the parcels*, etc.).

We can see that the dialogue and stage directions interact with each other. They both, through interaction, make up the chain of actions happening on the stage. From the above excerpt, we can see a happy couple, with Nora, the housewife, being in high spirits back from shopping, while Helmer, the husband, welcoming the housewife by greeting her (*calls out from his room*) and addressing her as " my little lark" and " my little squirrel". Even the address of "my little spendthrift", though containing a little blame, gives a sense of love and cherishing.

Now I will try out our deletion procedure on this excerpt by withdrawing the stage directions from it. After the deletion procedure, this sample becomes sample 5' as follows:

(5ˣ)

(1) **Nora**. Hide the Christmas Tree carefully, Helen. Be sure the children do not see it until this evening, when it is dressed. How much?

(2) **Porter**. Six pence.

(3) **Nora**. There is a shilling. No, keep the change. Yes, he is in.

(4) **Helmer**. Is that my little lark twittering out there?

(5) **Nora**. Yes, it is!

(6) **Helmer**. Is it my little squirrel bustling about?

(7) **Nora**. Yes!

(8) **Helmer**. When did my squirrel come home?

(9) **Nora**. Just now. Come in here, Torvald, and see what I have bought.

(10) **Helmer**. Don't disturb me. Bought, did you say? All these things? Has my little spendthrift been wasting money again?

Henrik Ibsen, *A Doll's House*, Act I (stage directions deleted)

This type of dramatic text seldom exists, since most drama contains some stage directions. But for the purpose of understanding the importance and functions of stage directions, I have deleted them from the original play text.

After removing the stage directions, we find it much more difficult to understand the dialogue. We simply do not know who these people are. Of course, we may try to infer from the dialogue the status of and relationship between the characters, but we are uncertain of them. We even have doubt about where this conversation takes place. From turn 1, we know that Nora is talking with Helen, but we do not know who Helen is. She might be a maid or a younger sister or a sister-in-law of Nora. We even cannot deny the possibility of this conversation happening in a kindergarten. Of course, we may rule out this possibility after we hear the conversation between Helmer and Nora, as the forms of address like "my little lark", "my little squirrel" and "my little spendthrift" are too intimate for a workplace situation. But we immediately have confusions again: who is Helmer? He might be the husband of Nora. But he might be a grandfather too, as many old people also call their children or young people they love by such intimate address forms.

It is quite obvious in the above discussion that without stage directions, the play text would be more difficult or even impossible to understand. A lot of confusion or trouble is caused. Much information is lost. We have more difficulty in constructing the context, identifying the status of and the relationship between the characters, and comprehending what the characters are doing.

If this deletion procedure is still not adequate enough to prove the importance of stage directions, we will see it more clearly in our substitution procedure, i.e., substituting new stage directions for the original ones. I am not trying to replace the original ones with entirely new ones, which might make the play totally different. What I am to do here is to make only a few changes in the original to make people see that even minor changes to the stage directions can cause major difference in the meaning the play conveys.

In the following sample 5", I have substituted new stage directions for the original ones. As I said, the new stage directions are actually not entirely new. They are almost the same as the original ones, except for some minor changes, which I have under-dotted for identification.

(5")

(SCENE. — A room furnished comfortably and tastefully, but not extravagantly. At the back, a door to the right leads to the entrance-hall, another to the left leads to Helmer's study. Between the doors stands a piano. In the middle of the left-hand wall is a door, and beyond it a window. Near the window are a round table, arm-chairs and a small sofa. In the right-hand wall, at the farther end, another door; and on the same side, nearer the footlights, a stove, two easy chairs and a rocking-chair; between the stove and the door, a small table. Engravings on the walls; a cabinet with china and other small objects; a small book-case with well-bound books. The floors are carpeted, and a fire burns in the stove. It is winter.

A bell rings in the hall; shortly afterwards the door is heard to open. Nora sneaks in, nervously. She is in outdoor dress and carries a number of parcels; these she lays on the table to the right. She leaves the outer door open after her, and through it is seen a porter who is carrying a Christmas Tree and a basket, which he gives to the MAID who has opened the door.)

Nora. (*In a low voice*) Hide the Christmas Tree carefully, Helen. Be sure the children do not see it until this evening, when it is dressed. (*To the porter, taking out her purse.*) How much?

Porter. Six pence.

Nora. There is a shilling. No, keep the change. (*The porter thanks her, and goes out. Nora shuts the door. She fearfully listens for a while. Then goes cautiously to her husband's door and listens.*) Yes, he is in. (*Quietly and cautiously, she goes to the table on the right.*)

Helmer. (*calls out from his room*) Is that my little lark twittering out there?

Nora. (*busy hiding some of the parcels into the drawer*) Yes, it is!

Helmer. Is it my little squirrel bustling about?

Nora. Yes!

Helmer. When did my squirrel come home?

Nora. Just now. (*After finishing putting some of the parcels in the drawer, she nervously pushes it close.*) Come in here, Torvald, and see what I have bought.

Helmer. Don't disturb me. (*A little later, he opens the door and looks into the room, pen in hand.*) Bought, did you say? All these things? Has my little spendthrift been wasting money again?

Henrik Ibsen, *A Doll's House*, **Act I (stage directions substituted)**

Even with a few minor changes in the stage directions, the play looks quite different. The characteristics of the characters have changed: Nora, instead of being a happy housewife, has become a repressed one. Helmer, instead of being an affectionate husband, has become a tyrant or dictator in the family. Their relationship has apparently become an unhappy and unequal one. Even the use of words like "my little lark" and "my little squirrel" or "my little spendthrift" has become ironic or symbolic. These words do not show any love or affection any more. They show the husband's treatment of his wife as a toy or a play doll at once.

People may argue: Aren't these changes wonderful?! Isn't it the play's intension to show Nora's rebellion against being treated as a toy or play doll? I would say, yes. But these changes have made Nora's realization of her inferior status later much less dramatic, and therefore much less impressive to the audience.

After the deletion and substitution procedure, we are now more aware of the importance of stage directions for both drama and drama stylistics. We are already convinced that stage directions, although previously neglected (as in most earlier stylistic studies) or used only to tell the writer-reader relationship (as in Feng & Shen, 2001 and Feng, 2002), should be included in stylistics of drama as a way, by itself as well as through their interaction with the dialogue, to reveal the aesthetic values of the drama.

3. Conclusion

In this paper, I have discussed the importance of stage directions as an indispensable component of drama and as an important object of stylistic analysis both in theory and by experiment.

Empirically, I have conducted some experiments by deleting and replacing the stage directions on excerpts from a famous play. These experiments show that stage directions are indispensable for the interpretation of the play. Deleting or even making minor changes to the stage directions will result in different interpretations of the plays.

I have also touched upon stage directions in classical plays before Ibsen's time. On the one hand, I illustrated with an example that even in these plays where stage directions are rare, some of them are inferable from dialogue, and others, those which cannot be inferred, still exist in the drama. On the other hand, a discussion on the reasons for the scarcity of stage directions in those classical plays shows that stage directions hold a more significant place in modern drama.

I would again compare drama to music. Stage directions are inseparable from drama as rhythm is from music. There is music without melody (such as in some African folk music that features a variety of local percussion instruments), but there is no music without rhythm. Likewise, there are plays without dialogue, but there are no plays without stage directions.

Of course, I am not under-evaluating the importance of the dialogue. There are reasons to argue that the drama is an art of dialogue. In most cases this is true because the dialogue is often the major component of the dramatic text. What I am trying to argue is that stage directions should not be neglected. Both the dialogue and stage directions play their part in drama, and in most cases, it is their interaction rather than either component alone that is providing meaning or inference for the audience.

Notes

① For a general picture of modern stylistics of drama, please refer to works relevant to modern stylistics of drama. For example, Jakobson (1960) and Jakobson & Jones (1970) claim the importance of stylistics by calling upon linguists and critics to work together to achieve a better understanding of the aesthetic values of literary works through the analysis of the text. Leech (1969) analyzed some lines of drama by treating them as poetry. Eliopulos (1975) tries to locate the stylistic features of Beckett's plays by trying to combine rhetoric with poetics. Burton (1980), Nash (1989), Herman (1991), Leech (1992), Short (1989, 1996, 1998), Thornborrow & Wareing (1998) and Simpson (1989) suggest that the aesthetic values of drama can be better understood by applying various linguistic theories and techniques such as pragmatics, sociolinguistic, discourse analysis. Culpeper, Short, & Verdonk (1998) compile the first book (a collection of papers) solely devoted to stylistics of drama. Culpeper (2001) outlines an interdisciplinary approach to characterization by drawing upon theories from social and cognitive psychology. In China, Yang (1989, 1991), Yu (1993, 1996, 1999), Li & Yu (2001), Feng (2002), Yu & Zuo (2004) and Wang (2006) represent the major effort by Chinese scholars in developing the field of drama stylistics.

② For example, Burton (1980), Herman (1991), Simpson (1989), Leech (1992), Short (1989, 1996, 1998), Culpeper, Short, & Verdonk (1998), Culpeper (2001), Yu (1993, 1996, 1999), Li & Yu (2001), Feng (2002), Yu & Zuo (2004), Wang (2006), etc.

③ For example, Leech (1969), Eliopulos (1975), Burton (1980), Yang (1989, 1991), Herman (1991), Leech (1992), Short (1989, 1996, 1998), Thornborrow & Wareing (1998), Simpson (1989), Culpeper, Short, & Verdonk (1998), Culpeper (2001), Yu (1993, 1996, 1999), Li & Yu (2001), Yu & Zuo (2004), Wang (2006), etc.

④ There are exceptions where the dialogue is not the main body of a play, such as Samuel Beckett's *Act without words*. Hence I use "usually" here rather than "always" when I say the dialogue constitute the main body of a play.

References

Austin, J. L. 1962. *How to Do Things with Words*. Oxford: The Clarendon Press.

Brecht, B. 1964. *Brecht on Theatre*. Trans. John Willett. London: Methuen.

Burton, D. 1980. *Dialogue and Discourse: A Sociolinguistic Approach to Modern Drama Dialogue and Naturally Occurring Conversation*. London: Routledge and Kegan Paul.

Culpeper, J. 2001. *Language and Characterization: People in Plays and Other Texts*. Essex: Pearson Education Ltd.

Culpeper, J., M. Short, & P. Verdonk (eds.). 1998. *Exploring the Language of Drama: From Text to Context*. London: Routledge.

Eliopulos, J. 1975. *Samuel Beckett's Dramatic Language*. The Hague: Mouton.

Feng, Z. 2002. *Pragmastylistics of Dramatic Texts: The Play off the Stage*. Beijing: Tsinghua University Press.

Feng, Z. & D. Shen. 2001. The play off the stage: The writer-reader relationship in drama. *Language and Literature*, 10 (1): 79–93.

Gu, Y. 1999. Towards a model of situated discourse analysis. In K. Turner (ed.). *The Semantics/Pragmatics Interface from Different Points of View*. Oxford: Elsevier.

Gu, Y. 2002. Towards an understanding of workplace discourse: A pilot study for compiling a spoken Chinese corpus of situated discourse. In C. N. Candlin (ed.). *Research and Practice in Professional Discourse*. Hong Kong: City University of Hong Kong Press.

Herman, V. 1991. Dramatic dialogue and the systematics of turn-taking. *Semiotica*, 83 (1–2): 97–121.

Ibsen, H. 1958. *A Doll's House*. 1879. Excerpted from: *Four Great Plays by Henrik Ibsen*. New York: Bantam Books, Inc.

Jakobson, R. 1960. Closing statement: Linguistics and poetics. In T. A. Sebeok (ed.). *Style in Language*. Cambridge: MIT Press.

Jakobson, R. & L. G. Jones. 1970. *Shakespeare's Verbal Art in Th'Expence of Spirit*. The Hague: Mouton.

Leech, G. N. 1969. *A Linguistic Guide to English Poetry*. London: Longman.

Leech, G. N. 1992. Pragmatic principles in Shaw's *You Never Can Tell*. In M. Toolan (ed.). *Lauguage, Text and Context: Essays in Stylistics*. London: Routledge.

Li, H. & D. Yu. 2001. Power relations, characterization, and plot development revealed by a turn-taking analysis. *Journal of PLA University of Foreign Languages*, 3 (2).

Lu, W. 2001. On style of drama. *Theoretical Studies in Literature and Art*, (6).

Morris, C. W. 1938. Foundations of the theory of signs. In O. Neurath, R. Carnap, & C. Morris (eds.). *International Encyclopedia of Unified Science*. Chicago: University of Chicago Press, 1: 77–138.

Nash, W. 1989. Changing the guard at Elsinore. In R. Carter & P. Simpson (eds.). *Language, Discourse and Literature*. London: Routeledge.

Searle, J. 1969. *Speech Acts: An Essay in the Philosophy of Language*. Cambridge: Cambridge University Press.

Short, M. 1989. Discourse analysis and the analysis of drama. In R. Carter & P. Simpson (eds.). *Language, Discourse and Literature*. London: Routledge.

Short, M. 1996. *Exploring the Language of Poems, Plays and Prose*. Essex: Addison Wesley Longman Ltd.

Short, M. 1998. From dramatic text to dramatic performance. In J. Culpeper, M. Short, & P. Verdonk (eds.). *Exploring the Language of Drama: From Text to Context*. London: Routledge.

Simpson, P. 1989. Politeness phenomena in Ionesco's *The Lesson*. In R. Carter & P. Simpson (eds.). *Language, Discourse and Literature*. London: Routledge.

Styan, J. L. 1971. *The Dramatic Experience*. Cambridge: Cambridge University Press.

Thornborrow, J. & S. Wareing. 1998. *Patterns in Language: Stylistics for Students of Language and Literature*. London: Routledge.

Wang, H. 2006. *Stylistics of Drama: Dialogue as Discourse*. Shanghai: Shanghai Foreign Language Education Press.

Wells, S. 1970. *Literature and Drama*. London: Routledge and Kefan Paul.

Yang, X. 1989. On linguistic stylistic analysis of drama. *Foreign Languages*, (1).

Yang, X. 1991. Discourse analysis and stylistic analysis of drama. *Foreign Language Teaching and Research*, (2).

Yu, D. 1993. Scope, nature and methodology of stylistics of drama. In D. Wang & T. Qiu (eds.). *On Study of English*. Chengdu: Sichuan Science and Technology Press.

Yu, D. 1996. Style of drama and stylistics of drama. *Journal of Zhejiang University*, (1).

Yu, D. 1999. *Style in Drama: Towards a Pragmatic Approach to the Study of Dramatic Texts*. Diss. Shanghai International Studies University.

Yu, D. & J. Zuo. 2004. Pragmatic ambivalence, conversation strategies and characterization of drama. *Foreign Language Teaching and Research*, (5).

The Interpersonal Meanings of News Discourse: A Perspective of Appraisal Theory

Wu Sumei （**Sichuan University of Arts and Science**）

Abstract: The reporter's viewpoint, attitude and ideology loaded in the news discourse are part of the total meaning of a discourse — the interpersonal meanings. This article investigates the interpersonal meanings of one sample news discourse under the framework of the Appraisal Theory in hope of helping the reader to gain a critical comprehension of news discourse, and also bringing some enlightenment to the English Reading and Writing Teaching.

Key words: news discourse; interpersonal meaning; Appraisal Theory

1. Introduction

With the fast development of technology and science, what is happening in one part of the world can be immediately known by people in the other part of the world. News is changing people's life at a sweeping speed. Every day innumerable pieces of news report not only tell people what is happening, has happened and will happen, but also influence the readers with the viewpoint, attitude and ideology loaded in the news. At the same time, different people may have quite different understandings and insights when they read the same news discourse, because the writer of the news discourse and the reader of the news discourse may have totally different social-cultural and ideological background. Even if they share the same social-cultural and ideological background, their understanding may vary with age, educational level and some other factors. Any news report cannot be utterly neutral or value-free as some journalists have often claimed to be. In other words, the reporter's viewpoint, attitude and ideology loaded in the news discourse, in fact, will be part of the total meaning of a discourse. To the readers, this kind of additional meanings — interpersonal meanings, is just the non-objectivity of news discourse that makes their diverse levels of understanding and insight.

As one of the most influential written text types in the fast-developing society, news discourse reflects typical interpersonal relations which are worth exploring. In fact, the function of newspapers is not limited to conveying the "hard" news of the day, let alone news comments which represent one of the most typical sub-genres of the field of media. Appraisal framework has been applied to the analysis of media discourse, including hard news, news stories and news comments (Iedema, Feez, & White, 1994; White, 1998; Martin, 2003). The most famous domestic scholars who concentrated on media discourse are Wang Zhenhua (2004) and Li Rongjuan (2005). The former explores attitudinal meaning in hard news; the latter probes into the attitudinal meanings of English political column texts. This article attempts to investigate the interpersonal meanings of news discourse under the framework of a newly developed theory — Appraisal Theory in hope of offering a new angle to gain a critical comprehension of news discourse.

2. Appraisal Theory

Appraisal Theory isn't a totally new theory, which is the further development of Interpersonal Metafunction. The initial motivation for its development has come from work conducted in the 80s and 90s for the *Write It Right* project of the New South Wales Disadvantaged Schools Program. In 1997, J. R. Martin first adopted the term of Appraisal, and his two books, *Working with Discourse: Meaning beyond the Clause (2003, 2007)* and *The Language of Evaluation: Appraisal in English (2005, 2008)*, mark the development and maturity of this theory.

Within the Appraisal Theory framework, the evaluative resources, according to their semantic sense, are classified into Attitude, Engagement and Graduation, among which Attitude is subdivided again into Affect, Judgment and Appreciation, referring to the emotional, ethical and aesthetic categories respectively; Engagement is further divided into two categories: Monogloss and Heterogloss; Graduation is subdivided into Force and Focus.

This article attempts to explore the interpersonal meanings hidden behind one sample discourse by way of Appraisal Theory, which is taken from NEWSWEEK, dated May 23, 2005.

3. Appraisal Analysis of the Sample News Discourse

Reading news discourse is not at all a single and unidirectional process which involves the continuing and interactive contact between the reader and the reporter. In a news discourse, the reporter not only conveys the information to the reader, but also expresses his point of view, explicitly or implicitly, while the reader, on the one hand, tries to figure out the reporter's point of view, and on the other hand, is encouraged to voice his own point of view based on his own knowledge and ideology system. By applying Appraisal Theory to news discourse, the reader can discern positioning, understand underlying values and ideology and even challenge the reporter's view. Therefore they can achieve a critical comprehension of reading in the discourse based on these analyses. The reporter's attitude towards the person, thing and happenings or situation in the report is generally reflected by the language resources, especially by the evaluative words.

Sample discourse one "Equality, of a Sort (Kuwaiti Democracy)", extracted from the American famous magazine NEWSWEEK, May 23, 2005 by Carla Power, talks about the status quo of women in Kuwait (revised). This news discourse is made up of five paragraphs. By the Gulf standards, Kuwait is a democratic superstar. Its citizens enjoy quite a lot of freedom. Kuwaiti women drive, work and travel freely. They manage multibillion-dollar businesses and serve as ambassadors. 70 percent of university students in Kuwait are females. However, as far as women's right to vote is concerned, ironically, the traditionalists, tribal leaders and the democratically-elected legislature unanimously opposed it. Even the Kuwaiti women are very content with their present situation, and most of them think men are better at politics. This is the so-called "Kuwaiti democracy".

The following analysis will first identify the linguistic resources that realize the evaluation, and then try to demonstrate how they contribute to the interpersonal or subjective meaning of the text. (In the following appraisal analysis, "+" stands for positive, "−" for negative, and overstriking for the most relevant appraisal values. All the appraisal analyses are put in the square brackets. The sample discourse is in italicized form.)

> *Getting to the heart of Kuwaiti democracy seems **hilariously*** [Graduation: intensification] ***easy*** [Appreciation: + reaction]. *Armed only with a dog-eared NEWSWEEK ID, I ambled through the gates of the National Assembly last week.* ***Unscanned, unsearched*** [Judgment: −capacity], *my satchel **could easily have held*** [Appreciation: −reaction] *the odd grenade or an anthrax-stuffed lunchbox. The only person who stopped me was a guard who **grinned and invited*** [Affect: + happiness] *me to take a swig of orange juice from his plastic bottle.*

At the very beginning of this passage, the reporter tastes the light atmosphere in Kuwait that is very rare in Middle Eastern countries. It is generally acknowledged that probing into the democracy of any country in Middle East sounds a tough task, because Middle Eastern countries always give people an impression of tradition, mystery and conservation. But the attitudinal meaning of the word "*easy*[Appreciation: + reaction]" and emotional meaning of the word "*hilariously*[Graduation: intensification]" makes things quite different. To some degree, this kind of appreciative evaluation coincides with the main idea conveyed in the whole passage — Kuwait has its own distinctive features of democracy. The reporter's negative appraisals of the security measures she encounters at the gate of the National Assembly are implicitly held in the two words both of which have a negative prefix " *unscanned, unsearched* [Judgment: −capacity]", and of course, this kind of encounter more or less is out of her expectation. This idea may begin to affect the readers' rooted impression of Middle Eastern counties. But, the subjunctive mood expresses that getting into National Assembly with the odd grenade or an anthrax-stuffed lunchbox is just sort of the writer's hypothesis. Whatever, the whole thing goes very smoothly. She walked into the National Assembly quite easily, and the only one who stopped her was a guard. The words " *grinned* " and "*invited*" indicate a sense of happiness when the guard sees the reporter, at the same time it poses a kind of welcome attitude towards outside visitors. The attitudinal meaning implied in the word "*grinned*" and "*invited*" in fact sets a basic mood in Kuwait when it treats the outside visitors.

> *Were I a Kuwaiti woman wielding a ballot, I would have been a clearer and more present **danger*** [Judgment: −normality]. *That very day Parliament **blocked*** [Affect: −happiness] *a bill giving women the vote; 29 M. P. s voted **in favor***

[Affect: + happiness] *and 29* ***against*** [Affect: −happiness] , *with two abstentions.* ***Unable to decide*** [Judgment: −capacity] *whether the bill had passed or not, the government scheduled another vote in two weeks* — ***too late*** [Appreciation: −reaction] *for women to* ***register*** [Judgment: − capacity] *for June's municipal elections. The next such elections aren't until 2009.*

In the second paragraph, the authorial attitudinal positioning to the democracy of Kuwait is reflected in the first sentence that is constructed in subjunctive mood. Her hypothesis is that Kuwaiti women once involved in the politic conflicts would be a *"****danger****"* [Judgment: − normality]. This kind of attitudinal positioning may virtually shed light on the unanimous prudence of different sides in Kuwait about the women's right to vote. The affection of the different sides are totally divulged by the linguistic resources of evaluation: *"****blocked****"* [Affect: −happiness], *29 M. P. s voted "****in favour****"* [Affect: + happiness] *and 29 "****against****"* [Affect: −happiness]. This vote proves to be a failure. The future of another vote seems not very bright also under a negative attitudinal evaluation of Appreciation (*"****too late****"* [Appreciation: −reaction]) and a negative attitudinal evaluation of Judgment (*"****to register****"* [Judgment: −capacity]).

In this paragraph, there are 3 authorial positioning, all of which are negative; there are 4 non-authorial positioning, among which there are 3 negative and 1 positive. Whether the reporter or the others concerned, they show no optimistic attitudes towards the present situation and the future of the political rights for the women in Kuwait.

> *Inside the elegant, marbled Parliament itself, a sea of mustachioed men in white robes sat in green seats, debating* ***furiously*** [Affect: −security]. *The ruling emir has* ***pushed for*** [Judgment: + capacity] *women's political rights for years.* ***Ironically*** [Appreciation: − reaction] [Engagement: counter-expect], *the democratically elected legislature has* ***thwarted*** [Affect: − happiness] *him. Traditionalists and tribal leaders are* ***opposed*** [Affect: −happiness]. *Liberals* ***fret*** [Affect: −security] [Engagement: attribute], *too, that Islamists will let their multiple wives vote, swelling conservative ranks. "When I came to Parliament today, people who voted yes* ***didn't even shake hands with me*** [Affect: −happiness]", ***said one Shia clerk*** [Engagement: attribute]. "Why can't we respect each other and work together?"*

Different sides have specifically different attitudes towards the women's political rights in Kuwait. Based on the statistical analysis of the evaluation values in this paragraph, one thing is sure that negative positioning foregrounds positive positioning by 6 : 1. The debate about the women's political rights at least makes the members in the Parliament feel very uneasy and restless because giving women the vote right means the first step to shake some rooted traditional ideas and concepts. The word "*furiously*" realizes this kind of interpersonal meaning that can make the reader form their own judgment about the so-called Kuwaiti style of democracy. Then what are represented to the reader are the specific attitudes towards it. The ruling emir supports it ("*pushed for*" [Judgment: + capacity]); the democratically elected legislature tries every means to stop it (" *thwart* " [Affect: −happiness]); Traditionalists and tribal leaders are against it ("*opposed*" [Affect: −happiness]); Liberals worries the potential consequence of the bill ("*fret*" [Affect: −security]) . Only the ruling emir is positive and active in the movement for women to gain vote right. The others show different degree of negative attitudes towards it. This kind of discourse structure is not a choice by the writer at random, and, in fact, it has appraisal values: the elaboration of the different attitudes towards the bill implies the author's doubt of the title of " democratic superstar" given to Kuwait and criticism of this kind of superficial and hypocritical democracy. Of course, these appraisal values are based on the reporter's own ideological foundation.

The most important feature of the genre as news report is thought to be objectivity. Except for the reporter's own voice, the other voices involved in it may let the reader close to the truth. In this part there are 3 Engagement values ("*ironically*" [Engagement: counter-expect] , *Liberals* "*fret*" [Engagement: attribute] and "*said one Shia clerk*" [Engagement: attribute]) . The first one is categorized into dialogic contraction and the next two are categorized into dialogic expansion. Frequently, counters are aligning rather than disaligning in that they construe the reporter's as sharing this axiological paradigm with the reader. The reporter is presented as just as surprised by this exceptional case as it is assumed the reader will be. In this case, the reporter and the reader both take for granted that the democratically elected legislature will hold the same democratic attitudes towards the women's vote right. Of course, solidarity between the writer and the reader may be at risk if there are any actual readers who don't subscribe to the taken-for-granted axiological paradigm. Under the other two engagement values of attribute, the reader may interpret that the reporter invests nothing in the proposition advanced in the reported material. In fact, the different voices in the news play a role in the negotiation between the reporter and the readers. This kind of negotiation may result in different comprehension among the readers because they are affected by their different social and cultural background. This, to a certain degree, contributes to the subjectivity of the news discourse.

> *Why not indeed? By Gulf standards, Kuwait is a* **democratic superstar** [Appreciation: + reaction] [Engagement: proclaim]. *Its citizens* **enjoy** [Affect: + happiness]*free speech (as long as they don't insult their emir, naturally) and* **boast** [Judgment: −veracity] *a Parliament that can* **actually pass** [Judgment: + capacity] *laws. Unlike their Saudi sisters, Kuwaiti women* **drive, work and travel freely** [Judgment: + capacity]. *They* **run multibillion-dollar businesses** [Judgment: + capacity] *and* **serve as ambassadors** [Judgment: + capacity]. *Their academic* **success** [Affect: + satisfaction] *is* **such** [Appreciation: + reaction] *that colleges have actually lowered the grades required for male students to get into medical and engineering courses. Even then, 70 percent of university students are females.*

This paragraph mainly introduces democracy in Kuwait. From the number of attitudinal analysis, positive values foreground negative value by 8: 1. Therefore, the reporter gives very positive appraisals of democracy in Kuwait. The non-authorial Affect value ("**enjoy**" [Affect: + happiness]) in fact expresses that people in Kuwait are very content with the right to voice their opinions. The word "**boast**" under the Judgment value of negative veracity may influence the reader in their judgment of the proposition advanced, at the same time, it leave room for other alternatives. Bill of the women's vote right may be a good case in point to show that this proposition is not very creditable and at risk of exaggeration. Women in Kuwait, the appraisal of their behaviors are realized by the following linguistic resources ("*Unlike their Saudi sisters, Kuwaiti women* **drive, work and travel freely** [Judgment: + capacity]. *They* **run multibillion-dollar businesses** [Judgment: + capacity] *and* **serve as ambassadors** [Judgement: + capacity]."). The image of Kuwaiti women supported by the appraisals at odds with the traditional and conservative figure covered by the burka in the readers' mind, which seems to have no difference from the western women.

But the second sentence ("*By Gulf standards, Kuwait is a **democratic superstar*** [Appreciation: + reaction].") in this paragraph, on the one hand explicitly realizes the reporter's first-rank evaluation of the democracy in Kuwait, and on the other hand, is implicitly invested with the writer's suspicion of this kind of democracy. By the Engagement analysis of the sentence, it is dialogical contraction: proclaim. This statement is represented as a bare assertion. As we all know, there is no such kind of bare assertion; nothing is completely neutral. All verbal communication occurs against a heteroglossic backdrop of other voices and alternative viewpoints that a rather different picture emerges. The honor granted to Kuwait is based on limited standards: Gulf standards. Hence, on the surface, the sentence is represented as an actual fact, in fact, it opens up channels to different positions, at the same time, the reporter's subjective appraisal of Kuwaiti democracy is implicitly expressed.

> *In Kuwait, the Western **obsession*** [Affect: + security] *with the higab finds its equivalent. At a fancy party for NEWSWEEK's Arabic edition, some Kuwaiti women wore them. Others **opted for*** [Affect: + happiness] *tight, spangled, sheer little numbers in peacock blue or parrot orange. For the party's entertainment, Nancy Ajram, the Arab world's answer to Britney Spears, sang **passionate*** [Appreciation: + reaction] *songs of love in a white **mini-dress*** [Appreciation: + reaction]. *She **couldn't dance*** [Judgment: −capacity] *for us, alas, since shaking one's body on stage is **illegal*** [Judgment: −propriety] *in Kuwait. That didn't stop whole tables of men from raising their camera-enabled mobile phones and clicking her picture.*

Women's life in Kuwait is colorful, and they have much say in the style of their clothing. Higab may let some of them feel a sense of protection that can be seen from the Affect analysis of the word "***obsession***" [Affect: + security]. Others may choose to wear something more fashionable or bright ("***opted for***" [Affect: + happiness]). Nancy Ajram, the most famous pop singer in Lebanon who is comparable to Britney Spears still couldn't shake her body on stage. Based on the two appraisal analyses ("***couldn't dance***" [Judgment: −capacity] and "***illegal***" [Judgment: −propriety]), the reporter continues her doubt and criticism of democracy in Kuwait. Especially, in Kuwait, if a female shakes her body in public, she will be in danger of violating the law. The readers will tend to be influenced by this description and they may reconsider their perception of Kuwaiti democracy especially when they compare it with that of their own countries.

> *You'd think* [Engagement: entertain] *not being able to vote or dance in public would* **anger** [Affect: −happiness] *Kuwait's younger generation of women. To find out, I headed to the malls — Kuwait's archipelago of civic freedom. Eager to* **duck** [Affect: −happiness] *strict parents and the social taboos of dating in public, young Kuwaitis* **have taken to** [Affect: + happiness] *cafes, beaming flirtatious infrared e-mails to one another on their cell photos. At Starbucks in the glittering Al Sharq Mall, I found* **only** [Graduation: quantification] *tables of men, puffing cigarettes and grumbling about the service. At Pizza Hut, I thought I'd got an answer after encountering a young woman who looked every inch the modern suffragette — drainpipe jeans, strappy sliver high-heeled sandals and a higab studded with purple rhinestones.* **But** [Engagement: count-expect] , *no, Miriam Al-Enizi, 20, studying business administration at Kuwait University,* **doesn't think** [Engagement: denial] *women need the vote. "Men are* **better** [Judgment: + capacity] *at politics than women." she explained, adding that women in Kuwait already have everything they need. Welcome to democracy,* **Kuwait style** [Appreciation: − valuation] [Graduation: focus: soften].

In the last paragraph, the authorial and subjective voice assumes that the readers may hold the view that the younger generation of women in Kuwait would be unhappy with the prohibition to vote and dance. The reporter also opens up dialogical room for more alternatives while she introduces what is true about democracy in Kuwait. That is to say, the authorial voice entertains the dialogical alternatives (or potential possibilities). The arrangement may further enhance interactivity between the reporter and the readers. Young Kuwaitis have two totally different affections to their strict parents and the social taboos of dating in public [Affect: −happiness] as well as cafes and flirtatious infrared e-mails [Affect: + happiness]. This contrast clearly shows that Kuwaiti democracy is in question and that Kuwaiti youngsters' concrete behaviors speak louder than words. Of course, this paragraph also gives example to show that some youngsters, including some females, don't care much about the vote right. That is greatly out of the reporter's expectation (*"but"* [Engagement: count-expect]). Miriam Al-Enizi, a young college student, who looked every inch the modern suffragette, gives a negative position that men are better at politics than women. This negation, at the same time, introduces the opposite position that may meet the reporter's expectation.

Hence, the denial in fact is in dialogical context. At last, the reporter gives a final but important evaluation of Appreciation directed at the democracy in Kuwait — Kuwait style. This Appreciation value is not concerned with what is traditional and known as aesthetic, but is based on social qualities the appraiser live with. Democracy in Kuwait, to the reporter and the readers from a western ideological system and values, is not a prototype example. This appraisal value in fact marginalizes the status of Kuwaiti democracy. This appraisal is also open to negotiation, hence it will vary with different social, cultural and ideological backgrounds.

In a summary, this news is full of the reporter's personal experience of democracy in Kuwait, so it carries a comparatively subjective attitude towards the democracy in Kuwait. First, the reporting angle of this news is special, and this news is developed by taking the reporter as the participant of the news. Second, the subjectivity of the news is realized by explicit lexical devices and implicit expressions. Among all the 16 evaluations of Affect, 12 evaluations of Judgment and 8 evaluations of Appreciation, a dominant proportion is realized by lexis carrying strong and obvious emotion. As a reporter with cultural and ideological background of western world, she has quite different understanding about the criteria of democracy. Her evaluation of democracy in Kuwait is conveyed in an indirect way. For example, "*By Gulf standards, Kuwait is a **democratic superstar**"* and "*Welcome to democracy, **Kuwait style**"*, these two Attitudinal evaluations of Appreciation seems positive, but in fact they are implicit ways of expressing the reporter's implied viewpoint that Kuwaiti democracy sounds not very satisfactory. Hence, the subjectivity of this news is mostly realized by lexis with strong emotion and implicit ways of expression.

4. Conclusion

The purpose of the present investigation is to study the realization of the interpersonal meanings in news discourse by Martin's Appraisal Theory. Firstly, Judgment and Appreciation are shown to be dominant attitudes in the sample discourse while Affect scores a low frequency of employment. It indicates that the reporter pays more attention to the human behavior and objects than people's emotions. This also indicates that the reporter's attitudinal tendency is more vaguely implied in linguistic resources of Judgment and Appreciation in the discourse, Secondly, the analysis shows that there is an active interaction between the reporter's voice and other voices. More contraction resources are found in sample discourse (57%). Thirdly, the reporter of the sample discourses employs more "force" than "focus" to amplify the evaluation with a percentage of 67%. It can be concluded that the reporter tends to intensify her evaluation and to enhance the proposition being advanced in the discourse by using more force-raising. At the same time the reporter try her best to align the readers in the proposition.

This analysis will help the reader to gain a critical comprehension of news discourse and therefore form their own judgment, at the same time it will bring some enlightenment to the English Reading and Writing Teaching.

References

Iedema, R. S. Feez & P. R. R. White. 1994. *Media Literacy*. Sydney: Disadvantaged Schools Program, NSW Department of School Education. Available at: www. grammatics.com/appraisal/Medialit-Comment.pdf.

Martin, J. R. & P. R. R. White. 2008. *The Language of Evaluation: Appraisal in English*. Beijing: Foreign Language Teaching and Research Press.

Martin, J. R. & D. Rose. 2007. *Working with Discourse: Meaning beyond the Clause*. Beijing: Peking University Press.

Martin, J. R. 2003. *Introduction*. (Special Issue on *Negotiating Heteroglossia: Social Perspectives on Evaluation*). *Text*, 23 (2): 171–181.

White, P. R. R. 2001. *Appraisal: An Overview*. Available at: www. grammatics. com/appraisal/AppraisalGuide/Framed/Frame.

White, P. R. R. 1998. *Telling Media Tales: The News Story as Rhetoric*. Unpublished PhD. Dissertation, Department of Linguistics, University of Sydney, Sydney.

李荣娟. 2005. 英语专栏语篇中态度意义的评价理论视角.《山东外语教学》,(4):30—35.

王振华. 2004. 硬新闻的态度研究——"评价系统"应用研究之二.《外语教学》,(5):31—35.

The Characterization of Lady Bracknell: Conversation Analysis in *The Importance of Being Earnest*

Luo Jianting (**Sichuan University of Arts and Science**)

Abstract: Conversation Analysis (CA hence forth), based on pragmatics, can be an effective means to the exploration of the dramatic dialogue in *The Importance of Being Earnest*. Lady Bracknell's power in the conversation and her role in creating dramatic conflicts are illustrated by analyzing the topic control, turn-taking, turn length and turn type in CA.

Key words: *The Importance of Being Earnest*; Conversation Analysis; pragmatic stylistics

1. Introduction

As the last and one of the most famous dramas of Oscar Wilde, *The Importance of Being Earnest* enjoyed most revivals for its conversations, and is different from Wilde's previous comedies. The play presents us with two young men with fictitious identities to escape unwelcome social obligations. It is replete with witty dialogues and satirizes some of the foibles and hypocrisy in religion, love, marriage, education and politics of late Victorian society (Wilde, 1994). Though critics and scholars abroad or at home try various approaches to analyze and study *The Importance of Being Earnest* from different perspectives for different purposes and therefore come out a large number of articles and books which do help to understand this play, it is still necessary to make further research on this novel from a brand-new angle.

According to Richards (1992: 156), CA refers to "the analysis of natural conversation in order to discover what the linguistic characteristics of conversation are and how conversation is used in ordinary life". CA investigates conversations of all kinds from all walks of life in all areas at all levels through all channels, thus as the written conversation, dialogues in plays can also be analyzed by CA. The analytic aspects of CA is generally agreed to include the topic control, turn-taking, turn length, turn type, interruption, monologue and so on. As in the written conversation, interruption and overlaps are usually reduced; therefore the thesis is mainly to discuss the former several aspects.

2. Conversation Analysis

There are several terms associated with CA. One of the most basic elements of conversation is turn-taking, which is seen as everything one speaker says before another speaker begins to speak. Turns can be words, phrases, clauses, or sentences and so on. And one of the linguistic features of conversations which tend to be modified in dramatic texts is the way turns are taken, i.e. the way people have a conversation organizes who is going to speak next. If one speaker keep talking at the same time as the other one do, over long stretches of the other one's turn, then the talk would probably become less of a collaborative conversation, and more of a confrontation.

How much a character talks can be indicative either of their relative importance in the play, or of how important they appear to think they are. Generally, central characters have longer and more speeches than minor characters. However, some main characters may have fewer long speeches, and the minor characters may have a big talk, which is of great significance in the characterization and the development of the plots (Gee, 1999). As to this play, Lady Bracknell is always found producing lengthy utterance, which is, of course, a striking feature of this character.

For adjacency pair, it is a model frequently proposed as a common structure for exchanges between speakers, and used subsequently in much work in conversation analysis, or, we say, a sequence of two related utterances by two different speakers, with the second utterance being a response to the first. Typical adjacency pairs are two-part exchanges such as greeting-greeting, question-answer, and request-response. A question predicts an answer and a reply "presupposes" a question (Grice, 1975). And some responses in oral discourse could be expected. Adjacency pairs underlie some principles governing the ways in which interlocutors respond to specific utterances. For example, adjacency pairs are determined by one of the rules agreed on by speakers such as "Having produced a first part of some pair, current speaker must stop speaking, and next speaker must produce at that point a second part to the same pair." (Levinson, 1983: 304)

3. Turn Distribution and Their Pragmatic Implicatures in the Play

3.1 The Initiation and Control of Topics in the Play

Jack, the protagonist of the play, is in love with Lady Bracknell's daughter, Gwendolen, and proposes to her without the permission of Lady Bracknell. While Lady Bracknell is against their relationship for she knows nothing about Jack, thus after departing Gwendolen, she initiates the conversation with Jack.

Conversation 1

> **T1. _Lady Bracknell_.** *[Sitting down.] You can take a seat, Mr. Worthing. (1) [Looks in her pocket for note-book and pencil.]*
>
> **T2. _Jack_.** *Thank you, Lady Bracknell, I prefer standing. (2)*
>
> **T3. _Lady Bracknell_.** *[Pencil and note-book in hand.] I feel bound to tell you that you are not down on my list of eligible young men, although I have the same list as the dear Duchess of Bolton has. (3) We work together, in fact. (4) However, I am quite ready to enter your name, should your answers be what a really affectionate mother requires. (5) Do you smoke? (6)*
>
> **T4. _Jack_.** *Well, yes, I must admit I smoke. (7)*
>
> **T5. _Lady Bracknell_.** *I am glad to hear it. (8) A man should always have an occupation of some kind. (9) There are far too many idle men in London as it is. (10) How old are you? (11)*
>
> **T6. _Jack_.** *Twenty-nine. (12)*
>
> **T7. _Lady Bracknell_.** *A very good age to be married at. (13) I have always been of opinion that a man who desires to get married should know either everything or nothing. (14) Which do you know? (15)*
>
> **T8. _Jack_.** *[After some hesitation.] I know nothing, Lady Bracknell. (16)*
>
> **T9. _Lady Bracknell_.** *I am pleased to hear it. (17) I do not approve of anything that tampers with natural ignorance. (18) Ignorance is like a delicate exotic fruit; touch it and the bloom is gone. (19) The whole theory of modern*

education is radically unsound. (20) Fortunately in England, at any rate, education produces no effect whatsoever. (21) If it did, it would prove a serious danger to the upper classes, and probably lead to acts of violence in Grosvenor Square. (22) What is your income? (23)

T10. *Jack*. Between seven and eight thousand a year. (24)

T11. *Lady Bracknell*. [Makes a note in her book.] In land, or in investments? (25)

T12. *Jack*. In investments, chiefly. (26)

T13. *Lady Bracknell*. That is satisfactory. (27) What between the duties expected of one during one's lifetime, and the duties exacted from one after one's death, land has ceased to be either a profit or a pleasure. (28) It gives one position, and prevents one from keeping it up. (29) That's all that can be said about land. (30)

(P19-20, Act I)

In **Conversation 1**, the initiation and control of the topic is obviously made by Lady Bracknell. And from the context, we know that Jack proposes to her daughter and Lady Bracknell is absolutely against it, and she believes she has the right to know everything about Jack, and then she just initiates the topic and controls topic throughout the conversation, "*You can take a seat.*", "*Do you smoke?*", "*How old are you?*", "*What is your income?*", while what Jack does is nothing but make response to her questions, "*Thank you, Lady Bracknell, I prefer standing.*", "*Well, yes, I must admit I smoke.*", "*Twenty-nine.*" and "*Between seven and eight thousand a year.*" The power and the domination of the character can be easily revealed by their conversation.

Each time Jack replies her question, Lady Bracknell does not go on with the next question immediately but makes some comments on the issue concerned, however, Jack never says anything more than required, which shows us the power and authorities of Lady Bracknell in the conversation and in their relationship.

More disquieting than questions themselves is the order in which Lady Bracknell asks them. Before she gets to such matters as age, income and family, she wants to know if Jack smokes (T3), and she is pleased to hear that he does, since she considers smoking the cure to idleness. Such trivial questions suggest the vacuity of London society, where more weighty issues are of secondary importance. Wilde uses Lady Bracknell's interview of Jack to make fun of the values of London society, which put a higher value on social connections than on character or goodness.

The same can be perceived in the following conversation, when Lady Bracknell follows her daughter to Jack's house in the country and finds the four young people there.

Conversation 2

> **T1. Lady Bracknell.** *Come here. (1) Sit down immediately. (2) Hesitation of any kind is a sign of mental decay in the young, of physical weakness in the old. (3) [Turns to Jack.] Apprised, sir, of my daughter's sudden flight by her trusty maid, whose confidence I purchased by means of a small coin, I followed her at once by a luggage train. (4) Her unhappy father is, I am glad to say, under the impression that she is attending a more than usually lengthy lecture by the University Extension Scheme on the Influence of a permanent income on Thought. (5) I do not propose to undeceive him. (6) Indeed I have never undeceived him on any question. (7) I would consider it wrong. (8) But of course, you will clearly understand that all communication between yourself and my daughter must cease immediately from this moment. (9) On this point, as indeed on all points, I am firm. (10)*
>
> **T2. Jack.** *I am engaged to be married to Gwendolen Lady Bracknell! (11)*
>
> **T3. Lady Bracknell.** *You are nothing of the kind, sir. (12) And now, as regards Algernon! (13)... Algernon! (14)*
>
> **T4. Algernon.** *Yes, Aunt Augusta. (15)*

(P56, Act III)

In this conversation, what is most significant is the turn initiated, dominated and controlled by Lady Bracknell. Her first turn is really a long one (more than 130 words) without any room or willingness for others to interrupt or, we say, to take their turns, though, we know there are quite a lot of people present. First, she chooses her first interlocutor, her daughter, by asking her to come and sit down beside her with two direct and firm imperatives ((1) and (2) in T1), and Gwendolen, we can imagine, just follows her direction, for if she had not done so, her mother would not have turned to Jack and chosen him as her second interlocutor. After a long narration and comments on what has happened, she tells Jack that he must stay away from her daughter, which of course arouses Jack's objection. However, regardless of Jack's pretest, Lady Bracknell confirms her ground on the matter and then continues to choose her next interlocutor Algernon. So, although there are many people present, Lady Bracknell firmly controls the topic and the turn sequence of the conversation. It is she who decides what to talk about and which person to talk with.

As a social climber and spokesperson for the status quo, Lady Bracknell's behavior enforces social discrimination and excludes those who do not fit into her new class. Her daughter's unsuitable marriage is an excellent example of how she flexes her muscles. She sees marriage as an alliance for property and social security; while love or passion is not part of the mix. Jack will be placed on her list of eligible suitors only if he can pass her unpredictable and difficult test. Lady Bracknell's authority and power are extended over every character in the play. Her decision about the suitability of both marriages provides the conflict of the story. She interrogates both Jack and Cecily, bribes Gwendolen's maid, and looks down her nose at both Chasuble and Prism. Wilde humorously makes Lady Bracknell the tool of the conflict, and much of the satire. For the play to end as a comedy, her objections and obstacles must be dealt with and overcome.

3. 2 Turn Length in the Play

How much a character talks can be indicative either of their relative importance in the play, or of how important they appear to think they are. Generally, central characters have longer and more speeches than minor characters. However, there may be some deviation in case a particular character is to be portrayed in the play. Let us look at the turn distribution in **Conversation 1**:

Fig. 1 Turn Distribution in Conversation 1

Characters	Words	Turns	Average Number of Words in Each Turn	Sentences	Average Number of Words in Each Sentence
Jack	30	6	5	6	5
Lady Bracknell	264	7	37.5	22	12
Total	294	13	23	28	10.5

In the play, Jack is, undoubtedly, one of the central characters; however, compared with Lady Bracknell, he speaks less. This is not because Lady Bracknell is relatively more important in the play, but because she, being bossy, social snobbish and sophisticated, believes she is important in her social circle. As in **Conversation 1**, Lady Bracknell has seven turns and Jack has six; however there are 264 words in her speech and 30 words in Jack's. Jack, the hero, has much fewer speeches than Lady Bracknell, since he is just in the position to provide necessary information she asks, and more speeches would have implied that he is somewhat aggressive and lacks respect to the senior. The dialogue just presents us a vivid picture of Lady Bracknell who is powerful, arrogant, and ruthless to the extreme. As a ruthless social climber and spokesperson for the status quo, Lady Bracknell's behavior enforces social discrimination and excludes those who do not fit into her new class. However, as a guardian who has got the fortune from Cecily's father, and as a young man interrogated by the elder lady who would be his mother-in-law, Jack wisely knows how to behave in the dialogue. To be modest and docile seems to be the best strategy in his conversation.

And in **Conversation 2**, among the four turns of the three main characters, two for Lady Bracknell, one for Jack and one for Algernon, a striking difference between the turn lengths can be applied to perceive the personality and inner world of the characters. **T1** is incredibly long with 136 words in which a vivid picture of a bossy, talkative and imperial woman from the upper-class is presented to the reader, that is to say, she is able to go round and round with other characters on witty epigrams and sharp replies, and she never fails to comment on anything: society, marriage, religion, money, illness, death, and respectability. She is powerful, arrogant, ruthless to the extreme, and conservative. In many ways, she represents Wilde's impression of Victorian upper-class negativity, conservative and repressive values. Just like Algernon, she is one of Wilde's inventions to present his satire on these subjects.

Fig. 2 Turn Distribution in Conversation 2

Characters	Words	Turns	Average Number of Words in Each Turn	Sentences	Average Number of Words in Each Sentence
Lady Bracknell	148	2	74	13	11
Jack	10	1	10	1	10
Algernon	3	1	3	1	3
Total	161	4	40	15	11

Both Jack and Algernon are central characters in the play, the pace-setters of the plot. In **Conversation 2**, however, how much they talk is strikingly different from their previous conversations, in which they always have hot debate and give each other tit for tat. In **Conversation 3**, though Jack has six turns, he just produces 68 words, while Algernon has two turns with 81 words. In the six turns of Jack, he produces 10 sentences, and each sentence has less than 7 words in average, from which we can sense that Jack is so indignant that he just utters short sentences to show his indignity and disgust towards Algernon. On the other hand, in the two turns of Algernon, he comes up with 4 sentences (20 words each), for he has predicted the situation and seems much calmer to say longer sentences to comfort Jack and defense himself as well.

3. 3 Turn Type and Adjacency Pair in the Play

To understand turn type, we should know what is adjacency pairs first. An adjacency pair is a term used in CA to refer to a pair of conversational turns by two different speakers and the production of the first turn (a first-pair part) makes a response (a second-pair part) of a particular kind of relevance. These involve the patterns like greeting-greeting, question-answer, and request-response.

For example, in **Conversation 1**, the pattern of the first adjacency pair is request-response, but that of the rest is definitely question-answer:

> **T1. Lady Bracknell.** [*Sitting down.*] *You can take a seat, Mr. Worthing.* [*Looks in her pocket for note-book and pencil.*]
>
> **T2. Jack.** *Thank you, Lady Bracknell, I prefer standing.*
>
> (P 19, Act I)

Lady Bracknell asks the question and Jack answers without any intention to initiate a new topic or to control the conversation due to his social position and immediate situation (being questioned by the would-be mother-in-law from the upper-class). That is to say, Lady Bracknell totally controls the topic and turn-taking, which just shows Lady Bracknell's dominating power over her interlocutor and her imperious manner in the conversation. However, Jack, as his fake name "Ernest" suggests, appears to be a docile and sincere, who just tries to be cooperative as much as he can.

And in **Conversation 2**, the last two sentences in **T1** serve as an implied request: *You should cease the communication with Gwendolen*. And T2 functions as an implied response or protest: *I would not cease the communication with Gwendolen*. It can also be put into the category of a new request: *I want to continue the communication with Gwendolen*. Therefore, in **T3**, Lady Bracknell makes a response to it by refusing his request. And she initiates a new adjacency pair with a request to call Algernon's attention in this turn, to which Algernon responses immediately. So, in the four turns, we can find three adjacency pairs of request-response instead of two, because some turns can be categorized into both the second part in the first pair and the first part in the second pair.

In **Conversation 3**, the adjacency pairs are not clear-cut. In **T3** and **T4**, it's request-response (**T3**. *Cecily. Uncle Jack, you are not going to refuse your own brother's hand?* **T4**. *Jack. Nothing will induce me to take his hand. I think his coming down here disgraceful. He knows perfectly well why.*) , and in **T6** and **T7**, it's question-answer (**T6**. *Jack. Oh! He has been talking about Bunbury, has he?* **T7**. *Cecily. Yes, he has told me all about poor Mr. Bunbury, and his terrible state of health.*). Though **T3** seems like a question, it serves to be a request to ask Jack to shake hands with Algernon, to which Jack rejects in **T4**. And in **T6**, Jack raises the question though he surely knows what the fact will be, about which Cecily gets no idea, and provides him the answer.

4. Summary

Lady Bracknell is not the protagonist of the play, but she impresses the reader a lot with the conversations she is involved in. A lot about her character and her authorities over the other characters can be perceived from CA, in which the initiation and control of topics, the turn length, the turn type as well as the adjacency pair have been discussed in this paper. The detailed analysis of CA is given to the three conversations of the play, and immediately followed by a statistic and contrastive analysis of the linguistic resources to reveal Lady Bracknell's authority in these conversations and her image as a powerful, arrogant and ruthless upper-class woman.

References

Gee, J. P. 1999. *An Introduction to Discourse Analysis: Theory and Method*. London: Routledge.

Grice, P. 1975. Logic and conversation. In Cole, P. & J. Morgan. (eds.). *Syntax and Semantics*. New York: Academic Press, (3): 41–58.

Levinson, S. C. 1983. *Pragmatics*. Cambridge: Cambridge University Press.

Richards, J. C. & R. Schmidt. 1992. *Longman Dictionary of Language Teaching and Applied Linguistics*. London: Longman.

Wilde, O. 1994. *The Importance of Being Earnest*. Penguin Popular Classics.

Part VI Style and Translation Studies

The Style(s) of a Classic in Translation and Back-Translation

Feng Zongxin (**Tsinghua University**)

Abstract: The study of style or styles in literary texts had not explicitly taken the translational perspective into account until very lately; and back-translation, generally assumed as putting a text back to its original language, has attracted even less scholarly attention in translation studies. This paper, taking Jakobson's ideas as points of departure, discusses several aspects of translation and deals with the style(s) of a literary classic in more than a hundred languages and its back-translation in a recent worldwide project. Focusing on an excerpt of the text back-translated from several languages, the paper displays how some key points in the classic were linguistically and stylistically dealt with by the original translators into their own languages and how translations of translations were done. It proposes that the enterprise of back-translating can take a literary classic as an object of linguistic and stylistic reflection and literary appreciation; it not only brings subtle issues of stylistic concern to the fore, but also serves as a practical approach to translation studies from linguistic and stylistic perspectives.

Key words: style; stylistics; translation; back-translation; translation of translation; *Alice in Wonderland*

1. Introduction

The study of style or styles in literary texts had not explicitly taken the translational perspective into account until the late 1990s. In fact, Roman

Jakobson (1896-1982), the Russian-American linguist and literary theorist, did mention the translation of a few typical lines from Russian wedding songs (about the apparition of the bridegroom) in his seminal "Closing Statement: Linguistics and Poetics" at the Indiana Style Conference in 1958. This only instance of dealing with style from a translational perspective (Jakobson, 1960: 369) in the modern era may have been eclipsed by the theme of the whole paper, but his important observations on the linguistic aspects of translation (Jakobson, 1959) have not aroused sufficient attention in the study of literary style, either. This paper, by taking as the point of departure Jakobson's ideas on the linguistic aspects of translation and his trichotomy of translation practices, will discuss issues in the translation and back-translation of a world classic and see what roles translational perspectives can play on the study of style or styles of a world classic that has been translated into over a hundred languages.

2. Linguistic Aspects of Translation

Jakobson is one of the earliest linguists and semioticians to attach great importance to linguistic aspects of translation. In his "On Linguistic Aspects of Translation", Jakobson (1959) observes that equivalence in difference is the "cardinal problem of language and the pivotal concern of linguistics"; like any receiver of verbal messages, the linguist acts as their "interpreter". Since no linguistic specimen may be interpreted by the science of language without a translation of its signs into other signs of the same system or into signs of another system, translating activities "must be kept under constant scrutiny by linguistic science". He also distinguishes "three ways of interpreting a verbal sign", i.e., it may be translated into other signs of the same language, into another language, or into another, nonverbal system of symbols". He labels these three kinds of translation as (1) "intralingual translation or rewording", (2) "interlingual translation or translation proper", and (3) "intersemiotic translation or transmutation". He observes that the most frequent practice is "interlingual translation" or "translation proper", which "substitutes messages in one language not for separate code-units but for entire messages in same other language". It is a "reported speech", in which the translator recodes and transmits a message received from another source, involving "two equivalent messages in two different codes".

Lambert (2009: 85–86) writes that "the simple one-to-one translation is an illusion", specifically in law, since one-to-one translation may mean the kind of formal correspondence and imply translating the terms in the original language by the same number of terms in the target language, more or less in the same order and with parallel or identical syntactic functions. However, translation seems to function well only as long as no quarrel comes up. While the relationship between two or more texts is supposed to be unproblematic in both directions, scholars know that translation is never symmetrical, and that "back-translation is an illusion", meaning that equivalence is dependent on conventions, even on the illusion of similarity, and that any translated text is "another text".

In the Introduction to his *The Pragmatics of Translation* (1998), Leo Hickey writes, since the mechanisms available to signal the distinction between theme and rheme (or given information and new information) may vary from language to language, a translator then has to decide how to convey the theme-rheme structure of an original text using whatever means the target language can offer. A "good fit" requires replication of the original theme-rheme structure, communicative value, message and thrust, while respecting the target language's grammar and style. Yet, just as willingness to risk deviance may mark a good writer, so also it may mark a good translator (Hickey, 1998: 6–7).

3. Back-Translation as a Technique and Strategy

Back-translation, namely, the process of translating back a statement or paragraph to its original language, has not attracted much scholarly attention, although it has been playing some important roles in cross-linguistic studies.

In discussing "grammatical translation", Catford (1965: 71) mentions a back-translation of an Arabic clause-structure into English to show an approximate morpheme-rank-bound. Miracle (1988) carried out an empirical study of the usefulness of back-translation as a "technique" for international advertising messages.

In discussing "creativity in translation" in his *Paragraphs on Translation*, Newmark (1993: 39) writes that the creative element is "circumscribed" and it "hovers" when translation is impossible or the standard translation procedures fail; if creativity dominates a text, the translation becomes an adaptation, an idiosyncratic interpretation which can hardly be verified. Thus, he thinks that at least an approximate verification is the scientific element in an appraisal of any translation, and this can be done "where there are correspondences to be assessed through back-translation". In the same book, Newmark (1993: 118) simply calls back-translation as "translation of translation", and declares his interest (common with Baker's) in it "to explain an example from a language the reader may not know" and "as a yardstick for the truth".

For the purpose of introducing readers to "the world of translation", Baker uses an example of translation by cultural substitution from Stephen Hawking's *Brief History of Time*, and then quotes the target text back-translated from Greek. The only study of back-translation mentioned in the second edition of Baker and Saldanha's *Routledge Encyclopedia of Translation Studies* (2009: 107) was done by Klaudy (1996). It was the back translation between English and Hungarian as "a tool for detecting explicitation strategies in translation" on the assumption that such strategies are "universal" and "independent of language pair and direction of translation".

In his "Text Politeness: A Semiotic Regime for a More Interactive Pragmatics", Basil Hatim (1998) elaborates on the procedure of assessing how a given rendering can secure optimal reception in the target language which would most certainly take precedence over all other criteria. In doing this, he uses some "samples" of back-translation from Arabic to show his points. In one case, he observes that when source-text function is not purely information-imparting, departures from norms of politeness must be appreciated for what they are and rendered intact, if only to draw attention to them or even to shock the target reader. An example is taken from a novel to show how text politeness is compromised predominantly due to sociocultural factors, with the conclusion that the published translation into English misleadingly re-negotiates predominantly socio-cultural politeness of text (or the deliberate absence of it). In another case, he observes that in the absence of the translator's much-needed intervention, a sample (abstract of an academic article) would by all the criteria be deemed to have contravened norms of text politeness in English.

Newmark (1998: 205) writes that a target language to source language dictionary is always useful for the purposes of back-translation which is "normally a part of any checking or revision process in translation". As he has observed, in the middle stages, translation from language 2 to language 1 of words and clauses may be useful in dealing with errors; therefore interference, interlanguage or unconscious translationese can be illuminated by back-translation, as an aid in the production of creative discourse or texts. He assumes that texts as such will not be translated, but occasionally translation from language 2 to language 1 is useful for the expansion of source language vocabulary, particularly for items within one semantic field or topic, and this becomes an "exercise in synonymy" (Newmark, 1991: 61).

Against this background, the case to be discussed is the checking of the translations of a world classic into over a hundred languages and back into modern English.

4. *Alice* in Translation

Certainly *Alice's Adventures in Wonderland* by the English mathematician Lewis Carroll is not the only work that has been translated worldwide, but perhaps no other work has aroused as much attention as *Alice* has. It is a children's book, and due to its comic nature and its primary target readership, it can hardly fall into the category of "elite" literature. Yet, since its publication in 1865 under the pseudonym of Lewis Carroll, *Alice* has fascinated adults as well as youngsters across the world — by the time of Carroll's death in 1898, *Alice* had become the most popular children's book in England. By the time of Carroll's centenary in 1932, *Alice* had become one of the most popular and perhaps the most famous literary work in the world. Up till now, it has been translated into over 120 languages (and 174 varieties of languages or different systems of codes). Of all western literary masterpieces introduced/translated to China in the twentieth century since the May Fourth Movement, no other work has enjoyed such popularity (Feng, 2009: 242; 2015a: 187).

Alice had not drawn much scholarly attention from a translational perspective until very recently. On October 24, 1866, Lewis Carroll wrote to his publisher Macmillan that his friends in Oxford seemed to think that "the book is untranslatable into either French or German, the puns and songs being the chief obstacles". But only several months later, he wrote to Macmillan that he had been strongly advised to try a translation of it into French, and that the great difficulty is "to find a man fit to try it", and "to find someone ... to have some sort of sympathy with the style" (Weaver, 1964: 33).

The earliest translations of *Alice* into other languages are the 1869 German and French editions. The other seven editions in the nineteenth century are the 1870 Swedish *Alices Äventyr i Sagolandet*, the 1872 Italian *Le Avventure di Alice nel Paese delle Meraviglie*, the 1875 Dutch *De avonturen van Alice in Wonderland* (abridged), the 1875 Danish *Alice i eventyrland*, the 1879 Russian Соня въ царствѣ дива, the 1889 Callendar's Cursive Shorthand (Chapter VII only), and the 1899 Dutch (the first complete Dutch translation).

The nine editions in the twentieth century prior to the first Chinese translation (by Zhao Yuanren, or better known as Yuen Ren Chao, 1922) are the 1903 Norwegian, the 1906 Finnish, the 1906 Edition for the Blind (printed in embossed type rather than modern Braille), the 1909 Pitman Shorthand, the 1910 Esperanto, the 1915 Gregg Shorthand, the 1920 Japanese, and the 1921 Braille (Cf. Weaver, 1964).

The first comprehensive and scholarly study of *Alice* in translation is Warren Weaver's *Alice in Many Tongues* (1964). When the book was published, there were translations of *Alice* in only 47 languages (with Shorthand and Braille editions included, although they are not exactly translations, as stated in a note by Weaver (1964: 110)). Half a century later, when a more comprehensive and scholarly study of *Alice* in translation is published in the three-volume *Alice in a World of Wonderlands* (Lindseth, 2015b), there are *Alice* translations in 174 languages, variations of languages and codes.

The year 2015 will witness the Sesquicentennial for the publication of *Alice's Adventures in Wonderland*. The Lewis Carroll Society of North America will hold a conference and host other related activities in New York in October, 2015: "*Alice* 150: Celebrating Wonderland". At the time the *Alice* Project started in around 2009, it was known that there were *Alice* translations in 90 languages. As the Project proceeded, many more were known and the number of languages in translation became 120 plus, and finally reaching 174, including dialects and variations of a number of languages.

These translations fall into two of Jakobson's classification, i.e., "interlingual" and "intersemiotic". Although the project does not include the third type of translation, the "intralingual", the number of editions for simplified versions of *Alice* in English can be very large, along with even larger numbers of simplified editions in other languages.

The 144 interlingual translations range alphabetically from Afrikaans to Zulu, with seven dialectal translations, in Appalachian, Cockney, Cornish-English, Middle English, Old English, Scouse, and Sussex. There are 13 intersemiotic translations such as English in other alphabets, including 7 unusual orthographies (i.e., Deseret, Ewellic, International Phonetic Alphabet, Nyctographic Square Alphabet, QR Barcode, Shaw and Unifon) and the Alphagram, Braille, Ciphers and Codes, Wakeling, Ñspel, and the Shorthand. And there are translations in 8 constructed languages, such as Blissymbols, Esperanto, Lingua Franca Nova, Lingwa de Planeta, Lojban, Neo, Sambahsa, and Volapük (Cf. Lindseth, 2015).

One of the principal and remarkable points in this worldwide activity is a special case of back-translation. It is noteworthy in several respects: the nature of the text in question, the variety of the translated texts worldwide, the number of languages, the original purpose of the activity, the number of back-translators involved, and the light that the whole enterprise can shed on the stylistics of translation and Translation Studies.

5. *Alice* in Back-Translation

Of the 47 translations collected for the first time in the history of *Alice*, Weaver (1964) "re-translated" (i.e., back-translated) only 14: Chinese, Danish, French, German, Hebrew, Hungarian, Italian, Japanese, Pidgin, Polish, Russian, Spanish, Swahili and Swedish. He particularly studied the translation of the "Twinkle, twinkle" verse (in Chapter 7) and listed some "principal problems" as he sees "from the adult point of view", which are: (A) verses; (B) puns; (C) the use of specially manufactured words or nonsense; (D) jokes which involve logic; and (E) words with a twist of meaning. And these became largely the points to be continued in the back-translation in the project of *Alice* 150.

The *Alice* Project recruited over the years more than 200 translators to back-translate pages 103 to 110 of the Macmillan red cloth edition of *Alice* (Carroll, 1865). In addition to back-translating these pages, participants for back-translating are requested to interpret what the original translator did and how he or she approached the problem; and to explain the word choices and customs of the region that affected the original translator. In cases where the original translator made significant changes from Carroll (as the English nonsense made little sense in the foreign language) and the translator wanted to appeal to local readers, back-translators are requested to bring the specific point out for the targeted reader of the *Alice* Project.

Following Weaver's practice in 1964, the guiding principles of back-translating in the Project 150 are as follows (designed by Jon A. Lindseth, the Organizer and the General Editor of the 2015 books): While Weaver selected those pages as they test the ability of the translator to handle a number of difficult parts of Carroll nonsense writing, the new project focuses on these pages as a handy piece to examine many more points of interest to a larger group of translators and for a wider audience. He later adds that a back-translation is not necessarily the same as Lewis Carroll's original, and explicitly spells out the guideline that literal translation is preferred even if the original translator meant to represent Carroll's wording in his or her original.

While the main concerns of the back-translation project is to analyze the original translator's method of translating the five aspects as Weaver labels in 1964, this paper will only take the book title ("Alice's Adventures in Wonderland") and the first 13 lines of the *Alice* Chapter text corresponding to pages 103 to 110 of the Macmillan red cloth edition (Carroll, 1865) for display and analysis, since they contain several aspects worthy of linguistic and stylistic analysis:

> "'*Twinkle, twinkle, little bat!*
> *How I wonder what you're at*!'
> You know the song, perhaps?"
> "I've heard something like it," said Alice.
> "It goes on, you know," the Hatter continued, "in this way: —
> '*Up above the world you fly,*
> *Like a tea-tray in the sky.*

Twinkle, twinkle —'"

Here the Dormouse shook itself, and began singing in its sleep "*Twinkle, twinkle, twinkle, twinkle* —" and went on so long that they had to pinch it to make it stop.

(Carroll, 1865: 103−104)

I have omitted all the extra spacing between certain lines in the text quoted here and the back-translated texts that will follow, not because they are stylistically unimportant, but only to save space.

An overwhelming majority of the 174 languages are foreign and unintelligible to us. Although we do not read, for instance, Indonesian or Hebrew or Thai, we can get some rough ideas about what the original translators did simply by reading their back-translations in the 2015 book.

The book title of the 2009 Jakarta edition of the Indonesian *Alice* remains in English, and the part of the text is back-translated as:

"'Flicker-flicker, cute little bat.

From where do you protrude?'

Do you know that song?"

"Yes, I've heard a song like that," said Alice.

"The next bit," said the Hat Maker, "is like this:

'Above the world you fly

Like a tea tray in the clouds.

Flicker-flicker —'"

The Dormitory Mouse [Dorm Mouse] shook his body and began to sing in his sleep. "*Flicker-flicker, flicker-flicker, flicker-flicker* —" He continued singing for a long time until they had to pinch him to make him stop.

(Lindseth, 2015b: 287)

It is really interesting to read the back-translated text from a stylistic perspective. Obviously, the indention, italicization, and the single quotation marks for the verse lines are not exactly those in the original. And variations in phonological, lexical, and syntactic aspects are all there for the reader to see what actually happened in the 2009 translation from English into Indonesian.

The back-translated text part of the 1997 Hebrew edition is:

"'Wink-a-wink, [2] you little bat! [3]

But you're blinking, [4] why is that?'

Do you happen to know this poem?"

"I've heard something like it," said Alice.

"There's more," the Hatter went on, "It goes like this:

'There above our heads you fly:

Tray-like on the cypress high!

Wink-a-wink —'"

At this point the Dormouse[5] shook itself and started singing in its sleep:
"Wink-a-wink-a-wink-a" — and went on for so long that they had to pinch it to
make it stop.

(Lindseth, 2015b: 258−259)

The uppercase numbers [2] to [5] indicate four notes in the back-translation,
which are altogether 229 words. Note 1, which is not quoted here, explains
the title, saying that the original translator "strives for functional equivalence"
and "it is accompanied by Gardner's notes and additional notes by Litvin (the
original translator)". Note 2 explains that the original Hebrew translation has a
note also including Litvin's translation of Jane Taylor's poem, "The Star",
which is the object of Carroll's parody according to Gardner"; Carroll's
"twinkle" has been replaced with the Hebrew word for "wink"; the two-
syllable Hebrew word for "twinkle" does not fit the rhythm and "wink" has
been preferred because it is funny and similar to "twinkle". Note 3 says:
Gardner explains that "Bat" was the nickname of an Oxford professor of
mathematics. Litvin adds another explanation based on Mavis Batey's *Alice's
Adventures in Oxford* (1980): Carroll had a bat-toy which once "flew" out of
the window, scared a servant walking near-by and made him drop the tea-tray
he was carrying. Note 4 says: In Hebrew: *te'af'ef*. Positioned in the Hebrew
translation at the end of the second line, *te'af'ef* rhymes with *atalef*, Hebrew
for "bat", which ends the first line. It also creates a pun because it echoes
te'ofef ("you will fly"). Note 5 says: Litvin uses the Hebrew idiom *la-harog
et ha-zman* which literally means "to kill time". She explains that while in
English "to murder time" means to distort the rhythm of a song, in Hebrew
"killing time" means "spending it somehow so as not to get bored". Despite
the difference in meaning, she has translated the English idiom literally
because the resulting Hebrew idiom fits in quite well.

The title in the 2009 Bangkok edition of the Thai *Alice* is back-translated
as "Alice in the Land of Amazement", and the part of the text is back-
translated as follows:

> " ' *Twinkle, twinkle, little bat!*
> *How I wonder what you're at*! [1]
> Twinkan, twinkan, [2] littan bat
> I wonder what you will do. ' [3]
> You've probably heard this song, yes?"
> "I've heard one very alike," replied Alice.
> "There's more to it," the Hat-maker [4] said, "It's sung...
> ' *Above our heads you fly back and forth*
> *Like a tea-tray on the distant sky.*
> *Twinkan, twinkan...* ' "

Mouse lifted his body and sang along while still asleep, repeating the word over and over, "Twinkan, twinkan, twinkan, twinkan," until his friends had to pinch him to stop his mouth.

(Lindseth, 2015b: 678-679)

Obviously there are changes in uses of indention, punctuation marks, and other features in the English version of the Thai text. Many more subtle things have been explained in notes. Note 1 says "Words in italics appear in English in the original", implying that the Thai text copied these original lines exactly, followed by a translation. Note 2 says that the two instances of "Twinkan" are "transliterated", and that Thai converts a final "l" into an "n". Note 3 says: Throughout, the translator presents the verse in both English and a rendering in Thai using Thai verse forms. The longer pieces, such as "You are old, Father William", are brilliantly done. Thai verse forms have complex rhymes, linking syllables at the end and middle of lines. Here, each line divides into two hemistiches, and there are three sets of rhymes in the four lines. The joke depends on the fact that most Thai readers will know the English original. The first three words, transliterated phonetically from English, lead the reader to expect "star" in English so there is a double surprise when it is not only a different word but a different language. Note 4 says: At his first appearance, there is a footnote explaining that the name, Mad Hatter, derived from the phrase "as mad as a hatter" which in turn came from a reputation which European hat-makers acquired from sniffing glue in the course of their work. These notes are quite explanatory from stylistic and translational perspectives.

The title of the 1922 Chinese edition (The Commercial Press) is back-translated as "Story of Ālìsī's Roaming in a Land of Miracles", with a note, and the part of the text is back-translated as:

> "'Ting-ge'er, ting-ge'er,[2] little bat!
> Just tell us all that you want!'[3]
> You know this piece of poem,[4] don't you?"
> Ālìsī said,[5] "I once heard a piece[6] that sounds sort of like it."
> That Hat-maker[7] went on saying, "The lines that follow are like this, do you remember?
> 'Flying in the sky so high,
> Like a tea tray fly 'n fly.[8]
> Ting-ge'er, ting-ge'er-'"
> Singing till this point that Idle Mouse[9] shook [its] body once, and began singing as loud as it could in [its] dream,[10] "Ting-ge'er, ting-ge'er, ting-ge'er, ting-ge'er —" singing without a pause, and only stopped when they pinched it.[11]

(Feng, 2015b: 122-127)

Many things have to be said about this back-translation, which is only one of the many possible ways of doing it. Obviously, due to various differences between Chinese and English, many points have to be noted and explained for the English reader knowing little or no Chinese in order to let them know what Chao really did in 1922.

Note 1 has to explain that the original Chinese title on the cover image (記境奇遊漫思麗阿), along with the translator and the publisher's names, reads from the right to the left. Readers viewing the image of the cover may not know that titles in Chinese books in the first half of the 20th century and earlier were in top-down or right-left lines but quoting of the titles in modern writings always goes from the left to the right, even in the original traditional characters. It also has to explain that texts of such a format go from top to the bottom, starting on the right of each page. More importantly, there are several transliterations for back-translating the title, and this is not the most literal, which could be "ālìsī roams in weird land: notes". Alternatives include "ālìsī wanders in wonderland: a story", "story of ālìsī's travel in a land of wonders", "notes on ālìsī's journey in a land of surprises", or "records of ālìsī's roving in an odd place", etc. Chao or Hu (the philosopher who suggested the Chinese title) might not agree with any of these titles if they were alive today, as they certainly meant Lewis Carroll's original. Chao might have back-translated the title differently for Warren Weaver in the 1960s, but it is not known. These transliterations are semantic representations of what the Chinese title means rather than rigid etymological and morphological translations. The same is true of the text, which cannot be as literal as "etymological translation", as was professionally shown by Chao in Weaver (1964: 94-95). It is a list of characters/words with linguistic explanations rather than a piece of meaningful discourse, and certainly not what Chao actually meant to do as "re-translation" for Weaver. In explaining his own back-translating ("the actual in-text meanings of whole syntactic words" rather than "the bound monosyllables into their etymological meanings if they are not being used in the text"), Chao implied that there had been "some translations [of etymological nature] from Chinese" (Weaver, 1964: 92). However, virtually no such decontextualized translation of literary texts in publication exists.

Note 2 says: Throughout the notes, characters linked by the hyphen (-) are inseparable in a phrase, while all others can be written either together or separately. *Tīng-gē'er* (汀格儿) is onomatopoeic in Chinese, closer to "jingle" rather than to "twinkle"; "儿" is a bound morphophonemic unit having no meaning of its own, only giving a sound /r/ to its preceding syllable. Chao (1922: 19) in fact made a note on his distinction of *er* (儿) as sound "not to be counted as a character/word" and *er* (兒) as a character/word. Yet in his example of etymological translation for Weaver (1964: 94-95), Chao used "兒" instead.

Note 3 says: The original rhyme for "bat" and "at" are realized by *fú* (蝠) and *yù* (欲), with a slight difference in tones. Chao's text has no typographic notation (i.e. italicization or different fonts) for the verse or extra spacing before and after. Note 4 says: Chao used *shǒu* (首) "piece", a quantifier for song or poem, and *shī* (詩) "poem, verse" for "song", possibly because in Chinese *gē* (歌) "song" can be without rhyme and less literary. Note 5 says: Chinese characters *ā lì sī* (阿麗思), along with those for other names and proper nouns, are underlined as a convention throughout the text. Chao's actual character for this "said" in many places is *dào* (道) "express verbally" instead of *shuō* (說) "say". Note 6 says: Chao used a quantifier *shǒu* (首) "piece" alone. Note 7 says: There is no definite or indefinite article in Chinese, and Chao used a demonstrative pronoun *nà*

（那）/ *nà-ge*（那個）"that", which is normally not necessary. And *mào jiàng*（帽匠）"hat-maker" does not imply anything of madness in Chinese. Note 8 says: The original rhyme for "fly" and "sky" was realized in Chao by *gāo*（高）"high" and *piāo*（飄）"fly", whose right part 風（*fēng*）is the character for "wind". In Weaver（1964: 94 – 95）, Chao changed it to its homophone *piāo*（漂）, which, as its left part 氵 suggests "water", means "float on water". Chao's own back-translation was accordingly "float" in the verse: "Like a tea tray float-a-float."（Weaver, 1964: 91）

These notes may seem a little bit over-informative. But considering the principles of back-translating for the project and the target readers who may not know anything of Chinese, these notes do not only provide necessary information, but also serve as detailed linguistic descriptions and stylistic analyses for the points in question. From these, target readers will not only read in English what Chao actually did the 1922 Chinese *Alice* but also why he did as he did, from linguistic and stylistic perspectives.

The title of the 2010 Chinese edition（Nanjing Yilin Press）is back-translated as "Aìlìsī wanders in the wonderland", and the text part is back-translated as:

> ... "'Flickering, flickering,[1] little *bian-fu*![2] Don't know where you're heading to!' Perhaps you know this song?"
>
> "I've heard something similar to this," Aìlìsī said.
>
> "You know, there's more next, like this."
>
> The Hatter went on singing:
>
> *High off the ground you fly,*
>
> *Like a tea-tray hanging in the sky.* [3]
>
> *Flickering, flickering —*
>
> Now, the Sleeping Mouse wiggled a bit and picked up the line in his sleep, "Flickering, flickering, flickering, flickering —"
>
> He went rattling on, showing no sign of stopping. This was too much for his friends. They nudged him and wanted him to stop.
>
> （Huang, 2015: 128-131）

The back-translator provided three notes to explain what the original translator of the 2010 Chinese edition did, and why. Note 1 says: In the translated Chinese version, the word "twinkle", which is more often used to invite in children pleasant image of a star, is rendered "*shǎn*"（閃）which, when referring to a flying bat in darkness (here possibly mocking the Dormouse because Chinese tend to see bat as a flying mouse) increases the joking atmosphere of the mad tea party. The word "twinkle" is therefore better rendered with these two words that suggest mysterious image of a bat fluttering against a canopy of darkness. Note 2 says: *Biān fú* (蝙蝠) "bat" rhymes well with *pū* (扑) "flying to" in the following line. Note 3 says: The end of the two lines are *dì miàn* (地面) "ground" and *tiān kōng* (天空) "sky", without a rhyme.

This excerpt is only a small part of the *Alice* chapter that was back-translated from some editions in some languages. And these are only some of the many different languages and editions for back-translation in the project (Lindseth, 2015b). The whole picture is much larger. The "texts" in consideration are not only in standard modern languages, but also in historical, geographical, and other variations of languages, dialects and even branches of dialects, such as Latin, Middle English, Appalachian English, Welsh, Scots, North-East Scots, Ulster Scots, Scottish Gaelic, Irish, German, Palatine German, Viennese German, Mennonite Low German, Serbian Albanian, Serbian Romanian, Serbian Hungarian, etc. Moreover, they include transcriptions in other semiotic systems, such as Gregg shorthand, Pitman shorthand, Braille, Ciphers and Codes, Esperanto and other artificial and imaginary languages. One will get a fuller view if he reads Volume 2 of the 2015 book in which over a hundred such texts are back-translated into modern English.

6. Discussion

Conventional translation studies focus on the similarities and differences between the source language text and the target language text. Comparative studies of translation generally focus on the features of the same text translated into different target languages. What is important is to observe stylistic differences in the same text in different languages; and what is equally, or even more, important is to observe stylistic differences in different versions of the same text in the same language in the same or different historical periods. Back-translating, as a practice and a method of study, adds another dimension, on which different versions of the same text in the same or different target languages are translated back into the source language. It not only serves the purpose of comparative studies of "translation", but also serves the purpose of comparative studies of "translation of translation" in one target language, which is also a working language.

The present discussion narrows down on the differences between the two Chinese translations, which are back-translated into English. Firstly, the two original translations are of different literary, linguistic and social values in different times, one the earliest (1922) and the other a more recent (2010) at the start of the project. Secondly, the two back-translators are working under the same principle, although from different backgrounds, one from literary studies and the other from linguistic stylistics.

The 1922 Chinese edition obviously draws more attention simply because of the values therein. The time of its translation followed the 1919 May Fourth Movement, which was a landmark when intellectuals started using spoken Chinese in writing, and modern Chinese grammar was at the beginning stage of development. It is possible that certain lexical, syntactical and metalinguistic usages at Chao's time no longer sound "modern" and "standard" enough to readers after 1980. In spite of the many new translators' "new" or "updated" versions of *Alice*, "no new version has shown significant signs of betterment, except those of apparent disappointment, compared against Chao's classic, at least from a linguistic and metalinguistic point of view". (Feng, 2009: 246)

As I have discussed in detail in my 2009 paper, if there were anything that Chao could not linguistically and metalinguistically accomplish in his translation in the early 1920s, it is true that no new translator over the years since has done equally well, let alone better, in the Chinese context up till now. The crux of the matter is that *Alice* is abundant with linguistic, metalingual and metalinguistic devices, among many others, for the creation of verbal art. While these devices help push the story forward on the level of nonsensical and illogical "message", they make themselves felt on the level of "code" in the Jakobsonian sense (Jakobson, 1960: 353). As the second-order metalanguage is largely the linguist's professional tool for description and analysis, translating metalanguage is actually a task of transforming the second-order code from a linguist's perspective. This is one more reason why many parts of *Alice* seem untranslatable and so many new translators striving to surpass Chao have sadly failed.

On the logical and philosophical level, some points in *Alice* can be properly dealt with only by a linguist and linguistic philosopher. Instances of nonsense and illogical reasoning in *Alice* are numerous, working within semantically-closed logical systems of their own. It is only an annotated Chinese *Alice* or a back-translated version into English that can foreground the points to show where the difficulties are and how they are actually dealt with. Meanwhile, back-translations can be used to judge and display how a competent translator faithfully represented and reconstructed or what an incompetent translator missed due to his or her ignorance of linguistic philosophy or philosophical logic and failed to find functionally and contextually appropriate equivalents to re-present or create similar semantically-closed logical systems in Chinese in particular and any other language in general. In general, a back-translating practice as such is functionally a linguistic and stylistic account (i.e., description, exposition, and explanation) for the *Alice* text in translation.

7. Conclusion

The enterprise of re-writing, translating, and back-translating can take any of the world classics of literature as an object of linguistic reflection and literary appreciation in terms of re-presentation. A practice such as back-translating can not only bring serious issues of stylistic concern to the fore and get us to see more about the values in the work in question, but also serve as a practical approach to the current translation studies from linguistic and stylistic perspectives.

The significance and practical values of back-translating can be numerous. Among the many, at least they include: (1) *Alice* in back-translations is a significant project for the study of "translation of translation". (2) Back-translations present the part of the *Alice* chapter in over 200 styles in over 120 languages, dialects, and code systems. And the reader knowing only English can at once read translations of translations in many languages. (3) The reader can compare the stylistic features and variations in different editions in different languages in the world as well as in different editions in the same language over different spans of time. (4) The reader can get much more than back-translated texts, since back-translators provide as many notes as possible to explain how the principal problems outlined by Weaver (1964) were handled by those original translators to their target language readers, who will be in a better position to make stylistic evaluations. (5) The academic nature of the project is that it probes into the linguistic, cultural, and historical aspects of the translation of *Alice* in particular and of any other literary work in general. (6) Back-translating a classic from different editions into the original source language is a feasible approach to diachronic and synchronic studies of style, and a valid means of carrying on studies of style in literature and of literary translation.

References

Baker, M. & G. Saldanha. 2009. *Routledge Encyclopedia of Translation Studies* (2nd Ed.). London: Routledge.

Batey, M. 1980. *Alice's Adventures in Oxford*. London: Jarrold Publishing.

Carroll, L. 1865. *Alice's Adventures in Wonderland*. London: Macmillan.

Catford, J. C. 1965. *A Linguistic Theory of Translation*. Oxford: Oxford University Press.

Chao, Y. 1922. *Alìsī mànyóu qíjìng jì* (Lewis Carroll: *Alice's Adventures in Wonderland*). Shanghai: The Commercial Press.

Feng, Z. 2009. Translation and reconstruction of a wonderland: *Alice's Adventures* in China. *Neohelicon*, 36 (1): 237–251.

Feng, Z. 2015a. *Alice* in Chinese translation. In J. Lindseth (ed.). *Alice in a World of Wonderlands* (Volume 1: Essays), 187–198. New Castle, DE: Oak Knoll Press.

Feng, Z. 2015b. Chinese *Alice* 1922. In J. Lindseth (ed.). *Alice in a World of Wonderlands* (Volume 2: Back Translations), 122–127. New Castle, DE: Oak Knoll Press.

Hatim, B. 1998. Text politeness: A semiotic regime for a more interactive pragmatics. In L. Hickey (ed.). *The Pragmatics of Translation*, 72 – 102. Clevedon: Multilingual Matters.

Hickey, L. 1998. "Introduction" to *The Pragmatics of Translation*, pp. 1–9. Clevedon: Multilingual Matters.

Huang, B. 2015. Chinese *Alice* 2010. In J. Lindseth (ed.). *Alice in a World of Wonderlands* (Volume 2: Back Translations), 128–131. New Castle, DE: Oak Knoll Press.

Jakobson, R. 1959. On linguistic aspects of translation. In R. A. Brower (ed.). *On Translation*, 232 – 239. Cambridge, MA: Harvard University Press. (In *Roman Jakobson Selected Writings II*, 260–266. The Hague: Mouton, 1971.)

Jakobson, R. 1960. Linguistics and poetics. In T. Sebeok (ed.). *Style in Language*, 350–377. Cambridge, MA: MIT Press.

Klaudy, K. 1996. Back translation as a tool for detecting explicitation strategies in translation. In K. Klaudy, J. Lambert, & A. Sohár (eds.). *Translation Studies in Hungary*, 99−114. Budapest: Scholastica.

Lambert, J. 2009. The status and position of legal translation: A chapter in the discursive construction of societies. In F. Olsen, A. Lorz, & D. Stein (eds.). *Translation Issues in Language and Law*, 76−95. Basingstoke: Palgrave Macmillan.

Lindseth, J. 2015a. *Alice in a World of Wonderlands* (Volume 1: Essays). New Castle, DE: Oak Knoll Press.

Lindseth, J. 2015b. *Alice in a World of Wonderlands* (Volume 2: Back Translations). New Castle, DE: Oak Knoll Press.

Miracle, G. E. 1988. An empirical study of the usefulness of the back-translation technique for international advertising messages in print media. *Proceedings of the 1988 Conference of the American Academy of Advertising*.

Newmark, P. 1991. *About Translation*. London: Multilingual Matters.

Newmark, P. 1993. *Paragraphs on Translation*. London: Multilingual Matters.

Newmark, P. 1998. *More Paragraphs on Translation*. London: Multilingual Matters.

Schaffner, C. 1995. *Cultural Functions of Translation*. London: Multilingual Matters.

Weaver, W. 1964. *Alice in Many Tongues*. Madison, WI: The University of Wisconsin Press.

Translation of English for Electric Power from the Stylistic Perspective

Lv Liangqiu Liu Xiaotong Li Lijun   (North China Electric Power University)

Abstract: Translation of English for electric power is an indispensable tool for technology exchange nowadays. Meanwhile, the translation methods are various, but most of which are concentrated on "complete translation" method. This paper will attempt to study on a new translation one for the translation of English for electric power based on the stylistic perspective, and combined with the "translation variation" proposed by Prof. Huang Zhonglian. This flexible method is expected to be significant in guiding translation practice on the translation of English for electric power. Therefore, the translated text could better convey the meanings of original text or reflect the original author's intentions and satisfy readers' needs. The kind of characteristic method that used to direct the translation of English for electric power will get improved.

Key words: stylistic perspective; translation variation strategy; English for electric power

1. Introduction

As electric power is one of the main driving forces in the economic development, translation of English for electric power is becoming more and more important. Then specific words should be applied in the translation of English for electric power which is subordinate to the scientific translation. Unlike literary translation, hardly will the translation of English for electric power take the culture or emotion factors into account. It is a kind of formal style — well-structured, well-organised, standardized language, objective description, etc. — which is the reason why "complete translation" method will always be applied to articles of electric power when translating.

However, it is not the case that all words or sentences can be translated "completely". In recent years, the "translation variation" theory is developing and readers' demands are increasing, the combination of the "translation variation" theory and translation of English for electric power is still at the blank stage, the necessity and importance of applying the "translation variation" theory to the translation of English for electric power are attracting people's broad attention gradually. To sum up, this paper will open a new "window" for the translation of English for electric power through the strategies of "translation variation" theory under the stylistic perspective.

2. Necessity and Feasibility of Combination of the "Translation Variation" Theory and Translation of English for Electric Power

As discussed above, the reasons of using the "translation variation" theory to study translation of English for electric power are as follows:

2.1 Stylistic Perspective

In mordern times, only scientific texts, like electric power articles, are mainly used to deliver information. As a result, translators are required to keep it simple and do it quick when translating these kinds of articles, which could better catch up with the trends of this era of science and technology. Prof. Huang Zhonglian also pointed out through cases that while working on the translations of scientific passages, "First is to be quick; second is to be reduced; and third is to satisfy the readers' needs". In other words, compared to the complete translation, the "translation variation" theory can absorb information from abroad more economically and efficiently. Thus, it can be concluded that the "translation variation" theory is suitable for scientific articles. It is essential that translation variation is an activity which aims at reproducing the contents of the original by using appropriate adaptations such as expansion, deletion, edition, commentary, condensation, combination and reformation to meet the special needs of the special readers under special circumstances (Huang, 2002c: 570).

2. 2 Practical Point

No matter what kind of translation theory should be used to direct electric power articles, the final purpose is to produce a perfect translated work. According to the so-called "perfect translated work", the practical operations such as how to handle an imported transformer could be operated correctly, accurately and rapidly. That is, such requirements which have determined those complete translation methods are not to meet the rapid era's development any more. What is really needed is not the detailed word-to-word translated text, but the most important instructions or a core description or something like that. In order to be understood easily, some simple translated works using the "translation variation" theory such as deletion, edition and other strategies could make the focal points stand out and cater to the needs of practical operations.

2. 3 Complexity of Language

Even if the requirements of translation of English for electric power possess relative certainty, owing to the essentials such as the vagueness of language definitions, the complexity of language itself and sentence structures, translations are still required to be more flexible to meet readers' needs.

2. 4 Diversity and Complexity of Electric Power Industry

With more detailed divisions and a wide range, electric power industry is rather systematic and complicated. It covers professional fields such as electricity, physics, maths just from the narrow perspective. Accordingly, the articles involved need to be translated completely. Nevertheless, from a broader perspective, the whole electric power industry also covers many business fields, so we have to translate various kinds of documents such as legal contracts, bidding documents.

All in all, the article need to be translated are involved in different text types, which ask for different linguistic organizations.

Moreover, readers of the translated text of electric power may be leaders, electrical engineers, operators and ordinary people. Based on the fact that different people have different knowledge background on electric power, when translating articles, on one hand, translators should first be clear that who are the target readers and what kind of article they are going to translate. For instance, if the translated articles are used to direct workers or ordinary people to operate a machine, translators should focus on particular operational program and delete the unimportant information. If the articles are for business use, then translators should focus on the properties, prices superiorities of products. Only in this way, can the translated works be easily accepted by readers from different levels. There is no doubt that the "translation variation" theory could cater to the requests of translation nowadays.

3. Characteristics of Electric Power Texts

Electric power text is subordinate to scientific articles, it has its own special characteristics: accurate, standard, concise, clear, formal, objective and logical, which are manifested in extensive uses of specialized vocabularies, terms, complex sentences, long articles etc. In addition, electric power texts also contain numerous professional samples, formulas, diagrams and other non-verbal expressions. Expressions of science and technology in electric power texts must be accurately translated. The main aspects are as follows:

3. 1 Vocabulary Aspects

Generally speaking, scientific English uses specialized vocabularies largely on lexical. Specialized vocabularies are generally divided into three forms: the inherent formats of electric power texts, such as lightning rod (避雷针), circuit breaker (断路器), inductive reactance (感抗) etc., which rarely appear in other articles; the multi-specialization of the same word in different articles, such as "power" (电力— in electric power, 功率— in physics), which should be identified according to their applicable ranges; the format of both common words and specialized vocabularies such as "current" which could refer to both specialized vocabulary "电流" and common word "当前的".

　　In electric power texts, apart from the large amount of specialized expressions, there are also lots of common expressions. In order to improve the formality of translated texts and reflect the accurateness of scientific and technical articles, these non-specialized expressions tend to be standard written English, so some long vocabularies are often used. For example, "discover" or "research" should be used to express "发现、找出" instead of "find out" in electric power texts.

Because there is no lack of mutural transformation between word classes of English for electric power, some flexible strategies should be employed during translating process.

3. 2　Syntax Aspects

Owing to the fact that electric engineers always pay more attention to the objective reality and rules of information, then scientific and technological texts for electric power have their own stylistic characteristics.

3.2.1　More Passive Sentences

The frequency of utilization of passive tense in English is much more than in Chinese. In addition, the utilization of passive tense in scientific and technological texts are needless to say much more, because the main purpose of these kinds of articles is to state facts, test reports and other various instructions.

3.2.2　More Complex and Long Sentences

With strict language structures, tight ratiocination and accurate statements, articles in electric power field also possess large amount of regular formulas, datas and terms. Plusing the information content to express the scientific facts or realities is huge enough, so complex and long sentences are used more. Above all, the so-called long sentences are always expanded on the basis of fundamental structure, adding various modifiers such as attribute and adverbial, sometimes parentheses, appositive, inverted sentences or elliptical structures. Thus, to make the translated texts look more authentic, translators must master good language skills so that they can use appropriate translation methods flexibly when translating. For instance, complex or long sentences could be decomposed into several appropriate sub-clauses from English to Chinese.

3.2.3 More Conditional Sentences and Non-Predict Structures

The scientific analysis of electric power is reflected on the aspect of the language with conditional sentences because it often put forward some hypothesis and inferences. There is no doubt that the sentence structures will be more complex, hence, more analyses should be done to ensure that appropriate methods could be used during translating process.

In fact, the scientific and technological texts for electric power have no differences with common stylistics texts originally. As for the pronunciation, the scientific and technoloical texts for electric power and common stylistics belong to the same phonetic system. Meanwhile, in spite that there is a large amount of specialized vocabularies in scientific and technological articles, the proportion of common words is far more than that of the specialized ones; as for the grammar, scientific and technological articles use the same gramma systems as common stylistics do.

To sum up, the stylistic characteristics such as vocabularies, syntax and text should be took into account during the process of translating electric power articles as usually as the common stylistics.

4. Specific Application of the "Translation Variation" Theory on the Translation of Electric Power Articles

Prof. Huang Zhonglian put forward the idea that the core of translation variation lies in "variation"— to be flexible. Thus it can be seen that to achieve multiple benefits and cooperation among original texts, translated texts, translators and readers. The "translation variation" theory is the very one to break the routine of complete translation methods and also the one to create a compromising solution and method. And the particluar strategies of translation variation are usually "explanatory translation, comment on translation, commentary, translation and writing, abridged translation, reference translation, translation and editing, translated narration, condensed translation, translated summarization, translation and rearrangement" etc. In the following part, this paper will state how the "translation variation" theory can be applied on the scientific articles particularly. According to the limitation of length, this paper will only state five strategies for analysis as follows:

4. 1　Condensed Strategy

Condensation means deleting unimportant parts generally. To save the reading time and pick out the most important parts from an article, condensed strategy is the condensation of original contents and information in quantity. In short, the condensed strategy always shrinks the length of original texts when it will be employed. The corresponding variaties are condensed translation.

> Example 1: Stainless steel possesses good hardness and high strength.
> Translated Version：不锈钢硬度大、强度高。
> Example 2: With regard to their products, they have the same concerns of the interrelationship of design, materials, and manufacturing process.
> Translated Version：关于产品,他们同样要考虑其设计、材料和制造工艺之间的相互关系。
>
> (Zhao, 2013: 70)

The verb "possess" in Example 1 adopts the condensed strategy, and is not translated into its literal meaning "拥有……", but in the translated version the adjectives "大"、"高" are used as predicate instead.

In Example 2, the verb "have" adopts the condensed strategy, and the word "concerns" is translated into "考虑".

4. 2　Combined Strategy

Combination means combining two or more parts which have the same type or logical relationship together. The relative parts may be sentences, sentence groups, paragraphs, pieces of writing, chapters and books.

> Example 3: The most common application is in the service entrance boxes of residences, where fuses may be used to protect the main lines and each of the several individual circuits into the house.
> Translated Version：熔断器一般多用在进线盒中,用来保护主要线路和入户的每一个独立电路。

Example 3 is a complex sentence, which involves a non-restrictive attributive clause and this clause is to describe "entrance boxes". In the translated version, these two clauses are combined logically into a long sentence with various modifiers, thus the translated text like this can not only avoid repetition, but also make it more compact and precise.

4. 3　Explanatory Translation Strategy

Explanatory translation is the translation variation which combines explanatory and translation and refers to add explanatory translation to original text. It aims to present the cultural value of original text by releasing the condensed cultural information for target readers.

> Example 4：Combine digital technology with advanced software, smaller and more powerful microprocessors, and exponential growth in fiber and wireless bandwidth, and you get something far more powerful — seamless, universal connectivity.
>
> Translated Version：把数字技术与先进的软件、体积更小、功能更强大的微型处理器以及快速增长的光纤和无线带宽度发展相结合，你就可以获得功能更加强大的无缝隙全方位的连接。

In the translated version, "体积" is added before the word "smaller", "功能" added before the word "powerful" and "发展" is added before the phrase "fiber and wireless bandwidth". By using the explanatory translation strategy, the translated text of scientific and technological for electric power can be more authentic and understandable.

> Example 5：Since energy is defined as the capacity to do work, we measure energy in units of work.
>
> (Feng, 2008：36)
>
> Translated Version：既然能定义为做功的能力，因此我们就用功的单位来计量能的大小。

In this example, the proper unknown or unclear contents "energy" is explained as "能的大小". This strategy used can benefit non-professionals to deal with the difficult and obscure texts, such as the accurate meaning of "energy".

4. 4　Comment on Translation

Comment on translation is one kind of translaion variation activities which refers to comment on the contents of original works after translation. This strategy not only helps readers understand original articles deeply, but also improves the connoisseurship, and promotes cross-cultural communication. It contains translating, comment and the combination of both.

Example 6：蒸汽机几乎已不再作为钻井动力。后来大型柴油机——电力混合驱动产生了。但最初人们认为它只适合于作为内陆海域中的钻井船动力。

Translated Version：Steam had all but disappeared as a source of drilling power. The big diesel-electric drives were coming in the future, but they were first thought of as power for drilling barges in inland waters. *There, size and weight and highway transportation was not a problem.*

(Li, 2013: 27)

In the translated version, it involves the translating and comment parts. The former part is the translated information of the original text, and the italic part is obviously the commentary. It can be seen that the italic information " size and weight and highway transportation was not a problem " serves as suggestions and summarization of the ways dealing with the pollution of petroleum hydrocarbon in soil. In this way, comments here give readers some specialized knowledge and straightaway expressions to understand the text easily. The translation, loyal to the original text, merely focuses on readers.

4. 5　Deletion Strategy

Deletion means deleting unimportant information from original text for reader's sake. Specifically, the translators will do their best to delete some repeated expressions, superfluous words, notes and explanations from a sentence or just select the core sentences to translate from a paragraph or even translate some important paragraphs related to the main idea from a piece of article. What's more, the corresponding translation varieties are divided into abridged translation and reference translation generally. The following part will just introduce the abridged translation.

Abridged translation is a translation variation activity that selects the main sources of original text to be translated according to readers for special needs. (Huang, 2004: 73)

According to Prof. Huang, the situations satisfying the definition are to translate the deletion parts of vocabulary or phrase, to translate the selective sentences which are not related with the core meaning can be deleted and to translate the sentence group. These strategies should obey the rule of loyalty.

The following example will introduce how the abridged translation method is applied to the electric power texts.

Example 7: Typically, electricity is generated at 13,800 volts, It is stepped up to 345,000 volts for transmission.

(Liu, etc. 2006: 34)

Translated Version: 典型的发电机出口电压为 13,800V,升压至 345,000V 用来输送。

As can be seen, the translated version is more precise and simple by breaking the sentence structure of the original text and translating the adverb "typically" as an adjective to modify the "electricity". In addition, the sentence pattern "It is stepped up to …" is used to express helpfully, so the unimportant information is deleted and the two parts of original text are combined into one sentence with only one structure as "subject-predicate".

5. Conclusion

For the scientific translation of electric power, the complete translation strategy with word to word or sentence by sentence should be suspended. Considering different requirements and focuses, translators should respect the objectivity of flexibility to guarantee their objectivity, accuracy and pertinence. Therefore, the original texts must be better analysed before translating so that the judgements on the translated purpose could be accurate and the appropriate translation method could be guaranteed correctly, so the subjective initiative should be played fully during the whole process of translating. All in all, since the "translation variation" theory itself is used to guide the application practice, its employment on the scientific and technological articles for electric power could also provide a more systematical theoretical support to the scientific translation for electric power.

References

Dai, P. 2013. *The Chinese Translation of English Complex Sentences in Electric Major*. Tianjin: Tianjin University of Technology.

Feng, J., X. Wang, Y. Liu, & Y. Yin. 2008. *The Basic Study Guide of English in Electrical Major*. Beijing: China Electric Power Press.

Fu, Y. & Y. Tang. 2012. *Scientific Translation*. Beijing: Foreign Language Teaching and Research Press.

Huang, Z. 2000. *The Study on Translation Variation*. Beijing: China Translation and

Publishing Corporation.

Huang, Z. 2002a. *The Translation Variation Theory.* Beijing: China Translation and Publishing Corporation.

Huang, Z. 2002b. The translation variation and complete translation: A couple of new category of translation. *Shanghai Journal of Translators for Science and Technology*, (3).

Huang, Z. 2002c. Seven flexible strategies of the translation variation Theory. *Foreign Language Research*, (1).

Huang, Z. & Y. Li. 2004. *The Science of Translation Studies.* Beijing: China Translation and Publishing Corporation.

Jin, P. & F. Lu. 2012. A study about translation of English for electric power from the theory of equivalence. *China Electric Power Education*, (19).

Li, Y. 2013. *E-C Translation of Technical Texts from the Perspective of Translation Variation Theory.* Sichuan: Southwest Petroleum University.

Liu, R., L. Bao, & Z. Jing. 2006. *English for Electric Power.* Beijing: China Electric Power Press.

Wang, H. 2011. The application of translation variation theory on the scientific English translation. *China Scientific Translation*, (5).

Zhao, Y. & L. Lv. 2013. *Theory and Practice of Electric Power Translation between English and Chinese.* Hebei: Hebei University Press.

Zhou, J. 2010. *Study on E-C and C-E Scientific Translation from Stylistic Perspective.* Shaanxi: Xi'an Polytechnic University, (12).